FILM AWARDS

Volume Two
1960 – 1979

About the Author

Brian Lindsay was awarded a PhD from the University of New South Wales for his thesis "Darkening Frontier, Vanishing Outback: Film, Landscape and National Identities in Australia and the United States". His articles about the Academy Awards have appeared in *The Sydney Morning Herald* and *The Australian*. Passionate about film and theatre history, he lives in Sydney, Australia with his partner, Simon.

His previous publication, *Category Fraud*, examined how studios have gamed the Oscar nominations for decades by campaigning for lead performances to be nominated in the supporting categories, and argued that it was past time the Academy reformed its rules to end the practice and restore integrity to the Oscars. *Category Fraud* was published by Tranter Ward Books in 2016.

The first volume of *Film Awards: A Reference Guide to US & UK Film Awards*, the only film awards reference book to cover the annual awards season category by category, was published in 2017. The third volume will be published by Tranter Ward Books in 2019 with the fourth following in 2020.

FILM AWARDS

A Reference Guide to US & UK Film Awards

Volume Two
1960 – 1979

Brian Lindsay

Tranter Ward Books

Tranter Ward Books
Sydney NSW Australia
www.tranterward.com

First Edition 2018

ISBN: 978-0-9804909-5-4

Cover design by Simon Moore, Elton Ward Creative

A catalogue record for this book is available from the National Library of Australia

To Simon

Introduction

Each year the Academy Awards ceremony is the culmination of a season of award presentations by critics' associations, industry guilds and other prestigious organisations. As the season unfolds, debate invariably unfolds as to whether each set of accolades portend Oscar glory or are merely curious anomalies.

There are numerous books and websites that diligently list the various nominees and winners, many providing commentary on which films were favoured by the critics and which swept the Globes on the way to the Oscars. Without exception, they chronicle the annual awards season the same way, taking each set of awards in turn – the winners of the major film critics' groups, then the Golden Globe Award nominees and winners, then the various Guild honourees and so forth, concluding with the Academy Awards.

It's only on rare occasions, however, that we want an overview of an entire awards season or even a snapshot of all the winners of the Los Angeles Film Critics Association prizes from a given year. More often, we reach for such reference books because, at that moment, we are interested in a certain film or a particular performance. Having just watched *The Godfather*, for example, you're curious to see how Marlon Brando and Al Pacino fared during that year's awards season. Which groups nominated their legendary performances? Who were they up against? When did they go head-to head for Best Actor honours? Which accolades did they win? Who did they lose out to? When you have such questions, this is the book to grab.

Film Awards takes a fresh and long overdue approach to the annual awards season: category by category. No more looking up the Best Actor winner from one critic's group, then turning the page to look up the winner from a different critic's group later in that season, then flicking to another page to find out who was nominated for the Golden Globes, and then finally turning to yet another page and scanning through a list of all the Academy Award nominees to find out who was in contention for the Oscar. In this book, the nominees and winners for Best Actor from all the major awards groups in a given year are listed together in one quick-reference table on the same page. At a glance, you can see which awards Marlon Brando won for *The Godfather*, who he was nominated alongside and to whom he lost.

Reference tables are compiled in *Film Awards* for Best Picture, Director, Actor, Actress, Supporting Actor and Supporting Actress. In this second volume, covering the years 1960 through to 1979, the tables include the nominees and winners of the Academy Awards, Golden Globe Awards, British Academy Awards, Directors Guild of America Awards, New York Film Critics Circle

Awards, Los Angeles Film Critics Association Awards, National Board of Review Awards and the National Society of Film Critics Awards where relevant in each instance (depending on which year the awards commenced and in which categories they were presented). Information about major film festival prize winners are not included as only a small number of selected candidates are eligible rather than all the films released throughout the year as is the case with the major annual awards.

The reputation of a film can diminish or become enhanced with the passage of time. In 2012, for example, leading film critics and academics polled by the British Film Institute's Sight & Sound magazine placed Stanley Kubrick's science-fiction masterpiece *2001: A Space Odyssey* as one of the ten greatest films of all time. The film did not, however, win any Best Picture prizes in the year of its original release. It was not even nominated for the top prizes at the Academy Awards or the Golden Globes. In 1968, reaction to *2001: A Space Odyssey* ranged from mixed to dismissive. The New York Times called it "a very complicated, languid film ... somewhere between hypnotic and immensely boring" and remarked "the uncompromising slowness of the movie makes it hard to sit through". Variety, meanwhile, said the film was "a major achievement" but "not a cinematic landmark." To better understand why certain films and performances garnered awards recognition while others were overlooked, *Film Awards* quotes from leading film critics in the United States, the United Kingdom and Australia to reveal the critical opinion contemporaneous to each film's initial release. Such quotes are reproduced with original spellings.

Throughout the book, films are referred to by the title under which they were originally released in their country of origin. Alternate titles by which a film was known in the United States are included in parentheses.

References to directors and performers in the index relate only to instances when the individual was an awards season contender. For example, only instances when Jack Nicholson is listed or referred to as a winner, nominee or contender for Best Actor or Best Supporting Actor appear in the index. Other incidental references to him in the book, such as when he was a presenter of the Best Actress statuette or was the star of a Best Picture nominee are omitted.

Film Awards has been designed to place the annual Oscar winners for Picture, Director and Acting into historical context alongside the other winners and nominees from that season as well as the opinions of the leading newspaper and magazine film critics of the day. Hopefully it will be an interesting and informative companion as you discover (or rediscover) the lauded films and performances of the years 1960 to 1979.

Abbreviations

AMPAS	Academy of Motion Picture Arts and Sciences
BAFTA	British Academy of Film and Television Awards
DGA	Directors Guild of America
HFPA	Hollywood Foreign Press Association
NBR	National Board of Review
NSFC	National Society of Film Critics
CT	Chicago Tribune
FQ	Film Quarterly
G	The Guardian
HRp	The Hollywood Reporter
HT	Herald Tribune
LAT	Los Angeles Times
MFB	Monthly Film Bulletin
Obs	The Observer
NYDN	New York Daily News
NYer	The New Yorker
NYP	New York Post
NYT	The New York Times
S&S	Sight & Sound
SMH	The Sydney Morning Herald
Sp	The Spectator
TT	The Times
V	Variety
WP	Washington Post

Note on income figures quoted for Best Picture Academy Award nominees: Figures quoted are for United States theatrical rental receipts during period of original release unless preceded by "gr:" indicating United States box office gross during period of original release.

1960

BEST PICTURE

ACADEMY AWARDS

The Alamo
(Batjac, United Artists, 192 mins, 24 Oct 1960, $7.9m, 7 noms)

• *The Apartment*
(Mirisch, United Artists, 125 mins BW, 15 Jun 1960, $6.9m, 10 noms)

Elmer Gantry
(Lancaster-Brooks, United Artists, 146 mins, 14 Jul 1960, $5.2m, 5 noms)

Sons and Lovers
(Wald, Twentieth Century-Fox, 103 mins BW, 3 Aug 1960, 7 noms)

The Sundowners
(Warner Bros., 133 mins, 8 Dec 1960, 5 noms)

GOLDEN GLOBE AWARDS

(Drama)
Elmer Gantry
Inherit the Wind
Sons and Lovers
• *Spartacus*
Sunrise at Campobello

(Comedy)
• *The Apartment*
The Facts of Life
The Grass is Greener
It Started in Naples
Our Man in Havana

(Musical)
Bells Are Ringing
Can-Can
Let's Make Love
Pepe
• *Song Without End*

BRITISH ACADEMY AWARDS

(Film)
The Angry Silence
• *The Apartment*
L'Avventura (The Adventure)
La Dolce Vita
Elmer Gantry
Hiroshima, Mon Amour
Inherit the Wind
Let's Make Love
Orfeu Negro (Black Orpheus)
Pote tin Kyriaki (Never on Sunday)
Les Quatre Cents Coups (The 400 Blows)
Saturday Night and Sunday Morning
Shadows
Spartacus
Le Testament d'Orphee (The Testament of Orpheus)
The Trials of Oscar Wilde
Tunes of Glory

(British Film)
The Angry Silence
• *Saturday Night and Sunday Morning*
The Trials of Oscar Wilde
Tunes of Glory

1960

NEW YORK – *The Apartment* and *Sons and Lovers*
BOARD OF REVIEW – *Sons and Lovers*
SCREEN PRODUCERS GUILD – *The Apartment*

A few days before Christmas, the National Board of Review presented its Best Picture award to *Sons and Lovers*, a drama about a drunken coalminer and his family (NYT "sensitively felt and photographed … picture poetry"; FQ "not really long enough … fails to achieve a firm personality of its own"). The group also honoured the film's director, former cinematographer Jack Cardiff.

A week later, in the voting for the New York Film Critics Circle prize, *Sons and Lovers* led the first five ballots, but on the sixth and final vote it tied with Billy Wilder's popular film *The Apartment*, a satirical comedy about a clerk who allows his superiors to use his apartment for their illicit trysts (NYT "brilliant", "gleeful, tender and even sentimental"; TT "both bitterly satirical and innocently amusing"; SMH "tremendous"). The two films shared the New York award – the first time that the circle had declared a tie in the top category. The group also named both Cardiff and Wilder as Best Director.

At the Golden Globe Awards, the two New York champions were the frontrunners for the Best Picture prizes. *Sons and Lovers* was nominated for the Drama award alongside Stanley Kubrick's *Spartacus* (NYT "a spotty, uneven drama"; V "a rousing testament to the spirit and dignity of man"), and three films that had featured in the voting for the New York prize: *Elmer Gantry*, a drama about an evangelist (NYT "exciting … a living, action-packed, provoking screen study … that captures both the eye and mind"; TT "powerful, passionate"; SMH "may be dismissed as a shallow and fairly unsavoury piece of work"); *Inherit the Wind*, a dramatisation of the 1925 Tennessee court case about the teaching of the theory of evolution in public schools (V "rousing and fascinating"; SMH "an engrossing study of character [and] a compelling drama … among the finest [pictures] of the year"); and *Sunrise at Campobello*, a biopic about President Franklin D. Roosevelt and his wife, Eleanor (NYT "a well-done, moving biographical film"; V "ferociously sentimental"; S&S "hard to dislike"; MFB "utterly conventional"). Surprisingly, the Globe went to *Spartacus*.

The winner of the Globe for Best Picture (Musical) was another surprise. *Song Without End*, a biopic about composer Franz Liszt (NYT "it is thus an excess of riches, musical and visual, telescoped in order to pack as much in as possible, that makes for distraction in this film"), outpolled the other nominees which included: *Pepe*, starring Cantinflas (NYT "a great mass of Hollywooden dross"); Vincente Minnelli's *Bells are Ringing* (V "better Broadway musicals than 'Bells Are Ringing' have come to Hollywood, but few have been translated to the screen so effectively"); and *Can-Can*, which, despite poor reviews, was the year's second most popular release (NYT "tedious", "foolish"; V "more discriminating film-goers will find it wanting").

Wilder's *The Apartment* won the Globe for Best Picture (Comedy), as expected. Among the other nominees were *The Facts of Life* (NYT "hilarious") and Carol Reed's *Our Man in Havana*, which was written by Graham Greene and starred Alec Guinness (NYT "disarmingly humorous"; V "polished, diverting entertainment").

Three weeks before the Globes were handed out, the Academy announced its nominees and the east coast prizewinners, *Sons and Lovers* and *The Apartment* were both short-listed for the top Oscar. Wilder's comedy topped the list of contenders with ten nominations.

Also nominated were: *Elmer Gantry*; Fred Zinnemann's *The Sundowners*, a drama about an Australian drover and his wife (NYT "deeply and poignantly revealing"; V "wonderfully warm, rich and compelling"; TT "pleasant" but "slow"; S&S "likeable"; MFB "warm, simple"; SMH "the Australian idiom is here, if sometimes self-conscious, but the essence of Australia is largely absent"); and John Wayne's expensive, nearly three-and-a-half hour long, historical epic *The Alamo* (NYT "another beleaguered blockhouse Western"; V suffers from "an absence of feeling"; TT "impresses favourably"; FQ "too long, too dull, too sentimental and, at crucial times, historically inaccurate").

Wayne's film did significant business at the box office, but its returns were nonetheless disappointing given its cost and industry expectations. Following the negative reviews, *The Alamo* received no recognition from the critics' groups, and was overlooked for the top Globes. Despite this, Wayne launched a massive campaign for Oscar recognition. Although Wayne himself was overlooked by the Academy as both actor and director, *The Alamo* was mentioned in seven categories.

Unexpectedly omitted from the Academy's Best Picture category, despite earning six nominations, was Kubrick's *Spartacus*. It was the second winner of the Globe (Drama) to be missing from Oscar consideration.

Other contenders overlooked were: Globe nominee *Inherit the Wind*; Alfred Hitchcock's thriller *Psycho* (NYT "frightening"; V "an unusual, good entertainment"; TT "neither so horrifying nor so surprising as might have been expected"; FQ "one of the most technically exciting films of recent years"); Otto Preminger's three-and-a-half hour epic *Exodus* (NYT "the best blockbuster of the year"; V "falls somewhat short of artistic greatness"; FQ "a bad film", "unimaginative" and "laughably pretentious"); *The Fugitive Kind*, an adaptation of Tennessee Williams' play 'Orpheus Descending' starring Marlon Brando, Anna Magnani and Joanne Woodward (NYT a "piercing account of loneliness and disappointment"); and, despite seven nominations, the musical *Pepe*.

1960

The Academy also ignored *Cimarron*, an expensive CinemaScope remake of the 1930/31 Best Picture Oscar winner which critics had slammed (NYT "stereotyped", "superficial" and "labored"; S&S "reality dogged by absurdity"; MFB "unwieldy and unimaginative").

The Academy nominated five American films, passing over such acclaimed foreign films as: Ingmar Bergman's *Jungfrukallan (The Virgin Spring)*, which won both the Oscar and the Globe as Best Foreign-Language Film (NYT "powerful and poignant"; TT "dark magnificence", "outstanding"); the French drama *Hiroshima, Mon Amour* which won the New York critics' prize for Best Foreign-Language Film (NYT "a complex yet compelling tour de force", "a searing, sophisticated philosophical drama"; TT "an important film"); Jules Dassin's *Pote tin Kyriaki (Never on Sunday)* (NYT "hilarious"; TT "delightful"; S&S "a curious mixture of abstract wit and light-hearted romantic comedy"; SMH "the adult comedy of the year"); the Russian drama *Letjat Zhuravli (The Cranes are Flying)* which won the Palme d'Or at the 1958 Cannes Film Festival (NYT "extraordinary"); Akira Kurosawa's 1958 samurai film *Kakushi-toride no san-akunin (The Hidden Fortress)* (NYT "essentially a superficial film"; V "a long, interesting, humor-laden picture"); the British comedy *I'm All Right Jack* (NYT a "sharp screen satire"); and the British drama *The Angry Silence* (NYT "convincing and emotionally disturbing"; V "absorbing"; SMH "little short of brilliant … a major achievement ").

In the days immediately following the announcement of the nominations, the American Associated Press was touting *The Sundowners* as the early favourite for the Best Picture Academy Award. On 5 March 1961, however, the Screen Producers Guild hosted its annual dinner for the recipient of its prestigious Milestone Award for significant contributions to film over the course of a distinguished career. In addition to honouring that year's recipient, Adolph Zukor, chairman of the board of Paramount Pictures, the guild presented prizes for best film and best television film. In the feature film category, the guild chose *The Apartment* from a slate of sixteen nominees that included *The Sundowners* as well as *Elmer Gantry*, *Exodus*, *Psycho, Sons and Lovers, Spartacus,* and *Sunrise at Campobello*. The guild had not included *The Alamo* on its short-list. Victory at the Golden Globes followed, in early April, by a Best Film win at the British Academy Awards, firmly placed *The Apartment* in the box seat heading into the Oscars.

Ten days after the BAFTAs, Wilder's comedy also triumphed in Hollywood receiving the Best Picture Oscar. It was the second film directed by Billy Wilder to claim the Academy's top prize and the first Golden Globe (Comedy) winner to be honoured with the Oscar. It would also be the last black-and-white film to win the Best Picture Oscar for over thirty years.

1960

BEST DIRECTOR

ACADEMY AWARDS
Jack Cardiff for *Sons and Lovers*
Jules Dassin for *Pote tin Kyriaki (Never on Sunday)*
Alfred Hitchcock for *Psycho*
• Billy Wilder for *The Apartment*
Fred Zinnemann for *The Sundowners*

GOLDEN GLOBE AWARDS
Richard Brooks – *Elmer Gantry*
• Jack Cardiff – *Sons and Lovers*
Stanley Kubrick – *Spartacus*
Billy Wilder – *The Apartment*
Fred Zinnemann – *The Sundowners*

DIRECTORS GUILD AWARD
Jack Cardiff – *Sons and Lovers*
Alfred Hitchcock – *Psycho*
Vincente Minnelli – *Bells Are Ringing*
• Billy Wilder – *The Apartment*
Fred Zinnemann – *The Sundowners*

NEW YORK – Jack Cardiff – *Sons and Lovers* and **Billy Wilder – *The Apartment***
BOARD OF REVIEW – Jack Cardiff – *Sons and Lovers*

Jack Cardiff was named Best Director by the National Board of Review and the New York Film Critics Circle for the literary adaptation *Sons and Lovers* (NYT "has filled it with picture poetry"; V "smoothly directed"). And, in the circle's first tie in the category, shared the latter honour with Billy Wilder for the comedy *The Apartment* (NYT "his direction is ingenious and sure"; V "cinematic skill"). It was Wilder's second citation from the east coast critics.

Both Cardiff and Wilder were among those short-listed by the Directors Guild of America, considered along with: Alfred Hitchcock for the thriller *Psycho* (NYT "expert and sophisticated command"; FQ "superbly constructed"); Fred Zinnemann for the drama *The Sundowners* (S&S "solid"); and Vincente Minnelli for the musical comedy *Bells Are Ringing* (V "Minnelli's graceful, imaginative direction puts spirit and snap into the musical sequences, warmth and humor into the straight passages, and manages to knit it all together without any traces of awkwardness in transition [from stage to screen]"). Wilder won the DGA prize for the first time at his record sixth nomination.

Cardiff, Wilder and Zinnemann were all mentioned for the Golden Globe alongside Richard Brooks for *Elmer Gantry* (NYT "a tribute to the artistry of Richard Brooks, the scenarist-director"; NYer "skillfully directed") and Stanley Kubrick for *Spartacus* (V "demonstrates a technical talent").

Mentioned on the Academy's list of nominees were: Cardiff (who had won an Oscar for Best Cinematography in 1947); previous winners Wilder (for the eighth and final time) and Zinnemann (for the fifth time); DGA nominee Hitchcock (for a fifth and final time); and the blacklisted Jules Dassin for *Pote tin Kyriaki (Never on Sunday)* (NYT "neatly and nimbly handled"). Globe nominees Brooks and Kubrick were unexpected omissions.

Overlooked for both the Globe and the Oscar were: Stanley Kramer for *Inherit the Wind* (NYT "has wonderfully accomplished not only a graphic fleshing of his theme but he also has got one of the most brilliant and engrossing displays of acting ever witnessed on the screen"; V "in top form"; SMH "thoughtfully presented … [in a] clear, fluent style", "superbly composed"); Otto Preminger for *Exodus*; Vincent J. Donehue for *Sunrise at Campobello* (NYT "has been reproduced on the screen with a photographic fervor that gives it, for better or worse, a wider exposure and sharper focus than it had on the stage"); Carol Reed for *Our Man in Havana*; Ronald Neame for *Tunes of Glory* (NYT "brilliant"); Tony Richardson for *The Entertainer*; Alain Resnais for *Hiroshima, Mon Amour* (NYT "expertly sustains the fragile mood of his theme"); Akira Kurosawa for *Kakushi-toride no san-akunin (The Hidden Fortress)* (V "the picture is really director Akira Kurosawa's, who takes what could have been a terribly unwieldy subject and makes it believable and highly entertaining"); Satyajit Ray for *Apur Sansar (The World of Apu)* (NYT "demonstrates that he is a master of a complex craft and style"); and Ingmar Bergman for *Jungfrukallan (The Virgin Spring)* (V "tremendous"; SMH "superb filmcraft").

In March, Cardiff received the Globe, but a month later, the Oscar went to Wilder. It was the second golden statuette he had won in the Best Director category.

1960

BEST ACTRESS

ACADEMY AWARDS

Greer Garson as 'Eleanor Roosevelt' in *Sunrise at Campobello*
Deborah Kerr as 'Ida Carmody' in *The Sundowners*
Shirley MacLaine as 'Fran Kubelik' in *The Apartment*
Melina Mercouri as 'Ilya' in *Pote tin Kyriaki (Never on Sunday)*
• Elizabeth Taylor as 'Gloria Wandrous' in *Butterfield 8*

GOLDEN GLOBE AWARDS

(Drama)
Doris Day – *Midnight Lace*
• Greer Garson – *Sunrise at Campobello*
Nancy Kwan – *The World of Suzie Wong*
Jean Simmons – *Elmer Gantry*
Elizabeth Taylor – *Butterfield 8*

(Comedy/Musical)
Lucille Ball – *The Facts of Life*
Capucine – *Song Without End*
Judy Holliday – *Bells Are Ringing*
Sophia Loren – *It Started in Naples*
• Shirley MacLaine – *The Apartment*

BRITISH ACADEMY AWARDS

(Foreign Actress)
Pier Angeli – *The Angry Silence*
• Shirley MacLaine – *The Apartment*
Melina Mercouri – *Pote tin Kyriaki (Never on Sunday)*
Emmanuelle Riva – *Hiroshima, Mon Amour*
Jean Simmons – *Elmer Gantry*
Monica Vitti – *L'Avventura (The Adventure)*

(British Actress)
Hayley Mills – *Pollyanna*
Wendy Hiller – *Sons and Lovers*
• Rachel Roberts – ***Saturday Night and Sunday Morning***

NEW YORK – Deborah Kerr – *The Sundowners*
BOARD OF REVIEW – Greer Garson – *Sunrise at Campobello*

At the start of the awards season, the Best Actress Oscar contest looked like it would be a close race between previous winner Greer Garson, nominated for a seventh time, and Deborah Kerr, mentioned for a sixth time. It would prove to be the last occasion either would receive a nomination during their career.

Garson won the National Board of Review award and the Golden Globe (Drama) for her performance as the former US First Lady, Eleanor Roosevelt in

Sunrise at Campobello (NYT "plays the role most sweetly, and with firmness and humor"; V "a deeply moving, multi-faceted characterization"; FQ "brings dignity and warmth to the role"; MFB "artificial"; SMH "a blushingly bad caricature of Eleanor Roosevelt"). Kerr, an unexpected omission from the list of Globe nominees, won a record third prize from the New York Film Critics Circle for her turn as an Australian sheep drover's wife in *The Sundowners* (V "a luminous and penetrating portrayal"; TT "sterling"; SMH "gives an impression of scrawny, warm toughness, although she lags behind [co-star Robert] Mitchum in her accent").

In addition to Garson and Kerr, the Academy's shortlist included three other strong contenders. The winner of the Globe (Comedy/Musical), the Best Foreign Actress BAFTA and the Venice Film Festival honour, Shirley MacLaine received her second Oscar nomination as the elevator operator in *The Apartment* (NYT "splendid"; SMH "on the hair's breadth line between amusement, comedy and sympathy, [MacLaine] gives perhaps her finest performance"). The Cannes Film Festival's Best Actress winner and runner-up in New York (she led on the first three ballots), Greek actress Melina Mercouri was included as the warm-hearted prostitute in *Pote tin Kyriaki (Never on Sunday)*, which was directed by her husband, Best Director Oscar nominee Jules Dassin (NYT "superb"; V "a brilliant execution of a larger than life character"; S&S "personifies sex and plays outrageously to the audience"; SMH "superb", "ideal"). The fifth candidate was Golden Globe nominee Elizabeth Taylor, who was mentioned for a fourth consecutive year, for her turn as a prostitute in *Butterfield 8* (NYT "lends a certain fascination to the film"; V "a torrid, stirring overall portrayal with one or two brilliantly executed passages"; S&S "rather splendid"; SMH the two leads "remain stock figures out of a novelette").

Notable omissions from the Academy's list were Globe and BAFTA nominee Jean Simmons as an evangelist in *Elmer Gantry* (NYT "finely etched portrayal"; NYer "impressive"; V "finely balanced"; TT "has never acted better") and BAFTA nominee Wendy Hiller in *Sons and Lovers* (NYT "plays with magnificently eloquent suggestions of barrenness and poignancy"; V "superbly acted"; TT "quite magnificent"). Independent producer Ross Hunter mounted a large campaign for the previous year's surprise nominee, Doris Day, for her portrayal of a terrified heiress in *Midnight Lace* (NYT "a golden impersonation"). While she received a Globe nod, Day was not shortlisted for the Oscar.

Others overlooked were: surprise Globe nominee Nancy Kwan in *The World of Suzie Wong* (NYT "plays her so blithely and innocently that even the ladies should love her … she and the scenery are the best things in the film"; V "fairly believable"; SMH "makes a quite nifty little Suzie"); Globe nominee Lucille Ball in *The Facts of Life* (V "exceptionally fine"; MFB "adept"); Globe nominee

Judy Holliday in the musical comedy *Bells Are Ringing* (NYT "succeeds"; V "[an] outstanding turn … steals [the] show with a performance of remarkable variety and gusto"); BAFTA nominee Pier Angeli in *The Angry Silence* (NYT "outstanding"; SMH "compelling"); Anna Magnani in *The Fugitive Kind* (NYT "brilliant"); Joanne Woodward in *From the Terrace* (NYT "skillful"; V "excellent"); Dorothy McGuire in *The Dark at the Top of the Stairs* (V "persuasively acted", "tops"; SMH "delicate"); Lee Remick in *Wild River* (V "splendid work in a difficult role"; TT "played with remarkable restraint"); Marilyn Monroe in *Let's Make Love* (V "a sheer delight"); Tatyana Samoilova in *Letjat Zhuravli (The Cranes are Flying)* (NYT "excellent"); and Emmanuelle Riva in *Hiroshima, Mon Amour* (NYT "gives each word and phrase meaning and tenderness").

According to popular Oscar lore, it was a prolonged stay in hospital culminating in an emergency tracheotomy due to a near-fatal bout of pneumonia, that swayed the Best Actress contest from Garson and Kerr in favour of Taylor. This myth gains much of its credence from Taylor's own words from her 1967 autobiography in which she wrote, "I got the Academy Award for 'Butterfield 8'. The reason was, I am afraid, that I had come within a breath of dying of pneumonia only a few months before. I was filled with profound gratitude at being considered by the industry an actress and not a movie star".

While she certainly garnered considerable sympathy as a result of her illnesses and operation, the truth is that Taylor had already emerged as the favourite for the Oscar before she was admitted to hospital. The American Associated Press was reporting that Taylor was the frontrunner in her category as early as 1 March 1961, just four days after the announcement of the Academy Award nominations and more than a week prior to the actress' admission to hospital. Rather than swinging the race Taylor's way, the media coverage of her illness and brush with death simply put her already expected win beyond any doubt. The other four candidates cancelled their plans to attend the ceremony. Kerr told reporters, "the Oscar should go to Elizabeth not because of her grave illness, but because her performance in *Butterfield 8* is superb."

On Oscar night, Yul Brynner announced that Taylor was the winner of the year's Best Actress Oscar. Sufficiently recovered to attend the ceremony, Taylor was helped to the stage by her husband Eddie Fisher and gracefully thanked the Academy. She later admitted that she did not believe her performance was worthy of the statuette and that she had only accepted the role because she was impatient to conclude her contractual obligations to M-G-M and move on to her million dollar pay check for Twentieth Century-Fox's *Cleopatra.*

Taylor's Oscar win left Kerr in the unenviable position of the Academy's record Best Actress loser – six nominations without a victory.

1960

BEST ACTOR

ACADEMY AWARDS
Trevor Howard as 'Walter Morel' in *Sons and Lovers*
• Burt Lancaster as 'Elmer Gantry' in *Elmer Gantry*
Jack Lemmon as 'C. C. Baxter' in *The Apartment*
Laurence Olivier as 'Archie Rice' in *The Entertainer*
Spencer Tracy as 'Henry Drummond' in *Inherit the Wind*

GOLDEN GLOBE AWARDS
(Drama)
Trevor Howard – *Sons and Lovers*
• Burt Lancaster – *Elmer Gantry*
Laurence Olivier – *Spartacus*
Dean Stockwell – *Sons and Lovers*
Spencer Tracy – *Inherit the Wind*

(Comedy/Musical)
Dirk Bogarde – *Song Without End*
Cantinflas – *Pepe*
Cary Grant – *The Grass is Greener*
Bob Hope – *The Facts of Life*
• Jack Lemmon – *The Apartment*

BRITISH ACADEMY AWARDS
(Foreign Actor)
George Hamilton
– *Crime and Punishment*
Burt Lancaster – *Elmer Gantry*
• Jack Lemmon – *The Apartment*
Fredric March – *Inherit the Wind*
Spencer Tracy – *Inherit the Wind*
Yves Montand – *Let's Make Love*

(British Actor)
Richard Attenborough
– *The Angry Silence*
• Peter Finch
– *The Trials of Oscar Wilde*
Albert Finney
– *Saturday Night and Sunday Morning*
John Fraser
– *The Trials of Oscar Wilde*
Alec Guinness – *Tunes of Glory*
John Mills – *Tunes of Glory*
Laurence Olivier – *The Entertainer*

NEW YORK – Burt Lancaster – *Elmer Gantry*
BOARD OF REVIEW – Robert Mitchum – *Home from the Hill* and ***The Sundowners***

Two of the strongest contenders for the year's Best Actor honours were previous Oscar winners Spencer Tracy and Fredric March as the lawyers in *Inherit the Wind*. In The New York Times, Bosley Crowther said their collaboration was "one of the most brilliant and engrossing displays of acting ever witnessed on the screen" while Variety commented that "if they aren't top contenders in the next Academy sweepstakes, then Oscar should be put in escrow for another year." When the film opened in Australia, The Sydney Morning Herald said, "Each of the main protagonists gives a potent analysis of his man: and Fredric March wins over Tracy because of the subtle complexities of his role. Here is compassion as well as skill". At the Berlin Film Festival, March was named Best Actor.

The year's other highly acclaimed performances were: Burt Lancaster as an evangelist in *Elmer Gantry* (NYT "outstanding"; NYer "impressive"; V "memorable"); Jack Lemmon as an insurance clerk in *The Apartment* (NYT "brilliantly played"); Anthony Perkins in *Psycho* (V "remarkably effective"; S&S "excellent"); Robert Mitchum in both *Home from the Hill* (NYT "garishly overplayed"; V "delivers his strongest performance in years") and *The Sundowners* (V "this may be the finest work he has done"; TT "sterling"; SMH "is surprisingly close to his Australian original in accent as well as lounging, feckless humour … a sound, admirable study"); Marlon Brando in *The Fugitive Kind* (NYT "brilliant"); Ralph Bellamy, reprising his Broadway success, as President Franklin D. Roosevelt in *Sunrise at Campobello* (NYT "every bit as strong, as full of feeling and characteristic gesture, as Mr Bellamy made it on the stage … one of the finest [performances] this year on the screen"; V "brilliant"; FQ "impressive" but "too calculated"; MFB "less a performance than a close, adulatory study of Roosevelt's mannerisms"; SMH "repeating his astonishing theatre performance"); Kirk Douglas in *Spartacus* (V "succeeds admirably"); Trevor Howard as a drunken miner in *Sons and Lovers* (NYT "played brilliantly"; V "superbly acted", "moving and wholly believable"); Laurence Olivier both as a former music-hall showman in *The Entertainer* (NYT "brilliant"; V "tremendous"; FQ a "virtuoso performance"; S&S "dazzlingly skilful") and as a Roman noble in *Spartacus* (V "exceptionally good"); 1959 BAFTA winner Peter Sellers in the comedy *I'm All Right Jack* (NYT "sensational", "side-splittingly funny"; SMH "a beautifully observed and richly funny performance … perfect"); Richard Attenborough in *The Angry Silence* (NYT "outstanding"; V "has done nothing better on the screen for a long time"; SMH "excellent"); and both Alec Guinness (NYT "superlative"; V "outstanding"; TT "splendid"; SMH "an uncanny performance") and Venice Film Festival Best Actor winner John Mills (NYT "brilliant", "tremendously revealing"; V "extremely moving"; TT "splendid"; S&S "impressive"; SMH "flawlessly played") in *Tunes of Glory*.

These performances overshadowed other portrayals such as: James Cagney in *The Gallant Hours* (NYT "one of the quietest, subtlest jobs that Mr Cagney has ever done"); Sidney Poitier in *All the Young Men* (NYT "commendable"); Bob Hope in *The Facts of Life* (V "exceptionally fine"); Richard Burton in *The*

Bramble Bush (NYT "remarkably substantial and aptly sensitive"); Stanley Baker in *Yesterday's Enemy* (NYT "the best performance of his career"); Dirk Bogarde in *Song Without End* (NYT "handsome and flamboyant as Liszt but he shows us little more than a troubled face"; V "brilliant"); Best Director nominee Jules Dassin in *Pote tin Kyriaki (Never on Sunday)* (NYT "superb"); Vittorio de Sica in *General della Rovere* (NYT "brilliant"); Peter Finch in *The Trials of Oscar Wilde* (V "moving and subtle"); and Richard Todd in *Never Let Go* (V "excellent").

The National Board of Review prize was awarded to Mitchum for both *Home from the Hill* and *The Sundowners*. Surprisingly, he was not considered for any of the other awards.

In New York a week later, Howard and Lemmon, the stars of the circle's two Best Picture winners, *Sons and Lovers* and *The Apartment*, were by-passed in favour of Lancaster, who had previously been honoured by the group in 1953. Howard finished as runner-up, followed by Olivier.

When the Golden Globe nominees were announced, March was a shock omission. The unexpected candidate was twenty-four-year old Dean Stockwell in *Sons and Lovers* (V "superbly acted"; FQ "fails to sustain the burning intensity so necessary for an adequate realization"; S&S "makes virtually no impression at all"). Surprisingly, the Academy also excluded March. Tracy was nominated, however – for a record seventh time.

The British Academy included March and Tracy for the Best Foreign Actor prize, along with Lancaster and Lemmon, but in a major upset, Howard was snubbed for the Best British Actor award.

Lancaster and Lemmon emerged as the frontrunners for the Oscar with victories at the Globes. Soon after, Lemmon won the BAFTA for Best Foreign Actor. Olivier's Oscar chances were not helped when he was outpolled for the British Academy's other award by Finch for *The Trials of Oscar Wilde*.

On Oscar night, Lancaster emerged victorious. He earned another nomination two years later, and then a fourth in 1981 when he was favoured by many to win a second statuette.

1960

BEST SUPPORTING ACTRESS

ACADEMY AWARDS
Glynis Johns as 'Mrs Firth' in *The Sundowners*
• Shirley Jones as 'Lulu Bains' in *Elmer Gantry*
Shirley Knight as 'Reenie Flood' in *The Dark at the Top of the Stairs*
Janet Leigh as 'Marion Crane' in *Psycho*
Mary Ure as 'Clara Dawes' in *Sons and Lovers*

GOLDEN GLOBE AWARDS
Ina Balin – *From the Terrace*
Shirley Jones – *Elmer Gantry*
Shirley Knight – *The Dark at the Top of the Stairs*
• Janet Leigh – *Psycho*
Mary Ure – *Sons and Lovers*

BOARD OF REVIEW – Shirley Jones – *Elmer Gantry*

In the 1950s, Shirley Jones was the popular star of musicals such as *Carousel* and *Oklahoma!*. In 1960, she was cast against type as a prostitute in *Elmer Gantry* and earned the National Board of Review prize, a Golden Globe nomination, and finally, the Oscar statuette for her performance (NYT "certainly different from the sweet heroine of 'Oklahoma!'"; V "impressive"). She later starred as the mother in the TV series 'The Partridge Family'.

The other main contender for the Oscar was Globe winner Janet Leigh as the petty thief murdered in a motel shower in Alfred Hitchcock's thriller, *Psycho*. Leigh's husband, Tony Curtis, had been a Best Actor nominee just two years earlier.

Also nominated for both the Globe and the Oscar were Shirley Knight as a travelling salesman's daughter in *The Dark at the Top of the Stairs* (V "fine"; TT "a tactful and warm-hearted performance"; SMH "touching") and Mary Ure in *Sons and Lovers* (V "superbly acted"; TT "a most intelligent study"). While the Hollywood Foreign Press Association completed the Golden Globe Award short-list by recognising Ina Balin in *From the Terrace* (NYT "beautifully played"; V "difficult to believe"), the Academy instead nominated Glynis Johns as the pub owner in *The Sundowners* (V "a vivacious delight"; TT "extraordinary"; MFB "all but bursts through the screen"; SMH "lively").

Surprisingly overlooked for both the Globe and the Oscar was previous Oscar winner Jo Van Fleet as the stubborn old matriarch in *Wild River*. Her performance was described by Variety as "a magnificent portrayal" which "steals the show" and has "Oscar written all over it."

Also overlooked were: Maureen Stapleton in *The Fugitive Kind* (NYT "touching"); both Brenda de Banzie (NYT "excellent"; V "irritating"; SMH "a superb performance") and Joan Plowright (V "excellent") in *The Entertainer*; Mildred Dunnock as the mother (NYT "excellent"), Betty Field as the mother's friend (NYT "excellent") and Kay Medford as the motel owner (NYT "amusing"; V "excellent") in *Butterfield 8*; Ann Shoemaker in *Sunrise at Campobello* (NYT "played extremely well"); Heather Sears in *Sons and Lovers* (V "superbly acted"; TT "touching"); both Eve Arden (NYT "showy and shallow"; V "convincing and highly effective") and Angela Lansbury (V "plays one of her better and more sympathetic roles … and she fills it well") in *The Dark at the Top of the Stairs*; Peggy Wood in *The Story of Ruth* (V "excellent"); Yvonne Mitchell in *The Trials of Oscar Wilde* (V "brilliantly understated"); and both Zhanna Prokhorenko (NYT "splendid") and Antonina Maksimova (NYT "beautifully conveyed") in the Russian drama *Ballada o Soldate (Ballad of a Soldier).*

1960

BEST SUPPORTING ACTOR

ACADEMY AWARDS
Peter Falk as 'Abe Reles' in *Murder, Inc.*
Jack Kruschen as 'Dr Dreyfuss' in *The Apartment*
Sal Mineo as 'Dov Landau' in *Exodus*
• Peter Ustinov as 'Lentulus Batiatus' in *Spartacus*
Chill Wills as 'Beekeeper' in *The Alamo*

GOLDEN GLOBE AWARDS
Lee Kinsolving – *The Dark at the Top of the Stairs*
• Sal Mineo – *Exodus*
Ray Stricklyn – *The Plunderers*
Woody Strode – *Spartacus*
Peter Ustinov – *Spartacus*

BOARD OF REVIEW – George Peppard – *Home from the Hill*

Several contenders for Best Supporting Actor honours appeared in the Roman epic *Spartacus*: Tony Curtis (V "a nicely balanced performance"), Charles Laughton (V "superb"), Woody Strode, and Peter Ustinov (NYer "good acting"; V "adroit"). The Academy only nominated Ustinov, for his portrayal of the owner of a gladiator school. He had also earned acclaim in *The Sundowners* (MFB "brilliantly funny"; SMH "flagrantly amusing and expert").

Also nominated for the Oscar were: Peter Falk as a gangland killer in *Murder, Inc.* (NYT "amusingly vicious"); Jack Kruschen as the neighbour in *The Apartment* (NYT "funny"; V "one of the film's hits"); Golden Globe winner Sal Mineo as a Zionist terrorist in *Exodus* (NYT "superb"; V "excellent"); and, following an infamously controversial campaign of self-promotion, Chill Wills in *The Alamo* (NYT "the best man in the cast"; SMH "gives an ingratiating account of a boisterous Tennessean").

The Academy included Wills ahead of National Board of Review winner George Peppard in *Home from the Hill* (NYT "garishly overplayed"; TT "striking"), and two Globe nominees: Lee Kinsolving in *The Dark at the Top of the Stairs* (V "persuasively acted") and Ray Stricklyn in *The Plunderers* (V "admirable").

Also overlooked were: Hume Cronyn in *Sunrise at Campobello* (NYT "a brilliant performance"); Felix Aylmer in *From the Terrace* (NYT "splendid"); both Victor Jory (NYT "simply superb") and R. G. Armstrong (NYT "smashing") in *The Fugitive Kind*; both Frank Gorshin and Bernie West in *Bells*

Are Ringing (V "excellent"); David Opatoshu in *Exodus* (S&S "excellent"); Roger Livesey in *The Entertainer* (V "completely believable"); Noel Coward in *Our Man in Havana* (NYT "standout"); Philip Ahn in *Yesterday's Enemy* (NYT "excellent"); William Hartnell in *Piccadilly Third Stop* (V "amusing"); Bernard Lee in *The Angry Silence* (SMH "exactly right"); James Mason in *The Trials of Oscar Wilde*; and Dean Stockwell, who had been a Golden Globe (Drama) nominee for Best Actor, for *Sons and Lovers* (NYT "played politely").

The Oscar frontrunners were Globe winner Mineo and Ustinov, both of whom were up for the award for a second time. Possibly because he had the advantage of two high-profile supporting turns in acclaimed and popular films, the Oscar went to Ustinov. He won a second Supporting Actor Oscar just four years later.

1961

BEST PICTURE

ACADEMY AWARDS

Fanny
(Mansfield, Warner Bros., 134 mins, 28 Jun 1961, 5 noms)

The Guns of Navarone
(Foreman, Columbia, 158 mins, 22 Jun 1961, $12.5m, 8 noms)

The Hustler
(Rossen, Twentieth Century-Fox, 134 mins BW, 25 Sep 1961, 9 noms)

Judgment at Nuremberg
(Kramer, United Artists, 178 mins BW, 1 Dec 1961, $5.0m, 11 noms)

• ***West Side Story***
(Mirisch-B&P, United Artists, 151 mins, 18 Oct 1961, $19.6m, 11 noms)

GOLDEN GLOBE AWARDS

(Drama)
El Cid
Fanny
• ***The Guns of Navarone***
Judgment at Nuremberg
Splendor in the Grass

(Comedy)
Breakfast at Tiffany's
• ***A Majority of One***
One, Two, Three
The Parent Trap
Pocketful of Miracles

(Musical)
Babes in Toyland
Flower Drum Song
• ***West Side Story***

BRITISH ACADEMY AWARDS

(Film)
Apur Sansar (The World of Apu)
• ***Ballada o Soldate (Ballad of a Soldier)***
• ***The Hustler***
The Innocents
Judgment at Nuremberg
The Long and the Short and the Tall (Jungle Fighters)
Rocco e i soui Fratelli (Rocco and His Brothers)
The Sundowners
A Taste of Honey
Le Trou (The Night Watch)
Whistle Down the Wind

(British Film)
The Innocents
The Long and the Short and the Tall (Jungle Fighters)
The Sundowners
• ***A Taste of Honey***
Whistle Down the Wind

NEW YORK – *West Side Story*
BOARD OF REVIEW – *Question Seven*
SCREEN PRODUCERS GUILD – *West Side Story*

1961

In mid-December 1961, the National Board of Review made a surprising choice for Best Picture: *Question Seven*, a West German English-language propaganda drama, funded by the Lutheran Church, about an East German youth's struggle to reconcile his religious beliefs with his Communist education (NYT has "an extraordinary timeliness and dramatic immediacy" … "becomes compelling"). The film was not considered for any of the other end of year accolades.

The main contenders for the Best Picture Oscar were *Judgment at Nuremberg*, a courtroom drama about the post-war Nazi war crimes trials (NYT "powerful, persuasive"; V "carefully, tastefully and upliftingly told"; TT "good and intelligent", "a brave and formidable achievement"; SMH "long, sobering drama", "a remarkable production") and *West Side Story*, a film version of the Broadway musical (NYT "superb", "a cinema masterpiece"; V "impressive", "powerful and sometimes fascinating"; S&S "striking"; SMH "powerful, moving and original"). Each received eleven Oscar nominations.

Also nominated for the top Oscar were: *The Hustler*, a drama about pool sharks which snared nine nominations (NYT "crackles with credible passions"; SMH "powerful"); *The Guns of Navarone*, a World War Two action film which was the year's biggest box office success and recipient of eight Oscar nominations (NYT "more emphasis is placed on melodrama than on character or credibility"; V "spectacular"; TT "first-rate", "tremendous and at moments even overwhelming", "outstanding"; Time "enjoyable"); and *Fanny*, a romantic drama which received five nominations (NYT "delightful and heart-warming").

Overlooked by the Academy were: *A Raisin in the Sun* (NYT "fine"; V "fine"; SMH "among the best films of the year"); Globe nominee *Splendor in the Grass* (NYT "a frank and ferocious social drama"; V "extremely intimate and affecting experience"; TT "a disappointment"); Globe nominee *El Cid* (NYT "the spectacle is terrific – only the human drama is stiff and dull"); Globe (Comedy) winner *A Majority of One* (NYT a "truly heartwarming and entertaining affair" but "overlong and occasionally too loquacious"); the popular Globe nominee *Breakfast at Tiffany's* (NYT "completely unbelievable but wholly captivating"; V "surprisingly moving"; SMH "elegant, raffish entertainment"); *Lover Come Back* (NYT a "sophisticated American comedy"); Globe nominee *One, Two, Three* (NYT "the sharpness of wit and satire is less conspicuous than the magnitude and speed of the obvious jokes and comic action … there is nothing subtle about it"); dual Best Film BAFTA nominee *The Innocents* (NYT lacks "sufficient incisiveness and candor to give us a first-rate horror or psychological film … [but it is] one that still has interest and sends some formidable chills down the spine"; SMH "a rare horror film for adults"); and *Saturday Night and Sunday Morning*, the previous year's Best British Film BAFTA winner (NYT "vivid"; V "absorbing but not very likeable"; S&S "engagingly frank"; FQ "a good film").

1961

In the year that the Academy first awarded a performance in a foreign-language film, the Best Picture Oscar list was again notably lacking any of the year's acclaimed non-English-language movies such as: *La Ciociara (Two Women)*, an Italian drama which won the Best Foreign-Language Film Globe and the Best Actress Oscar for Sophia Loren (NYT "a simple, honest film"); Federico Fellini's acclaimed *La Dolce Vita*, which won the New York award for Best Foreign-Language Film (NYT "sensational", "brilliant", "an awesome picture"; S&S "if 'La Dolce Vita' had been less grandiose and more private and personal it might have worked"; SMH "does not warrant the uproar it has caused … unexpectedly obvious in its story and derivative in style"); *Die Brücke (The Bridge)*, a German drama which won the NBR Best Foreign-Language Film prize (NYT "intense and compelling"); Jean-Luc Godard's French hit *À Bout de Souffle (Breathless)* (NYT "sordid" but "fascinating"; S&S "fascinating"); Luchino Visconti's Italian film *Rocco e i soui Fratelli (Rocco and His Brothers)* (NYT a "strong and surging drama"); the thriller *Plein Soleil (Purple Noon)*, a film version of Patricia Highsmith's novel 'The Talented Mr Ripley' (NYT "fascinating" and "dazzlingly beautiful"); and *Kumonosu jo (Throne of Blood)*, Akira Kurosawa's Japanese film version of William Shakespeare's 'Macbeth' (V "noteworthy"; TT "savage and turbulent"; S&S "impressive', "fascinating").

On December 28, *West Side Story* unexpectedly outpolled *Judgment at Nuremberg* on the third round of voting for the New York Film Critics Circle prize. It was the first musical and the first colour film honoured by the circle.

A month before the Oscars, *West Side Story* won the Golden Globe for Best Picture (Musical) and the Best Film award from the Screen Producers Guild. In a major surprise, however, *The Guns of Navarone*, the year's box office champion, won the Best Picture (Drama) Globe ahead of *Judgment at Nuremberg*, which had received the most Globe nominations that year.

Three days before the Oscar ceremony, *Judgment at Nuremberg* was unexpectedly outpolled again, this time for the Best Film BAFTA. Robert Rossen's *The Hustler* shared the award with the 1959 Russian war drama *Ballada o Soldate (Ballad of a Soldier)*, which the Academy in Hollywood had overlooked (NYT "touching"; V "warm, simple"; TT "outstanding"; FQ "an emotional film of exceedingly fine craftsmanship"; MFB "engaging"). Meanwhile, the Best British Film BAFTA was won by *A Taste of Honey*, an acclaimed comedy-drama about a teenager who becomes pregnant to a sailor which was eligible for Oscar consideration the following year (NYT "striking"; V "compelling"; S&S "first-rate").

On Oscar night, *West Side Story* triumphed with ten statuettes, including Best Picture and Best Director. Its haul was just one award short of the all-time record tally. It went on to finish 1962 as the year's highest-grossing film at the US box office.

1961

BEST DIRECTOR

ACADEMY AWARDS
Federico Fellini for *La Dolce Vita*
Stanley Kramer for *Judgment at Nuremberg*
• Jerome Robbins and Robert Wise for *West Side Story*
Robert Rossen for *The Hustler*
J. Lee Thompson for *The Guns of Navarone*

GOLDEN GLOBE AWARDS
• Stanley Kramer – *Judgment at Nuremberg*
Anthony Mann – *El Cid*
Jerome Robbins and Robert Wise – *West Side Story*
J. Lee Thompson – *The Guns of Navarone*
William Wyler – *The Children's Hour*

DIRECTORS GUILD AWARD
Blake Edwards – *Breakfast at Tiffany's*
Stanley Kramer – *Judgment at Nuremberg*
• Jerome Robbins and Robert Wise – *West Side Story*
Robert Rossen – *The Hustler*
J. Lee Thompson – *The Guns of Navarone*

NEW YORK – Robert Rossen – *The Hustler*
BOARD OF REVIEW – Jack Clayton – *The Innocents*

For the first time in the thirty-four-year history of the Oscars, the Academy included the director of a foreign-language film in the Best Director category: Federico Fellini for *La Dolce Vita* (NYT "splendid" direction). The acclaimed Italian film had won the Palme d'Or at the Cannes Film Festival the previous year and had become a very successful arthouse release in the United States. The New York critics' circle chose it as the year's Best Foreign-Language Film and the Academy nominated it in four categories.

In addition to Fellini, Oscar voters short-listed the winners of three of the other four major accolades, and the director of the year's biggest box office hit.

Robert Rossen won the New York Film Critics Circle award for *The Hustler* (NYT "strong"; LAT "directed in expert, if grim, fashion"). Although overlooked for the Golden Globe, Rossen was a candidate for the Directors Guild of America prize and received his second mention from the Academy.

1961

In the absence of Rossen, Stanley Kramer claimed the Globe for *Judgment at Nuremberg* and also earned a second nod from the Academy (LAT directed in a "measured, even meticulous manner"; SMH "skillful").

Outpolling Rossen and Kramer for the coveted Guild honour was the team of choreographer Jerome Robbins and film-maker Robert Wise for the musical *West Side Story*. Robbins and Wise had been the runners-up for the critic's prize in New York and were the first directorial pair to nominated for the Oscar.

Completing the list of nominees was J. Lee Thompson for *The Guns of Navarone*, the year's box office champion (TT deserves "major credit for the success" of the film; S&S "film lacks a firm controlling hand"; FQ "striking"; MFB "has not the ability to hold a long picture together"). Thompson had also been a contender for both the Globe and the DGA award.

The only one of the year's major Best Director winners to be excluded from the Oscar contest was Englishman Jack Clayton for the British thriller *The Innocents* (NYT "does a fine job of infusing this drama with spooky atmosphere and a certain sense of the weird and supernatural"). Clayton, an Oscar nominee two year's earlier for *Room at the Top*, won the National Board of Review plaudit, but did not receive any votes from the New York critics and was absent from consideration for both the Globe and the Directors Guild of America prize.

Also overlooked by the Academy were: DGA nominee Blake Edwards for *Breakfast at Tiffany's* (SMH "adroitly handles the [story]"); Globe nominee William Wyler for *The Children's Hour*, an adaptation of Lillian Hellman's play about slander which Wyler had previously directed as *These Three* in 1936 (NYT "should hang his head in shame … there is nothing about this picture of which he can be very proud"); John Huston for *The Misfits* (NYT "dynamic, inventive and colorful"; SMH "superb film craftsmanship"); Elia Kazan for *Splendor in the Grass*; Billy Wilder for the comedy *One, Two, Three*; Karel Reisz for *Saturday Night and Sunday Morning* (SMH "gives us some blinding passages of filmcraft"); Daniel Petrie for *A Raisin in the Sun*; Joshua Logan for *Fanny*, a Best Picture nominee (V "delicate direction"); Luchino Visconti for *Rocco e i soui Fratelli (Rocco and His Brothers)* (NYT "brilliant handling"); and Akira Kurosawa for *Kumonosu jo (Throne of Blood)* (NYT "Kurosawa's camera is handled with magnificent skill. There is exciting communication in its very movement and in the imagistic forms it evolves"; V "masterful direction").

Their DGA victory made the team behind *West Side Story* the strong favourites for the Oscar. For the previous twelve years, the DGA winner had subsequently been honoured with the Academy Award.

On Oscar night, Robbins and Wise became the first duo to be named as Best Director by the Academy. While Robbins never made the Oscar lists again, Wise won a second statuette just four years later.

1961

BEST ACTRESS

ACADEMY AWARDS
Audrey Hepburn as 'Holly Golightly' in *Breakfast at Tiffany's*
Piper Laurie as 'Sarah Packard' in *The Hustler*
• Sophia Loren as 'Cesira' in *La Ciociara (Two Women)*
Geraldine Page as 'Alma Winemiller' in *Summer and Smoke*
Natalie Wood as 'Wilma Dean Loomis' in *Splendor in the Grass*

GOLDEN GLOBE AWARDS
(Drama)
Leslie Caron – *Fanny*
Shirley MacLaine – *The Children's Hour*
Claudia McNeil – *A Raisin in the Sun*
• Geraldine Page – *Summer and Smoke*
Natalie Wood – *Splendor in the Grass*

(Comedy/Musical)
Bette Davis – *Pocketful of Miracles*
Audrey Hepburn – *Breakfast at Tiffany's*
Hayley Mills – *The Parent Trap*
• Rosalind Russell – *A Majority of One*
Miyoshi Umeki – *Flower Drum Song*

BRITISH ACADEMY AWARDS
(Foreign Actress)
Annie Girardot – *Rocco e i soui Fratelli (Rocco and His Brothers)*
Piper Laurie – *The Hustler*
• Sophia Loren – *La Ciociara (Two Women)*
Claudia McNeil – *A Raisin in the Sun*
Jean Seberg – *À Bout de Souffle (Breathless)*

(British Actress)
• Dora Bryan – *A Taste of Honey*
Deborah Kerr – *The Sundowners*
Hayley Mills – *Whistle Down the Wind*

NEW YORK – Sophia Loren – *La Ciociara (Two Women)*
BOARD OF REVIEW – Geraldine Page – *Summer and Smoke*

Since coming to Hollywood in the mid-1950s, Sophia Loren had been mainly given roles in romantic comedies. She attempted to escape this type-casting in 1961 by accepting starring roles in the epic *El Cid* and Vittorio de Sica's black-and-white drama *La Ciociara (Two Women)*. Her performance in the latter, as a woman escaping with her daughter from war-torn Rome, was honoured at the Cannes Film Festival, and earned her widespread critical acclaim (NYT "praiseworthy", "demonstrates herself an actress"; V "excellent", "impressive"; S&S "valiant"; MFB "authorative"; SMH "superb").

When the New York Film Critics Circle cast their votes for Best Actress, Loren tied on the first ballot with Geraldine Page, who only nine days earlier had won the National Board of Review award for her performance as a repressed spinster in *Summer and Smoke* (NYT "never falters"; TT "outstanding"; S&S "magnificent"; MFB demonstrates "sheer technical brilliance and richness of emotional range"; SMH "expressive, subtle and delicate gives the woman's performance of the year"). They both received four votes in the first round of voting, with three votes going to Piper Laurie as the alcoholic, crippled girlfriend of a pool shark in *The Hustler* (LAT "will tear at your heart as the strange, lonely girl"; V "establishes herself solidly"; TT "a highly intelligent performance"; MFB a "bravely off-beat show"; Life "proves herself a fine, perceptive actress"; SMH "superb"). On the sixth and final ballot, Loren obtained a winning edge with eleven votes to seven for Page and one for Laurie.

In the new year, Loren was overlooked for the Golden Globe (Drama) and Page was by-passed for the Best Foreign Actress BAFTA. Each actress, in the absence of the other, collected the accolade for which she had been nominated.

When the Academy announced its nominees, Page, Loren and Laurie were in contention for the Best Actress Oscar for the first time (Page had been a nominee in the supporting category in 1953). Loren's inclusion marked the first time that a performance in a foreign-language film had ever been recognised by the Academy.

Also nominated were Globe nominee Audrey Hepburn (her fourth nod) as an eccentric free-spirit in *Breakfast at Tiffany's* (NYT "displaying a fey, comic talent"; V "expressive"; S&S "a spellbinder … transforms the material"; MFB "plays her with a beautifully light touch"; SMH "Hepburn is an enchantment") and twenty-three-year old Globe nominee Natalie Wood (her second nomination) as the high school girl in *Splendor in the Grass* (NYT "played with amazing definition … in the end, the authority and eloquence of the theme emerge in the honest, sensitive acting of Mr Beatty and Miss Wood … there is poetry in her performance"; NYP "heartbreaking in her exquisite projection of the role"; LAT "Wood's response to her most demanding role is gratifying indeed – playful innocence, awakening desire, despair, coquetry, mental breakdown, rehabilitation and finally a maturity of sorts"; V "convincing"; TT "magnificent in an exacting part"). Hepburn had also been considered a contender for the drama *The Children's Hour* (NYT "gives the impression of being sensitive and pure"; V "a memorable portrayal – one of potential Oscar nomination calibre") while Wood had also starred in the musical *West Side Story* (NYT "outstanding"; V "entrancing"; SMH "touchingly true").

1961

The glaring omission from the Oscar list was Claudia McNeil in *A Raisin in the Sun*, the only actress nominated for both the Globe and the BAFTA (NYT "excellent"; LAT "repeats superlatively her role as the courageous mother … hers is a portrayal that brings nobleness, sympathy and warmth to this emotionally supercharged story"; V "repeats her towering stage portrayal", "sure to be remembered next Oscar time"; SMH "magnificently played").

Another notable omission was Rosalind Russell, who won a record fourth Globe as a Brooklyn widow who falls in love while holidaying in Japan in *A Majority of One* (NYT "does not readily come to mind as the obvious choice for the role, but she does an amazingly fine job, which has to be seen to be believed"; V "conveys the character almost to perfection").

Also by-passed for Oscar consideration were: Leslie Caron in *Fanny* (NYT "expressive"; V "scores with a warm enactment"); Shirley MacLaine in *The Children's Hour* (NYT "inclines to be too kittenish in some scenes and to do too much vocal hand-wringing toward the end"); Bette Davis in *Pocketful of Miracles*, in a role for which May Robson had been an Oscar nominee in 1932/3 (SMH "magnificent"); Marilyn Monroe in *The Misfits* (NYT "completely blank and unfathomable"; V "never quite fully submerges her own identity into the character"; MFB "has wonderful moments"); Annie Girardot in *Rocco e i soui Fratelli (Rocco and His Brothers)* (NYT "striking"; S&S "flawless"); Jean Seberg in *À Bout de Souffle (Breathless)* (V "lacks emotive projection"); 1960 BAFTA winner Rachel Roberts in *Saturday Night and Sunday Morning* (NYT "excellent"; FQ "excellent"; SMH "an arresting, vivid study"); Deborah Kerr in *The Innocents* (NYT "[the film is] let down by [her] lucent performance … neither acts nor looks a repressed or inhibited woman"; SMH "sensitively aware of her [character's time] period"); Ingrid Bergman in *Goodbye Again* (NYT "[the character] is neither that interesting nor is she sufficiently well played"; MFB "[played] remarkably convincingly"); and Anouk Aimee in *La Dolce Vita* (NYT '[makes a] most vivid impression"; S&S "brilliantly played").

The winner of the Best British Actress BAFTA, Dora Bryan for *A Taste of Honey*, and her co-star Rita Tushingham, would not be eligible for Oscar consideration until the following year.

Loren was too nervous to attend the Oscar ceremony, and chose to remain at home in Italy. She stayed up impatiently waiting for news from Hollywood and when dawn broke she decided that she must have lost and went to bed. Not long afterwards, she later told reporters, she received a telephone call from Cary Grant with the news that she had won. She was the first person to win an Oscar for a performance in a foreign-language film.

Three years later, Loren was a Best Actress nominee for another performance in a foreign-language film directed by Vittorio de Sica, the Italian comedy *Matrimonio all'italiana (Marriage, Italian Style)*.

1961

BEST ACTOR

ACADEMY AWARDS

Charles Boyer as 'Cesar' in *Fanny*
Paul Newman as 'Eddie Felson' in *The Hustler*
• Maximilian Schell as 'Hans Rolfe' in *Judgment at Nuremberg*
Spencer Tracy as 'Judge Dan Haywood' in *Judgment at Nuremberg*
Stuart Whitman as 'Jim Fuller' in *The Mark*

GOLDEN GLOBE AWARDS

(Drama)
Warren Beatty – *Splendor in the Grass*
Maurice Chevalier – *Fanny*
Paul Newman – *The Hustler*
Sidney Poitier – *A Raisin in the Sun*
• Maximilian Schell – *Judgment at Nuremberg*

(Comedy/Musical)
Fred Astaire – *Pleasure of His Company*
Richard Beymer – *West Side Story*
• Glenn Ford – *Pocketful of Miracles*
Bob Hope – *Bachelor in Paradise*
Fred MacMurray – *The Absent-Minded Professor*

BRITISH ACADEMY AWARDS

(Foreign Actor)
Montgomery Clift – *Judgment at Nuremberg*
Vladimir Ivashov – *Ballada o Soldate (Ballad of a Soldier)*
Philippe Leroy – *Le Trou (The Night Watch)*
• Paul Newman – *The Hustler*
Sidney Poitier – *A Raisin in the Sun*
Maximilian Schell – *Judgment at Nuremberg*
Alberto Sordi – *The Best of Enemies*

(British Actor)
Dirk Bogarde – *Victim*
• Peter Finch – *No Love for Johnnie*

NEW YORK – Maximilian Schell – *Judgment at Nuremberg*
BOARD OF REVIEW – Albert Finney – *Saturday Night and Sunday Morning*

The Best Actor Academy Award nominees were expected to be the three actors who had been in contention for the New York Film Critics Circle prize, along with the year's hottest new star and a veteran of pre-war musicals in his comeback role in a drama.

The winner in New York was thirty-one-year old Austrian Maximilian Schell, who attracted ten votes on the sixth and final ballot for his performance as a lawyer defending Nazi officers in *Judgment at Nuremberg* (NYT "performed masterly"; LAT "brilliant must surely be the word for Maximilian Schell's pounding projection of the defense lawyer"; V "not easily forgotten"; WP "persuasive"; FQ "dynamic"; MFB "overplays"; SMH "distinguished"). The runner-up, with four votes, was James Cagney as an American executive in West Berlin in the comedy *One, Two, Three* (NYT "the burden is carried by Mr Cagney ... he has seldom worked so hard in any picture or had such a browbeating ball ... he sure makes you laugh"). In the final round of voting, Paul Newman received two votes for his turn as a pool shark in *The Hustler* (NYT "plays with a master's control"; LAT "gives a powerful, restrained performance of the hustler ... builds his rather complex character admirably"; V "entirely believable"; MFB "competent"; SMH "superb").

The film sensation of the year was twenty-four-year old Warren Beatty, the brother of previous Best Actress nominee Shirley MacLaine. Beatty won acclaim for his debut as the heart-throb in *Splendor in the Grass* (NYT "played with amazing definition ... in the end, the authority and eloquence of the theme emerge in the honest, sensitive acting of Mr Beatty and Miss Wood ... [Beatty] shapes an amiable, decent, sturdy lad whose emotional exhaustion and defeat are the deep pathos in the film"; LAT "Beatty reflects sincerity and a boyish confidence that, while sometimes stumbling, will charm viewers"; V "convincing"). His almost instant popularity with the public was demonstrated in late February when Beatty was selected as the outstanding actor in the fortieth annual reader poll conducted by Photoplay magazine.

Maurice Chevalier, the popular French star of pre-war musicals who had been a Best Actor Oscar nominee in 1929/30, campaigned strongly to be recognised for his first non-singing role in an American film – the wealthy older suitor of a young woman in *Fanny* (NYT "wonderfully gentle"; V "walks off with the picture").

Beatty, Chevalier, Newman and Schell were all nominated for the Golden Globe (Drama) along with Sidney Poitier, for reprising his stage success in *A Raisin in the Sun* (NYT "excellent"; LAT "Poitier gives a vivid performance that commands great interest. He conveys self-torture with both expression and movement"; V "striking, commanding"; MFB "played with intelligence"; SMH "brilliant work"). In the Comedy/Musical category, however, Cagney was a surprise omission.

In an even bigger shock, Warner Bros. announced that it was putting Beatty forward for recognition in the Best Supporting Actor category at the Academy

Awards. Presumably the studio was hoping the move would secure a Best Actor nomination for Chevalier; *Fanny* was also a Warner Bros. film. Furious, Beatty said he would decline any nomination.

When the Academy revealed its short-list, New York and Globe winner Schell received his first nod and Newman earned his second mention in four years. The other nominees, however, were not as expected. Beatty was absent from both acting categories and both Cagney and Chevalier were overlooked.

Named instead of these front-runners were: Chevalier's co-star, Charles Boyer, who received his fourth (and final) mention as a cafe owner in *Fanny* (NYT "superbly portrayed"; TT "a full portrait"); Spencer Tracy as the judge in *Judgment at Nuremberg*, his record eighth nod (NYT "played superbly"; V "a performance of great intelligence and intuition"; FQ "expert"; SMH "a performance of matchless integrity"); and Stuart Whitman as an alleged child molester struggling to rehabilitate himself in the British film *The Mark* (NYT "does manage to convey the turmoil that would unnerve a physically strong, but mentally sensitive, man"; V "rather downbeat but absorbing").

Others overlooked were: Cannes Film Festival winner Anthony Perkins in *Goodbye Again* (NYT "plays [the role] in the most engaging fashion and almost carries the picture by himself… ranges from boyish excitement to deep and tear-popping grief and makes it believable and cogent"; LAT "engagingly played"; MFB "Perkins is mature and unusually unaffected"); National Board of Review winner Albert Finney in *Saturday Night and Sunday Morning* (NYT "brilliant realized and played by a fine young actor"; TT "succeeds"; FQ "he is constantly creating a human being"; SMH "Finney's lusty, profoundly dissatisfied graceless young worker is a creation that demanded his award"); Peter Sellers in *Two-Way Stretch* (NYT "dry and superior as the confident Cockney crook"; V "deft"); Laurence Harvey in *The Long and the Short and the Tall (Jungle Fighters)* (V "standout"); Berlin Film Festival prizewinner and BAFTA winner Peter Finch as a British politician in *No Love for Johnnie* (NYT "fascinating"; MFB "professional and intelligent playing"); and for their work in *The Misfits* both previous winner Clark Gable in his final screen appearance (SMH "unsure") and Montgomery Clift (V "excellent").

The Academy also by-passed several acclaimed non-English-language performances: Marcello Mastroianni in *La Dolce Vita* (NYT "played brilliantly"; V "excellent", "perfect"); Alain Delon in *Plein Soleil (Purple Noon)* (NYT "engaging"); Jean-Paul Belmondo in *À Bout de Souffle (Breathless)* (V "excellent" S&S "brilliant"); Vladimir Ivashov in *Ballada o Soldate (Ballad of a Soldier)* (NYT "splendid"); Renato Salvatori in *Rocco e i soui Fratelli (Rocco and His Brothers)* (NYT "unforgettable"); and Toshiro Mifune for *Kumonosu jo (Throne of Blood)*.

Meanwhile, Anthony Quayle's chances of receiving a nomination for his co-starring performance as Captain van der Poel in *Ice Cold in Alex*, for which he was a nominee for the Best British Actor BAFTA in 1958 (G "acting of a rare quality"), were thwarted when the film was finally released in the United States by Twentieth Century-Fox under the title *Desert Attack* with nearly an hour cut from the film's original two-hour-and-ten-minute length. The New York Times' Eugene Archer slammed the "hopelessly abbreviated form" in which the movie was screened. While the severe editing rendered the film's plot "totally pointless" and removed character development and motivation, Archer nonetheless called the acting "impeccable". Unsurprisingly, Quayle's performance went unnoticed during the North American film awards season.

Schell was the Oscar frontrunner but, as the night approached, support seemed to grow for Tracy, who hadn't won a statuette since his unprecedented back-to-back Best Actor victories in 1937 and 1938. The race became even harder to predict when, just days before the Oscars, Newman emerged as a darkhorse when he outpolled Schell to win the British Academy Award for Best Foreign Actor.

On Oscar night, however, there was no upset: Schell won the Best Actor Oscar. "This honors not only me, but the cast and that great old man who has been nominated for the eighth time now, Spencer Tracy," he told the audience. Back stage, he admitted to reporters that he had expected Newman to win.

Schell subsequently earned Oscar nominations for Best Actor for *The Man in the Glass Booth* in 1975 and for Best Supporting Actor for *Julia* in 1977. He also made several films as a director, one of which, *Der Fussgänger (The Pedestrian)* about the trial of an elderly war criminal, won the Golden Globe Award for Best Foreign-Language Film of 1973 and was nominated for the Best Foreign-Language Film Oscar for West Germany.

1961

BEST SUPPORTING ACTRESS

ACADEMY AWARDS
Fay Bainter as 'Mrs Amelia Tilford' in *The Children's Hour*
Judy Garland as 'Irene Hoffman' in *Judgment at Nuremberg*
Lotte Lenya as 'Contessa Terribili-Gonzales' in *The Roman Spring of Mrs Stone*
Una Merkel as 'Mrs Winemiller' in *Summer and Smoke*
• Rita Moreno as 'Anita' in *West Side Story*

GOLDEN GLOBE AWARDS
Fay Bainter – *The Children's Hour*
Judy Garland – *Judgment at Nuremberg*
Lotte Lenya – *The Roman Spring of Mrs Stone*
• Rita Moreno – *West Side Story*
Pamela Tiffin – *One, Two, Three*

BOARD OF REVIEW – Ruby Dee – *A Raisin in the Sun*

Seven years after she was narrowly outpolled for Best Actress, Judy Garland was overwhelmingly favoured to claim an Oscar with her second (and final) nod as the German housewife in *Judgment at Nuremberg* (NYT "amazingly real"; LAT "touching"; SMH "astonishingly good").

The other nominees were: Golden Globe winner Rita Moreno in *West Side Story* (V "scores hugely"; S&S "fine"; SMH a "triumph"); Una Merkel as the mother of a small-town spinster in *Summer and Smoke* (MFB "great fun"); Lotte Lenya as a corrupt aristocrat who runs a male escort agency in *The Roman Spring of Mrs Stone* (NYT "elaborately performs"; V "excellent"; TT "entertaining"; S&S "notable"; SMH "diabolically successful"); and previous winner Fay Bainter as the grandmother in *The Children's Hour* (NYT "fairly grim"; V "outstanding").

Surprisingly omitted from Oscar consideration was National Board of Review winner Ruby Dee as the hard-working wife in *A Raisin in the Sun* (NYT "quietly magnificent", "excellent"; LAT "underplays excellently"; MFB "a touching and skilful sketch"). Dee's co-star, Diana Sands, was also overlooked (NYT "fascinating"; LAT "plays well"; V "a standout").

Also passed over were: Globe nominee Pamela Tiffin in *One, Two, Three* (NYT "very good"; MFB "convincingly dizzy"); Marlene Dietrich in *Judgment at Nuremberg* (NYT "most sensitive"; LAT "subtly restrained but nonetheless effective"; V "persuasive"; S&S a "finely shaded performance"; MFB "persuasive"); Patricia Neal in *Breakfast at Tiffany's* (TT "excels"; S&S "a beautifully hard, glittering performance"); Audrey Christie in *Splendor in the Grass* (NYT "relentlessly engulfing"; LAT "standout"; V "truly exceptional ... worth serious Oscar consideration"); Thelma Ritter in *The Misfits* (MFB "thoroughly professional"); Megs Jenkins in *The Innocents* (SMH "the most telling and admirable work comes from Megs Jenkins as the housekeeper"); Yvonne Furneaux in *La Dolce Vita* (V "excellent"); Eleonora Brown in *La Ciociara (Two Women)* (V "amazing"); Katina Paxinou as the matriarch in *Rocco e i soui Fratelli (Rocco and His Brothers)* (S&S "flawless"); Isuzu Yamada in *Kumonosu jo (Throne of Blood)* (TT "stands out"; S&S "conveying perfectly all that her part demands"); and Antonina Maksimova in the Russian drama *Ballada o Soldate (Ballad of a Soldier)* (NYT "beautifully conveyed").

On Oscar night, Garland's dream of an Academy Award was dashed a second time. The upset winner of the statuette was Moreno. "I can't believe it!" she exclaimed from the stage after collecting the statuette from Rock Hudson.

Since her victory, Moreno has enjoyed continued success on Broadway, collecting a Tony Award in 1975 for 'The Ritz'. She is one of only a handful of performers to have won an Oscar, a Grammy, an Emmy and a Tony during her career.

1961

BEST SUPPORTING ACTOR

ACADEMY AWARDS
• George Chakiris as 'Bernardo' in *West Side Story*
Montgomery Clift as 'Rudolf Petersen' in *Judgment at Nuremberg*
Peter Falk as 'Joy Boy' in *Pocketful of Miracles*
Jackie Gleason as 'Minnesota Fats' in *The Hustler*
George C. Scott as 'Bert Gordon' in *The Hustler*

GOLDEN GLOBE AWARDS
• George Chakiris – *West Side Story*
Montgomery Clift – *Judgment at Nuremberg*
Jackie Gleason – *The Hustler*
Tony Randall – *Lover Come Back*
George C. Scott – *The Hustler*

BOARD OF REVIEW – Jackie Gleason – *The Hustler*

Warner Bros. decided to promote Warren Beatty's feature film debut as the heartbreaker in *Splendor in the Grass* for the Best Supporting Actor Academy Award even though he had one of the film's two leading roles and was a nominee at the Golden Globe Awards for the Best Actor (Drama) Award (NYT "played with amazing definition … in the end, the authority and eloquence of the theme emerge in the honest, sensitive acting of Mr Beatty and Miss Wood … [Beatty] shapes an amiable, decent, sturdy lad whose emotional exhaustion and defeat are the deep pathos in the film"; V "convincing"). Unimpressed by the studio's tactic, Beatty declared that he would decline any nomination.

Beatty's absence from the list of candidates, ironically, did not spare the Oscars from embarrassment. George C. Scott, nominated for the second time in three years for his performance as the manager of a pool shark in *The Hustler* (NYT "magnificent"; MFB "good"; SMH "superb"), denounced the idea of actors competing for prizes and asked that his name be removed from the ballot. It was the first time in the Academy's history that such a request had been made. The Academy refused, stating that it was the performance that was nominated rather than the performer. An anonymous official told The New York Times, "the nomination is not actually for the best actor or supporting actor but for the best achievement in those fields in which the person is only identified with that achievement. Despite his withdrawal, his name will remain on the ballot. If he wins an Oscar, he can refuse the award, but that, of course, is up to him."

The other nominees were: National Board of Review prizewinner Jackie Gleason as a tough pool player in *The Hustler* (NYT "excellent"; Life "covers himself with glory"); Golden Globe winner George Chakiris as the leader of the Sharks in the musical *West Side Story* (V "colorful"; S&S "fine"; SMH a "triumph"); Peter Falk as a gangster's bodyguard in *Pocketful of Miracles*, his second consecutive nod (V "just about walks off with the film"; SMH "beautiful support"); and Montgomery Clift (for the final time) in *Judgment at Nuremberg* (NYT "played touchingly"; S&S "embarrassingly mannered"; FQ "an extraordinary, almost nakedly painful performance").

Having been unsuccessfully nominated three times between 1948 and 1953, Clift was the sentimental favourite for the Oscar.

Passed over by the Academy were: Globe nominee Tony Randall in the romantic comedy *Lover Come Back* (NYT "wonderful"); Horst Buchholz in *Fanny* (NYT "intense"); Rod Steiger as the psychotherapist in *The Mark* (SMH "a sober, penetrating performance"); Annibale Ninchi in *La Dolce Vita* (V "fine"); Paolo Stoppa in *Rocco e i soui Fratelli (Rocco and His Brothers)* (S&S "flawless"); Yevgeni Urbansky in *Ballada o Soldate (Ballad of a Soldier)* (NYT "a performance of notable power"). The unsuccessful studio campaign for Beatty likely cost Pat Hingle any chance of an Oscar nomination for his performance as the wealthy father in *Splendor in the Grass* (NYT "a bruising performance"; LAT "standout" V "truly exceptional … worth serious Oscar consideration").

On Oscar night, *West Side Story* won ten Oscars. In the Best Supporting Actor category, Chakiris was swept to an upset win over Clift. Chakiris never made the Academy's lists again. He later starred in the television soap opera 'Dallas'.

1962

BEST PICTURE

ACADEMY AWARDS

• ***Lawrence of Arabia***
(Horizon-Spiegel-Lean, Columbia, 222 mins, 21 Dec 1962, $20.3m, 10 noms)
The Longest Day
(Zanuck-Twentieth Century-Fox, 180 mins BW, 4 Oct 1962, $15.2m, 6 noms)
The Music Man
(Warner Bros., 151 mins, 19 Jun 1962, $8.0m, 6 noms)
Mutiny on the Bounty
(Arcola, M-G-M, 178 mins, 8 Nov 1962, $9.8m, 7 noms)
To Kill a Mockingbird
(Pakula-Mulligan-Brentwood, U-I, 129 mins BW, 25 Dec 1962, $7.5m, 8 noms)

GOLDEN GLOBE AWARDS

(Drama)
Adventures of a Young Man
The Chapman Report
Days of Wine and Roses
Freud
• ***Lawrence of Arabia***
Lisa
The Longest Day
The Miracle Worker
Mutiny on the Bounty
To Kill a Mockingbird

(Comedy)
Boy's Night Out
The Best of Enemies
If a Man Answers
Period of Adjustment
• ***That Touch of Mink***

(Musical)
Girls! Girls! Girls!
Gypsy
Jumbo
• ***The Music Man***
The Wonderful World of the Brothers Grimm

BRITISH ACADEMY AWARDS

(Film)
L'Année dernière à Marienbad (Last Year at Marienbad)
Billy Budd
Le Caporal Épinglé (The Vanishing Corporal)
Dama s Sobachkoj (The Lady with the Dog)
Hadakano Shima (The Island)
Jules et Jim (Jules and Jim)
A Kind of Loving
The L-Shaped Room
• ***Lawrence of Arabia***

(British Film)
Billy Budd
A Kind of Loving
The L-Shaped Room
• ***Lawrence of Arabia***
Only Two Can Play

1962

Lola
The Manchurian Candidate
The Miracle Worker
Only Two Can Play
Phaedra
Såsom i en Spegel (Through a Glass, Darkly)
Tu Ne Tueras Point (Thou Shalt Not Kill)
Une Aussi Longue Absence (The Long Absence)
West Side Story

BOARD OF REVIEW – *The Longest Day*
SCREEN PRODUCERS GUILD – *Lawrence of Arabia*

Due to a newspaper strike, the New York Film Critics Circle did not present awards for the first time since 1934. The absence of a New York champion probably contributed to the Academy's selection of four studio epics (only one of which had been praised by critics) and one small, acclaimed drama as the nominees for Best Picture. The year's other lauded films, the kinds of small pictures usually highlighted by critics' prizes, were overlooked.

The four major studio releases selected by the Academy's voters were: National Board of Review Best Picture winner *The Longest Day*, a popular three-hour drama about the Allied landings in Normandy, which featured an international all-star cast and was the only Best Picture Oscar nominee cited by The New York Times as one of the year's ten best films (NYT "a strong, dramatic re-enactment"; V "a solid and stunning war epic"; S&S "solemnly spectacular"); David Lean's *Lawrence of Arabia*, a three-and-a-half hour biopic about T. E. Lawrence, which led the Oscar field with ten nominations (NYT "awe-inspiring" but "barren of humanity"; LAT "one of the most magnificent pictures, if not the most magnificent, and one of the most exasperating … [it] will be tremendous box office anyway – helped rather than hindered by the very fact that it makes such an aggravating question mark out of Lawrence himself"); the historical drama *Mutiny on the Bounty*, a lavish three-hour remake of the 1935 Best Picture Oscar winner (LAT "glorious escapism … has so many things going for it that I don't see how it can miss [at the box office]"; V "short of genuine dramatic greatness … [but] overwhelmingly spectacular"; TT "unsatisfactory"; S&S "directionless"; FQ "a slovenly, incoherent production"); and *The Music Man*, an extravagant two-and-a-half-hour version of the hit Broadway musical about a travelling con-man (LAT "an infectious and charming blockbuster of a musical"; V "ultimately endearing"; SMH "over-long, over-elaborate").

1962

Completing the Best Picture Oscar list was *To Kill a Mockingbird*, a modest, black-and-white adaptation of Harper Lee's popular novel about a Southern defence lawyer and his children (LAT "one of the finest [pictures] in a long time"; V "a major film achievement", "captivating and memorable"). The film amassed the year's second biggest tally of Academy Award nominations

The most notable omissions from the Oscar list were: the BAFTA nominated espionage thriller *The Manchurian Candidate* (LAT "a vigorous suspense melodrama, intrepidly daring in treatment, often unbelievable but on the whole thoroughly entertaining"; V "fascinating", "must inevitably come up for a bundle of Oscar nominations"; TT "a most ingenious piece of work"; S&S "refreshingly un-American"; FQ "impressive"); Globe and BAFTA nominee *The Miracle Worker* (NYT "a powerful emotional experience"; LAT "the miracle picture … there is a fixity, an intensity of purpose that gives it the breathless excitement of a mystery story"); Globe nominee *Days of Wine and Roses* (V "a film of emotional impact"); 1961 BAFTA winner *A Taste of Honey* (NYT "striking"; LAT "extraordinary"; V "compelling"; S&S "first-rate"; SMH "a brilliant film"); and BAFTA nominee *Såsom i en Spegel (Through a Glass, Darkly)*, Ingmar Bergman's Swedish drama which had won the previous year's Oscar for Best Foreign-Language Film (NYT "starkly realistic"; V "great"; SMH "[a] distinguished film").

Also overlooked were: Globe nominee *The Best of Enemies* (NYT "a potent comedy"; LAT "amusing production"; V "splendid"); BAFTA nominee *L'Année dernière à Marienbad (Last Year at Marienbad)* (V "a difficult, daring film"; S&S "hauntingly beautiful"); BAFTA nominee *Billy Budd* (NYT "splendid"; LAT "mainly talk, but toward the last we get caught up in it, thanks chiefly to the sympathy evoked by young Terence Stamp in the title role" FQ "very good"); *Victim*, a ground-breaking 1961 British drama about homosexuality (NYT "extraordinarily fine"; TT "intelligent"; SMH "deliberately unsensational in style, singularly frank"); *Birdman of Alcatraz* (NYT "a thoughtful yet powerful portrait"; LAT "an enthralling and compassionate picture … one of the finest pieces of film-making to come out of Hollywood in many a disappointing day"; V "outstanding"); *Long Day's Journey into Night* (NYT "generally stunning motion picture … a fine, fair picture of a tough and maybe tedious O'Neill play"); *Freud* (LAT "[an] enthralling, remarkable motion picture … a masterpiece, very probably one of the great motion pictures"); the independently-produced American teenage drama *David and Lisa* (NYT "crudely but courageously played"; LAT "this unusual film may not be everyone's idea of cinema fare but it is intelligently and compassionately made and well deserves the awards it has won thus far"); the Italian comedy *Divorzio all'italiana (Divorce, Italian Style)* (NYT "a dandy satirical farce"; LAT "a funny comedy, and also one of the cruelest … it's all very amusing, but it cuts deeply too"); *Kakushi-toride no san-akunin (The Hidden Fortress)* (TT "splendid", "technically brilliant"); and two notable Westerns, *Ride the High Country* (NYT "a downright pleasure to watch … disarming") and *The Man Who Shot Liberty Valance* (LAT "some may find this western old-hat").

Neither *The Longest Day*, *Mutiny on the Bounty* nor *The Music Man* received Oscar nominations in any of the other major categories – acting, directing or writing. That left the year's two most nominated films as the main contenders for the Best Picture Oscar. With more nominations, a victory at the Golden Globes, the best feature film citation from the Screen Producers Guild and the Directors Guild of America honour for its director, *Lawrence of Arabia* was strongly favoured ahead of *To Kill a Mockingbird.*

When the Academy Award winners were announced in early April, *Lawrence of Arabia* received six statuettes, including the Oscar for Best Picture. It was the first film to win the Academy's top accolade despite failing to be listed by The New York Times as one of the year's ten best movies since the comedy *You Can't Take It With You* in 1938. It was also the first film with not a single line of dialogue by a female character to win the Academy's top accolade.

Nearly a month later, the British Academy (which had changed the timing of its annual awards ceremony to early May) voted *Lawrence of Arabia* as both Best Film and Best British Film. It was the fourth film in six years to be honoured with the top awards in both Hollywood and London.

1962

BEST DIRECTOR

ACADEMY AWARDS
Pietro Germi for *Divorzio all'italiana (Divorce, Italian Style)*
• David Lean for *Lawrence of Arabia*
Robert Mulligan for *To Kill a Mockingbird*
Arthur Penn for *The Miracle Worker*
Frank Perry for *David and Lisa*

GOLDEN GLOBE AWARDS
George Cukor – *The Chapman Report*
Morton Da Costa – *The Music Man*
Blake Edwards – *Days of Wine and Roses*
John Frankenheimer – *The Manchurian Candidate*
John Huston – *Freud*
Stanley Kubrick – *Lolita*
• David Lean – *Lawrence of Arabia*
Mervyn LeRoy – *Gypsy*
Robert Mulligan – *To Kill a Mockingbird*
Martin Ritt – *Adventures of a Young Man*
Ismael Rodríguez – *The Brothers*

DIRECTORS GUILD AWARD
Ken Annakin, Andrew Marton and Bernhard Wicki – *The Longest Day*
John Frankenheimer – *The Manchurian Candidate*
Pietro Germi – *Divorzio all'italiana (Divorce, Italian Style)*
John Huston – *Freud*
Stanley Kubrick – *Lolita*
• David Lean – *Lawrence of Arabia*
Sidney Lumet – *Long Day's Journey into Night*
Peter Ustinov – *Billy Budd*

BOARD OF REVIEW – David Lean – *Lawrence of Arabia*

Against a field of four first-time nominees, previous winner David Lean was overwhelmingly favoured to win a second Oscar for *Lawrence of Arabia* (S&S "impeccably academic direction"). In the lead-up to the Academy Awards, he swept the other end of year awards, claiming his third National Board of Review prize, his second Golden Globe and his second Directors Guild of America honour. There was no New York critics' prize due a lengthy newspaper strike.

The potential darkhorse was Globe nominee Robert Mulligan, who earned his only nomination for the drama *To Kill a Mockingbird* (LAT "sensitive"; V "instinctively observant"; TT "direction is merely solid"). Mulligan was the only other candidate whose film had been shortlisted for the Best Picture award.

For the second year in a row, the Academy nominated the director of a foreign-language film: DGA candidate Pietro Germi for *Divorzio all'italiana (Divorce, Italian Style)* (NYT "wonderful"; TT "unexpectedly resourceful").

Surprisingly, despite a record numbers of nominees for both the Globe and the DGA honour, the Academy completed its ballot with two directors whose names did not appear on either of those other lists: Arthur Penn for *The Miracle Worker* and Frank Perry for the independently-produced *David and Lisa.*

The unexpected inclusion of Perry resulted in what Los Angeles Times critic Philip K. Scheuer called "two conspicuous omissions": John Frankenheimer, who had been nominated for both the Globe and the DGA prize for *The Manchurian Candidate* (NYT "exciting"; LAT "fine"; V "ripe for kudos") and who had also handled *Birdman of Alcatraz* (NYT "notable"); and Stanley Kubrick for the controversial *Lolita* (LAT "Kubrick's cinematic brilliance often making up for the loss of Nabokov's untranslatable literary brilliance"). Also considered for both the Globe and DGA honour, but snubbed by the Academy, was previous winner John Huston for his biopic *Freud* (LAT a "masterpiece").

The directors of three of the year's Best Picture nominees were also left out of contention: Globe nominee Morton Da Costa for *The Music Man*; previous winner Lewis Milestone for *Mutiny on the Bounty*; and the DGA nominated team of Ken Annakin, Andrew Marton and Bernhard Wicki for *The Longest Day.* Others passed over by the Academy were: Globe nominee Blake Edwards for *Days of Wine and Roses* (NYT "taut direction"); DGA nominee Sidney Lumet for *Long Day's Journey into Night*; DGA nominee and previous Best Supporting Actor Oscar winner Peter Ustinov for *Billy Budd* (S&S "inspired"); J. Lee Thompson for the thriller *Cape Fear* (NYT "frightening adroitness"); Sam Peckinpah for *Ride the High Country*; previous winner John Ford for *The Man Who Shot Liberty Valance* (NYT "handled with consummate professionalism"); Tony Richardson for *A Taste of Honey* (NYT "finely directed"; V "imaginatively directed"); Basil Dearden for *Victim*; Ingmar Bergman for *Såsom i en Spegel (Through a Glass, Darkly)*; and 1959 Berlin Film Festival winner Akira Kurosawa for *Kakushi-toride no san-akunin (The Hidden Fortress).*

On Academy Awards night in early April 1963, as expected, Lean collected his second Oscar as Best Director. His victory preserved the flawless record of the DGA in foreshadowing the eventual Oscar winner – it was the thirteenth consecutive year that the DGA winner had also been honoured by the Academy.

1962

BEST ACTRESS

ACADEMY AWARDS

• Anne Bancroft as 'Annie Sullivan' in *The Miracle Worker*
Bette Davis as 'Jane Hudson' in *What Ever Happened to Baby Jane?*
Katharine Hepburn as 'Mary Tyrone' in *Long Day's Journey into Night*
Geraldine Page as 'Alexandra Del Lago' in *Sweet Bird of Youth*
Lee Remick as 'Kirsten Arnesen' in *Days of Wine and Roses*

GOLDEN GLOBE AWARDS

(Drama)
Anne Bancroft – *The Miracle Worker*
Bette Davis – *What Ever Happened to Baby Jane?*
Katharine Hepburn – *Long Day's Journey into Night*
Glynis Johns – *The Chapman Report*
Melina Mercouri – *Phaedra*
• Geraldine Page – *Sweet Bird of Youth*
Lee Remick – *Days of Wine and Roses*
Susan Strasberg – *Adventures of a Young Man*
Shelley Winters – *Lolita*
Susannah York – *Freud*

(Comedy/Musical)
Doris Day – *Jumbo*
Jane Fonda – *Period of Adjustment*
Shirley Jones – *The Music Man*
• Rosalind Russell – *Gypsy*
Natalie Wood – *Gypsy*

BRITISH ACADEMY AWARDS

(Foreign Actress)
Anouk Aimee – *Lola*
Harriet Andersson – *Såsom i en Spegel (Through a Glass, Darkly)*
• Anne Bancroft – *The Miracle Worker*
Melina Mercouri – *Phaedra*
Jeanne Moreau – *Jules et Jim (Jules and Jim)*
Geraldine Page – *Sweet Bird of Youth*
Natalie Wood – *Splendor in the Grass*

(British Actress)
• Leslie Caron – *The L-Shaped Room*
Virginia Maskell – *The Wild and the Willing*
Janet Munro – *Life for Ruth*

BOARD OF REVIEW – Anne Bancroft – *The Miracle Worker*

1962

For the second year in a row, Geraldine Page won the Globe (Drama) and received an Oscar nomination (her third) for playing a Tennessee Williams character, this time the faded movie star in *Sweet Bird of Youth*, a role she had originated on Broadway (NYT "brilliant"; LAT "a performance of such diversity and depth-in-shallowness by Geraldine Page it virtually breathes a new dimension onto the screen"; V "a topflight performance of definite Academy potential"; TT "superb"; MFB "tremendous"; SMH "gives a bravura performance … she has an extraordinary cutting edge to her dialogue").

Also for the second year in a row, the Globe (Comedy/Musical) was won by Rosalind Russell, as the mother determined to make her daughter into a star in the musical *Gypsy* (NYT "simply doesn't have it"; LAT "works like a demon … she's especially delightful in early sequences. However, in late scenes and on into the complete disillusionment Roz's Rose engenders little if any sympathy"; V "deserves commendation"; MFB "her timing is impeccable"). It was Russell's fifth Globe – a record – and her third in the category in five years. She was again overlooked, however, by the Academy.

Bette Davis become the first person to earn a tenth Oscar nomination in the acting categories (all as Best Actress) for her performance as a grotesque former vaudeville child-star in *What Ever Happened to Baby Jane?* (NYT "chews the scenery to shreds"; LAT "gotten up as a simpering, ghastly horror of a harridan, acting all over the place, makes one laugh even as one recoils; you see it but you simple can't believe it"; V "earns the credit"; TT "marvellous"; MFB "magnificent"). Davis' chances of claiming a third Oscar, which she had desperately coveted for years, were considered strong when her co-star, previous winner Joan Crawford, was overlooked (NYT "chews the scenery to shreds"; LAT "has to do most of her acting with her great, expressive eyes"; V "a quiet, remarkably fine interpretation"; TT "one of her best acting performances").

Desperately jealous of her rival, Crawford openly campaigned for another of the nominees – National Board of Review winner Anne Bancroft, who had received her first Oscar nomination for reprising her Broadway success as the teacher of a blind-deaf-mute girl in *The Miracle Worker* (NYT "absolutely tremendous and unforgettable display of physically powerful acting"; LAT "quite, quite wonderful"; V "remarkable"; S&S "sterling").

Also nominated (for the ninth time) was previous winner Katharine Hepburn as the drug-addicted mother in *Long Day's Journey into Night* (NYT "tricky and uneven, probably because she has too much to do … she is put to so much repetition in the first hour or so of the film that she strains her own gifts of airy acting … a little less of Miss Hepburn would help the film"; LAT "a marvelous, miraculous" performance … "Hepburn is more or less continuously present for two of the three hours, and again and again she transfigures and lifts them by her seemingly inexhaustible powers of expression"; S&S "fascinating"). The fifth nominee was Lee Remick as an alcoholic in *Days of Wine and Roses* (NYT "extremely well-played", "brilliant"; V "effective"; TT "looks hopelessly miscast"). It was Remick's only Oscar nomination.

In the Los Angeles Times, critic Philip L. Scheuer opined that the omission of Shirley MacLaine from the Academy's ballot paper for her performance in *Two for the Seesaw* was "perhaps most surprising" of all the snubs across the four acting categories (LAT "is able to impart, with her transparent face, an irresistible humor to the kookier side of [her character]" but is miscast as "with an off-and-on accent, seldom if ever manages to look, speak and act like a girl from the Bronx, particularly a Jewish girl from the Bronx, simultaneously"). Also overlooked for Oscar consideration were: Globe nominee Glynis Johns in *The Chapman Report* (NYT "delightful"; V "spirited"); Globe nominee Natalie Wood as the daughter in *Gypsy* (NYT "inspiring"; LAT a "rather amazing transformation … her mannerisms are right on the button"); Globe nominee Jane Fonda in *Period of Adjustment* (LAT "mines humor from her role, chiefly by overplaying the part"; S&S "quite splendid"; MFB "excellent", "a superbly judged comedy performance tinged with genuine pathos"); Globe nominee and previous Best Supporting Actress Oscar winner Shirley Jones as the librarian in the musical *The Music Man* (LAT "delightful"; V "utterly charming"); BAFTA and Globe nominee Melina Mercouri in *Phaedra* (NYT "luminous with fervor and honesty"; LAT a "strong performance" … "tremendously vital, vibrant"); Globe nominee Susannah York in *Freud* (LAT "only the highest praise"; V "vivid"); Jeanne Moreau in *Jules et Jim (Jules and Jim)* (NYT "bewitching"); BAFTA nominee Harriet Andersson in *Såsom i en Spegel (Through a Glass, Darkly)* (NYT "beautifully expressive"; TT "startling"; S&S "brilliant"; MFB a "brilliant three-dimensional performance"; SMH "poignantly perceptive", "touching"); nineteen-year-old Rita Tushingham for her film debut as the pregnant girl in the British comedy-drama *A Taste of Honey* (NYT "brilliantly acted"; LAT "capable of reflecting, like the changing skies in a rain puddle, every emotion as it comes and goes"; V "handles comedy, drama and pathos with equal facility"; S&S "beautifully acted", "embodies the role"; SMH "is simply the character come to life on film"); Iya Savvina for her film debut in *Dama s Sobachkoj (The Lady with the Dog)* (NYT "a truly professional performance"; TT "exquisitely responsive performance"); Irene Papas in *Electra* (NYT "played to absolute perfection") and Daniela Rocca in *Divorzio all'italiana (Divorce, Italian Style)* (NYT "Mastroianni's performance is thoroughly complemented by the humorous uxorial enthusiasm that Miss Rocca provides"; V "excellent").

It is commonly accepted Hollywood lore that Davis was the favourite for the golden statuette, as evidenced by the depiction of events in the 2017 TV series 'Feud: Bette and Joan'. Press reports at the time, however, tell a different story.

On the eve of the ceremony, for example, Scheuer picked Page for the win writing, "Third time up in as many Hollywood roles, and a startlingly brilliant performer as Tennessee Williams' fading movie star … I am giving Miss Page a 51-49 edge over Katharine Hepburn … Closest runner-up to both is Anne Bancroft." Scheuer gave Remick a "a shooting-at-the-moonshine chance" and dismissed Davis entirely as the rank outsider. Davis, he wrote, "is galaxies away in outer space." And he wasn't alone. His colleague at the Los Angeles Times, gossip columnist Hedda Hopper thought "her magnificent performance" in *Long Day's Journey into Night* "might make it a pair" of golden statuettes on the mantelpiece at home for Hepburn.

On Academy Awards night, Davis' hopes of becoming the first person to win three Best Actress Oscars were indeed thwarted once again. The winner was Bancroft. As she was appearing on stage in New York in Bertolt Brecht's 'Mother Courage', Bancroft could not be present at the ceremony. To Davis' further vexation, the award was accepted on Bancroft's behalf by Crawford. A month later, Bancroft also won the Best Foreign Actress BAFTA.

After winning the Oscar, Bancroft successfully made the transition from stage actress to movie star. She earned a further four Oscar nominations during her career.

1962

BEST ACTOR

ACADEMY AWARDS

Burt Lancaster as 'Robert Stroud' in *Birdman of Alcatraz*
Jack Lemmon as 'Joe Clay' *in Days of Wine and Roses*
Marcello Mastroianni as 'Ferdinando' in *Divorzio all'italiana (Divorce, Italian Style)*
Peter O'Toole as 'T. E. Lawrence' in *Lawrence of Arabia*
• Gregory Peck as 'Atticus Finch' in *To Kill a Mockingbird*

GOLDEN GLOBE AWARDS

(Drama)
Bobby Darin – *Pressure Point*
Jackie Gleason – *Gigot*
Laurence Harvey – *The Wonderful World of the Brothers Grimm*
Burt Lancaster – *Birdman of Alcatraz*
Jack Lemmon – *Days of Wine and Roses*
James Mason – *Lolita*
Paul Newman – *Sweet Bird of Youth*
Peter O'Toole – *Lawrence of Arabia*
• Gregory Peck – *To Kill a Mockingbird*
Anthony Quinn – *Lawrence of Arabia*

(Comedy/Musical)
Stephen Boyd – *Jumbo*
Jimmy Durante – *Jumbo*
Cary Grant – *That Touch of Mink*
Charlton Heston – *The Pigeon that Took Rome*
Karl Malden – *Gypsy*
• Marcello Mastroianni – *Divorzio all'italiana (Divorce, Italian Style)*
Robert Preston – *The Music Man*
Alberto Sordi – *The Best of Enemies*
James Stewart – *Mr Hobbs Takes a Vacation*

BRITISH ACADEMY AWARDS

(Foreign Actor)
Jean-Paul Belmondo – *Léon Morin, Prêtre (The Forgiven Sinner)*
Franco Citti – *Accattone*
Kirk Douglas – *Lonely are the Brave*
George Hamilton – *Light in the Piazza*
• Burt Lancaster – *Birdman of Alcatraz*
Charles Laughton – *Advise and Consent*
Anthony Quinn – *Lawrence of Arabia*
Robert Ryan – *Billy Budd*
Georges Wilson – *Une Aussi Longue Absence (The Long Absence)*

(British Actor)
Richard Attenborough – *The Dock Brief*
Alan Bates – *A Kind of Loving*
James Mason – *Lolita*
• Peter O'Toole – *Lawrence of Arabia*
Laurence Olivier – *Term of Trial*
Peter Sellers – *Only Two Can Play*

1962

BOARD OF REVIEW – Jason Robards – *Long Day's Journey into Night* and *Tender is the Night*

Nineteen actors were nominated for the Golden Globes, five of which were subsequently named by the Academy. Surprisingly, National Board of Review winner Jason Robards was overlooked for both awards. He had been cited by the NBR for his work on the 1961 drama *Tender is the Night* and for his performance as the elder son in *Long Day's Journey into Night* (NYT "could give [the film] a little more … his performance and his character do not take firm hold until the thundering scene with his brother … then he suddenly bursts like a volcano with the hot lava in the character").

Also overlooked for both awards were: Ralph Richardson as the father in *Long Day's Journey into Night* (NYT "controlled and magnificent … his explicit awareness and command of the fatal ambivalence of this old rascal, his voluminous, flowing sentiment and his terrible, corroding canker of pride and insecurity are brilliantly drawn"); 1961 BAFTA nominee Dirk Bogarde as a married man blackmailed over his secret homosexuality in *Victim* (V "subtle, sensitive and strong"; TT "exceptionally good"; S&S "one of his best performances"; SMH "a performance of remarkable intensity"); Anthony Quinn in *Requiem for a Heavyweight* (NYT "a genuinely striking and professionally drawn characterization"; LAT "excellent … all but unrecognizable"); Murray Melvin in *A Taste of Honey* (V "succeeds"; S&S "beautifully acted"; SMH "excellent"); Laurence Harvey in *The Manchurian Candidate* (NYT "impressive"; S&S "unusually persuasive"); previous winner Marlon Brando in *Mutiny on the Bounty* (LAT "comes off well enough [but] mannered"; V "the finest performance of his career"); Montgomery Clift in *Freud* (NYT "an eerily illuminating performance"; LAT "only the highest praise"; V "intense, compassionate and convincing"); both Randolph Scott and Joel McCrea in the Western *Ride the High Country*; Raf Vallone in *A View from the Bridge* (NYT "devastating"); 1961 Venice winner Toshiro Mifune in *Yojimbo (The Bodyguard)* (NYT "commanding"; V "splendidly acted"); Oskar Werner in *Jules et Jim (Jules and Jim)* (NYT "haunting"); previous winner Charles Laughton in *Advise and Consent*, his final film (S&S "runs away with the picture"; MFB "his best performance in some twenty years"; SMH "a natural for the shambling, opportunist Southern senator"); Kirk Douglas in *Lonely are the Brave* (NYT "superbly convincing"; LAT "the most likeable portrayal he has ever given us"); Robert Ryan in *Billy Budd* (NYT "taut and chilling"); and previous winner Laurence Olivier in *Term of Trial* (NYT "no matter how patiently and deftly Mr Olivier plays the role, with all of his skill in portraying discomfort and down-at-heel wistfulness, he cannot quite make this fellow absorbing – or even wholly real"; V "absorbing").

As a widowed lawyer in *To Kill a Mockingbird*, Gregory Peck won his second Golden Globe and – after four unsuccessful nominations in five years in the late 1940s – earned his fifth (and final) Oscar nod (NYT "played superbly"; LAT "a superb and virtually flawless delineation"; V "exceptional", "[he makes] an especially challenging role … appear effortless").

Three of the other Globe (Drama) nominees were also mentioned by the Academy: Burt Lancaster (for a third time) as a prisoner in *Birdman of Alcatraz*, a performance for which he was honoured in Venice (NYT "outstanding"; LAT "an astonishing tour de force" and "a dramatization of exceptional power"; V "a masterful, Oscar-calibre performance"; MFB "achieves a compelling subtlety"); Jack Lemmon (his third Best Actor nod in four years) as an alcoholic in *Days of Wine and Roses* (NYT "extremely well-played", "brilliant"; V "powerful"; HRp "magnificent"; TT "has his moments"); and twenty-nine-year old Englishman Peter O'Toole for his screen debut in *Lawrence of Arabia* (LAT "superb performance and a startlingly versatile one"; V "striking" and "skillful").

Globe (Drama) nominees overlooked by the Academy included: Bobby Darin as a racist psychopath in *Pressure Point* (NYT "should make anyone recoil"); James Mason in *Lolita* (LAT "Mason makes the complex Humbert at least half-successful"; S&S "brilliantly controlled"); and Paul Newman in *Sweet Bird of Youth* (LAT "penetrates beneath the fair skin to the twitching nerve ends [of his character]" V "some overly-mannered moments"; MFB "credible"; SMH "as good as the role allows him to be").

The Academy's fifth nominee was the Globe (Comedy/Musical) winner – Marcello Mastroianni as a man plotting his wife's murder in *Divorzio all'italiana (Divorce, Italian Style)* (NYT "a performance that hangs in one's mind as one of the most ingenious and distinctive comic characterizations that has lately been" … "a performance that should win him an Academy Award"; LAT "plays this spineless dandy to perfection"; TT "a refined piece of comedy acting"). He was the first person to win a Globe for a non-English-language performance and the first to be nominated for such a performance in the Best Actor category at the Academy Awards. Among the other Globe (Comedy/Musical) nominees were: Alberto Sordi in *The Best of Enemies* (LAT "the amusing production also spotlights a delightful Italian comic, Alberto Sordi"; V "excellent"; SMH "wonderfully expressive"); Berlin winner James Stewart in *Mr Hobbs Takes a Vacation* (LAT "effortless"); and Robert Preston, reprising his Broadway success, in *The Music Man* (LAT "repeats his stage role with enthusiasm and the ease of long acquaintance"; V "his acting has remarkable authority"; S&S "a once-in-a-lifetime performance"; SMH "nobody could fault the bravura of Robert Preston's 'Music Man', repeating his Broadway role").

Peck was the sentimental favourite for the Academy Award, and on Oscar night he was finally rewarded with the Best Actor statuette. "Few begrudged Gregory Peck his Oscar for his Atticus Finch portrayal from *To Kill a Mockingbird*. It was his fifth bid for it," reported the Los Angeles Times. "The audience cheered Peck, and he thanked everyone, even his own family." Peck appeared in films for another three decades and received nominations for the Best Actor (Drama) Golden Globe for both *MacArthur* and *The Boys from Brazil* in the 1970s, but he never again received an Oscar nomination. The Academy did, however, bestow the Jean Hersholt Humanitarian Award on him in 1968. He also served as the President of the Academy from 1967 to 1970.

Of the unsuccessful Oscar nominees, three subsequently received BAFTAs for their performances. Lancaster and O'Toole won trophies in London a month after the Oscar ceremony, while Mastroianni received the Best Foreign Actor BAFTA the following year.

1962

BEST SUPPORTING ACTRESS

ACADEMY AWARDS
Mary Badham as 'Scout Finch' in *To Kill a Mockingbird*
• Patty Duke as 'Helen Keller' in *The Miracle Worker*
Shirley Knight as 'Heavenly Finley' in *Sweet Bird of Youth*
Angela Lansbury as 'Raymond's mother' in *The Manchurian Candidate*
Thelma Ritter as 'Elizabeth Stroud' in *Birdman of Alcatraz*

GOLDEN GLOBE AWARDS
Patty Duke – *The Miracle Worker*
Hermione Gingold – *The Music Man*
Shirley Knight – *Sweet Bird of Youth*
Susan Kohner – *Freud*
• Angela Lansbury – *The Manchurian Candidate*
Gabriella Pallotta – *The Pigeon that Took Rome*
Martha Raye – *Jumbo*
Kay Stevens – *The Interns*
Jessica Tandy – *Adventures of a Young Man*
Tarita – *Mutiny on the Bounty*

BOARD OF REVIEW – Angela Lansbury – *All Fall Down* and ***The Manchurian Candidate***

As the power-mad mother of a Communist assassin in *The Manchurian Candidate*, Angela Lansbury won the National Board of Review prize and a second Golden Globe (NYT "intense"; LAT "excellent ... scoring in a most bizarre role"; V "poignant"; S&S "right on top of and inside the part which could so easily have toppled over into caricature"; FQ "brilliant"; MFB "splendidly played"). She was also cited by the NBR for her turn as another overbearing mother in *All Fall Down*. The victories positioned her as the overwhelming favourite for the Oscar. "Little opposition here," commented film critic Philip K. Scheuer in the Los Angeles Times as he confidently predicted Lansbury would take home the golden statuette on Oscar night.

Another nominee with sentimental support was fifty-seven-year-old Thelma Ritter, nominated for the supporting prize for a record sixth (and final) time in thirteen years, as a prison inmate's mother in *Birdman of Alcatraz* (NYT "weak"; V "distinguished").

The other nominees were: Shirley Knight (her second nod in three years) in *Sweet Bird of Youth*; sixteen-year old Patty Duke as a blind-deaf-mute girl in

The Miracle Worker, reprising her Broadway success (NYT "absolutely tremendous"; LAT "quite, quite wonderful"; V "remarkable"); and ten-year old Mary Badham as a lawyer's tomboy daughter in *To Kill a Mockingbird* (NYT "superb"; V "exceptional"; TT "flawless").

Notable contenders overlooked for consideration by Oscar voters included: 1961 BAFTA winner Dora Bryan as the vulgar, quarrelsome mother in *A Taste of Honey* (LAT "fine"; SMH "superb"); Globe nominee Hermione Gingold in *The Music Man* (S&S "magnificently absurd"); Globe nominee Jessica Tandy as the stern, religious mother in the episodic *Adventures of a Young Man* (NYT "is compelled to make the mother a conventional, two-dimensional shrew"; SMH "splendid"); Globe nominee Tarita in *Mutiny on the Bounty* (V "enchanting"); and Shelley Winters as the widowed mother in *Lolita* (LAT "is the complete neurotic, as ridiculous as she is pathetic").

On Oscar night, the highly-favoured Lansbury and the veteran Ritter once more went home empty-handed. The Oscar was presented to Duke, the youngest person (to that date) to have won a competitive Oscar. As a result, Ritter's Oscar tally became six Best Supporting Actress nominations without a win – equalling Deborah Kerr's record losing streak of six Best Actress nominations without a win. Lansbury, meanwhile, received an honorary statuette at the fifth Governors Awards in November 2013.

1962

BEST SUPPORTING ACTOR

ACADEMY AWARDS
• **Ed Begley as 'Boss Finley' in *Sweet Bird of Youth***
Victor Buono as 'Edwin Flagg' in *What Ever Happened to Baby Jane?*
Telly Savalas as 'Feto Gomez' in *Birdman of Alcatraz*
Omar Sharif as 'Sherif Ali' in *Lawrence of Arabia*
Terence Stamp as 'Billy Budd' in *Billy Budd*

GOLDEN GLOBE AWARDS
Ed Begley – *Sweet Bird of Youth*
Victor Buono – *What Ever Happened to Baby Jane?*
Harry Guardino – *The Pigeon that Took Rome*
Ross Martin – *Experiment in Terror*
Paul Newman – *Adventures of a Young Man*
Cesar Romero – *If a Man Answers*
Telly Savalas – *Birdman of Alcatraz*
Peter Sellers – *Lolita*
• **Omar Sharif – *Lawrence of Arabia***
Harold J. Stone – *The Chapman Report*

BOARD OF REVIEW – Burgess Meredith – *Advise and Consent*

Golden Globe winner Omar Sharif was the favourite for the Oscar heading into the big night in Hollywood. He was expected to be carried along by the anticipated Oscar night sweep of *Lawrence of Arabia* and Los Angeles Times film critic Philip K. Scheuer declared, "he is hardly likely to have had serious competition" from the other four nominees during the voting period.

Also nominated were: Ed Begley as a redneck political boss in *Sweet Bird of Youth* (NYT "splendidly played"; LAT "almost frighteningly wicked"; V "outstanding in a perceptive portrayal"); Victor Buono in his film debut as the piano player in *What Ever Happened to Baby Jane?* (V "superb"; "excellent"); Telly Savalas as a prison inmate in *Birdman of Alcatraz* (V "distinguished"); and Terence Stamp in his film debut as the idealistic sailor in *Billy Budd*, a British film directed by previous Best Supporting Actor Oscar winner Peter Ustinov (NYT "perfect"; LAT "mainly talk, but toward the last we get caught up in it, thanks chiefly to the sympathy evoked by young Terence Stamp in the title role" V "sensitive"; S&S "an open, unpretentious, extremely effective performance"; FQ "cannot be faulted").

1962

Overlooked for Oscar consideration were: National Board of Review winner Burgess Meredith as a frightened witness in the political drama *Advise and Consent*; Globe nominee Ross Martin in *Experiment in Terror* (NYT "as ugly and repulsive as one could ask any villain to be"); Globe nominee Harold J. Stone in *The Chapman Report* (V "satisfactory"); Dean Stockwell in *Long Day's Journey into Night* (NYT "a feeble representation of a restless, consumptive youth. He is out of his class with the others"; S&S "inadequate"; MFB "hardly rises to the play's demands"); Globe nominee Paul Newman in *Adventures of a Young Man* (NYT "It is Paul Newman's very good fortune that he isn't recognizable in the role of an addle-brained vagrant prize-fighter, for he is simply terrible"; LAT "the acting surprise, though, is Paul Newman's gnarled, grumpy old Battler. I would never have recognized him if I hadn't known he was in the cast"; SMH "startling"); Howard da Silva in *David and Lisa* (NYT "does a good, straight job"); both Robert Stephens (V "fine") and Paul Danquah (NYT "gentle and subtle in a small but demanding role") in *A Taste of Honey*; Jackie Gleason in *Requiem for a Heavyweight* (NYT "brilliantly underplayed"); Brock Peters for *To Kill a Mockingbird* (LAT "outstanding"); Raf Vallone in *Phaedra* (NYT "superb"); Paul Ford as the mayor in *The Music Man* (LAT "scores"; V "wonderful"); previous Melvyn Douglas in *Billy Budd* (MFB "excellent"); and previous winner Karl Malden in *Birdman of Alcatraz*.

What the Los Angeles Times later called "the first real surprise" of Oscar night came when Rita Moreno revealed that the upset winner of the Best Supporting Actor statuette was Begley, a sixty-one-year old Hollywood veteran. Although it was a shock result, Murray Schumach reported in The New York Times a few days later, "There was little doubt from the audience reactions at the Santa Monica Civic Auditorium that the award to Ed Begley, for best supporting actor, was probably the most popular of the night."

Surprisingly none of the five Oscar nominees – all of whom were first-time candidates – ever made the Academy's lists again.

1963

BEST PICTURE

ACADEMY AWARDS

America, America
(Warner Bros., 174 mins BW, 17 Dec 1963, 4 noms)
Cleopatra
(Wanger, Twentieth Century-Fox, 243 mins, 12 Jun 1963, $26.0m, 9 noms)
How the West was Won
(M-G-M, Cinerama, 165 mins, 20 Feb 1963, $20.9m, 8 noms)
Lilies of the Field
(Rainbow, United Artists, 94 mins BW, 3 Oct 1963, 5 noms)
• ***Tom Jones***
(Woodfall, Lopert, 121 mins, 7 Oct 1963, $16.0m, 10 noms)

GOLDEN GLOBE AWARDS

(Drama)
America, America
Captain Newman, M.D.
• ***The Cardinal***
The Caretakers
Cleopatra
The Great Escape
Hud
Lilies of the Field

(Comedy/Musical)
Bye, Bye Birdie
Irma La Douce
It's a Mad, Mad, Mad, Mad World
A Ticklish Affair
• ***Tom Jones***
Under the Yum Yum Tree

BRITISH ACADEMY AWARDS

(Film)
Billy Liar
David and Lisa
Days of Wine and Roses
Divorzio all'italiana
(Divorce, Italian Style)
Hud
Noz w Wodzie (Knife in the Water)
Otto e Mezzo (8½)
Le Quattro Giornatedi Napoli
(The Four Days in Naples)
The Servant
This Sporting Life
To Kill a Mockingbird
• ***Tom Jones***

(British Film)
Billy Liar
The Servant
This Sporting Life
• ***Tom Jones***

1963

NEW YORK – *Tom Jones*
BOARD OF REVIEW – *Tom Jones*
SCREEN PRODUCERS GUILD – *Tom Jones*

In 1963, the Best Picture Academy Award was won by the British-made farce *Tom Jones*, Tony Richardson's version of Henry Fielding's classic novel. When it was released *Tom Jones* divided critics. The New York Times labelled it a "great film", "brilliant" and "one of the wildest, bawdiest and funniest comedies ... ever brought to the screen" and the Chicago Tribune called it "a bold, brash picture, sexy but never snide" and a "smooth satire" that was "handsomely photographed and acted to perfection". In contrast, Variety considered it to be "overlong" and The Times said that it was "not a very good film". Although he found it be "bawdy, bellicose, sprintingly acted and photographically arresting", Philip K. Scheuer in the Los Angeles Times was troubled by "its two styles which seemed to me incompatible" and concluded "unquestionably, it is 1963's dark horse".

As the awards season unfolded, *Tom Jones* became the clear Oscar frontrunner. In late December, it was named Best Picture by both the National Board of Review and the New York Film Critics Circle. In February, it received ten Academy Award nominations, more than any other film that year. In March, it won the Golden Globe (Comedy/Musical), the Screen Producers Guild accolade and the BAFTAs for both Best Film and Best British Film.

At the Oscar ceremony in April, *Tom Jones* received four statuettes, including Best Picture. It was the second non-American film to be honoured by the Academy.

Also receiving four statuettes was the epic historical *Cleopatra*, starring Elizabeth Taylor. Although mentioned in nine categories at the Oscars, it was not nominated for Best Director which effectively ruled it out as a Best Picture winner. The critical reaction to the trouble-plagued production had been mixed (NYT a "stunning and entertaining film", "exciting", "one of the great epic films of our day"; LAT "magnificent ... a surpassingly beautiful film"; V "remarkable"; HT "at best a major disappointment, at worst an extravagant exercise in tedium"; TT "fails to impress"; S&S "pretty dull"). The movie finished the year as the second most successful release. However, even the film's eventual take of $26 million was dramatically short of the reportedly $44 million production cost. At four hours and three minutes, *Cleopatra* remains the longest film ever nominated for the Best Picture Academy Award.

The year's box office champion was also a Best Picture Oscar nominee: *How the West was Won*, an all-star history of the American frontier filmed in Cinerama. Although it was a success with the public, critics were less enthusiastic (NYT "everything in this latest feature on the king-size Cinerama screen is a dutiful duplication of something you've already seen in anywhere from one to a thousand Westerns in the past sixty years"; V "a magnificent and exciting spectacle"; S&S "mixes eye-catching spectacle with slabs of static narrative"; MFB "never really gets off the ground"). *How the West was Won* was the only one of the Best Picture Oscar nominees not to have been a Globe contender. Nonetheless, it received the third highest number of nominations from the Academy that year: eight.

The other epic considered for the Best Picture Oscar was *America, America*, Elia Kazan's three-hour black-and-white drama about a Greek immigrant's struggle to get to the United States, which had also been nominated for the Golden Globe (Drama) (NYT "splendid", "vivid"; LAT "engrossing, sometimes moving … original, for certainly there has never been anything quite like it before"; V "one of the outstanding motion pictures of the year", "penetrating, thorough and profoundly affecting"). Kazan had based the story on the life of his own father.

The remaining nominee for the Best Picture Oscar was the low-budget drama *Lilies of the Field*, the story of an itinerant labourer who helps a group of German nuns to build a chapel. Filmed in just fourteen days for less than $300 000, it was dismissed by critics upon its release in both the US and Britain (NYT "it's 'Going My Way' with a Negro … [a] chunk of sweetness"; LAT "so naïve, so almost-childlike in its simplicity"; TT "particularly repellent entertainment"; MFB "definitely not a film for the sophisticated"; SMH "delightful").

As awards season approached, however, *Lilies of the Field* began to be championed by conservatives, moral leaders and some newspaper columnists, who were outraged at what they believed to be the sexual content in *Tom Jones*. The modest and inoffensive *Lilies of the Field* was heralded as a clean and positive American alternative to Richardson's immoral British comedy. Largely because of the campaigning of these groups, *Lilies of the Field* was nominated for both the Globe (Drama) and the Oscar.

The nomination of *Lilies of the Field* resulted in the exclusion of several acclaimed candidates. The most notable of these were *Hud* and *The Cardinal*, which each received more Oscar nominations than either *America, America* or *Lilies of the Field*.

Martin Ritt's pseudo-Western family drama, *Hud*, was the runner-up for the New York critics' award, a nominee for both the Globe (Drama) and the Best Film BAFTA, and received seven Academy Award nominations including nods for Best Director, Actor, Actress and Screenplay. In The New York Times, Bosley Crowther had declared it "the year's most powerful film" and "an achievement that should be honored" and in the Los Angeles Times, John L. Scott had called it "a bewildering, at times brilliant, bitter look at life" that was an "absorbing, if troubling, cinematic experience." Variety, meanwhile, had said it was "a film of considerable merit with flashes of brilliance" and The Washington Post praised it as "an extraordinarily powerful, provocative movie."

The Cardinal, a drama about the career of an Irish-American Cardinal, was a box office hit and only the third winner of the Golden Globe (Drama) to be snubbed by the Academy (CT "engrossing entertainment"; V "superlative drama ... emotionally stirring, intellectually stimulating and scenically magnificent"; G "it is a film that is not to be missed by anyone who really cares about the cinema"; MFB "immensely well worth watching"; SMH "rarely becomes more than an expert display of showmanship"). It was a candidate for six Academy Awards, including Best Director.

Other lauded films overlooked by the Academy were: Alfred Hitchcock's thriller *The Birds*, which had been a contender for the New York critics' prize (NYT "terrifying ... a horror film that should raise the hackles on the most courageous"; LAT "the implausibilities show up glaringly", "contrived and even ridiculous"; CT "technically, the film is superb"); Globe nominee *It's a Mad, Mad, Mad, Mad World* (NYT "wonderfully crazy"); Globe nominee *The Great Escape* (NYT "artificial"; V "entertains, captivates, thrills"); Globe nominee *Irma La Douce* (NYT "a brisk and bubbly film"; V "misses on several important counts"); BAFTA nominee *Billy Liar* (V "imaginative, fascinating"; CT "highly humorous, sometimes poignant"); BAFTA nominee *This Sporting Life* (NYT "smashing"; V "powerful" and "superior"; S&S "a film of passionate conviction"; MFB "distinguished"; SMH "a most powerful accomplishment"); and 1962 BAFTA nominee *The L-Shaped Room* (TT "sensitive").

The Academy also by-passed the year's acclaimed foreign-language films: Federico Fellini's *Otto e Mezzo (8½)*, which was a BAFTA nominee, the winner of Best Foreign-Language Film awards from the Academy, the NBR and the New York critics (NYT "a movie endowed with the challenge of a fascinating intellectual game", "tremendous pictorial poetry"; V "an exciting, stimulating, monumental creation"; S&S "extraordinary"; MFB "a magnificent folly"; SMH "often hard going for the audience"); *Mélodie en Sous-Sol (Any Number Can Win)*, the winner of the Best Foreign-Language Picture Globe; Serge Bourguignon's *Cybèle ou les Dimanches de Ville d'Avray (Sundays and Cybele)*, which had won the Best Foreign-Language Film Oscar the previous year (NYT a "masterpiece"; LAT "a motion picture of extraordinary simplicity and beauty which scans like poetry"); the Polish thriller *Noz w Wodzie (Knife in the Water)*, a nominee for the Best Film BAFTA nominee and the Best Foreign-Language Oscar (S&S "taut and brilliant"; SMH "supremely clever and totally intriguing"); and *Il Gattopardo (The Leopard)*, the year's Palme d'Or winner at the Cannes Film Festival (V "magnificent').

1963

BEST DIRECTOR

ACADEMY AWARDS
Federico Fellini for *Otto e Mezzo (8½)*
Elia Kazan for *America, America*
Otto Preminger for *The Cardinal*
• Tony Richardson for *Tom Jones*
Martin Ritt for *Hud*

GOLDEN GLOBE AWARDS
Hall Bartlett – *The Caretakers*
George Englund – *The Ugly American*
• Elia Kazan – *America, America*
Joseph L. Mankiewicz – *Cleopatra*
Otto Preminger – *The Cardinal*
Tony Richardson – *Tom Jones*
Martin Ritt – *Hud*
Robert Wise – *The Haunting*

DIRECTORS GUILD AWARD
Federico Fellini – *Otto e Mezzo (8½)*
Elia Kazan – *America, America*
Ralph Nelson – *Lilies of the Field*
• Tony Richardson – *Tom Jones*
Martin Ritt – *Hud*

NEW YORK – Tony Richardson – *Tom Jones*
BOARD OF REVIEW – Tony Richardson – *Tom Jones*

Englishman Tony Richardson was the first person to win the Best Director Oscar for a non-American film. Having been recently overlooked for the modest, black-and-white dramas *The Entertainer* and *A Taste of Honey*, Richardson was honoured by the National Board of Review, the New York Film Critics Circle, the Directors Guild of America and the Academy for his direction of the lavish colour production *Tom Jones* (NYT "Richardson has done as fine a job of catching the spirit of an old tale, as well as its salient points, and conveying it to a modern audience in a modern idiom as has ever been done … [his] camera techniques are really most apt revitalizations of flavorsome tricks and stunts"; CT "handled deftly"; SMH "there is art in the control of this zestful romp"). It was Richardson's only nomination from the Academy.

1963

Also nominated for directing a foreign film, *Otto e Mezzo (8½)*, was Federico Fellini (NYT "wonderful", "tremendous pictorial poetry"; G "it testifies to Fellini's singular capacity to make use in the cinema of any possible material"; SMH "Fellini' extraordinarily bold imagination and use of the camera in this film are as startling and disturbing as they were in 'La Dolce Vita'"). It was his second mention in three years.

For his highly personal, black-and-white epic *America, America*, previous winner Elia Kazan received a record fourth Best Director Golden Globe and was named by the Academy for a fifth time (NYT "brilliantly visualized ... with some masterfully authentic staging and a fitly hard-focus camera, he gives us as fine an understanding of that drama as the screen has ever had"). Four years after he had been a shock omission, Otto Preminger was included on the Oscar list (for a second time) for *The Cardinal* (CT "Preminger is a sure craftsman. He has directed his film in abrupt, forceful style and covered an enormous amount of territory ... there is no subtlety in the manner of presentation – but there is a force and vividness which make [the film] an effective sermon against bigotry and hatred"; G "throughout the film Preminger supplies the film equivalent of literary style by the construction of his sequences, the disposition of the actors, by his complex and beautifully articulated camera movements"; S&S "has excelled"). The remaining candidate was first-time nominee Martin Ritt for *Hud* (NYT "directed in a powerfully realistic style"; WP "exceptional"). None of these three directors were nominated again.

The Academy made one change from the DGA list with Preminger cited ahead of Ralph Nelson for the Best Picture nominee *Lilies of the Field*. Also bypassed were: previous winner and Globe nominee Joseph L. Mankiewicz for *Cleopatra* (NYT "brilliant"); Alfred Hitchcock for the thriller *The Birds* (NYT "has constructed [the film] beautifully, so that the emotions are carefully worked up to the point where they can be slugged"; V "masterful"); Globe nominee George Englund for *The Ugly American* (V "skilfully and explosively directed"); John Schlesinger for *Billy Liar*; Bryan Forbes for *The L-Shaped Room* (V "tactful, sensitive direction"); Stanley Kramer for *It's a Mad, Mad, Mad, Mad World*; previous winner and Globe nominee Robert Wise for *The Haunting*; Serge Bourguignon for *Cybèle ou les Dimanches de Ville d'Avray (Sundays and Cybele)* (NYT "flawless"); Luchino Visconti for *Il Gattopardo (The Leopard)*; and Roman Polanski for his debut *Noz w Wodzie (Knife in the Water)* (TT "closely observant of mood and gesture").

1963

BEST ACTRESS

ACADEMY AWARDS
Leslie Caron as 'Jane Fosset' in *The L-Shaped Room*
Shirley MacLaine as 'Irma La Douce' in *Irma La Douce*
• Patricia Neal as 'Alma Brown' in *Hud*
Rachel Roberts as 'Mrs Hammond' in *This Sporting Life*
Natalie Wood as 'Angie Rossini' in *Love with the Proper Stranger*

GOLDEN GLOBE AWARDS
(Drama)
Polly Bergen – *The Caretakers*
• Leslie Caron – *The L-Shaped Room*
Geraldine Page – *Toys in the Attic*
Rachel Roberts – *This Sporting Life*
Romy Schneider – *The Cardinal*
Alida Valli – *The Paper Man*
Marina Vlady – *Una Storia Moderna (The Conjugal Bed)*
Natalie Wood – *Love with the Proper Stranger*

(Comedy/Musical)
Ann-Margret – *Bye, Bye Birdie*
Doris Day – *Move Over, Darling*
Audrey Hepburn – *Charade*
• Shirley MacLaine – *Irma La Douce*
Hayley Mills – *Summer Magic*
Molly Picon – *Come Blow Your Horn*
Jill St John – *Come Blow Your Horn*
Joanne Woodward – *A New Kind of Love*

BRITISH ACADEMY AWARDS
(Foreign Actress)
Joan Crawford – *What Ever Happened to Baby Jane?*
Bette Davis – *What Ever Happened to Baby Jane?*
• Patricia Neal – *Hud*
Lee Remick – *Days of Wine and Roses*
Daniela Rocca – *Divorzio all'italiana (Divorce, Italian Style)*

(British Actress)
Julie Christie – *Billy Liar*
Edith Evans – *Tom Jones*
Sarah Miles – *The Servant*
• Rachel Roberts – *This Sporting Life*
Barbara Windsor – *Sparrows Can't Sing*

NEW YORK – Patricia Neal – *Hud*
BOARD OF REVIEW – Patricia Neal – *Hud*

1963

Marina Vlady was named Best Actress in Cannes for the Italian film *Una Storia Moderna (The Conjugal Bed)* and she was later nominated for the Golden Globe (Drama) (NYT "Vlady's cool, initial primness, her avidity when released by the act of matrimony and her delicate, ladylike hauteur when she has accomplished her sexual and social mission are very tasty, indeed. It is no wonder that this job got her the laurel as best actress at the Venice [sic] festival this year"; CT "Vlady is a pretty girl, but when she gets that look in her eye, and the sound track produces raucous jazz, things get unnecessarily obvious and tiresome"). Academy voters, however, overlooked Vlady when selecting their list of nominees.

The Academy did, however, mention both of the actresses considered by the New York Film Critics Circle. Patricia Neal, who had earlier won the National Board of Review prize, received the New York critics' accolade for her performance as a housekeeper victimised by her employer's son on an isolated ranch in Martin Ritt's *Hud* (NYT "brilliant"; LAT "vivid", "wonderful"; WP "brilliantly played … Neal's awareness is expressed with a kind of wry, sad humor and she does not pretty up this earthy role"; V "excellent"; MFB "excellent"). The runner-up was the previous year's Best British Actress BAFTA winner, Leslie Caron as a pregnant French woman living in London in *The L-Shaped Room* (NYT "stunning"; V "sympathetic"; TT "walks with assured steadiness through the pitfalls of a difficult part"; S&S "too graceful and composed to convince as a girl on the edge of despair"; MFB "never been more appealing"). Neal's part in *Hud* was arguably a supporting role and so, notwithstanding her double win from the critics' groups, the Hollywood Foreign Press Association nominated her for the Best Supporting Actress Golden Globe. The Academy was expected to follow suit and leave the Best Actress field clear for Caron, who had taken on a straight dramatic role in sharp contrast to her roles in the musicals *An American in Paris* and *Gigi*. When the Oscar nominations were announced, however, both Caron and Neal were included in the Best Actress category – Neal for the first time, Caron for the second.

Both nominated for a third time were Shirley MacLaine as a Parisian prostitute in the comedy *Irma La Douce* (NYT "has a wondrously casual and candid air that sweeps indignation before it and leaves one sweetly enamored of her … she is cheerful, impudent and droll"; V "a winning performance"; S&S "captivating"; MFB "another tour de force of comedy playing") and Natalie Wood as the pregnant girlfriend of a musician in *Love with the Proper Stranger* (V "convincing"; S&S "a performance without depth"; SMH "sensitive and perceptive"). Making the list for the only time was Rachel Roberts as a widow in a violent relationship in *This Sporting Life* (NYT "striking"; V "commendable"; MFB "beautifully observed"; SMH "matches Harris in unfolding depths of character"). Roberts' husband, Rex Harrison, was a Best Actor nominee that her year for his performance in *Cleopatra*.

In addition to Vlady, the Academy overlooked several performers nominated for the Golden Globe Awards, including: Geraldine Page in *Toys in the Attic* (NYT "Miss Page, under Mr Hill's direction, is a pinwheel whenever she's on. She sizzles and pops and spins in circles. But what's at the core of her? Who knows!"; LAT "achieves a tour de force of sorts by having us hating and pitying her at the same time"; V "powerful"; S&S "dazzling"; MFB "magnificent theatrics"); previous winner Audrey Hepburn in the romantic comedy thriller *Charade*, for which she would win a Best British Actress BAFTA the following year (NYT "the players, too, have at it in a glib, polished, nonchalant way that clearly betrays their awareness of the film's howling implausibility. Miss Hepburn is cheerfully committed to a mood of how-nuts-can-you-be in an obviously comforting assortment of expensive Givenchy costumes"; CT "Hepburn is handicapped by a role which makes her pathetic ... some of her scenes have charm and piquancy, others are labored"; WP "amusing"); Ann-Margret in *Bye, Bye Birdie* (V "striking"); Romy Schneider in *The Cardinal* (NYT "stand out"; LAT "memorable"; V "captivating"; S&S "she brings life and pathos to what might have been merely a clever plot twist"); Molly Picon as the mother in *Come Blow Your Horn* (LAT "is very amusing"; CT "amusing"; V "shines brilliantly"); and previous winner Joanne Woodward for the sex comedy *A New Kind of Love* (NYT "entirely improbable and not particularly comic"; LAT "acted with enormous joie de vivre"; CT "handles her role with wit and humor").

Surprisingly overlooked for recognition at both the Golden Globes and the Oscars was perhaps the most high-profile and talked about performance of the year: previous winner Elizabeth Taylor's portrayal of the fabled Queen of Egypt in the costly epic *Cleopatra* (NYT "plays with a skill and understanding that she has never surpassed"; LAT "a positive revelation"; TT "however spectacular she may look, she somehow always has a fatal tendency to disappear into her surroundings"; FQ "unforgettable").

Also shut out by both the Hollywood Foreign Press Association and the Academy in Hollywood were: Lee Grant in *Pie in the Sky* (V "outstanding"); Julie Harris in *The Haunting* (SMH "illuminates the whole film"); and Judy Garland in *A Child Is Waiting* (NYT "Miss Garland's misty-eyed compassion [is] of a standard dramatic order"; LAT "performs straightforwardly, with minimum of histrionics, though [her] character lacks resolution"; CT "appealing").

In the lead-up to the Academy Awards, four of the Oscar nominees received trophies. At the Golden Globes, Caron won the award for Best Actress (Drama) and MacLaine won her second Best Actress (Comedy/Musical) Globe in four years. Although she was unexpectedly defeated in the Best Supporting Actress category at the Golden Globes, Neal added the Best Foreign Actress trophy at the British Academy Awards to her NBR and New York prizes. Roberts, meanwhile, was honoured with the BAFTA as Best British Actress.

On Oscar night, the winner of the Globe (Drama) was outpolled for the fifth year in a row. To a rousing ovation from the audience, Gregory Peck announced that Neal was the winner of the Best Actress Academy Award. Neal was not in attendance at the Santa Monica Civic Auditorium, however. Heavily pregnant with her fourth child, she was in London with her husband, the novelist Roald Dahl (whom she had married in 1953 following the end of her long-term affair with Gary Cooper). Her statuette was accepted on her behalf by the French actress Annabella.

The years immediately after her Oscar win were marred with tragedy for Neal. Two of her children unexpectedly died (one in a road accident and one from measles) and she suffered from a series of debilitating strokes that left her partially paralyzed and confined to a wheelchair. She was unable to accept the part of Mrs Robinson in *The Graduate* in 1967 as she had not yet recovered, but made a triumphant comeback the following year in *The Subject was Roses*. Her performance garnered her a second Best Actress Oscar nomination. She was a strong contender for a third nod in 1999 for her supporting role in *Cookie's Fortune*, but was overlooked. Two-time Best Actress Oscar winner Glenda Jackson portrayed Neal in the 1981 British television movie, 'The Patricia Neal Story'.

1963

BEST ACTOR

ACADEMY AWARDS
Albert Finney as 'Tom Jones' in *Tom Jones*
Richard Harris as 'Frank Machin' in *This Sporting Life*
Rex Harrison as 'Julius Caesar' in *Cleopatra*
Paul Newman as 'Hud Bannon' in *Hud*
• Sidney Poitier as 'Homer Smith' in *Lilies of the Field*

GOLDEN GLOBE AWARDS
(Drama)
Marlon Brando – *The Ugly American*
Stathis Giallelis – *America, America*
Rex Harrison – *Cleopatra*
Steve McQueen
– *Love with the Proper Stranger*
Paul Newman – *Hud*
Gregory Peck – *Captain Newman, M.D.*
• Sidney Poitier – *Lilies of the Field*
Tom Tryon – *The Cardinal*

(Comedy/Musical)
Albert Finney – *Tom Jones*
James Garner
– *The Wheeler Dealers*
Cary Grant – *Charade*
Jack Lemmon – *Irma La Douce*
Jack Lemmon
– *Under the Yum Yum Tree*
Frank Sinatra
– *Come Blow Your Horn*
• Alberto Sordi – *Il Diavolo (To Bed or Not to Bed)*
Terry-Thomas
– *The Mouse on the Moon*
Jonathan Winters
– *It's a Mad, Mad, Mad, Mad World*

BRITISH ACADEMY AWARDS
(Foreign Actor)
Howard da Silva – *David and Lisa*
Jack Lemmon
– *Days of Wine and Roses*
• Marcello Mastroianni
– *Divorzio all'italiana (Divorce, Italian Style)*
Paul Newman – *Hud*
Gregory Peck – *To Kill a Mockingbird*

(British Actor)
• Dirk Bogarde – *The Servant*
Tom Courtenay – *Billy Liar*
Albert Finney – *Tom Jones*
Hugh Griffith – *Tom Jones*
Richard Harris – *This Sporting Life*

NEW YORK – Albert Finney – *Tom Jones*
BOARD OF REVIEW – Rex Harrison – *Cleopatra*

1963

A contender for the Best Actor Oscar emerged at each of the three major European Film Festivals. In Berlin, African-American Sidney Poitier was honoured as a labourer who builds a chapel for a group of nuns in *Lilies of the Field* (NYT "played so sincerely and with such charm"; WP "Poitier digs deep into the fellow, showing his frustration, geniality and grudging efforts at self-awareness"; V "striking contrast to many of his earlier roles"; MFB "self-conscious"; SMH "superb understatement"). In Cannes, Irishman Richard Harris won as a rugby player in the British drama *This Sporting Life* (NYT "realistic"; V "a dominating, intelligent performance"; SMH "almost shockingly true"). English actor Albert Finney, meanwhile, triumphed in Venice in another British film, *Tom Jones* (NYT "wonderful", "an acting masterpiece", "he makes a completely candid, lusty, engaging Tom"; LAT "portrayed with an irresistible joy of living"; CT "plays Tom with great skill").

All three prize-winners received votes from the film critics in New York, with Finney declared the winner. Also in contention were: both Paul Newman (NYT "tremendous"; LAT "gives one of his finest portrayals"; WP "the title character is probingly realized"; V "excellent"; MFB "excellent") and supporting actor Melvyn Douglas (NYT "magnificent") in the family drama *Hud*; Gregory Peck in *Captain Newman, M.D.* (NYT "adroit"; V "restrained and intelligent"); and Jason Robards as George S. Kaufman in *Act One* (NYT "while the most noticeable character in the film, is still a conventional eccentric with mannerisms but no substance underneath").

Another Englishman, Rex Harrison, entered in to Oscar contention when he won the National Board of Review prize. While much of the focus on the filming of the expensive epic *Cleopatra* had been on the romance between Elizabeth Taylor and Richard Burton, critics had praised Harrison as Julius Caesar (NYT "played with magnificent comprehension and distinction"; LAT "the characterization that outshines the others … he seemed the full measure of a man [and] I was moved by him"; V "superb").

When the Academy Award nominations were announced, the three festival champs and the NBR winner were all mentioned, along with Newman (his third nod in six years). Poitier, previously mentioned in 1958, was the first African-American to receive a second nomination. The three foreigners – Finney, Harris and Harrison – were all named for the first time.

Overlooked for Oscar consideration in addition to New York critics' prize contenders Peck and Robards, were: previous winner and Globe nominee Marlon Brando in *The Ugly American* (NYT "at the top of his form" in "an intricate and charming revelation of a decent, daring man"; LAT "played with surprising effectiveness"; V "well-played"); Globe nominee Stathis Giallelis in *America, America* (NYT "incredibly good as the determined hero, putting fire and spirit into the role, as well as a poignant revelation of the navieté and gentleness of youth"; LAT "gradually opens out from an enigmatic inner self to a man fighting for his very survival – the actor, like his performance – grows on one"; V "incredibly good", "makes a striking debut"); Globe nominee Tom Tryon in *The Cardinal* (LAT "memorable" in "a hellishly difficult part to demand of any actor"; CT "a fine performance with no trace of artificiality"; V "plays it very well indeed"; SMH "cannot break through his pattern of manipulations to be a warm human being"); Globe nominee Jack Lemmon in *Irma La Douce* (NYT "wonderfully skilful … his magnificently keen and agile clowning is what really carries this film"; CT "works strenuously in a demanding role"; MFB "another tour de force of comedy playing"); Globe nominee Frank Sinatra in *Come Blow Your Horn* (NYT "appears so indifferent and coolly self-satisfied that he moves and talks in the manner of a well-greased mechanical man"; LAT "tries harder this time not just to do his usual walk-through, and generally succeeds"; CT "manages [the role] with his usual ease and humor"); BAFTA nominee Tom Courtenay in *Billy Liar* (LAT "worth seeing"; V "impressive"; S&S "compelling", "remarkable"; MFB "flexible and vital performance"; SMH "brilliant"); and Richard Burton in both *Cleopatra* (NYT "exciting"; FQ "unforgettable") and *The V.I.P.s* (V "a top-league performance"). Nominated for a Golden Globe for his work in *Love with the Proper Stranger* (LAT "brisk and amusing") and also appearing in the war film *The Great Escape* and the comedy *Soldier in the Rain*, Steve McQueen was another notable omission from the Oscar ballot.

Both the Academy and the Hollywood Foreign Press Association ignored Jerry Lewis in *The Nutty Professor*, a film which he also co-wrote and directed. His turn was cautiously praised at the time of the film's release and is now considered one of the great comedic performances (NYT "credit the effervescent Mr Lewis for trying something different – a comical character study, with an edge of pathos. The surprising, rather disturbing result is less of a showcase for a clown than the revelation (and not for the first time) of a superb actor"; LAT "the production, which comes close to being a one-man show, will delight that hard core of Lewis fans who dig his face-making and comic capering … Lewis cavorts in typical fashion, which by now needs no amplification and defies criticism").

Also by-passed for their performances in foreign-language films were: Golden Globe winner Alberto Sordi in *Il Diavolo (To Bed or Not to Bed)*; Charles Denner in *Landru (Bluebeard)* (NYT "brilliant"); Hardy Krüger as the shell-shocked young man in *Cybèle ou les Dimanches de Ville d'Avray (Sundays and Cybele)* (NYT "brilliant"; LAT "beautifully played"); and Marcello Mastroianni in both *Cronaca Familiare (Family Diary)* (NYT "impressive") and *Otto e Mezzo (8½)* (NYT "plays in a beautifully bored and baffled fashion"; V "excellent").

1963

At first it appeared that Finney, Newman and Poitier would be the main contenders for the Oscar. Poitier, however, soon emerged as the favourite. Even though *Tom Jones* was favoured to win Best Picture, Finney refused to campaign and although Newman had strong support – New Yorker magazine, for example, had said "the Academy may as well give him an Oscar right now and get it over with" – he stated publically that he hoped that Poitier would win. And in sharp contrast to Finney, Poitier campaigned hard, aggressively promoting his film at a whole range of events. In mid-October, for example, gossip columnist Hedda Hopper reported on the actor's attendance at a special screening of the film for six hundred Catholic nuns in Denver, commenting "Sidney Poitier is going all out to plug 'Lilies of the Field' which may get him an Oscar."

At the Golden Globes, Poitier won the Drama award over Harrison and Newman, while in the other category, Finney was unexpectedly outpolled by Sordi – it was the second year in a row that the Globe (Comedy/Musical) had been won for a performance in an Italian film.

In another surprise, Finney was passed over again, along with Harris, for the Best British Actor BAFTA in London. The winner was Dirk Bogarde in *The Servant*. He would be eligible for Oscar consideration the following year for his performance.

Against a national political backdrop of civil rights activism, Poitier was voted the year's Best Actor by the Academy. "It has been a long journey to this moment," he told the audience at the Santa Monica Civic Auditorium. He was only the second African-American to win a golden statuette for acting.

1963

BEST SUPPORTING ACTRESS

ACADEMY AWARDS
Diane Cilento as 'Molly Seagrim' in *Tom Jones*
Edith Evans as 'Miss Western' in *Tom Jones*
Joyce Redman as 'Mrs Waters' in *Tom Jones*
• Margaret Rutherford as 'the Duchess of Brighton' in *The V.I.P.s*
Lilia Skala as 'Mother Maria' in *Lilies of the Field*

GOLDEN GLOBE AWARDS
Diane Baker – *The Prize*
Joan Greenwood – *Tom Jones*
Wendy Hiller – *Toys in the Attic*
Linda Marsh – *America, America*
Patricia Neal – *Hud*
Liselotte Pulver – *A Global Affair*
• Margaret Rutherford – *The V.I.P.s*
Lilia Skala – *Lilies of the Field*

BOARD OF REVIEW – Margaret Rutherford – *The V.I.P.s*

A week out from the announcement of the annual Oscar nominees, influential gossip columnist Louella Parsons summed up the list of likely contenders in an article entitled, "It's Guessing Time Again on the Oscars". With regard to the Best Supporting Actress field she wrote, "That hilarious and hardy perennial from old England, Margaret Rutherford, is a sure thing for 'The V.I.P.s' and there's been much praise for Lilia Skala in 'Lilies of the Field'. You can win an easy bet if you can find a sucker who doesn't think at least one of the three supporting ladies from the ubiquitous 'Tom Jones' will get a nod. Dame Edith Evans, Joyce Redman and Joan Greenwood are all being mentioned. Personally, of the three, my money's on Joyce."

In the end, the Academy's short-list was almost exactly as Parsons had speculated. Rutherford was named for her performance as an eccentric aristocrat in *The V.I.P.s* (NYT "dandy"; V "a sheer joy"; TT "excellent") along with Skala as the leader of a group of German nuns in the Arizona desert in *Lilies of the Field* (NYT "Skala's performance as the mother superior is radiant of softness and goodness underneath its tough Germanic hide"; WP "Skala is staunchly possessed"; V "first rate"; MFB "incongruously theatrical"; SMH "matchless in her role, and manages, without almost altering a muscle, to bring one of [the film's] deeply moving scenes"). Included for their work in *Tom Jones* were

Evans (CT "contributes her share of the fun"; S&S "magnificent"; MFB "brilliant"), Redman and, in place of Greenwood, the Australian actress Diane Cilento. It was only the second time, all the Oscar nominees in one of the acting categories were foreigners (the previous occasion having been in 1932/33 when all three nominees for Best Actor were foreigners). Furthermore, for the first time, three actresses were recognised by the Academy in the same category for their performances in the same film.

Overlooked for Oscar consideration in addition to Globe nominee Greenwood were: Maggie Smith as the secretary in *The V.I.P.s* (NYT "excellent"; V "outstanding"; TT "does wonders with her thankless part"; MFB "a delicate performance"); previous winner Wendy Hiller in *Toys in the Attic* (NYT "there's a bit of a sense of deep disorder in her moods of loftiness and gravity"; LAT "attains some measure of anchoring solidity as the sterner, stronger Anna"; V "sensitive"; MFB "superbly restrained support"); Globe nominee Linda Marsh in *America, America* (NYT a "standout"); Globe nominee Diane Baker as the physicist's niece in *The Prize* (NYT "does very nicely"); Globe nominee Liselotte Pulver as a Russian agent in *A Global Affair* (NYT "well-played"; V "good impression"); Jessica Tandy in *The Birds* (CT "credible"; V "vivid"); Carol Lynley in *The Cardinal* (MFB "superb"); Edie Adams in *Love with the Proper Stranger*; both Best Actress BAFTA nominee Julie Christie as the adventurous girlfriend (V "impressive"; S&S "stunning") and Mona Washbourne as the mother (LAT "standout") in *Billy Liar*; and Nicole Courcel in *Cybèle ou les Dimanches de Ville d'Avray (Sundays and Cybele)* (NYT "brilliant").

On Oscar night, the National Board of Review and Globe winner, Rutherford, a veteran of British theatre and film who had been overlooked by the Academy in 1944 for *Blithe Spirit*, was honoured with the golden statuette. Absent from the ceremony she later issued a statement describing the prize as "the climax of my career after twenty-eight years of filming". She added, "This may sound presumptuous at my age – I'm seventy-two next month – but I like to feel that this will be the starting point of a new little phase in films. I certainly hope it will be."

1963

BEST SUPPORTING ACTOR

ACADEMY AWARDS
Nick Adams as 'Ben Brown' in *Twilight of Honor*
Bobby Darin as 'Corporal Jim Tompkins' in *Captain Newman, M.D.*
• Melvyn Douglas as 'Homer Bannon' in *Hud*
Hugh Griffith as 'Squire Western' in *Tom Jones*
John Huston as 'Cardinal Glennon' in *The Cardinal*

GOLDEN GLOBE AWARDS
Lee J. Cobb – *Come Blow Your Horn*
Bobby Darin – *Captain Newman, M.D.*
Melvyn Douglas – *Hud*
Hugh Griffith – *Tom Jones*
• John Huston – *The Cardinal*
Paul Mann – *America, America*
Roddy McDowall – *Cleopatra*
Gregory Rozakis – *America, America*

BOARD OF REVIEW – Melvyn Douglas – *Hud*

In its review of *The Cardinal*, Variety commented that John Huston and Raf Vallone were "captivating" and that "Academy members should be hard put to decide between them for supporting performance honours." In the end, Vallone was overlooked. Huston, who had won the Golden Globe and the Oscar as Best Director in 1948, received the Best Supporting Actor Golden Globe, and his only Oscar nomination in the acting categories, for his debut performance as an ageing Boston cardinal (NYT "fascinates ... reveals in just a few scenes toughness, authority, political acumen, compassion and a fine philosophical turn of mind ... adroit"; CT "amusing"; V "etches a vigorous, warmly human portrait"; S&S "so successful in this his acting debut that one is tempted to inquire whether he had not heretofore missed his vocation"; MFB a "triumph"; G "extremely well-acted", "superb"; SMH "successful").

Also nominated were: singer-turned-actor Bobby Darin in *Captain Newman, M.D.* (NYT "touching"; V "highpowered histrionics"; FQ "barely adequate"); National Board of Review winner Melvyn Douglas as an old rancher in *Hud* (NYT "magnificent ... it is Mr Douglas's performance in the great key scene of the film that helps fill the screen with an emotion that I've seldom felt from any film"; WP "his portrait of the old man is resourceful and vivid"; V "excellent"; MFB "excellent"); previous winner Hugh Griffith (his second nod) as the lusty squire in *Tom Jones* (NYT "one of the wildest characters ever seen in films"; LAT "great"; CT "romps thru his role in hilarious fashion"); and Nick Adams as the accused murderer in *Twilight of Honor* (LAT "plays broadly but well"; V "somewhat overdone"). Adams had caused a considerable stir in Hollywood by openly campaigning for the nomination with advertisements in trade papers and numerous interviews.

In a major shock, Roddy McDowall was shut-out of contention for his portrayal of Octavius in *Cleopatra*, after Twentieth Century-Fox mistakenly listed the entire cast for consideration in the lead categories (NYT "fine"; V "especially noteworthy", "excellent"). The studio publically apologised for its "regrettable error".

Also passed over were: Globe nominee Paul Mann in *America, America* (NYT a "standout"; V "superb"); Globe nominee Lee J. Cobb in *Come Blow Your Horn* (V "steals the show"); Edward G. Robinson in *The Prize* (SMH "the honours go to Edward G. Robinson, tenaciously inside his character"); Louis Jourdan as a fading international playboy in *The V.I.P.s* (NYT "excellent"; V "excellent"); William Hartnell as an elderly rugby talent scout in *This Sporting Life* (V "valiant support"); Leslie French in *Il Gattopardo (The Leopard)* (V "stands out"); and Jacques Perrin in *Cronaca Familiare (Family Diary)* (NYT "splendid").

On Oscar night, Huston did not repeat his father's 1948 victory. Instead, the winner was Douglas, whose co-star, the overlooked Brandon deWilde, accepted the award in his absence. Douglas won a second Best Supporting Actor Oscar in 1979.

1964

BEST PICTURE

ACADEMY AWARDS

Becket
(Wallis, Paramount, 148 mins, 11 Mar 1964, $5.0m, 12 noms)
Dr Strangelove – or How I Learned to Stop Worrying and Love the Bomb
(Hawk Films, Columbia, 93 mins BW, 29 Jan 1964, $4.1m, 4 noms)
Mary Poppins
(Disney, Buena Vista, 140 mins, 26 Aug 1964, $45.0m, 13 noms)
• ***My Fair Lady***
(Warner Bros., 170 mins, 22 Oct 1964, $34.0m, 12 noms)
Zorba the Greek
(Rochley, Twentieth Century-Fox, 142 mins BW, 17 Dec 1964, $3.2m, 7 noms)

GOLDEN GLOBE AWARDS

(Drama)
• ***Becket***
The Chalk Garden
Dear Heart
Night of the Iguana
Zorba the Greek

(Comedy/Musical)
Father Goose
Mary Poppins
• ***My Fair Lady***
The Unsinkable Molly Brown
The World of Henry Orient

BRITISH ACADEMY AWARDS

(Film)
Becket
• ***Dr Strangelove – or How I Learned to Stop Worrying and Love the Bomb***
The Pumpkin Eater
The Train

(British Film)
Becket
• ***Dr Strangelove – or How I Learned to Stop Worrying and Love the Bomb***
King and Country
The Pumpkin Eater

NEW YORK – *My Fair Lady*
BOARD OF REVIEW – *Becket*
SCREEN PRODUCERS GUILD – *My Fair Lady*

Five films received votes from the New York Film Critics Circle at the end of the year. The winner, after six rounds of voting, was *My Fair Lady*, the expensive feature version of the hit Broadway musical that had itself been based on George Bernard Shaw's play 'Pygmalion' (NYT "a most wonderful, cheery movie"; LAT "a total triumph"; V "stunningly effective screen entertainment"). The stage production had starred Rex Harrison and Julie Andrews. Warner Bros.'

boss Jack Warner had been keen to retain Harrison, who had already starred in *Cleopatra* and earned an Oscar nomination for his performance, but was not prepared to keep the unknown Andrews. He replaced her with Audrey Hepburn (whose singing voice was dubbed by Marni Nixon, the singer who had substituted for Deborah Kerr in *The King and I* and Natalie Wood in *West Side Story*). The re-casting controversy ensured enormous publicity for the film.

The musical's New York victory, however, was not easily won. Gaining a lead on the second ballot, but ultimately finishing as runner-up was *Dr Strangelove – or How I Learned to Stop Worrying and Love the Bomb*, Stanley Kubrick's satire starring Peter Sellers, which had been enthusiastically embraced by most critics (NYT "brilliant", "an extraordinary cinematic creation"; NYer "the best American movie in years"; LAT "snide … [a] most unfunny comedy"; WP "an often brilliant, sometimes crude combination of irony and comedy"; CT "sardonic, wryly witty, cleverly caustic, and ghoulishly gripping … taut, suspenseful, and acidly amusing"; V "a sharply satirical comedy"; TT "one of the funniest films of the year"; S&S "dazzlingly clever"; FQ "a madcap comedy"; MFB "preposterously, sharply funny").

Also garnering consideration by the east coast circle were: National Board of Review winner *Becket*, an historical drama starring Peter O'Toole and Richard Burton (NYT "magnificent"; LAT "impressive"; CT "rewarding and memorable … a gripping drama"; V "a very fine, perhaps great, motion picture"; SMH "an entirely new kind of period drama in which all its people come alive", "challenging and beautiful … a film of the year"); the 1963 British film *The Servant*, starring Dirk Bogarde (NYT "an engrossingly symbolic study", "superior melodrama"; V "strong, dramatic fare", "provocative"); and, despite poor reviews from critics, *Zorba the Greek*, starring Anthony Quinn (LAT "stakes early claim to possible several Academy Awards … even if [it] doesn't carry off the big prize, it will stand among the year's best"; V "excessive length and overabundance of incident"; TT "almost unbearably slow and dull"; S&S "pretentious and painfully overlong").

When the Academy Award nominees were announced, four of these films were named as candidates for the Best Picture, Director and Actor Oscars – *Becket* and *My Fair Lady* each received twelve nominations, *Zorba the Greek* garnered seven, and *Dr Strangelove* earned four. Surprisingly, *The Servant* was shut-out of Oscar consideration entirely, without even a nomination for its star.

Included as a Best Picture nominee, and unexpectedly topping the list of Oscar contenders with thirteen nominations, was *Mary Poppins*, Disney's musical about a magical English governess (NYT "superlative", "brilliant"; LAT "the complete fantasy … will amaze and delight more people than you can count"; V "the novelty picture of the year", "a stimulating cinematic experience", "might very well be an Academy contender"). Although one short of the record number of nominations garnered by *All About Eve* in 1950, *Mary Poppins* was the first film to be nominated in thirteen different categories. The tally was an impressive vindication for Disney which had gambled on the actress that Warner had passed over for *My Fair Lady*, Julie Andrews.

In addition to *The Servant*, the two other most notable omissions were John Frankenheimer's *Seven Days in May*, a political drama about an attempted military coup in the United States starring Burt Lancaster, Kirk Douglas and Fredric March (NYT "gripping"; V "a strikingly dramatic realistic and provocatively topical film", "fascinating"; TT "superlative ... [and] intelligent entertainment"; S&S "vigorously intelligent entertainment"), and the melodrama *Hush ... Hush, Sweet Charlotte*, Robert Aldrich's follow-up to *What Ever Happened to Baby Jane*, which starred Bette Davis, and was nominated in seven categories (NYT "disgusting and profoundly annoying"; V "a brilliant production").

Other films passed over for Oscar consideration were: Globe nominee *The Chalk Garden* (NYT "a cozy, compact drama that follows a comfortable, sentimental line"); Globe nominee *Night of the Iguana* (V "compelling"; SMH "the most fascinating, adult drama"); the hit musical *The Unsinkable Molly Brown*, which was a Globe nominee starring Debbie Reynolds; the British drama *The Pumpkin Eater*, a BAFTA nominee starring Anne Bancroft (TT "a disappointment"); Alfred Hitchcock's *Marnie* (NYT "fascinating" and yet "disappointing"); the political drama *The Best Man*, starring Henry Fonda (NYT "highly entertaining"); the British drama *The Girl with Green Eyes* (NYT "remarkably fresh and natural", "wonderfully tender, touching and humorous"; CT "excellent entertainment"); the British drama *Seance on a Wet Afternoon* (V "a skillful and admirable picture"); *Cheyenne Autumn*, the last Western directed by John Ford (NYT "beautiful and powerful", "stunning", "magnificent"); the Beatles movie *A Hard Day's Night*; and both the 1963 crime caper comedy *The Pink Panther* and its 1964 sequel, *A Shot in the Dark* (NYT "excellent"; MFB "slapstick of the crudest kind").

Despite Best Foreign-Language Film awards from the Hollywood Foreign Press Association and the New York critics respectively, the Academy also by-passed both Vittorio de Sica's comedy *Matrimonio all'italiana (Marriage, Italian Style)* starring Marcello Mastroianni and Sophia Loren (NYT "wonderful"; LAT "extraordinary ... moving"; CT "adult entertainment") and Philippe De Broca's French spoof of the James Bond films, *L'Homme de Rio (That Man from Rio)* starring Jean-Paul Belmondo.

At the Golden Globes, *Becket* outpolled *Zorba the Greek* to win the Best Picture (Drama) award, while *My Fair Lady* gained an edge over *Mary Poppins* to win the trophy for Best Picture (Comedy/Musical). *My Fair Lady* also snared the Best Director Globe for George Cukor.

1964

Kubrick's *Dr Strangelove* was a notable omission from the list of Globe nominees, but was rewarded in London with the BAFTAs for both the Best Film and Best British Film.

At the time, however, the most significant Oscar indicators were the prizes from the Directors and Screen Producers guilds. Over the previous fifteen years the DGA winner had always won the Best Director Oscar. And in eleven of those fifteen years, the same film had claimed both the Best Picture and Best Director statuettes. During the brief period in the early 1960s, meanwhile, during which the Screen Producers Guild presented a Best Film prize, the winner never failed to go on to collect the Academy Award as well. In early February, Cukor won the DGA accolade for *My Fair Lady* while in mid-March, the Screen Producers Guild named *My Fair Lady* as best motion picture of the year over a field of fifteen other releases that included Oscar contenders *Becket*, *Dr Strangelove* and *Mary Poppins*. Also short-listed for the Producers' honour were: both *The Pink Panther* and *A Shot in the Dark*; the James Bond films *From Russia With Love* and *Goldfinger*; *Behold a Pale Horse*; *Ieri, Oggi, Domani (Yesterday, Today and Tomorrow)*; *Matrimonio all'italiana*; *Night of the Iguana*; *Seven Days in May*; *Topkapi*; *The Unsinkable Molly Brown*; and *The World of Henry Orient*.

The twin guild victories for Cukor and *My Fair Lady* made the musical the frontrunner for the Academy Award. History, however, also gave Disney some reason to hope that another musical might yet cause an upset in the top category. Ten times in the previous fifteen years, the film (or one of the films) with the most Oscar nominations had won Best Picture and in 1964 the field was led by Disney's *Mary Poppins*.

On Oscar night, Globe (Drama) winner *Becket* claimed just one statuette. The majority of the evening's awards were split between the two musicals. In the technical categories, *Mary Poppins* won four awards while *My Fair Lady* collected five. The Best Director prize, as expected, went to DGA winner Cukor for *My Fair Lady*. The main acting prizes were then split – Rex Harrison won Best Actor for *My Fair Lady* and Julie Andrews was named Best Actress for *Mary Poppins*. At the end of the evening, the final prize was claimed by *My Fair Lady*. It was the fourth Globe (Comedy/Musical) winner in five years to be honoured with the Best Picture Oscar, and the first Warner Bros. film to receive the Academy's top prize since *Casablanca* in 1943.

The following year, *My Fair Lady* was again victorious at the British Academy Awards in London, receiving the BAFTA for Best Picture.

While both musicals were huge hits at the box office over the next few years, *Mary Poppins* ended up earning more than its Oscar-winning rival.

1964

BEST DIRECTOR

ACADEMY AWARDS
Michael Cacoyannis for *Zorba the Greek*
• George Cukor for *My Fair Lady*
Peter Glenville for *Becket*
Stanley Kubrick for *Dr Strangelove – or How I Learned to Stop Worrying and Love the Bomb*
Robert Stevenson for *Mary Poppins*

GOLDEN GLOBE AWARDS
Michael Cacoyannis – *Zorba the Greek*
• George Cukor – *My Fair Lady*
John Frankenheimer – *Seven Days in May*
Peter Glenville – *Becket*
John Huston – *Night of the Iguana*

DIRECTORS GUILD AWARD
• George Cukor – *My Fair Lady*
Peter Glenville – *Becket*
John Huston – *Night of the Iguana*
Stanley Kubrick – *Dr Strangelove – or How I Learned to Stop Worrying and Love the Bomb*
Robert Stevenson – *Mary Poppins*

NEW YORK – Stanley Kubrick – *Dr Strangelove – or How I Learned to Stop Worrying and Love the Bomb*
BOARD OF REVIEW – Desmond Davis – *The Girl with Green Eyes*

James Stewart, Ingrid Bergman, Ronald Colman and Judy Holliday all won Oscars for performances in films directed by George Cukor. Yet the director had never received a statuette himself despite four nominations. At the age of sixty-five, over thirty years after he had first been nominated for the award, Cukor was finally voted Best Director by the Academy. His win, however, was not a purely sentimental career victory. Cukor won for *My Fair Lady*, the Warner Bros. musical that also won Best Picture, and in the lead up to the Academy Awards he had collected both the Golden Globe Award and the Directors Guild of America honour (LAT "delicate direction"). Cukor was the oldest person to that date to have won the Best Director Oscar, a distinction he retained for nearly forty years.

1964

Also nominated for the Oscar were four first-time nominees: Michael Cacoyannis for *Zorba the Greek* (LAT "gives this film the double elements of tragedy and comedy … bold and brilliant"); Peter Glenville for *Becket* (CT directed with "a simplicity that makes it a gripping drama" and "at a pace that makes it a piece of taut suspense"; V "astute handling"; MFB "lacks a sufficiently vivid visual imagination and reveals an inadequate grasp of cinematic resources … his half-hearted attempts to open out the play seem clumsy or irrelevant"); New York Film Critic's Circle prizewinner Stanley Kubrick for *Dr Strangelove – or How I Learned to Stop Worrying and Love the Bomb* (V "skill and daring"; SMH "cleverly-made"); and Robert Stevenson for *Mary Poppins* (NYT "has directed with inventiveness"; V "sensitive and understanding"). It was the first time since 1957 that the directors of the five Best Picture Oscar nominees were all included.

Overlooked for consideration by the Academy were: National Board of Review winner Desmond Davis for his debut feature *The Girl with Green Eyes* (V "imaginative"; SMH "the mood is beautifully judged"); Globe nominee John Frankenheimer for *Seven Days in May* (NYT "deft"; LAT "clever"; CT "directed it with quiet understatement that is masterful"; V "taut and penetrating directorial guidance"; SMH "has wrung all the dramatic action he can out of his tale … keeps the pace so forceful that glaring inconsistencies are dimmed"); Globe nominee and previous winner John Huston for *Night of the Iguana* (V "resourceful and dynamic"); Blake Edwards for both *The Pink Panther* and *A Shot in the Dark* (V "very good"); Joseph Losey for *The Servant* (LAT "has not always succeeded … too merciless"); Bryan Forbes for *Seance on a Wet Afternoon* (NYT "has directed so that action and atmosphere blend in a flow of sensuous experience that has the eeriness and tension of a spell"; WP "instantly and surely asserts this film's all-important atmosphere and it never falters"; MFB "an excellent job"); and Vittorio de Sica for *Matrimonio all'italiana (Marriage, Italian Style)* (LAT "de Sica has kept it earthy and real like the artist he is"; WP "a stunning example of style in film … has created a uniquely complex design"; CT "has shaped all these talents with a deft hand… he has a perceptive eye for the foibles of humanity"; V "adroit").

1964

BEST ACTRESS

ACADEMY AWARDS
• Julie Andrews as 'Mary Poppins' in *Mary Poppins*
Anne Bancroft as 'Jo Armitage' in *The Pumpkin Eater*
Sophia Loren as 'Filumena Marturano' in *Matrimonio all'italiana (Marriage, Italian Style)*
Debbie Reynolds as 'Molly Brown' in *The Unsinkable Molly Brown*
Kim Stanley as 'Myra Savage' in *Seance on a Wet Afternoon*

GOLDEN GLOBE AWARDS
(Drama)
• Anne Bancroft – *The Pumpkin Eater*
Ava Gardner – *Night of the Iguana*
Rita Hayworth – *Circus World*
Geraldine Page – *Dear Heart*
Jean Seberg – *Lilith*

(Comedy/Musical)
• Julie Andrews – *Mary Poppins*
Audrey Hepburn – *My Fair Lady*
Sophia Loren – *Matrimonio all'italiana (Marriage, Italian Style)*
Melina Mercouri – *Topkapi*
Debbie Reynolds – *The Unsinkable Molly Brown*

BRITISH ACADEMY AWARDS
(Foreign Actress)
• Anne Bancroft – *The Pumpkin Eater*
Ava Gardner – *Night of the Iguana*
Shirley MacLaine – *Irma La Douce* and *What a Way to Go!*
Kim Stanley – *Seance on a Wet Afternoon*

(British Actress)
Edith Evans – *The Chalk Garden*
• Audrey Hepburn – *Charade*
Deborah Kerr – *The Chalk Garden*
Rita Tushingham – *The Girl with Green Eyes*

NEW YORK – Kim Stanley – *Seance on a Wet Afternoon*
BOARD OF REVIEW – Kim Stanley – *Seance on a Wet Afternoon*

When Jack Warner bought the rights to the hit Broadway musical 'My Fair Lady', he wasn't prepared to retain the show's female star, Julie Andrews, who had played the role for three and a half years. Warner wanted a star and Andrews had never made a film. Instead he cast Audrey Hepburn and had her singing voice dubbed by Marni Nixon, the actress who had also provided the singing voices for Deborah Kerr in *The King and I* and Natalie Wood in *West Side Story*.

Meanwhile, Andrews was cast in the lead role as the magical English nanny in Disney's musical *Mary Poppins*. When the film opened in August, she earned the praise of critics and the film became a box office smash (NYT "superb"; LAT "plays [her first film role] coyly and captivatingly … her singing voice, of course, is liquid sweetness and she swings a wicked soft shoe"; V a "triumph").

Two months later, when *My Fair Lady* opened, Hepburn was also lauded by critics (NYT "superb", "a sensation", "wondrous and enchanting; LAT "unquestionably as superb in her way as Julie Andrews was in hers"; WP "luminous, lovely… [but] Hepburn's casting is the basic flaw in the transition [from Broadway to the screen]"; V "thoroughly beguiling"; TT "splendid"; S&S "certainly effective, if strained"). As a result, she became the overwhelming favourite for the Oscar.

The stars of the two musicals each received two votes from the New York Film Critics Circle at the end of the year, but were easily outpolled on the second ballot by National Board of Review winner Kim Stanley, who garnered nine votes for her performance as a fake psychic medium on the verge of a nervous breakdown in *Seance on a Wet Afternoon* (NYT "played so finely"; LAT "scorning make-up, she conveys the most minute emotions on her plain face that is really anything but, clear up to her final breakdown and madness"; WP "utterly mesmerizing … this should remind film-makers of a unique talent"; V "intelligent"; S&S "arresting", "quite understanding"; MFB "genuinely superb performance").

When the Academy Award nominations were announced in late February, the Best Actress category provided one of the biggest shocks in Oscar history – the highly-favoured Hepburn was overlooked. Andrews and Stanley each received their first nominations, as did Debbie Reynolds as a backwards girl who finds fame and fortune in another musical, *The Unsinkable Molly Brown* (NYT "explosive … since her role is more grotesque than life, her unharnessed enthusiasm is a delight"; LAT "in the show-off performance of her career … audiences will scarcely be able to resist [her]"; V "the outstanding performance of her career"; Time "it is impossible not to admire her"; MFB "a deliciously attractive performance"). Each nominated for a second time were previous winners Anne Bancroft as the mother of eight children in the British film *The Pumpkin Eater*, a performance for which she'd been honoured at the Cannes Film Festival (NYT "over-agonized performance"; LAT "fine performance"; V "exceptionally good"; TT "excellent"; S&S "well-acted") and Sophia Loren as a woman trying to convince her long-time lover to marry her in the comedy *Matrimonio all'italiana (Marriage, Italian Style)* (NYT "delightful"; LAT "beautifully acted"; WP "masterful … Loren's performance is a marvel of details. At the surface are contrasting moods and reactions, at the core is gritty determination. So polished are these varied facets that the woman becomes an individual all of one piece"; CT "her range is unlimited, and she proves it beyond doubt in this film which, while it's extremely amusing, is far more than just a comedy, thanks to her … in every aspect, she's just right"; V "fine").

Other notable omissions included: previous winner Bette Davis in *Hush … Hush, Sweet Charlotte* (NYT "a straight melodramatic tour de force"; V "an outgoing performance"; TT "at the top of her form", "moments of real pathos amid the grotesque"; S&S "brilliant"; FQ "impressive"; MFB "is in total command"); Globe and BAFTA nominee Ava Gardner as the hotel-keeper in *Night of the Iguana* (V "superlative"; S&S "carries little conviction"; MFB "lacks the dimension of self-parody"; SMH "the most potent performance of the year"); Deborah Kerr in both *Night of the Iguana* (NYT "ambiguous"; LAT "stunning" and "curiously touching"; CT "impressive"; V "superlative"; MFB "superbly comic performance"; SMH "impeccable control of a caricature-possible personality") and *The Chalk Garden*, for which she was a BAFTA nominee (LAT "exactly right for her part"; WP "exceptionally fine"; V "understanding performance"); Cannes co-winner Barbara Barrie in *One Potato, Two Potato* (NYT "justifies the prize with a portrayal that is perceptively naturalistic"); BAFTA nominee Rita Tushingham in *The Girl with Green Eyes* (NYT "a performance that could win her an Academy Award"; LAT "electrifying"; CT "can portray all the pathos and vulnerability of youth in a touching fashion"; V "often moving … and always interesting"; TT "engaging"; MFB "funny and touching"); Globe nominee Jean Seberg in *Lilith* (NYT "a fresh, flighty, fearsome performance"; S&S "intelligent performance"); and Venice Film Festival winner Harriet Andersson in *Att Älska (To Love)* (V "excellent" in "a beautifully modulated performance").

In the absence of Hepburn, bandleader-turned-film distributor Artie Shaw campaigned hard for Stanley. "If Kim doesn't get an Oscar for this then they just don't give them for acting merit," he told influential gossip columnist Hedda Hopper. "Her portrayal of an Englishwoman is flawless."

At the Globes, however, it was Andrews who emerged as the Oscar favourite, winning the Comedy/Musical award (ahead of Hepburn). The Drama prize was won by Bancroft, who also later claimed the Best Foreign Actress BAFTA. The Best British Actress BAFTA, meanwhile, was won by Hepburn for her performance in the romantic comedy thriller *Charade* for which she had been snubbed by the Academy the previous year.

On Oscar night, the Best Actress statuette was won by Andrews. It was the sixth year in a row that the Globe (Drama) winner had been unsuccessfully nominated for the Oscar. "You Americans are famous for your hospitality, but this is really ridiculous," Andrews told the audience.

The following year, Andrews was a strong contender to claim a second consecutive Best Actress Oscar for another musical, *The Sound of Music*.

1964

BEST ACTOR

ACADEMY AWARDS

Richard Burton as 'Archbishop Thomas Becket' in *Becket*
• Rex Harrison as 'Prof. Henry Higgins' in *My Fair Lady*
Peter O'Toole as 'King Henry II of England' in *Becket*
Anthony Quinn as 'Alexis Zorbas' in *Zorba the Greek*
Peter Sellers as 'Group Captain Lionel Mandrake' and 'President Merkin Muffley' and 'Dr Strangelove' in *Dr Strangelove – or How I Learned to Stop Worrying and Love the Bomb*

GOLDEN GLOBE AWARDS

(Drama)
Richard Burton – *Becket*
Anthony Franciosa – *Rio Conchos*
Fredric March – *Seven Days in May*
• Peter O'Toole – *Becket*
Anthony Quinn – *Zorba the Greek*

(Comedy/Musical)
• Rex Harrison – *My Fair Lady*
Marcello Mastroianni – *Matrimonio all'italiana (Marriage, Italian Style)*
Peter Sellers – *The Pink Panther*
Peter Ustinov – *Topkapi*
Dick Van Dyke – *Mary Poppins*

BRITISH ACADEMY AWARDS

(Foreign Actor)
Cary Grant – *Charade*
Sterling Hayden – *Dr Strangelove – or How I Learned to Stop Worrying and Love the Bomb*
• Marcello Mastroianni – *Ieri, Oggi, Domani (Yesterday, Today and Tomorrow)*
Sidney Poitier – *Lilies of the Field*

(British Actor)
• Richard Attenborough – *Guns at Batasi* and *Seance on a Wet Afternoon*
Tom Courtenay – *King and Country*
Peter O'Toole – *Becket*
Peter Sellers – *Dr Strangelove – or How I Learned to Stop Worrying and Love the Bomb* and *The Pink Panther*

NEW YORK – Rex Harrison – *My Fair Lady*
BOARD OF REVIEW – Anthony Quinn – *Zorba the Greek*

In 1963, Dirk Bogarde won the Best British Actor BAFTA for his performance as a corrupt servant who preys on his employer's sexual weaknesses in *The Servant* (NYT "expertly played"; LAT "powerful"; CT a "forceful and skilful" performance; V "standout"; TT "excellent"; S&S his "best performance ever";

MFB "the performance of his career"). His victory came over a field of nominees that included three of that year's Oscar nominees. When the New York Film Critics Circle voted for their Best Actor prize for 1964, Bogarde led on the first three ballots. On the sixth and final ballot, however, he lost by a single vote to Rex Harrison, who was honoured for the musical *My Fair Lady* (NYT "great"; WP "superb … what a great performance this is! This is one of the classic screen performances, an absolute certainty for next year's Oscar"; V "powerhouse contribution"; TT "extraordinary"; S&S "definitive"). Harrison had previously won a Tony for his performance in the musical's Broadway production.

When the Oscar nominees were announced, Bogarde was a glaring omission. The Academy instead selected five other foreigners – the first time that all the Best Actor nominees were non-Americans since 1932/33. All, interestingly, were also the stars of films nominated as Best Picture.

Harrison was named for a second consecutive year.

National Board of Review winner Anthony Quinn was mentioned for a fourth (and final) time as the dancing Greek peasant in *Zorba the Greek*, a role turned down by Burt Lancaster (NYT "brilliant", "[a] bold portrayal", "out of the whole towers the singular, monumental portrait of Zorba, as evolved by Mr Quinn. And it's this unforgettable portrait that justifies the film"; LAT "Quinn puts this picture in his pocket … deserves an Oscar nomination"; V "beautifully played", "excellent"; TT "does his best, but he cannot make us believe in Zorba"; MFB "grows irritating and monotonous").

Making the list for the second time in three years was Peter O'Toole in *Becket* (NYT "sensitive acting"; V "steals the picture"; LAT "stunning bravura performance"; TT "a sad disappointment", "monotonous"; MFB "effective, if mannered"). O'Toole played King Henry II, a role for which he would again be nominated four years later.

Also nominated for *Becket* was Richard Burton (LAT "probably his best film role to date"; V "generally convincing"; MFB "Burton, though adequate in the early scenes, is detached, even distant, and hardly suggests Becket's spiritual development"). It was his third Oscar nomination. He had also been praised for *Night of the Iguana* (NYT "spectacularly gross ... without a shred of real sincerity"; LAT "Burton manages his most 'human' portrayal here, more animated, even capable of humor, despite lapses into his usual dolorous expression"; CT "dominates the screen and gives a tremendous performance"; V "superlative"; MFB "superbly comic performance").

The only first-time contender was Peter Sellers, who played three roles – an RAF pilot, the US President and a former Nazi scientist – in *Dr Strangelove – or How I Learned to Stop Worrying and Love the Bomb* (CT "marvellously versatile"; V "excellent"; TT "remarkable"; S&S "brilliant"; FQ "a little disappointing"; MFB "contributes three beautifully judged performances";

SMH "works himself to bravura limits"). He had also appeared as the accident-prone detective in *A Shot in the Dark* (NYT "wonderful"; MFB "absolutely out of hand").

Other foreigners by-passed by the Academy included: Albert Finney in *Night Must Fall* (NYT "impressive"; V "vivid and explosive"); Peter Finch in both *The Girl with Green Eyes* (NYT "dead-panned"; V "a standout"; TT "engaging"; SMH "finds wry humour and gently touched pathos") and *The Pumpkin Eater* (NYT "showiness but not much substance"; LAT "Finch is good in a vague role"; V "impressive"; S&S "well-acted"); Marcello Mastroianni in *Matrimonio all'italiana (Marriage, Italian Style)* (NYT "marvellous"; LAT "beautifully acted"; WP "effective"; CT "the perfect foil of [Loren]"); and Philippe Leroy in *Le Trou (The Night Watch)* (NYT "simple, natural").

Americans overlooked for the Oscar were: both Henry Fonda (LAT "has never played a part with more integrity"; CT "completely convincing"; TT "well-acted"; MFB "impeccable") and Cliff Robertson (NYT "excellent"; CT "the best performance of his career"; S&S "excellent") in *The Best Man*; Tony Randall in *The Seven Faces of Dr Lao* (V "histrionic tour de force"); and the stars of *Seven Days in May* – previous winner Fredric March (NYT "expertly played"; LAT "the role was wisely entrusted to Fredric March ... powerful"), previous winner Burt Lancaster (LAT "played with fanatical glint"; TT "excellent") and previous nominee Kirk Douglas (LAT "underplays"; V "masterful").

Sellers was the early frontrunner for the Oscar but undermined his chances with negative comments about Hollywood. As a result, Harrison and O'Toole became the favourites and claimed the Golden Globes.

In London, the much-favoured Sellers was surprisingly outpolled for the BAFTA by Richard Attenborough for his performance as the husband in *Seance on a Wet Afternoon* (NYT "finely played"; WP "has a difficult role which he understates with repressed tensions").

On Oscar night, Harrison became the first winner of the Best Actor (Comedy/Musical) Globe to be honoured with the Oscar for the same role.

1964

BEST SUPPORTING ACTRESS

ACADEMY AWARDS
Gladys Cooper as 'Mrs Higgins' in *My Fair Lady*
Edith Evans as 'Mrs St Maugham' in *The Chalk Garden*
Grayson Hall as 'Judith Fellowes' in *Night of the Iguana*
• Lila Kedrova as 'Madame Hortense' in *Zorba the Greek*
Agnes Moorehead as 'Velma' in *Hush ... Hush, Sweet Charlotte*

GOLDEN GLOBE AWARDS
Elizabeth Ashley – *The Carpetbaggers*
Grayson Hall – *Night of the Iguana*
Lila Kedrova – *Zorba the Greek*
• Agnes Moorehead – *Hush ... Hush, Sweet Charlotte*
Ann Sothern – *The Best Man*

BOARD OF REVIEW – Edith Evans – *The Chalk Garden*

Critics were divided over Agnes Moorehead's performance as the sarcastic housekeeper in *Hush ... Hush, Sweet Charlotte*. In the New York Times, Bosley Crowther commented that "Agnes Moorehead as [Charlotte's] weird and crone-like servant is allowed to get away with some of the broadest mugging and snarling ever done by a respectable actress on the screen. If she gets an Academy award – which is possible, because she's been nominated for it – the Academy should close up shop!" In contrast, Variety called her performance "outstanding", Sight & Sound magazine said she was "brilliant" and Monthly Film Bulletin praised her for "an irresistible performance." In the Los Angeles Times, meanwhile, Philip L. Scheuer took the middle road declaring her performance to be "the sheer overacting delight" of the film. Moorehead won the Golden Globe and went into the Academy Awards as the favourite at her fourth (and final) Oscar nomination.

Also nominated for the Oscar were: Gladys Cooper (her third nomination, twenty years after her last) as the mother of Professor Higgins in *My Fair Lady* (LAT a "standout"); National Board of Review winner Edith Evans (her second consecutive mention) as the elderly grandmother in *The Chalk Garden* (LAT "exactly right for her part"; WP "exceptionally fine"; V "a joy to watch"; TT "splendid"; S&S "overacts irrepressibly"); Grayson Hall as the puritanical schoolteacher unable to face her homosexuality in *Night of the Iguana* (NYT "incredibly frantic"; V "delivers strongly"); and Russian-born actress Lila Kedrova, in her first English-language performance, as an ageing French dancer who runs a hotel in *Zorba the Greek* (NYT "brilliantly realized"; LAT "scores memorably … has earned an Oscar nomination for her portrayal"; V "oddly interesting performance"; MFB "expertly played").

Passed over by the Academy were: previous winner Mary Astor in *Hush ... Hush, Sweet Charlotte* (TT "unforgettable in her two great scenes"); Ann Sothern in *The Best Man* (NYT "standout"; TT "brilliant character acting"); Ava Gardner as a US General's former mistress in *Seven Days in May* (NYT "excellent"); Mona Washbourne in *My Fair Lady* (V "especially fine"); Siân Phillips in *Becket* (V "heartbreaking"; SMH "exquisite"); Irene Papas in *Zorba the Greek* (V "strikingly effective"); Wendy Craig in *The Servant* (MFB "excellent"); Elizabeth Ashley in *The Carpetbaggers* (NYT "comes through as fairly real person"; LAT "the silver lining [of the entire film] is Elizabeth Ashley … enters like a breath of fresh air. A new star!"; MFB "especially good"); and Lynn Redgrave as the tall room-mate in *The Girl with Green Eyes* (CT "briskly played"; S&S "a debut of startling brilliance"; MFB "funny and touching").

In a major upset on Oscar night, the Academy Award was won by Kedrova.

1964

BEST SUPPORTING ACTOR

ACADEMY AWARDS
John Gielgud as 'King Louis VII of France' in *Becket*
Stanley Holloway as 'Alfred Dolittle' in *My Fair Lady*
Edmond O'Brien as 'Senator Raymond Clark' in *Seven Days in May*
Lee Tracy as 'President Art Hockstader' in *The Best Man*
• Peter Ustinov as 'Arthur Simpson' in *Topkapi*

GOLDEN GLOBE AWARDS
Cyril Delevanti – *Night of the Iguana*
Stanley Holloway – *My Fair Lady*
• Edmond O'Brien – *Seven Days in May*
Gilbert Roland – *Cheyenne Autumn*
Lee Tracy – *The Best Man*

BOARD OF REVIEW – Martin Balsam – *The Carpetbaggers*

Eleven years after he won the both the Globe and the Oscar, Edmond O'Brien won a second Globe and was once again an Oscar nominee for his performance as a loyal US Senator in *Seven Days in May* (NYT "excellent"; LAT "the standout performance"; V "a standout"; TT "shines").

Also nominated for both prizes were Stanley Holloway in the musical *My Fair Lady*, and Lee Tracy, in his last film role, as a dying former US President, in *The Best Man* (LAT "Tracy is great, just great"; CT "plays his role in terse, cracking fashion … completely convincing"; V "just about steals the show with his expressive, colorful portrayal"; TT "brilliant character acting"; S&S "magnificent"). The Academy also short-listed John Gielgud (for the first time) in *Becket* (S&S "steals most of the honours"; MFB "he brings a style and authority to his small part"; SMH "splendidly acted") and previous winner Peter Ustinov (for a third time) as the slow-witted heavy in *Topkapi* (NYT "the salvation of the film"; LAT "just about steals the picture"; CT "his bumbling provides much of the fun in the film").

National Board of Review winner Martin Balsam was overlooked for his roles in *The Carpetbaggers* (MFB "especially good") and *Seven Days in May* (NYT "excellent"; V "truly vivid"). Unexpectedly passed over for *Dr Strangelove – or How I Learned to Stop Worrying and Love the Bomb* were George C. Scott (LAT "I have never see him give a bad performance till now"; V "a top performance"; TT "brilliantly played"; FQ "the prize performance of the picture"), Sterling Hayden (V "realistic"; FQ "a top-notch comic performance") and Keenan Wynn (CT "raucously funny"; FQ "splendid").

Also shut-out of consideration were: Donald Wolfit in *Becket* (SMH "a steely underplayed study"); James Fox in *The Servant* (NYT "dazzling"; MFB "perfect"); Frank Overton in *Fail Safe* (V "a particular standout"); Aldo Puglisi as the valet in *Matrimonio all'italiana (Marriage, Italian Style)* (NYT "brilliant"); and Peter Sellers for his first portrayal of Detective Clouseau in *The Pink Panther* (NYT "violently funny"; V "superlative"; TT "superior finesse"; FQ "perfect").

James Mason, meanwhile, had refused to allow Columbia to promote him for his small role in the British film, *The Pumpkin Eater*.

The Oscar contest was considered a close race between Gielgud and Holloway, but in a major upset, the award went to Ustinov. It was his second Academy Award as Best Supporting Actor in five years.

1965

BEST PICTURE

ACADEMY AWARDS

Darling
(Anglo-Amalgamated, Embassy, 128 mins BW, 3 Aug 1965, $3.3m, 5 noms)
Doctor Zhivago
(Ponti, M-G-M, 197 mins, 22 Dec 1965, $60.9m, 10 noms)
Ship of Fools
(Kramer, Columbia, 149 mins BW, 30 Jul 1965, 8 noms)
• *The Sound of Music*
(Argyle, Twentieth Century-Fox, 174 mins, 2 Mar 1965, $79.9m, 10 noms)
A Thousand Clowns
(Harrell, United Artists, 118 mins, 15 Dec 1965, 4 noms)

GOLDEN GLOBE AWARDS

(Drama)
The Collector
• *Doctor Zhivago*
Flight of the Phoenix
A Patch of Blue
Ship of Fools

(Comedy/Musical)
Cat Ballou
The Great Race
• *The Sound of Music*
Those Magnificent Men in Their Flying Machines
A Thousand Clowns

BRITISH ACADEMY AWARDS

(Film)
Hamlet
The Hill
The Knack ... and How to Get It
• *My Fair Lady*
Zorba the Greek

(British Film)
Darling
The Hill
• *The Ipcress File*
The Knack ... and How to Get It

NEW YORK – *Darling*
BOARD OF REVIEW – *The Eleanor Roosevelt Story*

For the second time in three years, the New York Film Critics Circle gave their Best Picture award to a British film. The winner on the sixth and final ballot was John Schlesinger's *Darling*, a black-and-white drama about a selfish, ambitious model and the men she becomes involved with on her way to the top (NYT "a slashing social satire loaded with startling expositions and lacerating wit … a film that will set tongues to wagging and moralists to wringing their hands"; WP "pleasurable to watch if hollow in retrospect"; CT "an interesting character study", "wickedly clever; V "provocative"; TT "mercilessly observant and sleekly accomplished" but "never quite fulfills its promise"; S&S "sometimes clever, often ugly, always self-conscious"; FQ "a film of excessive and self-defeating brilliance", "dangerously facile"; SMH "devilishly clever"). The film garnered votes from eight of the seventeen voting critics.

The runner-up, with five votes, was Sidney Lumet's *The Pawnbroker*, a black-and-white drama about a New York man haunted by his traumatic experiences during the Holocaust (NYT "remarkable … a dark and haunting drama … [a] most uncommon film which projects a disagreeable subject with power and cogency"; WP "memorable … relentlessly searing … will be remembered for [its] shattering force on its viewers").

Among the other films to receive votes in the voting in New York was the comedy *The Knack ... and How to Get It*, which had been the first British film in over fifteen years to win the Palme d'Or (NYT "delightful"; LAT "stunning, dazzling, raw … boldly committed to stylistic experiment"; CT "a silly, sharp combination of sex and slapstick"; FQ "vital, exuberant, joyous").

Early in the new year, these three films were all passed over by the National Board of Review, which unexpectedly named the documentary *The Eleanor Roosevelt Story* as the year's Best Picture. All three were also overlooked for the two Best Picture Golden Globes. In the Drama category the Hollywood Foreign Press Association short-listed: William Wyler's thriller *The Collector* (NYT "[a] frequently startling, bewitching film"; LAT "too clinical … [but] still manages to pique intellectual curiosity"; V "solid, suspenseful"); David Lean's epic *Doctor Zhivago* (NYT "a sad romance that seems almost as far away from Russia as the surging revolution seems from them … closer to Hollywood than to the steppes"; LAT "poetic … fine film-making"; V "meticulously designed and executed"; TT "breathtakingly beautiful"; HRp "more than a masterful motion picture: it is a life experience"; MFB "an honest failure"; SMH "a masterpiece"); the adventure film *Flight of the Phoenix* (WP "an engrossing adventure"); the inter-racial romance *A Patch of Blue* (NYT "for the most part seems a compound of specious contrivance"; LAT "everything is made as orderly as could be arranged so that the maximum in drama and pathos could be extracted from it before the inevitable exposure is reached"; WP "should have been halted as self-inflicted technical knockout"; V "touching"; SMH "a little masterpiece of cinematic good taste and restraint"); and the all-star melodrama *Ship of Fools* (NYT "powerful"; LAT "a series of vignettes, mordantly funny as well as wrenching"; WP "a superb film … will be remembered for years"; V "appeals to the intellect and the emotions"; MFB "ponderous"; SMH "trite").

The candidates for the Comedy/Musical Globe were: the Western spoof *Cat Ballou* (NYT "nothing surprising or unusual … [but] a cheerful lampoon … mostly just juvenile"; LAT "about as funny as a soundtrack burp"; CT "a broad, fast-moving and frequently funny parody"); the two popular chase films *The Great Race* (NYT "a movie that is surely a mammoth comic strip on the screen – a cinematized funny paper that runs for two and a half hours and is full of all sorts of situations that only the comics and old movies dare to pose … a runaway show"; LAT "funny"; CT "the audience howled at the constant clowning for most of the footage but the reaction slowed down as the film went on and on and on. There can be too much of a good thing"; S&S "a lot of fun but hardly ever funny") and *Those Magnificent Men in Their Flying Machines* (NYT "a lively and harmless – indeed delightful – jape"; LAT "ingratiating and amusing ... plenty of laughs"; WP "a wonder to behold, and behold it you should … buoyantly witty, and at times outrageously funny"; CT "I can't imagine anyone who wouldn't enjoy [this] comedy"; MFB "it's all good fun"); the smash hit musical *The Sound of Music* (LAT "close to three hours of visual and vocal brilliance … its sound will ring out for a long time to come"; V "captivating" and "moving"; WP "probably will be the best loved picture of 1965"; CT "a delightful melange of Austria and Andrews, with the emphasis on the latter"; TT "much to please and nothing to disturb"; S&S "almost intolerably wholesome"; MFB "an exceedingly sugary experience"); and the stage adaptation *A Thousand Clowns* (NYT "maintains the spirit and humor of the Herb Gardner play on which it is based"; LAT "much more than the play … will be right up there with the year's few best"; WP "often hilarious, socially pertinent and acted with zestful zip … a joyfully refreshing comedy").

The Academy's list of Best Picture contenders included the New York winner, *Darling*, and four Globe nominees – the dramas *Doctor Zhivago* and *Ship of Fools*, the musical *The Sound of Music* and the comedy *A Thousand Clowns*. Topping the list of nominees were the two major Hollywood productions – *Doctor Zhivago* and *The Sound of Music* – which both garnered mentions in ten categories, including Best Director.

A week after the Oscar nominees were announced, the Academy's endorsement of *Doctor Zhivago* and *The Sound of Music* was confirmed when each was presented with a Best Picture Golden Globe. The award for Best Director was won by David Lean for *Doctor Zhivago*, but the coveted Directors Guild of America accolade had already been won by Robert Wise for *The Sound of Music* (his second DGA win). The DGA prize made the musical, which was already a huge success with the public, the favourite for the Oscar.

The same day as the Globes were announced in Los Angeles, the British Academy declared the candidates for its annual awards. Oscar frontrunner *The Sound of Music*, although eligible, was overlooked for the Best Film award (*Doctor Zhivago* would be in contention for the BAFTAs the following year). *Darling* was nominated for the Best British Film prize and *The Knack ... and How to Get It* was one of two pictures short-listed for both accolades – the other was Sidney Lumet's *The Hill*, a drama about a military prison camp which the Academy had ignored (NYT "intense", "unrelenting"; LAT "[a] savage and brilliant movie"; V "uncompromising").

Overlooked for the Best British Film BAFTA was *Repulsion*, Roman Polanski's first English-language film which had deeply divided critics (NYT "an absolute knockout of a movie", "shocking, shattering and sickening" but still "an outstanding piece of penetrating and pulsating cinema artistry", "undoubtedly one of the best films of the year"; LAT "revolting"; V "a classy, truly horrific psychological drama"; CT "a grim grisly tale"; TT "misses its mark"; S&S "an irresponsible fiction", "intolerably lethargic and portentous"; SMH "brilliant"). The previous year, the British Academy had similarly overlooked the British release *The Leather Boys*, which went on to be ranked among the top ten films of 1965 by The New York Times (NYT "not tackling new problems [but gives] them sincerity, reality and pathos"; LAT "a perceptive and sensitive study"; WP "both amusing and touching … exceptionally real"; TT "well made, sympathetic, though despairingly sad"). Neither was in contention at the Golden Globes or the Oscars.

Among the BAFTA nominees was *Hamlet*, a Russian version of the Shakespearean tragedy. Surprisingly, it was the only non-English-language film considered for the top prizes by the Hollywood Foreign Press Association or the Academies in Hollywood and London. Other foreign-language films by-passed for the Best Picture Academy Award were: Vittorio de Sica's *Ieri, Oggi, Domani (Yesterday, Today and Tomorrow)*, which had won the 1964 Best Foreign-Language Film Oscar (NYT "wonderful"); Federico Fellini's *Giulietta degli Spiriti (Juliet of the Spirits)*, winner of the Golden Globe, New York critics' and NBR Best Foreign-Language Film awards (NYT "a cinematographic miracle"); Jacques Demy's *Les Parapluies de Cherbourg (The Umbrellas of Cherbourg)* (NYT "romantic contrivance and sheer decorative artifice"; MFB "utterly charming", "an unequivocal spellbinder"); and the Japanese films *Suna no Onna (Woman of the Dunes)* (NYT "strongly allegorical, strangely engrossing"; SMH "mostly obscure") and *Kwaidan* (NYT "a horror picture with an extraordinarily delicate and sensuous quality … a film that commends itself mainly to those viewers who can appreciate rare subtlety and grace"; LAT "awesome and enthralling … weaves a spell of enchantment … [a] masterpiece").

On Academy Awards night, the Best Picture Oscar was won by *The Sound of Music*, a film that had not been listed by the New York Times as one of the year's ten best films and which had not received a single vote for Best Picture from the New York critics. It was the third musical in five years to receive the Academy's top prize. In the Best Feature Documentary category, meanwhile, *The Eleanor Roosevelt Story* added a golden statuette to its earlier NBR Best Picture citation.

1965

BEST DIRECTOR

ACADEMY AWARDS
David Lean for *Doctor Zhivago*
John Schlesinger for *Darling*
Hiroshi Teshigahara for *Suna no Onna (Woman of the Dunes)*
• Robert Wise for *The Sound of Music*
William Wyler for *The Collector*

GOLDEN GLOBE AWARDS
Guy Green – *A Patch of Blue*
• David Lean – *Doctor Zhivago*
John Schlesinger – *Darling*
Robert Wise – *The Sound of Music*
William Wyler – *The Collector*

DIRECTORS GUILD AWARD
Sidney J. Furie – *The Ipcress File*
Sidney Lumet – *The Pawnbroker*
John Schlesinger – *Darling*
Elliot Silverstein – *Cat Ballou*
• Robert Wise – *The Sound of Music*

NEW YORK – John Schlesinger – *Darling*
BOARD OF REVIEW – John Schlesinger – *Darling*

Englishman John Schlesinger won both the National Board of Review and New York Film Critics Circle Best Director prizes for his handling of the British drama *Darling* (NYT "brilliantly graphic and fluid"; LAT "no question that Schlesinger's technique is dazzling"; WP "has been keenly resourceful"; CT "brisk and incisive"; FQ "his approach is one-dimensional"; MFB "compelling"; SMH "keeps a crisp and compact touch"). Tied in second place in the New York critic's vote were Roman Polanski for the British thriller *Repulsion*, his first English-language film (NYT "builds a towering drama with a skilful mesh of incidental stimuli"; CT "told with a gripping simplicity"; SMH "a brilliant piece of film making; a director's triumph") and David Lean, a previous New York prizewinner, for *Doctor Zhivago* (NYT "skillful direction"; SMH "genius").

When the finalists for the Directors Guild of America award were announced, Schlesinger was a first-time candidate, but both Polanski and, most unexpectedly, Lean were overlooked. In addition to Schlesinger, the Guild nominees were: Sidney J. Furie for *The Ipcress File* (NYT "flashy camera style"; CT "polished"; S&S "is not likely to destroy his reputation but it won't vastly enhance it either"); Sidney Lumet for *The Pawnbroker* (NYT "he has brilliantly intercut flashes of the horrors of the concentration camps with the equally shocking visualizations of imprisonment in a free society"; WP "ruthlessly sharp … we are taken into the man's very mind"); Elliot Silverstein for *Cat Ballou* (NYT "under Elliot Silverstein's direction, [the film] is mostly just juvenile lampoon"); and Robert Wise for *The Sound of Music* (LAT "[has] taken this sweet, sometimes saccharine and structurally slight story and transformed it into close to three hours of visual and vocal brilliance").

Only two of these DGA nominees, however, were contenders for the Best Director Golden Globe: Schlesinger and Wise. The remaining candidates were Guy Green for *A Patch of Blue* (V "excellent direction") and two previous winners: Lean for *Doctor Zhivago*, and William Wyler for *The Collector* (LAT "careful and often perceptive direction"; S&S "really rather grippingly told").

On 12 February 1966, Wise was presented with the DGA for the second time, four years after he had received it for *West Side Story*. The result made him the overwhelming favourite for the Academy Award. Over the previous sixteen years the guild honouree had subsequently won the Oscar without exception.

The Academy Award nominees were revealed nine days later. *Doctor Zhivago* and *The Sound of Music* topped the list of contenders with ten nominations each, including mentions for Lean (his sixth nomination) and Wise (his third, and final, mention). Wyler was recognised for an unprecedented twelfth (and final) time. Schlesinger, the critics' choice, was named for the first time. The remaining nominee, also included for the first (and only) time, was a major surprise: Japanese director Hiroshi Teshigahara for *Suna no Onna (Woman of the Dunes)*, a drama that had won the Special Jury prize at the 1964 Cannes Film Festival (SMH "dominated by camera techniques, it gives a feeling of being fabricated"). Teshigahara was the first person nominated in the category for an Asian film.

As well as the various DGA and Globe nominees by-passed for Oscar consideration, the Academy overlooked: Stanley Kramer for *Ship of Fools* (LAT "has succeeded in giving it greater depth and significance"); Richard Lester for *The Knack … and How to Get It*; Jacques Demy for *Les Parapluies de Cherbourg (The Umbrellas of Cherbourg)*; and Masaki Kobayashi for *Kwaidan* (NYT "merits excited acclaim for his distinctly oriental cinematic artistry").

A week after the Oscar nominations were announced, Lean won the Best Director Golden Globe for the third time in a decade. Wise nonetheless remained the favourite for the Academy Award on the strength of his DGA victory. In mid-April, *The Sound of Music* was awarded the Best Picture Oscar and Wise won the Academy Award for Best Director for a second time.

1965

BEST ACTRESS

ACADEMY AWARDS
Julie Andrews as 'Maria' in *The Sound of Music*
• Julie Christie as 'Diana Scott' in *Darling*
Samantha Eggar as 'Miranda Grey' in *The Collector*
Elizabeth Hartman as 'Selina D'Arcey' in *A Patch of Blue*
Simone Signoret as 'La Condesa' in *Ship of Fools*

GOLDEN GLOBE AWARDS
(Drama)
Julie Christie – *Darling*
• Samantha Eggar – *The Collector*
Elizabeth Hartman – *A Patch of Blue*
Simone Signoret – *Ship of Fools*
Maggie Smith – *Othello*

(Comedy/Musical)
• Julie Andrews – *The Sound of Music*
Jane Fonda – *Cat Ballou*
Barbara Harris – *A Thousand Clowns*
Rita Tushingham – *The Knack ... and How to Get It*
Natalie Wood – *Inside Daisy Clover*

BRITISH ACADEMY AWARDS
(Foreign Actress)
• Patricia Neal – *In Harm's Way*
Lila Kedrova – *Zorba the Greek*
Simone Signoret – *Ship of Fools*

(British Actress)
Julie Andrews – *The Americanization of Emily* and *The Sound of Music*
• Julie Christie – *Darling*
Maggie Smith – *Young Cassidy*
Rita Tushingham – *The Knack ... and How to Get It*

NEW YORK – Julie Christie – *Darling*
BOARD OF REVIEW – Julie Christie – *Darling* and ***Doctor Zhivago***

"It may not be too early to start musing over the probable predicament next year of Academy Award nominators and voters in the peculiar case of Miss Julie Christie," wrote leading film critic Philip K. Scheur in the Los Angeles Times in late October 1965 in his review of the British film *Darling*. "For her portrayal of Diana Scott in *Darling* is certain to rank high among contenders, while her forthcoming Lara in *Doctor Zhivago* may well put her in competition with herself." Critics heaped praise on Christie for her portrayal of a selfish and ambitious fashion model in *Darling* (NYT "splendid"; LAT "[a] heady performance … certain to rank high among [Oscar] contenders"; WP "treads [the path of her character] beautifully"; CT "plays Diana with impressive flair"; V "almost perfectly captures the character"; TT "magnetic"; SMH "tremendous") and she won more acclaim at the end of the year for David Lean's epic *Doctor Zhivago* (LAT "electrifying"; V "outstanding"; TT "ideal").

At the end of the year, Christie outpolled the previous year's Best Actress Oscar winner, Julie Andrews, to collect the Best Actress award from the New York Film Critics Circle by a margin of eleven votes to four on the third ballot. Andrews had received votes for her performance as a novice nun appointed as governess to the family of a widowed naval captain in the smash hit musical *The Sound of Music*, the favourite for the Best Picture statuette (NYT "with her ability to make her dialogue as vivid and appealing as she makes her songs, brings a nice sort of Mary Poppins logic and authority to this role, which is always in peril of collapsing under its weight of romantic nonsense and sentiment"; LAT "warmer and more appealing than she was as Mary Poppins and just as irrepressible"; WP "whatever Miss Andrews does becomes true, watchful and infectious … the thorough professional"; CT "so brilliant in the role that when she's off-camera [the film] seems tone-deaf"; TT "perfect").

Finishing third in the New York voting was French actress Catherine Deneuve. Her portrayal of a mentally ill young woman who is terrified of men, in Roman Polanski's British thriller *Repulsion*, had divided critics, however, and Deneuve did not receive nominations for the Globe, the BAFTA or the Oscar (NYT "simply splendid", "harrowing and heart-breaking"; V "remarkable", "handles a very difficult chore with insight and tact"; TT "wooden"; S&S "adequate"; FQ "rather unconvincing"; SMH "a triumph"). Deneuve had a contrasting performance in *Les Parapluies de Cherbourg (The Umbrellas of Cherbourg)* which was also overlooked.

Two previous Oscar winners were also notably overlooked for the year's various Best Actress plaudits: Vivien Leigh in her final screen appearance in *Ship of Fools* (NYT "excellent"; WP "she makes [her role] memorable through invisible alchemy"; V "excellent"; TT "splendid"; MFB "deliciously funny"); and Sophia Loren in Vittorio de Sica's *Ieri, Oggi, Domani (Yesterday, Today and Tomorrow)* (NYT "is in her finest fettle … dazzling"; V "excellent").

In early January, Christie added the National Board of Review award to her New York prize. She was cited for her performances in both *Darling* and *Doctor Zhivago*. At around the same time, she and Andrews both received nominations from the Hollywood Foreign Press Association.

Christie was mentioned for the Globe (Drama) along with: English actress Samantha Eggar as the art student kidnapped by a psychopath in William Wyler's *The Collector* (NYT "Eggar is able to make the girl everything she should be"; LAT "beautifully played"; V "remarkably restrained", "convincing", "a cinch for critical acclaim"; S&S "looks fine, but seems to find the snob social background attributed to her something of a burden"); Elizabeth Hartman for her film debut as a young blind woman in *A Patch of Blue* (LAT "wonderfully appealing"; WP "extracts what she can from the mawkish, melodramatic script"; V "an exceptional screen debut"; SMH "she has indeed turned in an acting masterpiece"); French actress Simone Signoret in *Ship of Fools* (NYT "fine", "excellent"; LAT "depicted with great delicacy"; WP "inspired … [her scenes with Oskar Werner] tingle with exceptional vitality"; V "a finely balanced performance"; MFB "splendid"); and rising English actress Maggie Smith as Desdemona in *Othello* (FQ "excellent").

Andrews, meanwhile, was considered for the Globe (Comedy/Musical), which she had won the previous year. Also nominated were: Jane Fonda in *Cat Ballou* (LAT "unfunny"; WP "[her] best role to date"); Barbara Harris in *A Thousand Clowns* (NYT "sensational"; LAT "comes near to proving [Robard's] match"; S&S "very well played"); Natalie Wood in *Inside Daisy Clover* (LAT "works hard and sometimes well at being Daisy"; V "better than her part"; SMH "does a credible job"); and Rita Tushingham in *The Knack ... and How to Get It* (CT "most appealing"; V "exceptionally good"; S&S "hard to better the performance of Rita Tushingham"). Tushingham also garnered good notices for the 1964 British film *The Leather Boys* (NYT "[gives] depth, intensity and charm to her portrayal"; LAT "dazzling … has never been better")

In February, the Academy short-listed five of these Globe candidates. Previous winners Andrews and Signoret each received their second nomination, while the three newcomers – Christie, Eggar and Hartman – were all first-time nominees. Smith, the remaining Globe (Drama) contender, was also nominated, for the first time, but in the supporting category.

At the Golden Globes ceremony a week later, Christie's Oscar chances suffered a set-back for the first time. While Andrews, Christie's main Oscar rival, won her second consecutive Globe (Comedy/Musical) as expected, in a major upset, Christie was outpolled for the Globe (Drama) by Eggar.

A month later, at the British Academy Awards in London, Christie triumphed as the year's Best British Actress. She won the award ahead of both Andrews and Globe nominee Tushingham. In the Best Foreign Actress category, previous winner and Oscar nominee Signoret was unexpectedly outpolled by Patricia Neal in the war drama *In Harm's Way* (V "expert performance"). Neal had been overlooked for both the Globe and Oscar for her performance.

On Oscar night, *The Sound of Music* won five Academy Awards, including Best Picture. The musical's star, Julie Andrews, however, did not claim a second consecutive Oscar. The Best Actress statuette was won by Christie for *Darling*.

1965

BEST ACTOR

ACADEMY AWARDS
Richard Burton as 'Alec Leamas' in *The Spy Who Came in from the Cold*
• Lee Marvin as 'Kid Shelleen' and 'Tim Strawn' in *Cat Ballou*
Laurence Olivier as 'Othello' in *Othello*
Rod Steiger as 'Sol Nazerman' in *The Pawnbroker*
Oskar Werner as 'Dr Schumann' in *Ship of Fools*

GOLDEN GLOBE AWARDS
(Drama)
Rex Harrison
– *The Agony and the Ecstasy*
Sidney Poitier – *A Patch of Blue*
• Omar Sharif – *Doctor Zhivago*
Rod Steiger – *The Pawnbroker*
Oskar Werner – *Ship of Fools*

(Comedy/Musical)
Jack Lemmon – *The Great Race*
Jerry Lewis – *Boeing Boeing*
• Lee Marvin – *Cat Ballou*
Jason Robards
– *A Thousand Clowns*
Alberto Sordi
– *Those Magnificent Men in Their Flying Machines*

BRITISH ACADEMY AWARDS
(Foreign Actor)
Jack Lemmon – *Good Neighbor Sam* and *How to Murder Your Wife*
• Lee Marvin – *Cat Ballou* and *The Killers*
Anthony Quinn – *Zorba the Greek*
Innokenti Smoktunovsky – *Hamlet*
Oskar Werner – *Ship of Fools*

(British Actor)
Harry Andrews – *The Hill*
• Dirk Bogarde – *Darling*
Michael Caine – *The Ipcress File*
Rex Harrison – *My Fair Lady*

NEW YORK – Oskar Werner – *Ship of Fools*
BOARD OF REVIEW – Lee Marvin – *Cat Ballou*

Two Berlin Film Festival honourees were the frontrunners for the Oscar. The Berlin Best Actor winner in 1964 was Rod Steiger as a New York pawnbroker haunted by his memories of the Holocaust in *The Pawnbroker* (NYT "powerfully plays … with a mounting intensity"; WP "distinguished by the bravura performance of the star … completely the master of his demanding role"). The winner in Berlin in 1965 was Lee Marvin in the dual role of twin brothers in the Western spoof *Cat Ballou* (NYT "playing it in the broadest style

– so broadly, in fact, that there are moments when it looks as though he is going to spread himself right off the screen"; LAT "differentiates between [the dual roles] cleverly but both characterizations are coarse, undisciplined and, in their unbridled excesses of emotion, actually ugly to watch"; WP "a masterpiece of wild, exuberant farce"; CT "gets the lion's share of the laughs, and deserves them"; V "the standout of the picture"; TT "excellent"; S&S a "virtuoso performance"). Both men were strong contenders for the New York Film Critics Circle award, but tied as runners-up to Oskar Werner as the ship's doctor in *Ship of Fools* (NYT "poignant", "excellent"; LAT "depicted with great delicacy"; WP "inspired … [his scenes with Simone Signoret] tingle with exceptional vitality"; V "a most appealing, interesting portrait"; MFB "injecting his part with more honest feeling than it deserves"). A fortnight later, Marvin won the National Board of Review prize.

In early January, Steiger and Werner received nominations for the Golden Globe (Drama). Also named were: Rex Harrison as Pope Julius II in *The Agony and the Ecstasy* (NYT "interesting"; V "outstanding"; MFB "manages to make some of his lines sound witty"); Sidney Poitier in *A Patch of Blue* (NYT "has to act too much like a saint"; V "excellent"; SMH "tender without descending into sentimentality"); and Omar Sharif in *Doctor Zhivago* (LAT "remarkable")

Marvin was cited for the Comedy/Musical award for which the other nominees included: Jack Lemmon in *The Great Race* (NYT "there is something unique about this picture, and that can be expressed in two words (or one name) – Jack Lemmon … [he] is thoroughly delightful … consistently comical … as whacky and hilarious a cut-up as we have seen in a long time"; LAT "steals the movie … Lemmon's mugging was as eloquent as words"; V his "delineation is an event"); and Jason Robards, reprising his Broadway success, in *A Thousand Clowns* (NYT "full of spice with his clownish wise-cracks"; LAT "can be just as fiercesome in his humor as in his anger, but you just can't resist the big lug for long"; V "scenery-chewing"; TT "perfectly played").

The three main New York prize contenders were the only Globe nominees recognised by the Academy. Marvin and Werner were each named for the first (and only) time, while Steiger earned his second nomination. Receiving his fourth nod was Richard Burton as a Cold War agent in *The Spy Who Came in from the Cold* (NYT "expertly [played]"; WP "hard, matter-of-fact acting"; S&S "a self-absorbed performance of narrow range"; FQ "extraordinarily superficial"). Previous winner Laurence Olivier, meanwhile, garnered his sixth mention as the Moor in *Othello* (NYT "powerful and passionate"; LAT "one of the great enactments of our time … dwarfs all other stars I have respected during the year to date"; S&S "marvellous"; MFB "a towering, magnificent, bravura performance"; SMH "extended to the full capacity of his acting powers, gets into the very bones of the agent").

1965

The most surprising omission from the Academy's list of candidates was Sharif, especially as *Doctor Zhivago* was one of the two films which had topped the list of contenders with ten nominations. After he had been the unsuccessful favourite for the supporting prize in 1962, many had considered Sharif a certainty for an Oscar nod. His exclusion was highlighted just a week later when he won the Golden Globe over Oscar nominees Steiger and Werner.

In late March, the British Academy Awards highlighted another major oversight by the Academy. For *Darling*, Dirk Bogarde won his second Best British Actor BAFTA in three years (NYT "splendid"; LAT "exceptional"; V "always believable"; CT "a skilled and moving performance"; TT "exemplary"; S&S "excellent"; MFB "strongly sympathetic"; SMH "a firm, strong character performance"). Among those he bested was the previous year's Oscar winner.

Apart from the overlooked Globe nominees, other contenders by-passed for Oscar consideration were: James Stewart in both *Flight of the Phoenix* (WP "immensely engrossing"; V "particularly effective in underplaying his character") and *Shenandoah* (NYT "perfectly cast, plays his role to the hilt"; LAT "creates a unique character and sustains it convincingly"; MFB "one of the best performances of his career"); Cannes winner Terence Stamp as the psychopath in *The Collector* (NYT "fascinating at the start … [but] tends to become monotonous"; LAT "plays him deadpan, like a zombie"; "entirely believable"; S&S "one is throughout too conscious of the mechanics of the performance to be totally won over by it"); Sean Connery in *The Hill* (LAT "well-acted"; V "superbly acted"; MFB "convincing"); 1964 BAFTA winner Marcello Mastroianni in *Ieri, Oggi, Domani (Yesterday, Today and Tomorrow)* (NYT "hilarious"; V "excellent"); Michael Caine in *The Ipcress File* (V "skillful"; TT "could hardly be bettered"; S&S "superbly played"); and Eiji Okada in *Suna no Onna (Woman of the Dunes)* (FQ "remarkable").

While many media pundits favoured Steiger for the Oscar, others were not so sure. "The Oscars are an industry popularity contest," Hollywood reporter Guy Austin explained to his readers in Australia, "[and] Steiger is not too well liked in Hollywood generally and he has been away from here for a long time. 'The Pawnbroker' was made in New York. Lee Marvin, on the other hand, is a rough and tumble character who is much liked in the industry … [he] is considered first choice." On Oscar night, it was indeed Marvin who ended up taking home the golden statuette. Seemingly unaware of the predictions of Hollywood insiders like Austin, The New York Times commented, "Marvin's selection ranked as perhaps the only surprise of the evening."

At the British Academy Awards the following year, two of the unsuccessful Oscar nominees won awards. Steiger was named Best Foreign Actor for *The Pawnbroker* while Burton won as Best British Actor for *The Spy Who Came in from the Cold.*

1965

BEST SUPPORTING ACTRESS

ACADEMY AWARDS
Ruth Gordon as 'the dealer' in *Inside Daisy Clover*
Joyce Redman as 'Emilia' in *Othello*
Maggie Smith as 'Desdemona' in *Othello*
• Shelley Winters as 'Rose-Ann D'Arcey' in *A Patch of Blue*
Peggy Wood as 'the Mother Abbess' in *The Sound of Music*

GOLDEN GLOBE AWARDS
Joan Blondell – *The Cincinnati Kid*
• Ruth Gordon – *Inside Daisy Clover*
Joyce Redman – *Othello*
Thelma Ritter – *Boeing Boeing*
Peggy Wood – *The Sound of Music*

BOARD OF REVIEW – Joan Blondell – *The Cincinnati Kid*

In 1942, forty-six-year old Ruth Gordon, who had been overlooked for an Oscar nomination two years earlier for her portrayal of Mary Todd in *Abe Lincoln in Illinois*, married playwright Garson Kanin and, having made just eight films, abandoned her acting career in favour of writing. Over the next decade, she and Kanin received three Oscar nominations in the writing categories: for the drama *A Double Life* (for which Ronald Colman won the Best Actor Oscar) and the comedies *Adam's Rib* and *Pat and Mike* (which both starred Katharine Hepburn and Spencer Tracy). Gordon also wrote the 1953 film *The Actress*, which was based on her own early ambition to become an actress.

In the mid-1960s, Gordon resumed her on-screen career. At the age of sixty-nine, for her come-back performance in *Inside Daisy Clover*, she won the Best Supporting Actress Golden Globe and earned her first Oscar nomination in the acting categories (LAT "strikes just the right wacky note"; V "immense"; TT "good"). In so doing, Gordon became the first woman nominated by the Academy for both acting and writing.

Also nominated for the Oscar were: both Joyce Redman as Emilia, the wife of the villainous Iago (NYT "eloquently played"; LAT "if Joyce Redman tends to lose her lines during her shouted hysterics, the hysterics are certainly justified") and Best Actress (Drama) Golden Globe nominee Maggie Smith as the tragic Desdemona (NYT "beautifully sensitive, vibrant"; LAT "lovely" FQ "excellent") in *Othello*, a film adaptation of the William Shakespeare tragedy; previous winner Shelley Winters as the mother opposed to her blind daughter's relationship with an African-American man in *A Patch of Blue* (LAT "makes the girl's mother the prototype of a role she has appropriated as her own – petty, waspish, shrill, hysterical"; V "very good"); and Peggy Wood as the Mother Superior in the musical *The Sound of Music* (WP "winning … no one would guess that this gentle Abbess could have the strength of dynamic Miss Wood"; V "especially outstanding"; TT "does some effortless scene-stealing").

The Academy's list of nominees did not include either National Board of Review winner and Globe nominee Joan Blondell in *The Cincinnati Kid* (NYT "and fortunately, for spectators bored by cards, into that interminable climax there breezes Miss Blondell, like a blowsy, good-natured gale"; WP "sassy"; MFB "adds a nice dash of spice") or Globe nominee Thelma Ritter as the housekeeper in the comedy *Boeing Boeing* (NYT "has the tangiest lines and makes the withering most of them"; LAT "deadpans the play away from the rest of the cast"; V "outstanding"; SMH "gives her usual professional performance"). Ritter had been unsuccessfully nominated for the Best Supporting Actress Oscar six times over the previous fifteen years, but missed out on a record seventh mention in the supporting category.

Overlooked for both the Globe and the Oscar were: Eleanor Parker as the Baroness in *The Sound of Music* (WP "does quite well"; CT "excellent"); Angela Lansbury as Jean Harlow's mother in *Harlow* (LAT "workmanlike"; CT "adequate"; MFB "superb"); Gladys Henson as a grandmother in the British film *The Leather Boys* (NYT "[a] sharply etched cameo"; LAT "distinguished"; FQ "fine"); Mona Washbourne in *The Third Day* (V "a standout"); and both Yvonne Furneaux (NYT "splendid") and Valerie Taylor (S&S "excellent") in Roman Polanski's British thriller *Repulsion*.

Arguably the most glaring omission from the two lists of nominees, however, was Geraldine Fitzgerald as the welfare worker who tries to befriend a traumatised Holocaust survivor in *The Pawnbroker* (NYT "striking"; V "although appearing only in three scenes, Geraldine Fitzgerald makes a deep impression").

The favourite for the Oscar was Gordon who's triumphant return to Hollywood was the focus of newspaper features by columnists on both sides of the United States. But on the night the Academy Award went to Winters, who became the first woman to win a second statuette as Best Supporting Actress (she had first won six years earlier for *The Diary of Anne Frank*). She was a strong contender for a third Oscar seven years later when she received a third Supporting Actress nomination for the disaster film *The Poseidon Adventure*.

Globe winner Gordon had a second chance at the Best Supporting Actress statuette three years later with the occult thriller *Rosemary's Baby*.

1965

BEST SUPPORTING ACTOR

ACADEMY AWARDS
• Martin Balsam as 'Arnold Burns' in *A Thousand Clowns*
Ian Bannen as 'Crow' in *Flight of the Phoenix*
Tom Courtenay as 'Pasha' in *Doctor Zhivago*
Michael Dunn as 'Glocken' in *Ship of Fools*
Frank Finlay as 'Iago' in *Othello*

GOLDEN GLOBE AWARDS
Red Buttons – *Harlow*
Frank Finlay – *Othello*
Hardy Krüger – *Flight of the Phoenix*
Telly Savalas – *Battle of the Bulge*
• Oskar Werner – *The Spy Who Came in from the Cold*

BOARD OF REVIEW – Harry Andrews – *The Agony and the Ecstasy* and ***The Hill***

Oskar Werner won the Golden Globe as Best Supporting Actor for his performance as a German agent in Martin Ritt's *The Spy Who Came in from the Cold* (NYT "electrifying"; WP "hard, matter-of-fact acting … unrecognizable"). He had also been nominated for the Best Actor (Drama) Globe for his role in *Ship of Fools*. When the Academy Award nominations were announced, however, Werner was not a double nominee. He was passed over for the supporting prize and recognised only in the Best Actor category. Similarly, Rod Steiger received a Best Actor Oscar nomination for *The Pawnbroker* but was not included in the secondary category for his performance as Komarovsky in the epic *Doctor Zhivago* (NYT "very good"; LAT "electrifying"; TT "excellent"). On Oscar night, both men were outpolled for the Best Actor statuette.

Hardy Krüger essentially ruled himself out of Oscar contention for *Flight of the Phoenix* when he declined his Golden Globe nomination and had his name removed from the ballot (LAT "a particular delight"). The Academy instead recognised one of the other members of the ensemble cast, Ian Bannen (WP "[a] fine portrait"). Of the other three unsuccessful Globe contenders, both Red Buttons in *Harlow* (LAT "workmanlike") and Telly Savalas in *Battle of the Bulge* (NYT "overacts") were passed over by Oscar voters. Only Frank Finlay appeared on both the Globe and Oscar ballots, for his performance as Iago, the scheming villain in *Othello* (NYT "fluid and brash", "eloquently played"; LAT "terrifically effective"; FQ "excellent").

Nominated for the Academy Award alongside Bannen and Finlay were: Martin Balsam as the sensible brother of a social misfit in *A Thousand Clowns* (LAT "at a preview, an audience predominantly press and thus presumably hard-boiled, rewarded Balsam's [characterization] with spontaneous applause as he finished his exit line"); Tom Courtenay as a Russian revolutionary in *Doctor Zhivago* (NYT "very good"; LAT "electric"; TT "excellent"; SMH "the soundest and most sustained character work [in the film]"); and Michael Dunn for his film debut as the philosophising dwarf in *Ship of Fools* (NYT "superb"; LAT "played with a sly mixture of contempt and compassion"; WP "so brilliantly etched that further roles must be found for him"; MFB "superb"). It was the third time in fifteen years that the five Oscar candidates were all first-time nominees.

A notable omission from the lists of Globe and Oscar candidates was National Board of Review winner Harry Andrews, both for his BAFTA nominated turn as the prison commanding officer in *The Hill* (NYT "devastating"; LAT "performed no less than magnificently"; V "a standout"; MFB "couldn't be bettered") and for his portrayal of Bramate, the architect of St Paul's Basilica in the Vatican, in *The Agony and the Ecstasy* (V "excels"). That the Academy should exclude Andrews was not, however, entirely surprising. Of the eleven previous NBR winners in the supporting category, only four had been considered for the Oscar (and only two of those had been honoured with the Academy Award).

Also unrecognised by the Academy were: Alec Guinness in *Doctor Zhivago* (TT "excellent"); José Ferrer in *Ship of Fools* (V "excellent"); Laurence Harvey in *Darling* (V "exceptionally good"); Derek Jacobi as Cassio in *Othello* (V "excellent"); Michael Hordern in *The Spy Who Came in from the Cold* (S&S "very clever"); Raf Vallone as Jean Harlow's stepfather in *Harlow* (MFB "superb"); Ossie Davis in *The Hill* (NYT "superb"); Robert Morley as an actor in *The Loved One* (NYT "brilliant"); Dudley Sutton as the sexually ambiguous friend in the British film *The Leather Boys* (NYT "carefully indicates the deviate and his concomitant loneliness"; LAT "succeeds in both letting the audience know immediately the truth about the character and in gaining sympathy"; WP "acted with touching dignity"; S&S "excellent"); Henry Hull as a smelly old farmer in *The Fool Killer* (V "superbly played", a "brilliant vignette – big enough to remember when Oscar supporting choices come around"); and Edward G. Robinson in *The Cincinnati Kid* (NYT "is quiet, precise and deadly – all with his eyes"; LAT "superb").

On Oscar night, the established and respected Hollywood character actor outpolled the newcomer and the three foreigners. The statuette was won by Balsam. Despite another twenty-five years in films, Balsam was never again included on the Academy's lists of nominees.

1966

BEST PICTURE

ACADEMY AWARDS

Alfie
(Sheldrake, Paramount, 114 mins, 24 Aug 1966, 5 noms)

• ***A Man for All Seasons***
(Highland, Columbia, 120 mins, 12 Dec 1966, $9.2m, 8 noms)

The Russians are Coming, the Russians are Coming
(Mirisch, United Artists, 120 mins, 25 May 1966, $7.7m, 4 noms)

The Sand Pebbles
(Argyle-Solar, Twentieth Century-Fox, 179 mins, 20 Dec 1966, 8 noms)

Who's Afraid of Virginia Woolf?
(Chenault, Warner Bros., 134 mins BW, 22 Jun 1966, $10.3m, 13 noms)

GOLDEN GLOBE AWARDS

(Drama)
Born Free
• ***A Man For All Seasons***
The Professionals
The Sand Pebbles
Who's Afraid of Virginia Woolf?

(Comedy/Musical)
A Funny Thing Happened on the Way to the Forum
Gambit
Not With My Wife, You Don't
• ***The Russians are Coming, the Russians are Coming***
You're a Big Boy Now

BRITISH ACADEMY AWARDS

(Film)
Doctor Zhivago
Morgan!
The Spy Who Came in from the Cold
• ***Who's Afraid of Virginia Woolf?***

(British Film)
Alfie
Georgy Girl
Morgan!
• ***The Spy Who Came in from the Cold***

NEW YORK – ***A Man for All Seasons***
BOARD OF REVIEW – ***A Man for All Seasons***
NATIONAL SOCIETY – ***Blow-Up***

Finding that their views increasingly differed from those of the New York Film Critics Circle, a group of younger critics (who had been excluded from the circle because they worked for magazines rather than newspapers) established their own group: the National Society of Film Critics. Despite its name, the new association was New York-based and remained so into the early 1970s.

Interestingly, the rival groups each considered the same three films for Best Picture.

The winner of the New York Film Critics Circle accolade was *A Man for All Seasons*, an adaptation of Robert Bolt's acclaimed play (NYT "fine and impressive, albeit somewhat lengthy and verbose", "a picture that inspires admiration, courage and thought"; LAT "brilliant [and] moving"; V "an excellent, handsome and stirring film"; S&S "intelligent if rather academic"). It was the first film to win four accolades from the New York critics also taking out prizes for Best Director, Actor and Screenplay.

Finishing as runner-up was *Who's Afraid of Virginia Woolf?*, a critically acclaimed box office success, that starred Elizabeth Taylor and Richard Burton as a dysfunctional married couple (NYT "a notable event in our film history", "the eye-opener of the year"; LAT "monumental piece of American cinema … [a] masterwork"; CT "unlike most stage-to-screen metamorphoses, this one comes up brilliant, going a step beyond the original … unquestionably is the forerunner for the best motion picture of 1966"; WP "unquestionably will be one of the decade's remembered films"; V "brilliant"; HRp "shattering"; SMH "comes off even better on screen than it did on stage").

A week later, both *A Man for All Seasons* and *Who's Afraid of Virginia Woolf?* garnered votes from members of the National Society but were ultimately out-polled by the film which had finished third in New York: British release *Blow-Up* (NYT "fascinating", "stunning", "the sharpest piece of cinema of the year"; TT "interesting" but "superficially effective"; S&S "odd, beautiful, and desperately sad").

In early January, *A Man For All Seasons* also claimed the National Board of Review plaudit with *Who's Afraid of Virginia Woolf?* finishing in fourth place. *Blow-Up* did not appear in the group's top ten.

Blow-Up was also absent from lists of nominees for the two Best Picture Golden Globes. Both *A Man for All Seasons* and *Who's Afraid of Virginia Woolf?* were included in the Drama category, along with the NBR runner-up *Born Free* (NYT "this film casts an enchantment that is just about irresistible"; LAT "a film for all to see … its simplicity is deceptive"; WP "a rare, enchanting and, of all things, truthful movie … remarkable"; CT "a good, colourful, honest, and unpretentious movie … warm, sincere family fun … a refreshing oddity"; V "[an] outstanding artistic achievement").

Surprisingly overlooked for the Globe (Drama), despite nominations for its director and star, was the British film *Alfie* which had won a special Jury prize at the Cannes Film Festival and had finished third in the NBR vote (NYT "there is in this seemingly blithe film an annoyance of large proportions in the principal character … [but] the whole thing is played expertly"; LAT "another of those black comedies, which really means tragi-comedies, at which the English are so damnably expert … brilliantly cast and acted"; MFB "sharp, comic and sometimes sentimental"; SMH "exceptional").

In a major change to the way in which the annual film awards season unfolded, the Globes were, for the first time, presented prior to the announcement of the Oscar nominations. The winner of the Globe (Drama) was *A Man for All Seasons*, which also won the award for Best Director. That same week, the DGA award was won by Fred Zinnemann for *A Man for All Seasons*. As a result, the historical drama became the outright favourite for the Best Picture Oscar even though it did not receive nearly as many nominations as its main rival.

The list of Academy Award contenders was topped by *Who's Afraid of Virginia Woolf?* with thirteen nods in a record-equalling thirteen categories. Meanwhile, *A Man for All Seasons* earned eight nominations. They were the only films named for both Best Picture and Director.

The other Best Picture nominees were: *Alfie*; the war epic *The Sand Pebbles* (NYT "brooding and turbulent", "curiously turgid and uneven"; LAT "adventure on a grand scale … stirring"); and the winner of the Best Picture (Comedy/Musical) Golden Globe and surprise box office hit *The Russians are Coming, the Russians are Coming* (NYT "rousingly funny and perceptive"; V "outstanding"; WP "refreshingly witty topical comedy"; CT "a breezy comedy that disappointingly never gets its second wind … falls apart during the last hour as sporadic slapsticking and propaganda pitching replace the quiet subtleties"; MFB "film treads a dangerous path … and almost falls flat when it indulges in sententious philosophising … [climax] is false and artificial").

Missing out on nominations for the top Oscar despite recognition for their directors were NSFC champ *Blow-Up*, Globe nominee *The Professionals* (NYT "the scenery provided in this picture is clearly more profound than the script, and the sense of magnitude in the environment more engrossing than the plot"; LAT "for a good deal of its 116 minutes I kept telling myself it is one of the best westerns in years … then, a couple of times after I expected it to end and it didn't, what ensued slipped dangerously close to anti-climax and a coming-apart at the seams"; CT "little more than a B-plus Southwestern"), and the French film *Un Homme et une Femme (A Man and a Woman)*, which won both the Academy Award and the Golden Globe as Best Foreign-Language Film (NYT "beautiful and sometimes breath-taking"; LAT "dazzlingly difficult … in structure it is as complex as its story is simple"; TT "a witty, perverse comedy"; SMH "succeeds impeccably"). Nominated in seven categories but also overlooked for Best Picture was the all-star epic *Hawaii* (NYT "one comes out of the theatre not so much moved as numbed by the cavalcade of conventional if sometimes eyepopping scenes … big and familiar [but] heavy"; LAT "one of the outstanding Hollywood pictures of 1966"; WP "spoiled by the hyperlong sameness and a main character who lacks only the archetypal bad-guy moustache and whip"; S&S "thoroughly respectable").

Also passed over were: Billy Wilder's *The Fortune Cookie* (NYT "a fine, dark, gag-filled hallucination … a comedy of unrelieved vulgarity, but it has style and taste … it is also an explosively funny live-action cartoon"; WP "sharp"; V "overlong"); Berlin Film Festival prizewinner *Cul-de-Sac* (V "always absorbing"); the British film *Morgan!* (NYT "howlingly funny … but it is really much more than a swiftly moving farce. Within its absurdities is satire on some of the sad immaturities of our day … it may cause us all to have a bit too much sympathy for beatniks and their childishness in a vicious world"; LAT "[a] perverse picture"; CT "wonderfully wacky … [a] kooky kaleidoscope"); the 1964 British drama *King and Country* (NYT "an intense, compelling picture … smashing … stark and unrelenting … it is not an easy film to watch"; CT "but something is wrong. Such characters and situations should grab with a visceral force, but they don't"; SMH "excellently achieved purpose"); and the Czechoslovakian film *Obchod na Korze (The Shop on Main Street)*, which won Best Foreign-Language Film awards from the Academy in 1965 and the New York critics in 1966 (NYT "stunning" "one of the most arresting and devastating pictures I've seen from Europe or anywhere else in several years"; LAT "a masterpiece … not within recent memory has there been a picture with such emotional impact … superb in every way, this Czechoslovakian film should be a strong contender in the upcoming Oscar race"; WP "you will not want to miss it"; CT "compelling"; SMH "superlatives seem to be inadequate").

On Oscar night, the Best Picture Academy Award was won by *A Man for All Seasons*. The following year, Zinnemann's drama also won both the BAFTAs for Best Film and Best British Film. The NSFC prizewinner *Blow-Up*, meanwhile, received the Palme d'Or at the Cannes Film Festival.

1966

BEST DIRECTOR

ACADEMY AWARDS
Michelangelo Antonioni for *Blow-Up*
Richard Brooks for *The Professionals*
Claude Lelouch for *Un Homme et une Femme (A Man and a Woman)*
Mike Nichols for *Who's Afraid of Virginia Woolf?*
• Fred Zinnemann for *A Man for All Seasons*

GOLDEN GLOBE AWARDS
Lewis Gilbert – *Alfie*
Claude Lelouch – *Un Homme et une Femme (A Man and a Woman)*
Mike Nichols – *Who's Afraid of Virginia Woolf?*
Robert Wise – *The Sand Pebbles*
• Fred Zinnemann – *A Man for All Seasons*

DIRECTORS GUILD AWARD
Richard Brooks – *The Professionals*
John Frankenheimer – *Grand Prix*
Lewis Gilbert – *Alfie*
James Hill – *Born Free*
Norman Jewison – *The Russians are Coming, the Russians are Coming*
Claude Lelouch – *Un Homme et une Femme (A Man and a Woman)*
Silvio Narizzano – *Georgy Girl*
Mike Nichols – *Who's Afraid of Virginia Woolf?*
Robert Wise – *The Sand Pebbles*
• Fred Zinnemann – *A Man for All Seasons*

NEW YORK – Fred Zinnemann – *A Man for All Seasons*
BOARD OF REVIEW – Fred Zinnemann – *A Man for All Seasons*
NATIONAL SOCIETY – Michelangelo Antonioni – *Blow-Up*

Italian director Michelangelo Antonioni won the inaugural National Society of Film Critics Best Director award for his first English-language film *Blow-Up* (NYT "it is vintage Antonioni … beautifully photographed"; LAT "a brilliant master of the camera"). Although he was subsequently overlooked for the Golden Globe and the Directors Guild of America honour, he did receive his first (and only) nomination from the Academy.

The overwhelming favourite for the Best Director statuette on Oscar night, however, was fifty-nine-year old Hollywood veteran Fred Zinnemann, who had collected all of the other major end-of-year accolades for his handling of the acclaimed historical drama *A Man for All Seasons* (NYT "a fine job"; V "excellent"; S&S "sincere and unaffected"; MFB "sensitive and imaginative").

At the start of the film awards season, Zinnemann collected a record-equalling fourth plaudit from the New York Film Critics Circle. In addition to Zinnemann, the east coast critics considered: Antonioni; theatre director Mike Nichols for his feature film directorial debut, *Who's Afraid of Virginia Woolf?* (NYT "successful"; LAT "his perceptiveness, his feeling for what's right, is positively brilliant"; CT "a highly notable achievement, intelligently using the medium to its maximum potential"; V "outstanding"; MFB "the camera is constantly on the move, irritating, distracting, breaking up the play's finely calculated obsessional qualities"; SMH "good cinema thanks to the masterly way in which [he] uses film realism"); Karel Reisz for the British film *Morgan!* (LAT "brilliantly improvised quality"); and the partnership of Ján Kadár and Elmar Klos for *Obchod na Korze (The Shop on Main Street)* (LAT "creates a pathos that culminates in a heart-rending climax"; WP "have made words superfluous"' SMH "the direction flows as if in personal experience").

Zinnemann's status as the Academy Award favourite was confirmed when he collected the National Board of Review accolade, the DGA honour and the Globe, each for the second time in his career.

Nominated for both the DGA prize and the Globe were: Lewis Gilbert for *Alfie* (NYT "smartly done"; LAT "skilful"; WP "photographed with imaginative restraint"; CT "sprightly direction"); Claude Lelouch for *Un Homme et une Femme (A Man and a Woman)* (NYT "a first-rate demonstration of the artfulness of a cameraman and the skill at putting together handsome pictures"; LAT "an ambitious attempt to break down barriers between film and reality"); Nichols for *Who's Afraid of Virginia Woolf?*; and Robert Wise for the war epic *The Sand Pebbles* (NYT "beautifully mounted" but "uneven").

Five days after winning the Globe, Zinnemann was included on the Academy's list of Oscar contenders for the sixth time. Also nominated were Antonioni, Lelouch and Nichols (each for the first time) and Richard Brooks for *The Professionals* (LAT "he knows how to use the medium to tell [his story]"; CT "has developed the incredible ability of transforming gold into dross").

In addition to Wise and Gilbert, the most surprising omission was DGA nominee Norman Jewison for *The Russians are Coming, the Russians are Coming* (NYT "wisely gave this talented crew [of comic actors] their heads"; CT "neatly manipulates the sight gags"). Also overlooked were both Silvio Narizzano for *Georgy Girl* (CT "disturbingly erratic"; V "impressive"); and Joseph Losey for *King and Country* (CT "keenly sensitive").

On Oscar night, the faultless record of the DGA as an Oscar indicator was preserved when Zinnemann won the Best Director Oscar for a second time.

1966

BEST ACTRESS

ACADEMY AWARDS

Anouk Aimee as 'Anne Gauthier' in *Un Homme et une Femme (A Man and a Woman)*

Ida Kaminska as 'Rozalie Lautmannova' in *Obchod na Korze (The Shop on Main Street)*

Lynn Redgrave as 'Georgy Parkin' in *Georgy Girl*

Vanessa Redgrave as 'Leonie Delt' in *Morgan!*

• Elizabeth Taylor as 'Martha' in *Who's Afraid of Virginia Woolf?*

GOLDEN GLOBE AWARDS

(Drama)

• Anouk Aimee – *Un Homme et une Femme (A Man and a Woman)*

Ida Kaminska – *Obchod na Korze (The Shop on Main Street)*

Virginia McKenna – *Born Free*

Elizabeth Taylor – *Who's Afraid of Virginia Woolf?*

Natalie Wood – *This Property is Condemned*

(Comedy/Musical)

Jane Fonda – *Any Wednesday*

Elizabeth Hartman – *You're a Big Boy Now*

Shirley MacLaine – *Gambit*

• Lynn Redgrave – *Georgy Girl*

Vanessa Redgrave – *Morgan!*

BRITISH ACADEMY AWARDS

(Foreign Actress)

Brigitte Bardot – *Viva Maria!*

Joan Hackett – *The Group*

• Jeanne Moreau – *Viva Maria!*

(British Actress)

Julie Christie – *Doctor Zhivago* and *Fahrenheit 451*

Lynn Redgrave – *Georgy Girl*

Vanessa Redgrave – *Morgan!*

• Elizabeth Taylor – *Who's Afraid of Virginia Woolf?*

NEW YORK – Lynn Redgrave – *Georgy Girl* and **Elizabeth Taylor – *Who's Afraid of Virginia Woolf?***

BOARD OF REVIEW – Elizabeth Taylor – *Who's Afraid of Virginia Woolf?*

NATIONAL SOCIETY – Sylvie – *La Vieille Dame Indigne (The Shameless Old Lady)*

1966

For the first time in the history of the Academy Awards, all the Best Actress nominees were foreigners. Interestingly, the winner was the only candidate nominated for a performance in an American film.

At the end of the year, the New York Film Critics Circle announced that for the first time, two winners would share one of its acting awards. The co-winners of the Best Actress accolade were two English actresses: twenty-three-year old Lynn Redgrave for her portrayal of the ugly duckling title character in the British comedy *Georgy Girl* (NYT "it is her exceeding sensitivity to the nuances of this girl and her dexterity in expressing these nuances that are the core of the film"; LAT "not an unalloyed triumph"; V "a topflight comedy performance"; CT "makes a smashing film-starring debut, displaying hilarity, impudence, touching sensitivity and freshness"; TT "splendidly played") and thirty-four-year old Elizabeth Taylor as the foul-mouthed wife of an alcoholic university professor in *Who's Afraid of Virginia Woolf?* (NYT "the best work of her career, sustained and urgent", "illuminating"; LAT "sustained intensity"; CT "comes close to her husband's performance … her final sequences are especially moving"; V "topflight performance"; FQ "extremely good"; MGB "thoroughly sound in a familiar Hollywood tradition of screen acting"; SMH "playing Martha powerfully"). Both actresses had gained extra weight in order to play their characters.

Three other actresses were considered by the New York critics, all of them foreigners. Ida Kaminska, a sixty-seven-year old Ukrainian actress, finished as runner-up with her turn as an old Jewish shopowner during the Nazi occupation in the Czechoslovakian drama *Obchod na Korze (The Shop on Main Street)* (NYT "wondrous", "played superbly"; LAT "superlatively played … flawless"; WP "the most striking feature [of the film] is the creative performance by Ida Kaminska … builds her scenes from the comic to the tragic with brilliantly resourceful detail … magnificently effective"; CT "thoroughly charming and credulous"; TT "admirable"; SMH "[her] acting is no longer acting but life in process"). Also receiving votes were English actresses Wendy Hiller, for her supporting performance in *A Man for All Seasons*, and Vanessa Redgrave, the twenty-nine-year old sister of Lynn, for her role as the wife of the mentally unstable title character in the British film *Morgan!*, for which she had been honoured at the Cannes Film Festival (NYT "positively smashing"; CT "she waltzes thru the part of Leonie with great style and charm"; S&S "extraordinary"; MFB her performance is "[a] success with its suggestion of vulnerability held in check by parental prompting"). Vanessa Redgrave had also earned acclaim from critics for her part in another British film, Michelangelo Antonioni's *Blow-Up* (NYT "excellent", "pliant and elusive, seductive yet remote as the girl"; LAT "she plays well").

1966

Yet another foreign actress entered into Best Actress Oscar contention when the newly-established National Society of Film Critics announced their inaugural winners early in the new year. French character actress Sylvie had first appeared on the screen in the French silent film *Germinal* in 1913. At age eighty-three, she won Best Actress from the NSFC for what was her final role, the title character in *La Vieille Dame Indigne (The Shameless Old Lady)*, a part writer Bertolt Brecht had based on his grandmother (NYT "plays the leading role in a manner that should etch it forever on the memories of those who see the film … she has the great skill of being able to make us sense and comprehend a human soul"; LAT "a lifetime of acting has given her perfect simplicity and unobtrusive authority. She does much with little – a gesture, a look, tells all"; WP "played with beguiling understatement … indicates Berthe's reactions with brilliant subtlety, merely, it seems, hinting with her eyes. Whatever magic she uses, it works and through her careful understatement she says a mouthful"; CT "an altogether charming characterization").

A week later, the National Board of Review named Taylor as the year's Best Actress and observers began to declare husband and wife, Richard Burton and Elizabeth Taylor, as the Oscar frontrunners for their performances as the venomous married couple in *Who's Afraid of Virginia Woolf?*.

At the Golden Globe awards in February, however, the Oscar chances of Burton and Taylor began to look less certain when each was outpolled in the lead drama categories. In a huge upset, the Globe for Best Actress (Drama) was won by yet another non-American, French actress Anouk Aimee, as a woman who finds love while visiting her children at boarding school one weekend, in *Un Homme et une Femme (A Man and a Woman)* (NYT "disconcerting flatness").

In addition to Taylor, the Globe (Drama) category's unsuccessful nominees were: New York contender Kaminska; English actress Virginia McKenna in *Born Free* (NYT "gentle"; LAT "incredibly natural"; CT "a convincing performance"); and Natalie Wood as the flirtatious Southern girl in *This Property is Condemned* who was surprisingly included despite mixed reviews (LAT "comes through more artfully than at any time since 'Splendor in the Grass'"; WP "certainly good"; CT "seems to ring false"; V "a very good interpretation"; MFB "struggles helplessly"). Overlooked was previous Globe winner Julie Andrews as a missionary's wife in the historical epic *Hawaii* (V "excellent in a demanding dramatic role"; MFB a "warm portrayal").

In the Comedy/Musical category, the Globe was won by Lynn Redgrave. Her victory came over a field of nominees that included her elder sister and Shirley MacLaine in the heist caper *Gambit* (CT "shows welcome restraint").

When the Oscar nominees were announced, both Globe winners Aimee and Lynn Redgrave received mentions for the first time. Also nominated for the first time were Kaminska and Vanessa Redgrave. Just like her husband in the Best Actor category, Taylor was the only previous nominee listed in the category, and was the strong favourite to win. It was her fifth nomination in a decade.

The inclusion of both Lynn and Vanessa Redgrave was historic on several counts. Following the nomination of Joan Fontaine and Olivia de Havilland in 1941, they were the second pair of sisters nominated for the Best Actress Oscar in the same year. They were also second-generation nominees as their father, Michael Redgrave, had been a Best Actor candidate in 1947. Furthermore, Vanessa Redgrave was, at the time, the wife of Tony Richardson, the 1963 Best Director Oscar winner.

The Academy also made history by mentioning both Aimee and Kaminska. It was the first time that Oscar voters had shortlisted two performances in non-English-language films in the same category.

On Oscar night, Taylor won the Best Actress Academy Award for the second time, although she was not present to collect the statuette. Disappointed that Burton had not also won an Oscar, however, Taylor refused to issue a statement of thanks the following day.

Taylor's victory made it the eighth year in a row that the winner of the Best Actress (Drama) Globe had been an unsuccessful Oscar nominee.

Later in the month, Taylor was also presented with the BAFTA for Best British Actress (Burton was also honoured by the British Academy). Among the other nominees were the Redgrave sisters.

The following year, Burton and Taylor attempted to re-create the on-screen fireworks of *Who's Afraid of Virginia Woolf?* by appearing as the leads in *The Taming of the Shrew*, a film version of the William Shakespeare comedy. Critics, however, were unimpressed. Taylor made few notable films during the 1970s and since then appeared only rarely on the big screen. In 1994, she received praise for her comic turn, in a supporting role, in *The Flintstones*. Despite winning two Oscars from five nominations in just ten years, Taylor was never again nominated by the Academy.

1966

BEST ACTOR

ACADEMY AWARDS

Alan Arkin as 'Rozanov' in *The Russians are Coming, the Russians are Coming*
Richard Burton as 'George' in *Who's Afraid of Virginia Woolf?*
Michael Caine as 'Alfie Elkins' in *Alfie*
Steve McQueen as 'Jake Holman' in *The Sand Pebbles*
• Paul Scofield as 'Sir Thomas More' in *A Man for All Seasons*

GOLDEN GLOBE AWARDS

(Drama)
Richard Burton – *Who's Afraid of Virginia Woolf?*
Michael Caine – *Alfie*
Steve McQueen – *The Sand Pebbles*
• Paul Scofield – *A Man for All Seasons*
Max von Sydow – *Hawaii*

(Comedy/Musical)
• Alan Arkin – *The Russians are Coming, the Russians are Coming*
Alan Bates – *Georgy Girl*
Michael Caine – *Gambit*
Lionel Jeffries – *The Spy With a Cold Nose*
Walter Matthau – *The Fortune Cookie*

BRITISH ACADEMY AWARDS

(Foreign Actor)
Jean-Paul Belmondo – *Pierrot le Fou (Crazy Pete)*
Sidney Poitier – *A Patch of Blue*
• Rod Steiger – *The Pawnbroker*
Oskar Werner – *The Spy Who Came in from the Cold*

(British Actor)
• Richard Burton – *The Spy Who Came in from the Cold* and *Who's Afraid of Virginia Woolf?*
Michael Caine – *Alfie*
Ralph Richardson – *Doctor Zhivago* and *Khartoum* and *The Wrong Box*
David Warner – *Morgan!*

NEW YORK – Paul Scofield – *A Man for All Seasons*
BOARD OF REVIEW – Paul Scofield – *A Man for All Seasons*
NATIONAL SOCIETY – Michael Caine – *Alfie*

1966

British actors dominated consideration for all of the year's major Best Actor awards. Only three Americans made a notable impression on critics for performances in leading roles and all were nominated for both the Globe and the Oscar (although one was surprisingly named by the Academy in the supporting category).

Nominated for the Best Actor Oscar were the stars of the five films short-listed by the Academy for the Best Picture statuette. American actor Alan Arkin was included for his debut film performance as the Russian lieutenant who runs his submarine aground on the US Atlantic coast in Norman Jewison's comedy *The Russians are Coming, the Russians are Coming* (NYT "particularly wonderful"; WP "outstanding … reveals a deft comedy talent, indeed, and surely he is a performer who will be delighting us for the rest of his days … Arkin's most striking characteristics are his underplaying and his eyes, shifting, darting suspicious and affectionate"; CT "fine performance"; MFB "the best performance [of the cast] … handing his part with a sure comic touch"). The other American mentioned was Steve McQueen, for his portrayal of an American sailor on a gunboat in China in the 1920s, in the epic drama *The Sand Pebbles* (NYT "the most restrained, honest, heartfelt acting he has ever done"; LAT "Jake is a complex yet simple man, neither hero not anti-hero, and Steve McQueen illumines the complexity and the simplicity, often with the most fleeting change of expression, in every scene. In short, he is great"; V "outstanding").

Two Englishman were also recognised, each for the first time: Paul Scofield for reprising his stage portrayal of Sir Thomas More in *A Man for All Seasons* (NYT "superb", "brilliant in his exercise of temperance and restraint", "forceful", "throughout Mr Scofield manages to use the glowing words of Mr Bolt and his own histrionic magnificence to give luminescence and power, integrity and honor, to this man"; LAT "Scofield underplays superbly … his portrayal is a must for an Academy Award nomination"; V "excellent"; TT "vivid"; MFB "a masterpiece", "splendidly restrained"); and Michael Caine as the title character in *Alfie*, a role played on stage by Terence Stamp (NYT "played expertly [in an] easy and appealing good humor"; LAT "brilliantly acted … etches an exasperatingly clever portrait"; WP "superb … Caine's central performance has a cool sensitivity of meaning"; CT "brilliantly played"; V "a powerfully strong performance"; TT "excellent"; FQ "smashingly good"; MFB "Caine, who seems to be constantly straining after an accent that no longer comes naturally, tends to be monotonous"; SMH "fits into the whole spirit of the film for the direct way in which he handles the struggle of selfishness with glimpses of redeeming sympathy"). Nominated for the Globe (Drama) for his work in *Alfie*, Caine was also short-listed for the Globe (Comedy/Musical) for his performance in heist caper *Gambit* (CT "neatly underplays").

1966

The only previous nominee in contention was Welshman Richard Burton as an alcoholic professor in *Who's Afraid of Virginia Woolf?* (NYT "utterly convincing", "illuminating"; LAT "on film, at least, Burton has finally made it unequivocally … finely honed"; CT "outstanding"; V "a smash portrayal"; FQ "superb"; MFB "the performances are good, particularly that of Richard Burton playing a role that might have been written for him"). Burton's wife, Elizabeth Taylor, was a Best Actress nominee for the same film.

British actors overlooked for the Oscar included: Laurence Olivier as the Madhi in *Khartoum* (NYT "excels", "impressively and eloquently played"; LAT "is in his element, still playing Othello"; WP "to this part, largely limited to voice and face, Olivier gives brilliantly detailed suggestions"; CT "retains his 'Othello' make-up and mouth-mannerisms. But if the rolling eyes seemed ludicrous in the Shakespearean production, they seem credible for this role"; MFB "strangely weak … Olivier so strives after intonation that what should be an immense character is no character at all"); both 1964 Venice winner and 1964 Best British Actor BAFTA nominee Tom Courtenay as a deserter (NYT "plays the inarticulate private with quivering emotions", "sterling", "outstanding", "compelling"; LAT "fine"; CT "the acting is excellent, topped by Courtenay's engrossing performance as the simple boy"; S&S "agonisingly effective"; SMH "impressively stated") and Dirk Bogarde as the lawyer assigned to defend him (NYT "splendid"; LAT "fine"; CT "excellent"; V "outstanding", "a dramatic highlight") in the anti-war drama *King and Country*; Ralph Richardson in the comedy *The Wrong Box* (NYT "splendid"; V "superb"; S&S "beautifully performed"); David Hemmings in *Blow-Up* (NYT "excellent", "completely fascinating – languid, self-indulgent, cool, yet expressive of so much frustration"; LAT "with his inspired energy Hemmings really makes you believe he is a master of the still camera, and even his youthful cynicism is engaging … one more of those astonishing British finds"); and David Warner in *Morgan!* (NYT "excellent … plays him so that he is terrifying and droll, crafty and pathetic"; CT "played with extraordinary off-center oddity … Warner's zaniness is matched by a keen sense of pathos"; S&S "extraordinary").

Also by-passed for consideration were Russian Innokenti Smoktunovsky in the 1964 Soviet film production of *Hamlet* for which he had been a 1965 BAFTA nominee (NYT "excellent"); Slovak Jozef Kroner in *Obchod na Korze (The Shop on Main Street)* (NYT "played superbly"; LAT "gives a Chaplinesque performance … flawless"; WP "a role splendidly conceived"; CT "brilliantly steers the success of the film, as he makes the delicate transition from comedy to tragedy, from indifference to involvement"; TT "admirable"); Frenchman Jean-Louis Trintignant in *Un Homme et une Femme (A Man and a Woman)* (NYT "disconcerting flatness"); and Swedish actor Max von Sydow in the epic *Hawaii* (V "outstanding").

1966

American comedian Walter Matthau was a Globe nominee for his performance as an unscrupulous lawyer in *The Fortune Cookie* (NYT "makes a fine figure of a comic villain … superb ... dominates the film"; WP "played with gorgeous zest … it is a rich, racy role [and] Matthau enjoys every minute of it and so will you"; V "standout performance"; FQ "hams engagingly"). However, despite being one of the film's two leads, Matthau was included in the supporting category by Oscar voters. Overlooked by Oscar voters was his co-star, Jack Lemmon (NYT "perfect"; WP "Lemmon's performance is a joy you might easily ignore … it is Lemmon's responses which give Matthau his cues [and] Matthau couldn't begin to get away with his highflown antics were they not neatly set in motion by Lemmon … thus, for all Matthau's superb playing of Willie, don't neglect the bouncy wall Lemmon provides with his watchful, anxious eyes, his querulous, probing voice.").

The National Society of Film Critics gave their first Best Actor prize to Caine, but the other two critics accolades, the National Board of Review accolade and New York Film Critic's Circle award, both went to Scofield, who also won the Globe (Drama). The other Globe was won by Arkin. Despite this, the overwhelming favourite for the Academy Award was Burton, who was nominated for the third consecutive year and had never received a statuette, despite four previous nominations. It was widely expected that the husband and wife team of Burton and Taylor would both win Oscars for their performances as a warring married couple.

On Oscar night, Taylor won the Oscar as Best Actress. In an upset, however, the absent Burton was outpolled by the only other nominee not in attendance at the ceremony: Scofield. His award was accepted by his co-star, Wendy Hiller.

Two weeks later, Burton was named Best British Actor by the British Academy for his performances in both *The Spy Who Came in from the Cold* and *Who's Afraid of Virginia Woolf?*. Scofield won the same award the following year.

1966

BEST SUPPORTING ACTRESS

ACADEMY AWARDS
• Sandy Dennis as 'Honey' in *Who's Afraid of Virginia Woolf?*
Wendy Hiller as 'Alice More' in *A Man for All Seasons*
Jocelyne LaGarde as 'Alii Nui' in *Hawaii*
Vivien Merchant as 'Lily Clamacraft' in *Alfie*
Geraldine Page as 'Margery Chanticleer' in *You're a Big Boy Now*

GOLDEN GLOBE AWARDS
Sandy Dennis – *Who's Afraid of Virginia Woolf?*
• Jocelyne LaGarde – *Hawaii*
Vivien Merchant – *Alfie*
Geraldine Page – *You're a Big Boy Now*
Shelley Winters – *Alfie*

BOARD OF REVIEW – Vivien Merchant – *Alfie*

The year after she won a second Best Supporting Actress Academy Award, Shelley Winters was a contender for the accolade again. She was mentioned for the Golden Globe for her role as one of the title character's sexual conquests in the British film *Alfie*, but missed out on a nomination when the Oscar contenders were announced in late February (NYT "expertly played"; WP "excellently drawn"; MFB "makes a bright and entertaining guest appearance").

Film critics were more impressed with two of Winter's English co-stars in *Alfie*. FQ commented that Julia Foster and Vivien Merchant each "deserves special mention" while MFB commended them both for "beautifully subdued studies in resignation". At the end of the year, however, it was Merchant who earned the kudos. For her screen debut as the married woman who has an abortion, Merchant was named Best Supporting Actress by the National Board of Review (NYT "played expertly"; V "brilliant"; LAT "brilliantly acted … may well tear you into small pieces as the dowdy, pathetic Lily"; WP "superb"; TT "excellent"; S&S "touching"). At the time, Merchant was married to playwright Harold Pinter.

Although Winters was passed over by the Academy, the other four Globe candidates all received Academy recognition. Nominated for the first (and only time) were: NBR winner Merchant; Broadway actress Sandy Dennis as the fragile young wife in *Who's Afraid of Virginia Woolf?* (NYT "credibly bland"; NYer "triumphant"; LAT "movingly pathetic"; CT "right on target"; V "an impressive screen debut"; TT "too theatrical"; S&S "stunningly well played";

MFB "good"); and Globe winner Jocelyne LaGarde, a Tahitian who was named for her only screen appearance as the Island queen in the historical epic *Hawaii* (LAT "paradoxically emerges as a queen of great dignity in one of the few roles that allow for humor, making the queen's scenes all her own"; CT "the most captivating accomplishment is achieved by Jocelyne LaGarde … all the more remarkable since she has never acted before"; V "standout"; MFB "a magnificent performance"). LaGarde did not speak English and had to learn her lines phonetically. Included on the Academy's lists for a fourth time was Geraldine Page, as a possessive mother in *You're a Big Boy Now* (NYT "plays or was told to play the boy's mother like a monstrous, cawing parrot"; MFB "reliably portrays the older generation"). Mentioned for the Oscar ahead of Winters was another previous Best Supporting Actress winner, Wendy Hiller, who earned her third (and final) nod for her portrayal of the wife of Sir Thomas More in *A Man for All Seasons* (LAT "highest praise"; S&S "striking").

Arguably the most glaring absentee from the list of Oscar candidates was Charlotte Rampling as the bitchy housemate of the title character in *Georgy Girl* (NYT "splendid"; LAT "provides the right contrast to Miss Redgrave"; CT "not only proves to be the most delectable young actress in years, but deftly conveys general all-round nastiness"; V "fine").

Also overlooked were: Candice Bergen in *The Sand Pebbles* (NYT "beautiful and flawless"; LAT "fresh and lovely"); Irene Handl as the mother of the mentally unstable title character in *Morgan!* (V "excellent"); Eleanor Parker in *The Oscar* (LAT worthy of "some praise"); Kate Reid in *This Property Is Condemned* (NYT "Reid makes [her character] monstrously meaty and maudlin"; LAT "[fills the role] exceptionally well"; CT "the best performance is by Kate Reid who makes a sparkling film debut as the frowzy boarding house owner"; MFB "good"); and, despite a strong campaign, Stella Stevens as the well-intentioned klutz in *The Silencers* (NYT "runs off with the acting honors"; LAT "comes closest to managing an amusingly dumb characterization").

On Academy Awards night, only Hiller and Globe champ LaGarde were present at the ceremony, and both went home empty-handed (although Hiller did accept the Best Actor statuette for her co-star, the absent Paul Scofield). Sidney Poitier opened the envelope and announced that the winner was Dennis. The Oscar was accepted on her behalf by the film's director, Mike Nichols.

Dennis was a strong contender for Best Actress honours over the next two years with her performances in *Up the Down Staircase, The Fox* and *Sweet November*, but was overlooked on each occasion. After she starred in the original version of the comedy *The Out-of-Towners* in 1970, she went into semi-retirement making only occasional appearances on the screen until her death, aged fifty-four, in 1992. She never received a second nomination from the Academy.

1966

BEST SUPPORTING ACTOR

ACADEMY AWARDS
Mako as 'Po-han' in *The Sand Pebbles*
James Mason as 'James Leamington' in *Georgy Girl*
• Walter Matthau as 'Willie Gingrich' in *The Fortune Cookie*
George Segal as 'Nick' in *Who's Afraid of Virginia Woolf?*
Robert Shaw as 'King Henry VIII of England' in *A Man for All Seasons*

GOLDEN GLOBE AWARDS
• Richard Attenborough – *The Sand Pebbles*
Mako – *The Sand Pebbles*
John Saxon – *The Appaloosa*
George Segal – *Who's Afraid of Virginia Woolf?*
Robert Shaw – *A Man for All Seasons*

BOARD OF REVIEW – Robert Shaw – *A Man for All Seasons*

Over thirty years after Charles Laughton won the Best Actor Oscar for portraying King Henry VIII, actor and writer Robert Shaw was included on the Academy's list for his impersonation of the sixteenth century English monarch in Fred Zinnemann's acclaimed drama *A Man for All Seasons* (NYT a "tempestuous performance", "he shapes a frightening portrait of the headstrong, heretical King"; LAT "highest praise"; V "excellent"; MFB "excellent"). Shaw was named Best Supporting Actor by the National Board of Review, and was a contender for the Golden Globe as well as the Oscar. His wife, Mary Ure, had been a Best Supporting Actress nominee at the Globes and the Oscars six years earlier for *Sons and Lovers*.

The winner of the Globe was another Englishman, actor-director Richard Attenborough in the historical war epic *The Sand Pebbles* (NYT "the most hackneyed of the lot"; LAT "professional polish"). Despite the accolade, Attenborough was overlooked by the Academy, who nominated one of his co-stars instead.

Attenborough was excluded from Oscar consideration as a result of the inclusion of American comedian Walter Matthau for his leading performance in Billy Wilder's *The Fortune Cookie*. Matthau had been billed after his co-star, Oscar winner Jack Lemmon, but above the title of the film (NYT "makes a fine figure of a comic villain … superb ... dominates the film"; WP "played with gorgeous zest … it is a rich, racy role [and] Matthau enjoys every minute of it and so will you"; V "standout performance"; FQ "hams engagingly"). At the

Golden Globe awards, Matthau was nominated in the Best Actor (Comedy/Musical) category rather than for the Best Supporting Actor prize and, as The New York Times commented, his portrayal of an unscrupulous lawyer "dominates the film". Furthermore, Matthau was not an unknown when he made *The Fortune Cookie*, often a factor prompting performers to be included in the lesser category for substantial roles. Matthau had appeared on screen for over a decade, and was a respected Broadway star (he had already won a Tony for the stage production of Neil Simon's 'The Odd Couple').

Included alongside Matthau and Shaw on the Oscar list were: Japanese actor Mako for his screen debut in *The Sand Pebbles* (NYT "most credible"; LAT "standout" V "a good film debut"); George Segal as the young biology teacher in *Who's Afraid of Virginia Woolf?* (NYT "good"; LAT "hardly to be faulted"; CT "generally convincing"; V "first-rate performance"; TT "admirable"; S&S "stunningly well played"; FQ "deficient"; MFB "good"); and, only two years after he refused to be considered in the supporting category for *The Pumpkin Eater*, James Mason as the rich lover in *Georgy Girl* (NYT "most engaging", "splendid"; NYer "a stunning portrayal"; CT "drolly underplays"; V "adept").

Passed over for consideration for the Oscar were: Globe nominee John Saxon in the Western *The Appaloosa* (NYT "played with remarkably fearsome oiliness"); Alan Bates in *Georgy Girl* (NYT "almost always convinces"); Nigel Davenport as the Duke of Norfolk in *A Man for All Seasons* (S&S "striking"; MFB "excellent"); Richard Crenna in *The Sand Pebbles* (V "fine"); Brian Keith in *The Russians are Coming, the Russians are Coming* (WP "pleasingly natural"; CT "fine performance"; V "excellent"; MFB "particularly good"); Richard Harris in *Hawaii* (NYT "stands out"); Ralph Richardson as Prime Minister Gladstone in *Khartoum* (NYT "good performing"; LAT "among the first-rank"; WP "the finest role Ralph Richardson has had in years and he rewards it accordingly"; CT "disappointingly turns Gladstone into a huffy stereotype"; MFB "makes Gladstone something of an endearing old stick"); Peter Sellers in the comedy *The Wrong Box* (NYT "the best of the clowning"; LAT "hilarious"; S&S "superb"); Hugh Griffith in *How To Steal A Million* (LAT "takes every scene he comes stomping into and makes it his own"; SMH "acting honours must go to Hugh Griffith who hams it up marvellously"); and Leo McKern in *King and Country* (NYT "impressive"; V "faultless"). Despite a strong campaign, Milton Berle was not recognised in *The Oscar* (LAT "I was especially taken by the degrees of emotion Milton Berle seemed capable of expressing").

On Oscar night, Shaw's supporting performance was not rewarded with an Oscar, even though *A Man for All Seasons* won six statuettes, including Best Picture. Similarly, although both Elizabeth Taylor and Sandy Dennis collected Oscars for their performances in *Who's Afraid of Virginia Woolf?*, Segal went home empty-handed. The winner was Matthau.

1967

BEST PICTURE

ACADEMY AWARDS

Bonnie and Clyde
(Warner Bros., Seven Arts, 111 mins, 13 Aug 1967, $22.8m, 10 noms)
Doctor Dolittle
(Apjac, Twentieth Century-Fox, 152 mins, 19 Dec 1967, $3.5m, 9 noms)
The Graduate
(Nichols-Turman, Embassy, 105 mins, 21 Dec 1967, $44.0m, 7 noms)
Guess Who's Coming to Dinner
(Kramer, Columbia, 108 mins, 12 Dec 1967, $25.5m, 10 noms)
• ***In the Heat of the Night***
(Mirisch, United Artists, 109 mins, 2 Aug 1967, $11.0m, 7 noms)

GOLDEN GLOBE AWARDS

(Drama)
Bonnie and Clyde
Far from the Madding Crowd
Guess Who's Coming to Dinner
In Cold Blood
• ***In the Heat of the Night***

(Comedy/Musical)
Camelot
Doctor Dolittle
• ***The Graduate***
The Taming of the Shrew
Thoroughly Modern Millie

BRITISH ACADEMY AWARDS

(Film)
Bonnie and Clyde
Un Homme et une Femme
(A Man and a Woman)
In the Heat of the Night
• ***A Man for All Seasons***

(British Film)
Accident
Blow-Up
The Deadly Affair
• ***A Man for All Seasons***

NEW YORK – *In the Heat of the Night*
BOARD OF REVIEW – *Far from the Madding Crowd*
NATIONAL SOCIETY – *Persona*

The year after they had been Oscar frontrunners as a warring married couple in *Who's Afraid of Virginia Woolf*, Richard Burton and Elizabeth Taylor reteamed as another acrimonious couple in *The Taming of the Shrew*, a highly-anticipated screen adaptation of the William Shakespeare comedy. When released in March, however, critics were unimpressed (NYT "totally wild abstraction of the Bard … a florid and fustian film … forthrightly campy entertainment … it all grows a bit tedious"; LAT "photographically and technically it is magnificent … a genuine achievement" but "I wearied of it toward the last of two hours"; CT "a brawling, bawdy, barrel-throwing free-for-all"; S&S "weary farce, tasteless caricature, and a hysteria of grimaces"; MFB "a boisterous, bowdlerised version of the play", "if the film works at all, it is only on this level of a rollicking farce").

In August, however, two films emerged as definite candidates for Best Picture honours. The first was the anti-racism drama *In the Heat of the Night* (NYT "a film that has the look and sound of actuality and the pounding pulse of truth"; LAT "smooth and beguiling entertainment"; WP "absorbing … [despite] emphatic flaws, most notably a rushed, confused finale and a rather pushy start"; CT "a tense drama"; V "absorbing"; MFB "a splendidly integrated, entertaining and disturbing film"; SMH "a magnificent film").

Two weeks later, critics were sharply divided by *Bonnie and Clyde*, a violent dramatisation of the lives of two 1930s gangsters. In The New York Times, Bosley Crowther condemned the film as being "as pointless as it is lacking in taste" and Variety commented that it "leaves much to be desired." In contrast, Charles Champlin in the Los Angeles Times lauded it as a "stunning and disturbing film" while The Washington Post called it "brash and altogether brilliant" and the New Yorker said it was "exciting" and "entertaining". Overseas, the Monthly Film Bulletin called it "a beautifully modulated film … a film of levels, violent, tender and comic by turns" while the Sydney Morning Herald declared it to be "one of the best American films of the decade".

These two films remained the frontrunners for the top Oscar, until the last few weeks of the year. In mid-December, another drama with a strong anti-racism message was released, *Guess Who's Coming to Dinner* (NYT "a most delightfully acted and gracefully entertaining film"; LAT "must-viewing for anyone who has ever cared about movies", "deeply moving"; V "outstanding", "superior in almost every imaginable way"; S&S "not to be missed"; SMH "just another glossy, escapist Hollywood comedy … sentimental"). Released three days later was *In Cold Blood*, a black-and-white documentary-like drama about the murder of a Kansas family (NYT an "excellent quasidocumentary", "starkly realistic and electrifyingly illuminating", "vivid realism and literal quality"; LAT "a work of great power, honesty and importance"; V "probing, sensitive, tasteful, balanced and suspenseful"). Finally, opening just days before Christmas was *The Graduate*, a comedy about an affair between a university student and an older married woman (NYT a "delight ... one of the best of the year"; LAT "superior … a dazzling comedy, observant, sharp and spirited").

When the New York Film Critics Circle gathered for their annual vote on 28 December 1967 these five acclaimed American films each received support in the first round of voting for the Best Picture accolade, as did *Ulysses*, an Irish film version of James Joyce's novel (NYT "a surprisingly fine film", a "brilliant rendering of Mr Joyce's extremely complex book"; LAT "an engrossing experience – very often superbly funny, frequently moving"; CT "for the most part, an excellent effort"). The leader for the Best Picture prize after the first round of voting was *Bonnie and Clyde*. Appalled by this result, Crowther addressed the circle, blasting *Bonnie and Clyde* for its violence. He urged the circle to instead endorse *In the Heat of the Night*. Evidently swayed, the New York critics ultimately chose the anti-racism drama.

Three days later, the National Board of Review surprisingly selected *Far from the Madding Crowd* as its Best Picture winner (NYT "disappointing"; S&S "must be seen"; MFB "fails"). Neither *Bonnie and Clyde* nor *In the Heat of the Night* even appeared on the NBR's list of the ten best films of the year.

There was a further surprise another three days later, when the National Society of Film Critics passed over all the year's acclaimed American productions to honour Ingmar Bergman's Swedish drama *Persona* (NYT a "lovely, moody film which, for all its intense emotionalism, makes some tough intellectual demands"; CT "uneven", "intriguing [but then] starts falling apart, floundering in contrived chaos"; V "sometimes confusing ... but fascinating"; G "a film whose early simplicity is gradually stripped off to reveal a complex framework of meaning … a single viewing leaves one only wanting to see it again"; S&S a "masterpiece", "original and triumphant", "profoundly upsetting, at moments terrifying"; MFB "an undeniably difficult film, if only because it leaves itself open to so many interpretations").

In mid-February, the Golden Globe for Best Picture (Drama) was won by the New York champ *In the Heat of the Night* but the biggest winner on the night, was *The Graduate* which won the awards for Best Picture (Comedy/Musical) and Best Director for Nichols. Five days later, Nichols was named Best Director by the Directors Guild of America thus positioning *The Graduate* as the frontrunner for the Oscar. For the previous eighteen years, the DGA winner had always received the Best Director Oscar and the Academy had given the Best Picture and Best Director statuettes to the same film for the past decade.

When the Academy announced the Oscar nominees two days later, on 19 February 1968, there were, however, some major surprises. Leading the field of contenders, each with ten nominations, were *Bonnie and Clyde* and *Guess Who's Coming to Dinner*. Trailing these films by just one nomination was the musical *Doctor Dolittle*, which had been a critical and commercial disaster (NYT "fabricated", "the music is not exceptional" and "the fantasy is dull"; LAT "calculated", "anti-climactic"; CT "better left well enough alone", "interminable"; V "imperfect"; TT "never really takes fire"). The shock inclusion of *Doctor Dolittle* resulted in the omission of *In Cold Blood*. Completing the Oscar short-list, each with seven mentions, were the two Globe winners: *The Graduate* and *In the Heat of the Night*. It was only the second time that all the Best Picture nominees were in colour.

1967

Also nominated in seven categories, but by-passed for the top prize, was the musical *Thoroughly Modern Millie* (NYT "a joyously syncopated frolic"; WP "may not be thoroughly marvelous but, by jingo, it's fun"; CT "what can start out as the berries, can finish up a lemon … succeeds more as a comedy than a musical"; TT "thoroughly delightful"; S&S "a piece of good, and good-natured entertainment [that is] full of delightful small touches"). Also by-passed were: *Cool Hand Luke* (NYT "intelligent"; CT "a sharp, absorbing, extremely entertaining motion picture"; LAT "a remarkably interesting and impressive Hollywood film … has its flaws [but] remains an achievement, a starkly powerful parable, a simple tale with truths to tell"); and BAFTA nominee *Accident* (NYT "such a teapot tempest and it is so assiduously underplayed that it is neither strong drama nor stinging satire"; LAT a "triumph", "a breath-taking piece of virtuoso filmmaking, at once naturalistic and poetic", "compelling and thought-provoking; WP "an immensely absorbing, richly acted adventure"; G "a great film"; Sp "the film is masterly").

Although now celebrated by historians and critics, mixed reviews and various controversies led to the Academy at the time to ignore: *Point Blank* (NYT "spectacularly stylized and vividly photographed [but] relentless … a tangled, cryptic [film] that is likely to engross the viewer without enlightening or edifying … candid and calculatedly sadistic"; LAT "hard-hitting … leaves you reeling"; WP "pointless"); *Chimes at Midnight* (NYT "a confusing patchwork of scenes and characters"; S&S "a less than satisfactory experience for the audience"); and *Two for the Road* (NYT a "bitter account of domestic discord", one can only "endure the tedium of much of the picture"; LAT "a mature and memorable film, touching, romantic, funny, insightful and important"; S&S "would be a far better film if it could only decide which of three lanes it wanted to drive in – comedy, farce or philosophical comment").

In the early part of Academy Awards night, *Bonnie and Clyde* and *In the Heat of the Night* each won two Oscars and when Leslie Caron announced Best Director, the winner was Mike Nichols for *The Graduate*. The two screenplay awards and the two major acting awards were then split between *Guess Who's Coming to Dinner* and *In the Heat of the Night* before it fell to Julie Andrews to announce the winner of the evening's final award. In a major surprise, the award went to *In the Heat of the Night*, which emerged as the night's biggest winner with five statuettes. It was the first time that different films had won the Picture and Director Oscars since 1956.

At the British Academy Awards both *Bonnie and Clyde* and *In the Heat of the Night* were Best Film nominees, but were both out-polled by the previous year's Oscar winner, *A Man for All Seasons*. The following year *The Graduate* won the Best Film BAFTA.

1967

BEST DIRECTOR

ACADEMY AWARDS
Richard Brooks for *In Cold Blood*
Norman Jewison for *In the Heat of the Night*
Stanley Kramer for *Guess Who's Coming to Dinner*
• Mike Nichols for *The Graduate*
Arthur Penn for *Bonnie and Clyde*

GOLDEN GLOBE AWARDS
Norman Jewison – *In the Heat of the Night*
Stanley Kramer – *Guess Who's Coming to Dinner*
• Mike Nichols – *The Graduate*
Arthur Penn – *Bonnie and Clyde*
Mark Rydell – *The Fox*

DIRECTORS GUILD AWARD
Richard Brooks – *In Cold Blood*
Norman Jewison – *In the Heat of the Night*
Stanley Kramer – *Guess Who's Coming to Dinner*
• Mike Nichols – *The Graduate*
Arthur Penn – *Bonnie and Clyde*

NEW YORK – Mike Nichols – *The Graduate*
BOARD OF REVIEW – Richard Brooks – *In Cold Blood*
NATIONAL SOCIETY – Ingmar Bergman – *Persona*

For the fifth time (the last being in 1958), the Academy and the Directors Guild of America nominated the same five directors: Richard Brooks for *In Cold Blood* (NYT "Brooks exercises his admirable skill and good taste"; LAT "has worked a particular masterstroke"; V "remarkable"; SMH "only partly successful"); Stanley Kramer for *Guess Who's Coming to Dinner* (NYT "Kramer has made [a deliciously swift and pithy script] spin brightly in a stylish ambience of social comedy"; LAT "a well-made play in the form of a well-made movie, a picture of words [and] Kramer has seen to it that the words are well-delivered"); Norman Jewison, who earned his first nod from the Academy, for *In the Heat of the Night* (LAT "acute and satiric observations of attitudes prevailing in our society … the message is packaged as a smooth and beguiling entertainment"; WP "emphatic flaws"; CT "creates an interesting movie in spite of a bit of prefabricated poetic-licensing"; V "sometimes pretentious"; S&S "shows himself to be a director with a real feeling for a setting and its details … [but] Jewison is much helped by Haskell Wexler's hard, sharp lighting and imaginative framing"; MFB "the plot itself is so full of holes that it will scarcely bear examination, and the fact that this does not disturb one in the least during the film is in itself a tribute to the firm control of Norman Jewison's direction"); Mike Nichols, recognised by both groups for a second consecutive year, for *The Graduate* (NYT "[shows] fluency with camera, and sharpness and surprise in editing"; LAT "demolishes any lingering doubts that he is a brilliant, imaginative and free-wheeling movie director … confirms that he is a master of the motion picture form … the pace, the verbal timing, the visual excitements are superior"); and Arthur Penn for *Bonnie and Clyde* (LAT "has great visual strength and succeeds to a remarkable degree in capturing a time, a region and an atmosphere"; WP "developed under the tight rein and casual camera methods of director Penn … [film is] a professional accomplishment"; V "uneven"; S&S "handles the shift in mood quite brilliantly – and almost imperceptibly"; MFB "does a superb job of creating a pattern of moods, so that at the end of the film they coalesce to produce an odd sense of ambivalence … it is a long time since one has seen an American film so perfectly judged as this"; SMH "you get the feeling that [he] owes a lot to a hard-working film editor").

The list of Golden Globe nominees and the field considered by the New York Film critics circle each differed from this selection by only one candidate. The Hollywood Foreign Press Association excluded Brooks in favour of Mark Rydell for his debut *The Fox*, which would be eligible for the Academy Awards the following year. In the rounds of voting by the east coast circle for Best Director, no votes were cast for Kramer but there was support for Alain Resnais for *La Guerre est Finie (The War is Over)* (NYT "superb").

Overlooked by the Academy were: NSFC winner Ingmar Bergman for the Swedish drama *Persona* (NYT "has magnificently and sensitively composed a veritable poem of two feminine spirits"; LAT "really succeeds"; CT "sensitive, mature direction"; V "perfection"; S&S "a remarkable feat"); Joseph Losey for the British drama *Accident* (LAT "[has a] remarkable sense of place and character … virtuoso filmmaking"; S&S "masterly"; MFB "accomplished"; Sp "a dazzlingly good piece of movie-making"); John Schlesinger for *Far from the Madding Crowd* (NYT "he is sluggish, indecisive and banal in presenting the surface behaviour of the rural people in Hardy's solemn tale"); and John Boorman for *Point Blank*.

The similar field of nominees for the New York and Guild honours, the Globe and the Oscar all yielded the same winner: Nichols for the popular and acclaimed comedy *The Graduate*. The only major awards Nichols did not collect were the National Board of Review prize, which went to Brooks, and the National Society of Film Critics plaudit, which was won by Bergman.

1967

BEST ACTRESS

ACADEMY AWARDS

Anne Bancroft as 'Mrs Robinson' in *The Graduate*
Faye Dunaway as 'Bonnie Parker' in *Bonnie and Clyde*
Edith Evans as 'Mrs Margaret Ross' in *The Whisperers*
Audrey Hepburn as 'Susy Hendrix' in *Wait Until Dark*
• **Katharine Hepburn as 'Christina Drayton' in *Guess Who's Coming to Dinner***

GOLDEN GLOBE AWARDS

(Drama)
Faye Dunaway – *Bonnie and Clyde*
• **Edith Evans – *The Whisperers***
Audrey Hepburn – *Wait Until Dark*
Katharine Hepburn – *Guess Who's Coming to Dinner*
Anne Heywood – *The Fox*

(Comedy/Musical)
Julie Andrews – *Thoroughly Modern Millie*
• **Anne Bancroft – *The Graduate***
Audrey Hepburn – *Two for the Road*
Shirley MacLaine – *Woman Times Seven*
Vanessa Redgrave – *Camelot*

BRITISH ACADEMY AWARDS

(Foreign Actress)
• **Anouk Aimee – *Un Homme et une Femme (A Man and a Woman)***
Bibi Andersson – *Persona* and *Syskonbädd 1782 (My Sister, My Love)*
Jane Fonda – *Barefoot in the Park*
Simone Signoret – *The Deadly Affair*

(British Actress)
• **Edith Evans – *The Whisperers***
Barbara Jefford – *Ulysses*
Elizabeth Taylor – *The Taming of the Shrew*

NEW YORK – Edith Evans – *The Whisperers*
BOARD OF REVIEW – Edith Evans – *The Whisperers*
NATIONAL SOCIETY – Bibi Andersson – *Persona*

Thirty-four years after she won the Best Actress Academy Award for her performance in *Morning Glory*, Katharine Hepburn won her second statuette for her performance as the liberally-minded mother of the bride-to-be in *Guess Who's Coming to Dinner* (NYT "superior"; TT "splendid"). It was Hepburn's tenth nomination, equalling the record tally reached by Bette Davis five years earlier. Hepburn's win, however, was something of a surprise as the Oscar was the only major accolade that she received. Although a Golden Globe nominee, Hepburn had not been honoured by any of the critics' groups and in fact she had not received a single vote from any members of the New York Film Critics Circle when they had met to determine their annual awards.

The favourite for the Academy Award had been eighty-year old English actress Edith Evans, for her portrayal of a lonely old lady in the British drama *The Whisperers* (NYT "brilliant ... merits a shout of approval"; LAT "extraordinary … hard to forget – ever"; WP "here is what acting is really about: immersion so complete, so absolutely assured that a whole character is brought unforgettably to life", a "magnificent performance", a "deeply cut, wistful portrayal", "pure artistic triumph"; V "a finely chiseled performance ... it is difficult to see anyone else doing it so well, so believably"; S&S "magnificent"; MFB "while her minute variations in facial expression reveal a fine sensitivity to the film medium, she still remains essentially theatrical in gesture and movement … one catches oneself admiring her technique, but remains rather too conscious of its presence"). Evans won the Best Actress prize at the Berlin Film Festival, collected both the New York and National Board of Review prizes and won the Golden Globe (Drama). It was the third (and final) time she had been mentioned by the Academy.

Ironically, observers had not even considered Hepburn as the darkhorse for the Oscar. Evans' main challenger was thought to be twenty-six-year old Faye Dunaway, who made the Academy's list for the first time for her impersonation of the 1930s bank robber Bonnie Parker in *Bonnie and Clyde* (NYT "has Miss Dunaway squirming grossly"; LAT "can hardly be faulted …her skills are impressive"; WP "far from shallow in revealing the facets of the strange poetry-writing Bonnie"; V "a knockout", "registers with deep sensitivity"; TT "extraordinary"; SMH "is under-directed in several sequences").

Nominated for a third time in six years was Anne Bancroft, for her role as the older woman who seduces a university student in *The Graduate* (NYT "superior"; LAT "[handles] wrenchingly sharp shifts in tone … genuinely tragic and thoroughly Bancroftian … she is something to watch"; V "excellent"; TT "perfectly played"; S&S a "virtuoso performance"). The role had been turned down by numerous Hollywood stars, including Doris Day and Patricia Neal (who had not yet recovered from a series of strokes), before it was offered to thirty-six-year old Bancroft (who was only six years older than her co-star Dustin Hoffman). Bancroft won the Globe (Comedy/Musical) for her performance, adding to the Globe (Drama) she had won in 1962.

Another previous winner, Audrey Hepburn, completed the Academy's field of candidates. She was recognised (for a fifth, and final, time) for her turn as a blind woman terrorised by thieves in *Wait Until Dark* (NYT "the sweetness with which Miss Hepburn plays the poignant role, the quickness with which she changes and the skill with which she manifests terror attract sympathy and anxiety to her and give her genuine solidity in the final scenes"; WP "exceptionally resourceful"; V "superior", "superb"; MFB "Hepburn shows a resourcefulness which makes [the film] not unconvincing"). The role had been originated on stage by Lee Remick. Hepburn was also praised by critics for portraying the wife in *Two for the Road* (LAT a "superb performance"; WP "masterfully resourceful acting"; V "amazing", "completely believable, lovable and totally delightful"; MFB "successfully rings the changes from youthful candour to bored bitchiness and finally more mature understanding"). She was a nominee in both Globe categories.

The only Globe (Drama) nominee to be absent from the list of Oscar nominees was Anne Heywood as a lesbian in the drama *The Fox* (NYT "good"; LAT "fine performance"; CT "effective"; V "does a creditable job"; MFB "adequate"). The film garnered three nominations from the Hollywood Foreign Press Association after industry screenings were held in Los Angeles in December 1967. However, it was not eligible for Academy Award consideration until the following year as the studio delayed its commercial release until February 1968 in order that the film not undermine the Oscar campaigns of the other films on its slate. Heywood's co-star in *The Fox*, Sandy Dennis, who had won the Best Supporting Actress Oscar the previous year, was overlooked for *Up the Down Staircase* (NYT "engagingly natural, sensitive, literate and thoroughly moving", "walks away with the show, giving a vivid performance of emotional range and depth"; LAT "stunning", "superb", "provides a characterization as fully-realized as any you'll see all year", "she gives us that too-rare meeting of marvelous actress and marvelous role"; WP "unimpressive", "shows her inexperience"; V "excellent acting", "nearly perfect"; MFB "Dennis, whose vulnerability is her main asset, can only present [Sylvia] as a weak, well-meaning young creature"). Also by-passed were National Society of Film Critics winner Bibi Andersson (NYT she and Ullman "just about carry the film – and exquisitely too"; LAT "a remarkable performance that amounts to a virtual monologue", "outstanding in one of the most demanding roles in the history of movies"; CT "compelling"; V "a tour de force") and her co-star Liv Ullmann (NYT she and Andersson "just about carry the film – and exquisitely too"; CT "compelling") for their work in *Persona*.

Also unrecognised were: previous winner and Globe nominee Julie Andrews in the musical *Thoroughly Modern Millie* (NYT "absolutely darling – deliciously spirited and dry"; WP "immediately engaging"; TT "may not be quite at her best"); Vanessa Redgrave in the musical *Camelot* (NYT "almost dazzling at times", "charming"; LAT "breathtakingly beautiful and elegant … [has] a lovely charm"; CT "outstanding in portraying the lovely and vibrant young woman"; MFB "a Guenevere of character and charm"); Jane Fonda in *Barefoot in the Park* (NYT "evidently it was discovered that Miss Fonda couldn't do much of anything too well, except for hurling herself into the arms of her astonished husband"; LAT "handles [herself] with a fine, deft charm … has the harder job, since her nymphoid role teeters at the edge of a steamy and unattractive reality, but she keeps her balance"; WP "plays the bride with relish, and well she should because it makes her look better than any prior film role has"; V "excellent"; MFB "Fonda, finally cast in a role well within the rather limited range of her talents, gives an agreeable performance"); Pia Degermark in *Elvira Madigan* (NYT "perfect", "captures all the adoration and dignity of the girl"; CT "the acting more than measures up to the technical excellence with Pia Degermark wonderfully naïve and tender as the almost legendary entertainer"; MFB "played with grace and utter conviction"); and Annie Girardot in *Vivre pour Vivre (Live for Life)* (WP "a fine cast, especially Annie Girardot as the patient wife"; MFB "a sensitive and understated performance").

Among the BAFTA nominees ignored by the Academy were: previous winner Elizabeth Taylor in *The Taming of the Shrew* (NYT "extravagant overacting", "toss[es] about the language without much clarity or eloquence"; LAT "Taylor is to be credited for making Kate's softening-up reach us"; S&S "a shrill performance"; MFB "is no match for Shakespeare's words"); Barbara Jefford in *Ulysses* (NYT "absolutely perfect"; LAT "Jefford, though excellent, seemed to me a shade too intellectual, a shade too little the earthy sensualist I had expected"; CT "excellent"; MFB "Jefford's rendering of Molly's monologue is beautifully done"); and previous winner Simone Signoret whose role in *The Deadly Affair* was pivotal but brief (WP "has little to do … but hers is a crucial role with which Lumet manages to further the mystery"; MFB "war-torn, soiled and now betrayed, the character comes painfully to life as Signoret, majestically calm in Lumet's big close-ups, pours out her bitterness").

Katharine Hepburn's surprise Oscar victory made it the ninth successive year that the Globe (Drama) winner had been unsuccessfully nominated for the Academy Award. Evans never received a fourth nomination. Katharine Hepburn, however, won a third statuette the following year, and a record fourth in 1981.

1967

BEST ACTOR

ACADEMY AWARDS
Warren Beatty as 'Clyde Barrow' in *Bonnie and Clyde*
Dustin Hoffman as 'Benjamin Braddock' in *The Graduate*
Paul Newman as 'Luke Jackson' in *Cool Hand Luke*
• Rod Steiger as 'Bill Gillespie' in *In the Heat of the Night*
Spencer Tracy as 'Matt Drayton' in *Guess Who's Coming to Dinner*

GOLDEN GLOBE AWARDS
(Drama)
Alan Bates
– *Far from the Madding Crowd*
Warren Beatty – *Bonnie and Clyde*
Paul Newman – *Cool Hand Luke*
Sidney Poitier
– *In the Heat of the Night*
• Rod Steiger
– *In the Heat of the Night*
Spencer Tracy – *Guess Who's Coming to Dinner*

(Comedy/Musical)
Richard Burton
– *The Taming of the Shrew*
• Richard Harris – *Camelot*
Rex Harrison – *Doctor Dolittle*
Dustin Hoffman – *The Graduate*
Ugo Tognazzi
– *L'Immorale (The Climax)*

BRITISH ACADEMY AWARDS
(Foreign Actor)
Warren Beatty – *Bonnie and Clyde*
Sidney Poitier
– *In the Heat of the Night*
• Rod Steiger
– *In the Heat of the Night*
Orson Welles – *Chimes at Midnight*

(British Actor)
Dirk Bogarde – *Accident*
and *Our Mother's House*
Richard Burton
– *The Taming of the Shrew*
James Mason – *The Deadly Affair*
• Paul Scofield
– *A Man for All Seasons*

NEW YORK – Rod Steiger – *In the Heat of the Night*
BOARD OF REVIEW – Peter Finch – *Far from the Madding Crowd*
NATIONAL SOCIETY – Rod Steiger – *In the Heat of the Night*

Previous winner Sidney Poitier was praised by critics for his performances in three 1967 films: as the New York City detective who travels to the Deep South to assist a bigoted southern sheriff with a murder investigation in *In the Heat of the Night* (NYT "stinging performance", "magnificent", "Oscar-worthy"; LAT "quality … simply one of the finest actors around, and reconfirms it here"; WP "exceptionally strong central performance"; CT "coming in a close second" to Steiger for acting honours; V "excellent"; S&S "given the chance at last, is better than he has been for some time"; MFB "unusually disciplined and effective ... Poitier is never allowed to exploit his personal charm ... [and instead] effortlessly expresses the explosive possibilities that lurk just below his tightly controlled exterior"; SMH "exercises great control with a difficult character"); as the fiancé in *Guess Who's Coming to Dinner* (NYT "splendid"; LAT "a performance which cannot be faulted"); and as an inexperienced teacher assigned to a school in London's East End in the British drama *To Sir, with Love* (V "scores strongly"; SMH "certainly giving a performance of the year"). With the two acclaimed American films considered front-runners for the Academy Awards, it seemed certain that Poitier would be recognised with a third Oscar nomination, especially given the centrality of the civil rights movement in national affairs. Poitier was mentioned for both the Golden Globe (Drama) and the Best Foreign Actor BAFTA, but the Academy overlooked him.

Included ahead of Poitier, and considered the frontrunners for the Oscar, were the African-American actor's two Anglo-American male co-stars. Previous winner Spencer Tracy, who had died just ten days after the completion of filming, was posthumously nominated (for a record ninth time) for his portrayal of the ageing father in *Guess Who's Coming to Dinner* (NYT "superior"; LAT "by any standards a superb valedictory for one of Hollywood's greatest careers ... he is marvelous, and it is impossible to think of another actor who could have brought to the part anything like the same warm, troubled, eloquent humanity"; CT "[his] most shining hour"; TT "moving"). Rod Steiger, who had been the unsuccessful Best Actor Oscar favourite just two years earlier, earned his third nomination as the racist police officer in *In the Heat of the Night* (NYT "stinging performance", "magnificent", "Oscar-worthy"; LAT "it's hard to recall a role in which Steiger has seemed more engaging and less the studied actor"; WP "exceptionally strong central performance"; CT "an especially sharp performance"; V "outstanding"; S&S "a beautifully observed, inventive performance"; MFB "unusually disciplined and effective ... sinks his own intelligence with complete success"; SMH "dialogue is delivered beautifully by Steiger in his definitive characterisation of a small-town police chief ... his best performance since 'The Pawnbroker'.").

Paul Newman received his fourth nod in a decade, as a defiant chain-gang prisoner in *Cool Hand Luke* (NYT "splendid acting", "excellent, at the top of his sometime erratic form"; LAT "a triumph"; WP "a fine performance"; CT "brings off his usually competent performance"; V "excellent"; S&S "splendid"; MFB "brilliant") having been also praised for *Hombre* (LAT "meets the challenge of creating a character of few words but much force ... superb"; CT "Newman's casting as an uncivilized adopted Apache sometimes is a bit hard to take"; V "excellent"). Each mentioned for the first time were Warren Beatty in *Bonnie and Clyde* (NYT "clowning broadly"; LAT "can hardly be faulted ...a powerful screen performance, probably his best, but finally more Beatty than Barrow"; WP "earns honors as star as well as producer"; V "believable"; TT "never been better") and Dustin Hoffman as the university student in *The Graduate* (NYT "superior ... believable and sympathetic"; LAT "a marvelously comical performance with an underlying innocence which is one of the charms of the picture"; V "perfect"; TT "perfectly played"; MFB "excellent").

In addition to Poitier, the Academy overlooked: New York Film Critic's Circle prize contender Yves Montand in *La Guerre est Finie (The War is Over)* (NYT "played strongly"; LAT "thoroughly remarkable performance"); both National Board of Review winner Peter Finch in the supporting role of the wealthy farmer (NYT "conventionally stout and heavily shaken with bursts of passion"; LAT "could not be improved upon"; V "struggles"; TT "quite well played"; MFB "brilliantly suggesting all the barely suppressed violence that can lurk beneath a civilised exterior"; SMH "only player to bring his character alive") and Globe nominee Alan Bates as the shepherd (NYT "simply adorned with rustic humors"; TT "quite well played") in *Far from the Madding Crowd*; Globe and BAFTA nominee Richard Burton in *The Taming of the Shrew* (NYT "extravagant overacting", "toss[es] about the language without much clarity or eloquence"; LAT "may be his finest moment, at least on the screen ... he is robustious time and again"; CT "a riotous roughhouse performance"; S&S "undermines the wit of the piece"; MFB "lapses into mannerism"); Globe winner Richard Harris in the musical *Camelot* (NYT "broad and uneven, sometimes winning, more often brusque and on the verge of being boorish"; LAT "a captivating figure and sympathetic"; CT "artfully creates a masterful characterization of a monarch"; MFB "adequate"); both BAFTA nominee Dirk Bogarde (LAT "not less than stunning"; WP "striking"; V "superbly right"; TT "immaculate"; MFB "almost faultless"; G "[one of] the best performances I have ever seen"; Sp "the honours for sheer accomplishment and speed of reaction go to Dirk Bogarde") and Stanley Baker (LAT "not less than stunning"; WP "striking"; TT "a revelation"; S&S "miraculously good"; MFB "almost faultless"; G "quite unrecognisable ... brilliant"; Sp "among the best things [he] has done") in *Accident*; BAFTA nominee James Mason as the secret agent in *The Deadly Affair* (LAT "allow me to sing the praises of Mason ... very nearly making the role of a browbeaten, cuckolded husband sympathetic without being disgusting"; WP "ideal"; V "one of his best performances"; TT "superlative"); Alfredo Mayo as the tycoon in *La Caza (The Hunt)* (NYT "played superbly"); previous winner Lee Marvin in both *Point Blank* (NYT "taut and tough"; LAT "you believe him ... credible"; MFB "solid") and *The Dirty Dozen* (NYT "tough and terrifying"; LAT "dominates in still another superb performance"; WP "[an] assured portrait … resourceful enough in minute details to be credible and always interesting. Marvin has a trick of tossing away words, even lines, but his meanings simmer through"; CT "first-rate performance … outstanding"); and both Robert Blake and Scott Wilson in *In Cold Blood* (NYT "the subtle revelations and variations in the performances of Robert Blake and Scott Wilson in the principal roles. Their abilities to demonstrate the tensions, the torments and shabby conceits of the miserable criminals, give disturbing dimension to their roles"; LAT "are indelible, credible, the more frightening for being the more human and recognizable … outstanding acting capabilities"; SMH "faultless").

Mixed reviews apparently discouraged recognition for Albert Finney in *Two for the Road* (NYT "is compelled to play the husband role as though he were a hater of women and a slave driver to boot"; LAT "[a] superb performance"; V "[a] stodgy performance", "very bad"; MFB "almost manages to bring off the frequent sharp transitions from youthful student to young married [man] to discontented successful architect and back again") and BAFTA nominee Orson Welles as Falstaff in *Chimes at Midnight* (NYT "difficult to comprehend"; TT "[a] disappointment"; S&S "a highly intelligent and complex interpretation, and it is carried through with exactly the right degrees of force and subtlety and feeling"; MFB "can hardly be faulted").

Steiger collected a majority of accolades during the awards season. He won the Globe (Drama) and both the NSFC and New York prizes. While *The Graduate* was expected to win the Best Picture Oscar, its star was not seen as a major challenger for the Best Actor prize. At the Globes, Hoffman had been unexpectedly outpolled by Harris, and prior to the Oscars he admitted to reporters that he had actually voted for Steiger rather than himself. Pundits labelled Tracy as the darkhorse with many observers tipping *Guess Who's Coming to Dinner* as an upset winner in the top category. In the Chicago Tribune, Norma Lee Browning reported, "the talk of the town [in Hollywood] is that Spencer Tracy will win the first posthumous Oscar in history".

On Oscar night, however, the momentum was with Steiger and *In the Heat of the Night*. The film was a surprise winner in the Best Picture category and Steiger claimed the Best Actor statuette he had missed out on two years earlier. A month later he won the Best Foreign Actor BAFTA for a second year in a row.

The following year, meanwhile, Tracy was posthumously awarded the BAFTA for his work in *Guess Who's Coming to Dinner*.

1967

BEST SUPPORTING ACTRESS

ACADEMY AWARDS
Carol Channing as 'Muzzy Van Hossmere' in *Thoroughly Modern Millie*
Mildred Natwick as 'Mrs Ethel Banks' in *Barefoot in the Park*
• Estelle Parsons as 'Blanche Barrow' in *Bonnie and Clyde*
Beah Richards as 'Mrs Prentice' in *Guess Who's Coming to Dinner*
Katharine Ross as 'Elaine Robinson' in *The Graduate*

GOLDEN GLOBE AWARDS
• Carol Channing – *Thoroughly Modern Millie*
Quentin Dean – *In the Heat of the Night*
Lillian Gish – *The Comedians*
Lee Grant – *In the Heat of the Night*
Prunella Ransome – *Far from the Madding Crowd*
Beah Richards – *Guess Who's Coming to Dinner*

BOARD OF REVIEW – Marjorie Rhodes – *The Family Way*
NATIONAL SOCIETY – Marjorie Rhodes – *The Family Way*

Marjorie Rhodes won the inaugural National Society of Film Critics' award as well as the National Board of Review prize for her part as the mother in the comedy *The Family Way* (LAT "fine … comes close to stealing the show"; WP "splendid"; CT "fine support"; V the film's "best performance"). Astonishingly, she was overlooked for both the Golden Globe and the Oscar.

Also by-passed for both prizes were: Jo Van Fleet as the dying mother in *Cool Hand Luke* (NYT "a special word of commendation must be said for Jo Van Fleet ... in one scene [she] does as much to make us comprehend the background and the emotional hang-up of the loner as might have been done in the entire length of a good film"; LAT "marvelous characterization"; WP "plays the brief role so beautifully"; CT "masterfully played"); both Gladys Cooper (CT "the best portrayal") and Greer Garson (NYT "gives a performance that is pure Mrs Miniver"; LAT "regal warmth"; CT "the comedy wastes the talents of [this lovely and] gifted actress") in *The Happiest Millionaire*; both Barbara Rush (LAT "superb", she and Cilento "ultimately dominate"; V "outstanding") and Diane Cilento (LAT "superb", she and Rush "ultimately dominate"; CT "top honors must go to Miss Cilento who affected a remarkable American accent to play the thorny boarding-house boss") in *Hombre*; Vivien Merchant in *Accident* (WP "striking", "brilliantly suggests more than she knows"; TT "plays a complex character with just the right apparent simplicity"; S&S "miraculously good"; MFB "almost faultless"; G "[one of] the best performances I have ever seen"); Fiona Walker as the maid in *Far from the Madding Crowd* (S&S "excellent"); Ellen O'Mara as one of the students in *Up the Down Staircase* (NYT "outstanding", "makes [an] impression that you have to call indelible"; WP "a most expressive performance"); Katharine Houghton, the niece of Best Actress Oscar winner Katharine Hepburn, in *Guess Who's Coming to Dinner* (NYT "rapturously plays"); Geneviève Bujold in *La Guerre est Finie (The War is Over)* (NYT "convincing"); and Margaret Rutherford in *Chimes at Midnight* (S&S "makes a fine Mistress Quickly, and movingly delivers her speech after Falstaff's death"; MFB "can hardly be faulted … superb in her narration of the death of poor Jack").

Oscar voters also overlooked four of the Globe nominees, including Lillian Gish in *The Comedians* (LAT "expert work"; MFB "splendid") and Lee Grant in Best Picture winner *In the Heat of the Night* (LAT "neatly done"; WP "fine playing"), as well as Best Foreign Actress BAFTA nominee Simone Signoret whose role in *The Deadly Affair* was pivotal to the plot but brief in terms of screen time (WP "has little to do … but hers is a crucial role with which Lumet manages to further the mystery"; MFB "war-torn, soiled and now betrayed, the character comes painfully to life as Signoret, majestically calm in Lumet's big close-ups, pours out her bitterness").

The Academy short-listed five first-time nominees: Globe winner Carol Channing as the widow in the musical *Thoroughly Modern Millie* (NYT "comes closest to taking the cake … wonderful fun"; WP "still bigger than life and full of the ole pizzazz, comes on strong"; V "commands"); Mildred Natwick reprising her Broadway success as the widowed mother in *Barefoot in the Park* (NYT "plays with pretty much the same farcical flutters and simpleton sputterings she used in the play"; LAT "Miss Natwick in particular manages to invest the silliness with an honest warmth"; WP "the real joy of the movie … this is her role of a lifetime"; V "excellent"); Estelle Parsons as the frightened sister-in-law of 1930s bank robber Clyde Barrow in *Bonnie and Clyde* (LAT "done to a kind of perfection"; V "good"); Globe nominee Beah Richards as the mother of the prospective groom in *Guess Who's Coming to Dinner* (NYT "deeply touching"); and Katharine Ross as the daughter of Mrs Robinson in *The Graduate*.

On Oscar night, Parsons won the Academy Award as Best Supporting Actress. She is the only one of the five nominees to earn a second mention, garnering another nomination the following year for her repressed lesbian in *Rachel, Rachel*. She later won acclaim for playing the elderly mother on the television sitcom 'Roseanne'.

1967

BEST SUPPORTING ACTOR

ACADEMY AWARDS
John Cassavetes as 'Victor Franko' in *The Dirty Dozen*
Gene Hackman as 'Buck Barrow' in *Bonnie and Clyde*
Cecil Kellaway as 'Monsignor Ryan' in *Guess Who's Coming to Dinner*
• George Kennedy as 'Dragline' in *Cool Hand Luke*
Michael J. Pollard as 'C.W. Moss' in *Bonnie and Clyde*

GOLDEN GLOBE AWARDS
• Richard Attenborough – *Doctor Dolittle*
John Cassavetes – *The Dirty Dozen*
George Kennedy – *Cool Hand Luke*
Michael J. Pollard – *Bonnie and Clyde*
Efrem Zimbalist, Jr. – *Wait Until Dark*

BOARD OF REVIEW – Paul Ford – *The Comedians*
NATIONAL SOCIETY – Gene Hackman – *Bonnie and Clyde*

English actor-director Richard Attenborough won the Best Supporting Actor Golden Globe, for the second year in a row, for his performance as the circus manager in the expensive musical *Doctor Dolittle* (LAT "a rollicking delight ... one of the best things in the movie"; V "outstanding"; TT "spirited"). Although the film was unexpectedly nominated as Best Picture, Attenborough was overlooked by the Academy for a second consecutive year.

Also passed over for Oscar consideration were: both National Board of Review winner Paul Ford (LAT "expert work"; MFB "splendid") and James Earl Jones (NYT "impressively valiant"; LAT "excellent") in the all-star political drama *The Comedians*; both Globe nominee Efrem Zimbalist, Jr. as the husband (NYT "comes on aptly"; V "a smooth, professional job") and Alan Arkin as one of the thugs (NYT "a bit disconcerting at times ... Arkin is not that good as a serious villain"; LAT "makes a thoroughly repulsive psychopath"; WP "not always convincing"; MFB "chillingly effective") in the thriller *Wait Until Dark*; Harry Andrews in *The Deadly Affair* (WP "ideal"; MFB "walks away with the film"); John Gielgud as King Henry IV in *Chimes at Midnight* (MFB "can hardly be faulted"); Charles Boyer in *Barefoot in the Park* (NYT "acts the Duan Juan from upstairs with all his celebrated casual elegance, which isn't at all right for the character but may be valuable to the attractiveness of the film"; WP "an odd choice for the role"); and Michael Hordern as Baptista in *The Taming of the Shrew* (NYT "the best of the lot ... endows the harassed Baptista with a bit of character"; CT "excellent"; S&S "only Michael Hordern as Baptista sustains the grotesquerie with success"; MFB "make[s] the most of the few lines [he is] given").

Ahead of these contenders, the Academy short-listed three unsuccessful Globe nominees, the inaugural National Society of Film Critics winner and a previous Oscar contender.

Nearly twenty years after first being considered, Cecil Kellaway earned his second nod from the Academy as the priest in *Guess Who's Coming to Dinner* (NYT "played jovially"). Also nominated, all for the first time, were: actor-director John Cassavetes in *The Dirty Dozen* (NYT "bold"; LAT "in the first half of the film [Lee] Marvin gets a run for his money from John Cassavetes"; WP "allowed to shine"; CT "first-rate performance … outstanding"; V "first-rate"); both NSFC winner Gene Hackman as the brother of 1930s bank robber Clyde Barrow (LAT "done to a kind of perfection") and Michael J. Pollard as the slow-witted getaway driver (LAT "done to a kind of perfection") in the crime drama *Bonnie and Clyde*; and George Kennedy as a brutal chain gang leader in *Cool Hand Luke* (NYT "powerfully obsessive"; LAT "superb … [the film] will almost certainly do for George Kennedy what 'Cat Ballou' did for Lee Marvin – pay off with stardom in a long honourable hitch at lesser servitude"; WP "capitally acted"; CT "exceptionally strong support"; V "outstanding").

Although *Bonnie and Clyde* and *Guess Who's Coming to Dinner* were the year's most Oscar nominated films, the Best Supporting Actor Oscar was won by Kennedy. Despite a solid career as a respected supporting player over the following decade, Kennedy never made the Academy's lists for a second time.

1968

BEST PICTURE

ACADEMY AWARDS

Funny Girl
(Rastar, Columbia, 151 mins, 19 Sep 1968, $26.3m, 8 noms)
The Lion in Winter
(Haworth, Avco Embassy, 134 mins, 30 Oct 1968, $6.4m, 7 noms)
• ***Oliver!***
(Romulus, Columbia, 153 mins, 11 Dec 1968, $10.5m, 11 noms)
Rachel, Rachel
(Kayos, Warner Bros., Seven Arts, 101 mins, 26 Aug 1968, 4 noms)
Romeo and Juliet
(BHE-Verona-DeLaurentiis, Paramount, 138 mins, 8 Oct 1968, $14.5m, 4 noms)

GOLDEN GLOBE AWARDS

(Drama)
Charly
The Fixer
The Heart is a Lonely Hunter
• ***The Lion in Winter***
The Shoes of the Fisherman

(Comedy/Musical)
Finian's Rainbow
Funny Girl
The Odd Couple
• ***Oliver!***
Yours, Mine and Ours

BRITISH ACADEMY AWARDS

• ***The Graduate***
Oliver!
Ostre Sledovane Vlaky (Closely Watched Trains)
2001: A Space Odyssey

NEW YORK – *The Lion in Winter*
BOARD OF REVIEW – *The Shoes of the Fisherman*
NATIONAL SOCIETY – *Skammen (Shame)*

The two films that generated the most discussion amongst film critics were both overlooked for Best Picture Oscar nominations, even though each had received votes during the Best Picture balloting by the New York Film Critics Circle.

When Stanley Kubrick's science fiction epic *2001: A Space Odyssey* was released in the United States in April, most critics raved about it, although some others seemed unable to decide whether it was a cinematic masterpiece or an incredible bore, or both simultaneously (NYT "a very complicated, languid movie ... it is somewhere between hypnotic and immensely boring"; LAT "an ultimate statement of the science fiction film, an awesome realization of the spatial future … a milestone, a landmark in the art of film", "some of next year's Academy Awards are already bespoken"; WP a "marvellously exciting journey … spectacular"; CT "a decided disappointment in every respect except the visual"; V "a major achievement … [but] not a cinematic landmark"; TT "staggering" but of "somewhat excessive length"; S&S "marvellously ingenious, tantalising and intelligent"; FQ "one of the visual masterpieces of modern cinema"; MFB "outstanding"; SMH "spectacular").

In September, critical opinion was similarly polarised by *Faces*, John Cassavetes' extremely low-budget, improvised drama about infidelity (NYT "a really important movie"; LAT "remarkable … [has] a grainy, gritty realism overwhelming in its rawness", "impressive"; CT "a generally good, but uneven work"; V "at least an hour too long"; S&S "a film that lives and breathes"; MFB "a relentlessly probing study of loneliness").

When the New York critics voted at the end of the year, *Faces* was only very narrowly outpolled for the Best Picture award. The winner was *The Lion in Winter*, an adaptation of the historical stage drama about the power struggles between King Henry II of England and his wife, Eleanor of Aquitaine (V "intense"; S&S "an exciting visual experience of this essentially stagy material"). Finishing a very distant third in the New York voting was *Oliver!*, the lavish British musical version of Charles Dickens' novel (NYT "an elaborate and faithful movie enlargement of the Lionel Bart operetta"; LAT "lavish … [a] big, bright, expensive musical"; WP "good, solid entertainment"; V "bright, shiny, heartwarming").

In early January, the National Board of Review and the National Society of Film Critics both made unexpected choices for Best Picture. The NBR selected the poorly reviewed *Shoes of the Fisherman*, a drama about a Russian-born Pope's attempts to prevent a nuclear holocaust (NYT "unintelligible"; LAT "a stodgy, diffuse script, pedestrian direction and, above all, a subplot of staggering tastelessness"; WP "wholly absorbing"; CT "unhappily the film as a whole contains much more circumstance than pomp"). The NSFC, meanwhile, awarded its accolade to a film by Ingmar Bergman for the second year in a row: *Skammen (Shame)* (NYT "a simple, direct drama … a literal and unrelenting picture … smashing realism"; FQ "a disappointment").

The New York and NBR winners were both included on the list of Golden Globe (Drama) candidates, along with: *Charly* (NYT "the movie did not work for me"; LAT "contrived … it is sleek, efficient, empty, manipulative"; WP "too careful and too clinical"; MFB "the most distressing thing about 'Charly' is its insistent, persistent sentimentality"); the anti-Semitism historical drama *The Fixer* (NYT "failure"; LAT "heavy-handed"); and *The Heart is a Lonely Hunter* (NYT "at almost every dramatic moment, the story becomes frail"; LAT "the saddest, kindest picture in a long time"; WP "a touching, thoughtful mood piece").

In the Comedy/Musical category the nominees included New York contender *Oliver!* and two adaptations of Broadway hits: the comedy *The Odd Couple* (NYT "a very funny, professional adaptation"; LAT "will cause more people to do more laughing than any film you are likely to see all year"; WP "a riotously funny film"; V "excellent"); and the musical *Funny Girl* (NYT "an elaborate, painstaking launching pad [for Streisand]", "interminable"; LAT "an elaborate, expensive, entertaining movie in the glossiest tradition of high-gloss Hollywood ... [but] is essentially the same thin, musically inadequate and only average property it was on stage"; WP "unfunny and interminable", "a long, drippy bore"). Astonishingly, the comedy *The Producers* was overlooked by the Hollywood Foreign Press Association, an omission subsequently compounded by the Academy (NYT "some of it is shoddy and gross and cruel; the rest is funny in an entirely unexpected way... leaves one alternately picking up one's coat to leave and sitting back to laugh"; CT "one of the funniest films in recent years").

Victorious on the night were *The Lion in Winter* and *Oliver!* and the Academy included both on its list of Best Picture nominees. Of the remaining eight Globe candidates, however, Academy members selected only *Funny Girl*. All the unsuccessful drama nominees, including the NBR winner, were passed over.

Also overlooked in addition to *Faces*, *2001: A Space Odyssey* and *The Producers* were: the NSFC champion and Bergman's other film that year, *Vargtimmen (Hour of the Wolf)* (NYT "not one of Bergman's great films"; LAT "totally demanding, totally rewarding"; CT "quite good – a difficult film, both maddening and maddeningly intriguing"; S&S "brilliant"); the acclaimed and popular horror film *Rosemary's Baby* (NYT "doesn't quite work on any of its dark or powerful terms"; LAT "a gem"; CT "one of the most totally absorbing pictures in the last decade ... masterful"; V "excellent"); the family drama *The Subject was Roses* (NYT "the play has been brought to the screen with flat, fatal fidelity"; V "outstanding", "intimate, poignant and telling"); the lesbian drama *The Fox* (NYT "a really good and interesting movie"; LAT "what could have been tawdry and sensational instead engages our sympathy and our understanding"; CT "an uneven, but excellent, study of a tormented triangle"; MFB "leaves nothing whatever to the imagination"); and both the 1966 and 1967 Venice winners – the Italian war drama *La Battaglia di Algeri (The Battle of Algiers)* (NYT "a most extraordinary picture", "ferocious [and] starkly realistic", "an uncommonly dynamic picture"; LAT "[a] remarkable movie"; WP "stunning"; CT "a suspenseful, absorbing, masterfully-conceived work") and the French film *Belle de Jour* (NYT "a really beautiful movie"; LAT "less than a masterpiece"; WP "the film [has a] haunting fascination"; TT a "masterpiece"; S&S "exquisite, beautifully measured and tantalisingly enigmatic"; MFB "exquisite and spell-binding").

The Academy also excluded the lauded Russian epic *Vojna i Mir (War and Peace)*, which won a clean sweep of the major accolades as Best Foreign-Language Film: the Oscar, the Globe and the awards from the NBR and New York critics (NYT "a vulgarism and a failure … pretentious and devoid of life [and] not even as enjoyable as any number of lesser films"; LAT "the battle scenes are superb, immense, executed on a scale and with a fidelity previously beyond the reach of any movie maker anywhere. But the peaceful scenes, the private moments and the personal stories far from battle and burning, are static and tedious in the extreme … a monumental film [but] cold and academic"; WP "[a] towering achievement"). The seven-hour-and-fourteen-minute historical drama was edited down to six and a half hours for its release in North America where it screened in two parts. According to The New York Times it was "the longest movie ever offered for conventional commercial release" in the United States.

With eleven nominations, *Oliver!* was the most nominated film of the year, followed by *Funny Girl* with eight and *The Lion in Winter* with seven.

The other Best Picture nominees were: *Rachel, Rachel*, a drama about a small-town spinster that was the directorial debut of previous Best Actor nominee Paul Newman (NYT "the best written, most seriously acted American movie in a long time"; LAT "never makes a false move … a genuine achievement"); and *Romeo and Juliet*, a British-Italian co-production of William Shakespeare's romantic tragedy that was directed by Franco Zeffirelli (NYT "a lovely, sensitive, friendly popularization of the play … the sweetest, most contemporary romance on film this year"; LAT "unique and refreshing"; WP "vibrant, vital and vivid … fascinating … sets a standard for years to come").

The strong favourite for the Best Picture Oscar was *The Lion in Winter*, the Globe (Drama) winner for which Anthony Harvey had won both the Directors Guild of America award and Globe as Best Director. When Sidney Poitier opened the evening's final envelope, however, the surprise winner was *Oliver!*. It was the fourth musical in a decade to win the Academy's top prize and, even more significantly, it was the second British film in six years to win the Best Picture Academy Award.

Despite its historic win in Hollywood, however, *Oliver!* did not repeat its triumph in London. Surprisingly, it was outpolled for the British Academy's Best Film award by *The Graduate*, the American comedy that had been upset in the Best Picture Oscar category the previous year. Among the other nominees outpolled for the BAFTA was Kubrick's *2001: A Space Odyssey*.

1968

BEST DIRECTOR

ACADEMY AWARDS
Anthony Harvey for *The Lion in Winter*
Stanley Kubrick for *2001: A Space Odyssey*
Gillo Pontecorvo for *La Battaglia di Algeri (The Battle of Algiers)*
• Carol Reed for *Oliver!*
Franco Zeffirelli for *Romeo and Juliet*

GOLDEN GLOBE AWARDS
Anthony Harvey – *The Lion in Winter*
• Paul Newman – *Rachel, Rachel*
Carol Reed – *Oliver!*
William Wyler – *Funny Girl*
Franco Zeffirelli – *Romeo and Juliet*

DIRECTORS GUILD AWARD
• Anthony Harvey – *The Lion in Winter*
Stanley Kubrick – *2001: A Space Odyssey*
Paul Newman – *Rachel, Rachel*
Carol Reed – *Oliver!*
William Wyler – *Funny Girl*

BRITISH ACADEMY AWARDS
Lindsay Anderson – *if...*
• Mike Nichols – *The Graduate*
Carol Reed – *Oliver!*
Franco Zeffirelli – *Romeo and Juliet*

NEW YORK – Paul Newman – *Rachel, Rachel*
BOARD OF REVIEW – Franco Zeffirelli – *Romeo and Juliet*
NATIONAL SOCIETY – Ingmar Bergman – *Vargtimmen (Hour of the Wolf)* and *Skammen (Shame)*

While *The Lion in Winter* and *Faces* closely contested the New York Film Critics Circle Best Picture award, the directors of these films were both out-polled for the circle's Best Director plaudit by Paul Newman, the popular actor who had been a Best Actor Oscar nominee four times over the previous decade. Newman was honoured for his directorial debut, *Rachel, Rachel* (NYT "sensitive and discreet"; LAT "a great achievement"; V "directed with an uncertain hand ... awkward"; MFB handled with "depth and sincerity"). The New York critics also presented their Best Actress award to Newman's wife, Joanne Woodward, for her performance in the film. The runner-up was another actor-director, John Cassavetes for *Faces* (LAT "it vindicates Cassavetes' faith in himself as a director"; S&S "Cassavetes' modernity is that he manages to show thought in movement rather than characters in action. His characters' unpredictability is achieved by the very free staging of scenes"; MFB "a directorial triumph"). Cassavetes had been a Best Supporting Actor Oscar nominee the year before.

The two other critics' prizes were won by foreigners for their handling of non-American films. The National Board of Review gave its award to Italian director Franco Zeffirelli for *Romeo and Juliet* (NYT "beautifully thought out and staged"; LAT "[has] triumphantly infused life and vigor, color and credence into Shakespeare's poetic tragedy") while the National Society of Film Critics honoured Swedish director Ingmar Bergman, for the second year in a row, for both *Vargtimmen (Hour of the Wolf)* (LAT "no one more than Bergman forces us to see the truth about ourselves"; WP "measured") and *Skammen (Shame)*.

Yet another winner emerged from the Directors Guild of America voting: Anthony Harvey for *The Lion in Winter* (V "excellent work"; S&S "tactful direction"). Harvey received the accolade ahead of a field of contenders that included both Newman and Zeffirelli, as well as Carol Reed for *Oliver!* (NYT "his direction seems to be primarily concerned with moving the audience's attention – as gently as possible – from one big scene to another … he actually does it quite well"; CT "Reed's direction is robust and lively") and Stanley Kubrick for *2001: A Space Odyssey* (NYT "all kinds of minor touches are perfectly done"; LAT "as a technical achievement – a graduation exercise in ingenuity and the marking of film magic – it surpasses anything I've ever seen … a milestone, a landmark in the art of film … any annoyance of the ending cannot really compromise Kubrick's epic achievement, his mastery of the techniques of screen sight and screen sound to create impact and illusion"; MFB "Kubrick has won the ultimate technical triumph in that his film is beautiful to watch from start to finish").

Two days after the DGA result, a different winner triumphed out of a similar field of candidates at the Golden Globes. Newman won ahead of Harvey, Reed, Zeffirelli, and previous winner William Wyler for *Funny Girl* (NYT "almost every shot is held too long, every pointless scene is interminable").

Newman's Globe victory, however, was bittersweet. On the same day as the Globe ceremony, the Academy announced its list of Oscar candidates. In a major shock, Newman did not receive a nomination, even though *Rachel, Rachel* was included in the Best Picture category and Woodward was among the Best Actress contenders. He was the third Globe winner and fourth New York winner to be excluded from Oscar contention. In both instances, the last time such an omission had occurred had been in 1956.

The other glaring omission from the Academy's list of nominees was New York runner-up Cassavetes. Also passed over by the Academy were: Bergman;

previous winner Wyler; Luis Buñuel for *Belle de Jour* (NYT "beautifully directed"; WP "Bunuel's style may sometimes seem confusing"); Roman Polanski for *Rosemary's Baby* (LAT "has directed with the patient attention to detail which creates atmosphere and generates very great suspense"; CT "masterful"; V "superior direction"); John Frankenheimer for *The Fixer* (NYT "the direction, by John Frankenheimer, is powerful and discreet"; LAT "the principal difficulty with 'The Fixer' is that Frankenheimer's telling of the story is so strident, so heavy-handed, so charged, that it becomes less a human drama than a theatrical pageant"; CT "Frankenheimer's direction is uncharacteristically flat"); Sergei Bondarchuk for the epic *Vojna i Mir (War and Peace)*; and Akira Kurosawa for *Akahige (Red Beard)* (NT "consistently persuasive").

Another notable absentee was Mark Rydell for his directorial debut *The Fox* (NYT "interesting"; LAT "a remarkable debut ... left no doubt that [he has] won a place of prominence in the new generation of filmmakers"; CT "for the most part handles his subject with admirable artistry"; MFB "well made in its routine way"). Following a handful of industry preview screenings in December 1967, Rydell received a Golden Globe nomination as Best Director. The movie wasn't commercially released until early 1968, qualifying for Oscar consideration of that year.

Nominated ahead of Newman were Harvey, Kubrick, Reed, Zeffirelli, and, unexpectedly, Italian director Gillo Pontecorvo for *La Battaglia di Algeri (The Battle of Algiers)*, a war drama that had won Best Picture in Venice in 1966 (NYT "more commanding of lasting interest and critical applause is the amazing photographic virtuosity and pictorial conviction of this film ... so authentically and naturalistically were its historical reflections stage that it looks beyond any question to be an original documentary film"; LAT "[an] awesome achievement"; WP "so fascinating and demanding a cinema style requires responsible handling and this Pontecorvo seems to supply"; CT "masterfully-conceived").

The surprise absence of Globe winner Newman made DGA honouree Harvey the outright favourite for the Academy Award. Over the previous nineteen years, the DGA winner had never failed to receive the Best Director statuette.

On Oscar night, however, the winner of the Best Director award proved an even bigger shock than Newman's omission from the list of nominees. For the first time, the DGA victor did not collect the Oscar. In a major upset, the winner was sixty-two-year old veteran Reed, who had been unsuccessfully short-listed by the Academy in 1949 and 1950. Surprisingly, Reed was outpolled for the inaugural Best Director BAFTA.

Reed was not the only Best Director nominee to win an Oscar that year, however. Kubrick was a winner in the Best Special Effects category for *2001: A Space Odyssey*. It was the only statuette he ever won.

1968

BEST ACTRESS

ACADEMY AWARDS
• Katharine Hepburn as 'Eleanor of Aquitaine' in *The Lion in Winter*
Patricia Neal as 'Nettie Cleary' in *The Subject was Roses*
Vanessa Redgrave as 'Isadora Duncan' in *Isadora*
• Barbra Streisand as 'Fanny Brice' in *Funny Girl*
Joanne Woodward as 'Rachel Cameron' in *Rachel, Rachel*

GOLDEN GLOBE AWARDS
(Drama)
Mia Farrow – *Rosemary's Baby*
Katharine Hepburn
– *The Lion in Winter*
Vanessa Redgrave – *Isadora*
Beryl Reid
– *The Killing of Sister George*
• Joanne Woodward
– *Rachel, Rachel*

(Comedy/Musical)
Julie Andrews – *Star!*
Lucille Ball – *Yours, Mine and Ours*
Petula Clark – *Finian's Rainbow*
Gina Lollobrigida
– *Buona Sera, Mrs Campbell*
• Barbra Streisand – *Funny Girl*

BRITISH ACADEMY AWARDS
Anne Bancroft – *The Graduate*
Catherine Deneuve – *Belle de Jour*
• Katharine Hepburn – *Guess Who's Coming to Dinner* and ***The Lion in Winter***
Joanne Woodward – *Rachel, Rachel*

NEW YORK – Joanne Woodward – *Rachel, Rachel*
BOARD OF REVIEW – Liv Ullmann – *Vargtimmen (Hour of the Wolf)* and ***Skammen (Shame)***
NATIONAL SOCIETY – Liv Ullmann – *Skammen (Shame)*

The National Board of Review named Norwegian performer Liv Ullmann as Best Actress for her performances in two Ingmar Bergman films: as a painter's wife in *Vargtimmen (Hour of the Wolf)* (NYT "acting too good to be apparent"; LAT "superb"; WP "Ullmann's square, ruddy face and troubled, somber eyes convey the situation with striking clarity, an ideal performance for this forcefully personal film"; CT "fine") and as a musician in *Skammen (Shame)* (NYT "[a] gruelling performance"; S&S "fantastic").

The New York Film Critics Circle, meanwhile, selected Joanne Woodward as Best Actress for her performance as an unmarried schoolteacher in *Rachel, Rachel*, the directorial debut of her husband, previous Best Actor Oscar nominee Paul Newman (NYT "extraordinarily good"; LAT "unerring … one of the classic and definitive portraits of the movie form, a characterization more impressive because of its lack of extravagant dramatics"; TT "excellent"; S&S "convincing"; MFB "delicately balanced"). It was Woodward's first trophy from the east coast circle. The runner-up was twenty-five-year old Tuesday Weld as the immoral high-school girl in *Pretty Poison* (NYT "numbingly dull"; LAT "convincing … totally remarkable – natural, credible and affecting"; S&S "splendid"; FQ "overwhelmingly fascinating").

Woodward triumphed again at the Golden Globes, winning the Drama award for the second time. Her victory, however, was spoiled by the announcement that same day of the Oscar nominations. While *Rachel, Rachel* was short-listed for Best Picture and previous winner Woodward received her second Best Actress nomination, Newman was overlooked for Best Director. Bitterly disappointed, Woodward strongly criticised the members of the Academy. Her outburst probably quashed her chances of a second statuette.

Vanessa Redgrave, mentioned by the Academy for the second time in three years, also effectively ruled herself out when she spoke out against the Vietnam War. Redgrave was included on the ballot for her portrayal of the American dancer Isadora Duncan in a three-hour biopic *Isadora*, which had been given a qualifying run in Los Angeles (NYT a "funny, complex, grandly romantic evocation"; LAT "an actress of great gifts, here deployed in vibrant youth and ravaged age over one of the longest and most taxing roles in screen history … the proof of her excellence is that she remains interesting in spite of everything"; V "a major acting triumph"; FQ "evokes the complexities and exaggerated eccentricities of Isadora").

The favourite for the Oscar was twenty-six-year old Barbra Streisand who was lauded by critics and won the Globe (Comedy/Musical) for her debut in the musical *Funny Girl* in which she reprised her stage success as Broadway star Fanny Brice (NYT "has a power, gentleness and intensity that rather knocks all the props and sets and camera angles on their ear" but at moments "becomes mannered"; LAT "an engrossing, compelling, lavishingly talented and versatile lady … not to be missed … fine dramatic efforts … one of the great performances, one of the great congruences of personality and role, an interpretation perfected over the months on stage and enriched by the resources of the screen"; WP "unique … she communicates, especially in songs, for which she has a style all her own … seems intensely honest and you marvel at her vulnerability. There is no doubt that this is a striking performer"; V "highly successful"; TT "a beautifully exact, casually timed comedy performance"; S&S "hilarious and impeccably timed"; FQ "captivating"; MFB "exhilarating").

Also considered for the Oscar were two previous winners. Patricia Neal earned her second nod as a war veteran's bitter mother in *The Subject was Roses*, her first role since suffering a series of strokes (NYT "gives the film an emotional impact it wouldn't otherwise have"; LAT "triumphant … her performance is masterful in its complexity and its honesty"; V "outstanding"). The previous year's winner, Katharine Hepburn, meanwhile, became the first person to receive an eleventh nomination for her portrayal of Eleanor of Aquitaine, the wife of King Henry II in *The Lion in Winter*, a role played on Broadway by Rosemary Harris (V "outstanding"; S&S "one of her best-ever performances"; MFB "a beautifully judged rendering, perhaps the crowning achievement of an extraordinary career").

Both NBR and NSFC champion Ullmann and New York runner-up Weld were overlooked by the Academy. Also by-passed by Oscar voters were: Globe nominee Mia Farrow, then wife of Oscar winner Frank Sinatra, as the victim of a coven's evil plans in *Rosemary's Baby* (NYT "quite marvelous, pale, suffering, almost constantly on screen in a difficult role"; LAT "confirms that she is an exciting and sexy screen personality and a very good actress"; V "outstanding"; FQ "the main asset of the film"); Globe nominee Beryl Reid reprising her Tony Award-winning Broadway triumph as a hammy television actress in *The Killing of Sister George* (NYT "unconvincing"; LAT "luminous"; V "superb"); Globe nominee and previous winner Julie Andrews as the late Gertrude Lawrence in the musical *Star!* (WP "acts the off-stage Miss Lawrence, but in the songs she is herself"; V "carefully built-up performance"; MFB "convincing"); Globe nominee Lucille Ball in *Yours, Mine and Ours* (NYT "very funny"; LAT "at her best"; WP "not for years has the incomparable Miss Ball had so well-wrought a movie and she plays it with her unique skill"; MFB "[gives] the redoubtable Lucille Ball opportunities for the kind of eccentric comedy business she has made her own"); previous winner Julie Christie in *Petulia* (LAT "back in the contemporary scene where she seems to do her most impressive work"; CT "displaying a lack of range and conviction in a role that presumably is a natural for her"; S&S "seems miscast"; MFB "Christie's performance is permeated throughout with an insurmountable sadness"); Sandy Dennis in *Sweet November* (NYT "very good"; LAT "despite some quite familiar mannerisms, Sandy Dennis gives thin material an earnestness it didn't know it had"; CT "cluttering [her] performance with those annoying mannerisms"; MFB "piling on the kooky charm"); fifteen-year old Olivia Hussey in *Romeo and Juliet* (LAT "conveys the vigor and the innocence and the idealism of young passions … charming and somehow unutterably moving"; V "inexperienced"); Gena Rowlands as the prostitute in *Faces* (NYT "extraordinary acting"; MFB "painfully and overpoweringly real"; CT "excellent"); Maggie Smith in *Hot Millions* (NYT "marvelously funny … a perfect foil for Ustinov"; MFB "copes engagingly with incompetent secretary jokes, loyal wife jokes, and sudden plunges into intelligence behind a façade of total inanity"); and Catherine Deneuve in *Belle de Jour* (NYT "excellent"; MFB "perfect … demonstrates remarkable control").

Also omitted from the list of Oscar contenders was Anne Heywood as a lesbian in the drama *The Fox* (NYT "good"; LAT "fine performance"; CT "effective"; V "does a creditable job"; MFB "adequate"). Heywood had garnered a Golden Globe nomination for her performance the previous year following industry screenings in Los Angeles in December 1967, but was not eligible for Academy Award consideration until the picture received a commercial release in February 1968.

On Oscar night, for the first time in the history of the category, there was a tie. The winners were newcomer Streisand and veteran Hepburn, who became the first person to win three statuettes in the major acting categories. Hepburn later triumphed again at the British Academy Awards.

The last word on the unusual Best Actress contest, however, belonged to Redgrave. Shortly after the Oscar ceremony, a shorter, re-edited version of *Isadora* opened in New York as *The Loves of Isadora*. The New York Times declared "two weeks after the 1968 Academy Awards were announced, New Yorkers can see the performance that should have won the Oscar for Vanessa Redgrave." In 1969, she was named Best Actress at the Cannes Film Festival and subsequently won the National Society of Film Critics' Best Actress accolade.

1968

BEST ACTOR

ACADEMY AWARDS
Alan Arkin as 'John Singer' in *The Heart is a Lonely Hunter*
Alan Bates as 'Yakov Bok' in *The Fixer*
Ron Moody as 'Fagin' in *Oliver!*
Peter O'Toole as 'King Henry II of England' in *The Lion in Winter*
• Cliff Robertson as 'Charly Gordon' in *Charly*

GOLDEN GLOBE AWARDS
(Drama)
Alan Arkin
– *The Heart is a Lonely Hunter*
Alan Bates – *The Fixer*
Tony Curtis – *The Boston Strangler*
• Peter O'Toole – *The Lion in Winter*
Cliff Robertson – *Charly*

(Comedy/Musical)
Fred Astaire – *Finian's Rainbow*
Jack Lemmon – *The Odd Couple*
Walter Matthau – *The Odd Couple*
• Ron Moody – *Oliver!*
Zero Mostel – *The Producers*

BRITISH ACADEMY AWARDS
Trevor Howard – *The Charge of the Light Brigade*
Ron Moody – *Oliver!*
• Spencer Tracy – *Guess Who's Coming to Dinner*
Nicol Williamson – *The Bofors Gun*

NEW YORK – Alan Arkin – *The Heart is a Lonely Hunter*
BOARD OF REVIEW – Cliff Robertson – *Charly*
NATIONAL SOCIETY – Per Oscarsson – *Sult (Hunger)*

Having played the lead role in the one hour television drama 'Days of Wine and Roses' in 1958 only to be passed over when the project was developed into a feature four years later in favour of Jack Lemmon (who received a Best Actor Oscar nomination), Cliff Robertson himself purchased the feature film rights to another television drama in which he had starred: the 1961 teleplay 'The Two Worlds of Charlie Gordon'. It took the actor several years to secure financing, but in 1968 he starred in a feature version which was simply entitled *Charly*. For his performance as a cognitively-impaired man temporarily transformed into a genius by a scientific experiment, Robertson earned mixed reviews (NYT gives "an earnest performance" but he is "really impossible to identify with"; LAT "a first-rate dual performance"; WP "the kind of acting assignment that wins awards … gives a mature, thoughtful performance"; CT "one of his finest [performances]"; V "seems to overdo the external manifestations of retardation ... but is excellent in the post-operative scenes"; TT "plays with tact and finesse"; Obs "little short of brilliant"; FQ "quite effective"; MFB "a careful, sympathetic performance"). At the end of the year, he was named Best Actor by the National Board of Review and received Globe and Oscar nominations.

Nominated by the Academy for the second time in three years was New York prizewinner, Alan Arkin, as a deaf-mute who transforms the lives of the people around him in *The Heart is a Lonely Hunter* (NYT "Arkin is extraordinary, deep and sound"; LAT "splendid"; WP "without being a thrilling performance, Arkin's is quietly powerful"; V "erratic and mannered"; Obs "remarkable"; S&S "beautifully played"; MFB "[a] delicate performance"). Nominated for the first time were Englishmen Alan Bates as a Russian Jewish peasant accused of murdering a child in *The Fixer* (NYT "very fine"; V "indefinite"; TT "a performance which is distinguished in parts, but gives no sense of progression"; S&S "an extraordinarily thorough performance"; MFB "convincing") and Englishman Ron Moody reprising his West End triumph as Fagin in the British musical *Oliver!* (NYT "played in a London music hall style"; LAT "Moody, loping, leering and loose-jointed as a marionette with the audience on a string, emerges as a star character actor ... one of the great entertaining performances"; V "virtual showstopper"; WP "a truly memorable performance"; FQ "standout", "makes a delightfully deceitful and even touching figure – a sympathetic figure"). Moody had won the Globe (Comedy/Musical) for his performance.

The overwhelming favourite for the Academy Award, however, was another English actor, Peter O'Toole. Five years after he had received an Oscar nomination for portraying King Henry II in *Becket*, O'Toole made the lists for playing the monarch again in *The Lion in Winter* (NYer "the brightest thing in the movie ...[a] robust performance"; V "outstanding"; S&S "much more disciplined than his earlier portrayal in 'Becket'"). O'Toole finished third in the New York voting (he led on the first ballot) and won the Globe (Drama) for his impersonation of the English monarch.

Surprisingly overlooked by the Academy, despite Globe nominations for their performances as the mis-matched flat-mates in the comedy *The Odd Couple*, were previous Best Supporting Actor Oscar winners Walter Matthau, reprising his Broadway role (NYT "completely low key and lovable"; LAT "[a] stellar performance"; V "a superior characterization"; S&S "brilliant"; MFB "brilliant") and Jack Lemmon (NYT "sometimes overacts"; LAT "stellar ... gives a very straight and earnest performance"; CT "gives his best comedy performance since 'The Apartment'"; V "outstanding"; S&S "good").

Three other notable omissions were: New York runner-up George C. Scott in *Petulia* (CT "superb, blending humor and pathos"; MFB "poignant"); National Society of Film Critics winner and 1966 Cannes honouree Per

Oscarsson in *Sult (Hunger)* (NYT "extraordinary"; S&S "superb"; MFB "[a] brilliant performance"); and previous winner Rod Steiger in both *The Sergeant* (LAT "[an] impeccable performance … tempting to proclaim this picture as the pinnacle of Steiger's career"; V "generally excellent"; TT "a bravura performance"; MFB "competent") and *No Way to Treat a Lady* (NYT "a beautifully uninhibited performance"; WP "has a field day with seven characterizations"; MFB "[a] tour de force").

Others unrecognised by Oscar voters were: Globe nominee Tony Curtis as the title character in *The Boston Strangler* (NYT "ludicrously, but with evident sincerity"; LAT "compelling … perhaps so far the finest performance of his career"; WP "outstanding"; CT "surprisingly adequate"; V "quite convincing"); Globe nominee Zero Mostel in *The Producers* (NYT "overacting grotesquely"; CT "occasionally grates a bit"); Anthony Quinn as the Pope in *The Shoes of the Fisherman* (NYT "plays his role with a lack of warmth, soul and intellectuality that characterizes the whole production"; LAT "[a] winning portrayal"; WP "above all, there is the finest, most credible performance from Anthony Quinn … unforgettable"; CT "gives a better performance than the film deserves"; V "excellent"); Dirk Bogarde as the prosecutor in *The Fixer* (NYT "very fine"; TT "shines"; S&S "having a fine old time"); Anthony Perkins in *Pretty Poison* (LAT "interesting [and] totally remarkable – natural, credible and affecting"; S&S "splendid"; FQ "overwhelmingly fascinating"); Oskar Werner in *Interlude* (NYT "a thoroughly convincing performance"; WP "proves intensely persuasive and frequently quite charming"; CT "fails to arouse much involvement"; S&S "sharp playing"; MFB "gives one of his effective, slightly abstracted performances"); seventeen-year old Leonard Whiting in *Romeo and Juliet* (LAT "conveys the vigor and the innocence and the idealism of young passions"; V "inexperienced"); BAFTA nominee Nicol Williamson in *The Bofors Gun* (LAT "marvelous"; MFB "a shattering performance"; G "always watchable"); Steve McQueen as a detective in *Bullitt* (NYT "in a part that is perfect for him"; LAT "appropriate and effective"; S&S "convincing"); Peter Sellers in *I Love You, Alice B. Tolkas* (NYT "sometimes funny but quite often grotesque"; LAT "superlatively played"; MFB "[at first] gives a beautifully modulated characterisation [but then] generally descends to the level of costumed masquerade"); Max von Sydow in *Skammen (Shame)* (NYT "[a] gruelling performance"; S&S "fantastic"); and Toshiro Mifune in *Akahige (Red Beard)* (NYT "strong, brooding and exquisitely restrained").

Although O'Toole was the favourite, Robertson campaigned hard for the statuette. On Oscar night, his efforts were rewarded when he was named Best Actor. Robertson was not in Hollywood to collect his Oscar, however, as he was in The Philippines filming his next movie. He never made the Academy's shortlist a second time.

1968

BEST SUPPORTING ACTRESS

ACADEMY AWARDS
Lynn Carlin as 'Maria Forst' in *Faces*
• Ruth Gordon as 'Minnie Castevet' in *Rosemary's Baby*
Sondra Locke as 'Mick Kelly' in *The Heart is a Lonely Hunter*
Kay Medford as 'Rose Brice' in *Funny Girl*
Estelle Parsons as 'Calla Mackie' in *Rachel, Rachel*

GOLDEN GLOBE AWARDS
• Ruth Gordon – *Rosemary's Baby*
Barbara Hancock – *Finian's Rainbow*
Abbey Lincoln – *For Love of Ivy*
Sondra Locke – *The Heart is a Lonely Hunter*
Jane Merrow – *The Lion in Winter*

BRITISH ACADEMY AWARDS
Pat Heywood – *Romeo and Juliet*
Virginia Maskell – *Interlude*
Simone Signoret – *Games*
• Billie Whitelaw – *Charlie Bubbles* and *Twisted Nerve*

BOARD OF REVIEW – Virginia Maskell – *Interlude*
NATIONAL SOCIETY – Billie Whitelaw – *Charlie Bubbles*

The National Board of Review posthumously honoured Virginia Maskell in *Interlude* (NYT "remarkable"; LAT "a superbly dignified and compassionate performance"; CT "manages to turn in a fine performance as the conductor's wife"; S&S "sharp playing"; MFB "affectingly well played") while the National Society of Film Critics awarded Billie Whitelaw in *Charlie Bubbles* (NYT "believable"; CT "brings her own sense of loneliness and despair to the former wife … good"; V "scores"; S&S "convincing"). Although overlooked for both the Globe and the Oscar, both were shortlisted by the British Academy. Whitelaw won for both *Charlie Bubbles* and the controversial and poorly received *Twisted Nerve* (NYT "gives the best performance [in the film]"; LAT "flawless … the most notable [of the cast]"; CT "standout"; V "does wonders with her unconvincing role").

The Globe and the Oscar were won by seventy-two-year old Ruth Gordon as a witch in *Rosemary's Baby* (NYT "overplays"; LAT "cannot be faulted"; CT "smashingly strong"; V "pleasantly unrestrained"). When the film had opened back in June 1968, Charles Champlin had declared in the Los Angeles Times, "Gordon establishes an early claim on a nomination for best supporting actress". It was her second Oscar nod in the acting categories, having been previously mentioned in the writing categories. It was her second Golden Globe win.

Outpolled for the Oscar were: Lynn Carlin for her film debut as an unhappy wife in *Faces* (NYT "strong", "extraordinary acting"; CT "excellent"; MFB "painfully and overpoweringly real"); Sondra Locke for her film debut as a teenager in *The Heart is a Lonely Hunter* (NYT "Locke is as fine as she can be within the limits of a lot of rather mawkish business and corny lines"; LAT "fine"; WP "arresting"; V "excellent"); Kay Medford in *Funny Girl* (LAT "displays the vivid economy of musical comedy portraiture, larger and more succinct than life"; WP "a mere puppet"); and the previous year's winner Estelle Parsons as a lesbian teacher in *Rachel, Rachel* (NYT "extraordinarily good"; LAT "Miss Parsons' characterization seems a good deal more subtle and difficult than the one she gave in 'Bonnie and Clyde'. She is remarkable"; V "effective"; TT "excellent"; S&S "fine").

Surprisingly the Academy overlooked: Shirley Knight as the ex-wife in *Petulia* (LAT "a fine performance"; CT "fine support"; S&S "radiantly played"; MFB "conveys a poignant sense of loss"); Ava Gardner as the empress in *Mayerling* (NYT "the surprise of the picture ... movingly underplays her few scenes"); Globe nominee Jane Merrow in *The Lion in Winter* (V "a sensitive portrayal"; S&S "makes a human being out of the underwritten part of Alais"); Abbey Lincoln in *For Love of Ivy* (NYT "immensely appealing"; WP "as wise as she is beautiful as the dissatisfied maid"; CT "comes off better than anyone"; MFB "the cast, Abbey Lincoln in particular, come out of it with credit"); Eileen Heckart in *No Way to Treat a Lady* (NYT "extravagantly played"; WP "quite overdoes the cop's nagging mother, which is less her fault than director Jack Smith's"; S&S "a master stroke ... [her] ceaseless stream of derogatory remarks about her offspring, delivered with deadly indifference, makes the horrors of any sort of mother fixation all too tangible"; MFB "if there is too much of the Yiddisher Momma in Eileen Heckart's performance, her timing and the genuinely comic dialogue allotted to her are more than enough to smooth it over"); Beverly Garland in *Pretty Poison* (NYT "excellent"; LAT "terribly standard"); Genevieve Page in *Belle de Jour* (NYT "superb"; MFB "electrifying"); Shani Wallis in *Oliver!* (LAT "entirely sympathetic"; WP "the best singing performance [in the film] ... her performance throughout is buoyant and delightful"; CT "proves to be a solid actress"); Kate Herrington in *Rachel, Rachel* (TT "excellent"); Joyce Van Patten in *I Love You, Alice B. Tolkas* (NYT "excellent in a rather flat role ... funny and valiant"; LAT "shines"; CT "delightful"); Cicely Tyson in *The Heart is a Lonely Hunter*; and Liza Minnelli in *Charlie Bubbles* (CT "particularly impressive").

1968

BEST SUPPORTING ACTOR

ACADEMY AWARDS
• Jack Albertson as 'John Cleary' in *The Subject was Roses*
Seymour Cassel as 'Chet' in *Faces*
Daniel Massey as 'Noel Coward' in *Star!*
Jack Wild as 'the Artful Dodger' in *Oliver!*
Gene Wilder as 'Leo Bloom' in *The Producers*

GOLDEN GLOBE AWARDS
Beau Bridges – *For Love of Ivy*
Ossie Davis – *The Scalphunters*
Hugh Griffith – *The Fixer* and *Oliver!*
• Daniel Massey – *Star!*
Martin Sheen – *The Subject was Roses*

BRITISH ACADEMY AWARDS
• Ian Holm – *The Bofors Gun*
Anthony Hopkins – *The Lion in Winter*
John McEnery – *Romeo and Juliet*
George Segal – *No Way to Treat a Lady*

BOARD OF REVIEW – Leo McKern – *The Shoes of the Fisherman*
NATIONAL SOCIETY – Seymour Cassel – *Faces*

Daniel Massey won the Golden Globe and earned an Oscar nomination for his portrayal of his godfather, English actor-director-writer and previous Oscar nominee Noel Coward, in the musical *Star!* (NYT "acts beautifully"; WP "has a subtle base of impersonation, underdone but stylishly accurate"; CT "[a] delight"; V "uncanny … steals most of his footage"; MFB "delightful").

The winner of the Academy statuette, however, was Jack Albertson as the father of a war veteran in *The Subject was Roses* (NYT cast is "so good that they begin to look as if they're showing off"; V "outstanding"). Albertson had previously won a Tony for his performance in the Broadway production.

The other nominees for the Oscar were: National Society of Film Critics winner Seymour Cassel as a disillusioned wife's one-night stand in *Faces* (NYT "strong", "extraordinary acting"; CT "excellent"; MFB "painfully and overpoweringly real"); Gene Wilder as the accountant in *The Producers* (NYT "he is forced to be as loud and as fast as [Zero] Mostel, but he's fine"; CT "provides the proper shadowy support for his decibel-devouring partner, neatly underplaying"); and sixteen-year old Jack Wild as the young pickpocket in the musical *Oliver!* (NYT "played by gross stage professionalism"; LAT "beguiling"; WP "portrayed with absolute enjoyment"; V deserves "major honors"; MFB "Wild's tireless mugging creates an Artful Dodger who is as accomplished a scene stealer as he is a pickpocket").

Overlooked by the Academy were Australian actor Leo McKern, who won the National Board of Review award for *The Shoes of the Fisherman* (LAT "good … lends welcome strength"; WP "[a] shrewdly friendly performance"; V "topnotch") as well as his co-stars Oskar Werner (NYT "does very well"; WP "spoken with glorious simplicity") and Vittorio de Sica (LAT "good"; V both "excellent"). BAFTA winner Ian Holm was also passed over for both *The Bofors Gun* (LAT "especially good"; TT does "particularly well"; G "[a] performance of a high standard") and *The Fixer* (V "compelling"). His co-stars in *The Fixer*, Globe nominee Hugh Griffith (V "solid") and David Warner (NYT "very fine"; TT "shines in a relatively small role"), also went unrecognised.

Also absent from the list of nominees were: Globe nominee Martin Sheen as the war veteran in *The Subject was Roses* (NYT cast is "so good that they begin to look as if they're showing off"; V "excellent"); Donald Sutherland as the bumbling family friend in *Interlude* (NYT "remarkable"; LAT "conveys a good deal in a relatively short at time"); Globe nominee Beau Bridges in *For Love of Ivy* (NYT "adds individuality to what is essentially [a] stereotyped role"; LAT "proves again that he is a fine and attractive young actor, even in what is essentially a very silly part"; WP "I was immensely taken with Beau Bridges"); Globe nominee Ossie Davis in *The Scalphunters* (NYT "played with gusto … especially comic and even moving"; LAT "beautifully played"; CT "effectively blending the servile and the sardonic"); BAFTA nominee John McEnery in *Romeo and Juliet* (NYT "beautifully played"; LAT "gives a characterization of Mercutio which is a movie in itself, madcap and captivating"; WP "a fascinating realization"); BAFTA nominee Anthony Hopkins for his film debut in *The Lion in Winter* (NYT "solid"); BAFTA nominee George Segal in *No Way To Treat A Lady* (WP "fine"; MFB "excellent and unselfish support"); Oliver Reed in *Oliver!* (LAT "admirable"; WP "played very well"); Richard Chamberlain as the violent husband in *Petulia* (LAT "superbly played"; CT "in one of the year's casting coups, Richard Chamberlain – playing an immature, spoiled playboy – is smashingly repugnant"); and Robert Vaughn in *Bullitt* (NYT "excellently acted"; LAT "the stand-out performance"; CT "neatly played").

The most enduring of the supporting performances of 1968 is arguably that of Douglas Rain as the computer in *2001: A Space Odyssey* (WP "gives the voice of computer HAL 9000 a steely bite which suggests a cold, individualistic machine"). Bestowing a nomination on a performer who never appeared on screen was, however, perhaps too great a stretch for Academy members.

1969

BEST PICTURE

ACADEMY AWARDS

Anne of the Thousand Days
(Wallis, Universal, 143 mins, 18 Dec 1969, 10 noms)
Butch Cassidy and the Sundance Kid
(Hill-Monash, Twentieth Century-Fox, 110 mins, 23 Sep 1969, $45.9m, 7 noms)
Hello, Dolly!
(Chenault, Twentieth Century-Fox, 146 mins, 16 Dec 1969, $13.0m, 7 noms)
• ***Midnight Cowboy***
(Hellman-Schlesinger, United Artists, 113 mins, 25 May 1969, $20.4m, 7 noms)
Z
(Reggane Films, Cinema V, 127 mins, 8 Dec 1969, 5 noms)

GOLDEN GLOBE AWARDS

(Drama)
• ***Anne of the Thousand Days***
Butch Cassidy and the Sundance Kid
Midnight Cowboy
The Prime of Miss Jean Brodie
They Shoot Horses, Don't They?

(Comedy/Musical)
Cactus Flower
Goodbye, Columbus
Hello, Dolly!
Paint Your Wagon
• ***The Secret of Santa Vittoria***

BRITISH ACADEMY AWARDS

• ***Midnight Cowboy***
Oh! What a Lovely War
Women in Love
Z

NEW YORK – *Z*
BOARD OF REVIEW – *They Shoot Horses, Don't They?*
NATIONAL SOCIETY – *Z*

For the first time since 1938, a foreign-language film was nominated for the Best Picture Academy Award: Constantin Costa-Gavras' French-language political drama, *Z* (NYT "immensely entertaining", "one of the most entertaining thrillers in years", but "it is likely to be mistaken as a work of fine – rather than popular – movie art"; LAT "one of the year's most important pictures … exciting [and] authentic … a remarkable achievement"; CT "a totally absorbing adventure film that will have wide appeal and a razor-sharp indictment … an art film with an intelligible, exciting story … memorable"; V "punchy" and "suspenseful"). *Z* had received a special Jury prize at the Cannes Film Festival and become a serious Academy Awards contender when it won the Best Picture accolades from both the New York Film Critics Circle and the National Society of Film Critics. *Z* was the first foreign-language film to be honoured by the east coast circle as non-English language films had previously been eligible only for a separate award. This distinction had been abolished as part of recent reforms to the group's voting procedures.

While *Z* garnered a Best Picture Oscar nomination, the year's other non-American movies were passed over, including: Richard Attenborough's British vignette film *Oh! What a Lovely War*, which was the runner-up in the New York critics' balloting (NYT "accomplishes that most difficult of artistic tasks: it attacks with devastating understatement the folly of war without exploiting the violence of warfare"; LAT "a beautifully imaginative, unorthodox, uncompromising, emotionally powerful piece of cinema"; CT "deserves an Academy Award nomination for the best picture of the year"; TT "an almost complete triumph", "it is spectacular and it is very moving"; S&S "little short of a triumph"); François Truffaut's French film *Baisers Volés (Stolen Kisses)*, a sequel to his 1959 debut feature, *Les Quatre Cents Coups (The 400 Blows)* (NYT "wonderful", "strong, sweet, wise and often explosively funny"; LAT "warmly enjoyable … very genuinely funny, very honestly gently and affecting"); and *if...*, the British winner of the Palme d'Or (NYT "good and strong", "very human"; LAT "eerie and compelling … a powerful picture"; WP "the tone of the movie is always a bit too shrewd and calculating to convince"; V "entertaining and provocative"; CT "a tough, timely manifesto of today's youth"; TT "extraordinary"; FQ "extraordinary").

The most surprising omission from the Academy's list of nominees, however, was an American film: *They Shoot Horses, Don't They?*, a drama about a 1930s dance marathon (NYT "far from being perfect, but it so disturbing in such important ways that I won't forget it very easily, which is more than can be said of much better, more consistent films"; LAT "[an] unrelenting study in despair", "remains a piece of theater, stagey and occasionally exciting but never, I believe, truly convincing"; FQ "a commendable film, in fact in many ways a remarkable film"). It was named Best Picture by the National Board of Review and was a Golden Globe nominee, but when the Oscar nominations were announced *They Shoot Horses, Don't They?*, mentioned for nine Oscars, became the most nominated film overlooked for a Best Picture nomination.

Other acclaimed American films overlooked were: the hugely successful road trip movie *Easy Rider* (LAT "an astonishing work of art and an overpowering motion picture experience [and] a social document which is poignant, potent, disturbing and important", "confirms the revolutionary new day in motion picture making"; V "perceptive"; Time "one of the ten most important motion picture events of the decade"; TT "no film before has caught the precise quality of life in the drifting generation of young Americans as well as this"; S&S "succeeds where it matters most, in communicating a yearning vision of a different way of life"; FQ "remarkable"); *Bob & Carol & Ted & Alice* (NYT "a conventional comedy [which] manages to be offensive … the movie is unpleasant because it acts superior to the people in it"; LAT "a scintillating social comedy"; CT "the best comedy of the year"; WP "the sharpest American comedy in several years"; FQ "a genuinely intelligent American comedy"); *Alice's Restaurant* (NYT "a sort of folk movie – wise, fantastic, technically superb, sometimes wildly funny, sometimes touching"; LAT "untraditional … while this new work seems to be less consistently successful in its own terms than either 'Easy Rider' or 'Midnight Cowboy', it is still a fresh, captivating and important piece"; CT "a free-wheeling, lyrical film"; S&S "a film of considerable beauty, no rancour and not a little ambiguity, an episodic, elegiac movie"); *The Prime of Miss Jean Brodie* (NYT "a very decent movie, but it will probably be underrated"; LAT "consistently engrossing, swift, revealing, rising from charm and humor to tragedy"; S&S "[suffers from] a serious imbalance"); Alfred Hitchcock's thriller *Topaz* (NYT "a huge success, a quirky, episodic espionage tale", "most entertaining"; LAT "diverting [but] one of those pictures in which the whole is not greater than the sum of its parts … not among the master's very best"; WP "may be the least thrilling thriller ever made"; S&S "disappointing"); and three Westerns – *True Grit*, starring John Wayne (NYT "a marvellously rambling frontier fable"; LAT "as straight-shootin' a western as ever was to celebrate all westerns … a joy"; WP "merely good enough by contemporary industry standards"); Sam Peckinpah's *The Wild Bunch* (NYT "very beautiful and the first truly interesting American-made Western in years", "a classic Hollywood Western"; LAT "the most graphically violent western ever made, and one of the most violent movies of any kind … a brilliantly made thought-provoking movie"; WP "a remarkable film … the most fascinating and explosive American movie to come along since 'Bonnie and Clyde' – a violent, quirky action epic") and Sergio Leone's *Once Upon a Time in the West* (NYT "granting the fact that it is quite bad, [it] it is almost always interesting", "has moments of genuine impact"; LAT "a triumphantly bravura shoot-em-up … a most elegant and most enjoyable western"; CT "he made the western so big that much if its snap and tension are diluted over too many minutes"; WP "almost three hours of pictorialism, nostalgia, homage, historical recreation, anachronistic humor and choreographed gunplay … endearing and irresistible"; TT "much too long").

Leading the field of Oscar contenders with ten nominations was the Globe (Drama) winner, *Anne of the Thousand Days* (NYT "one of those almost unbearably classy movies that have a way of elevating the reputations of moviemakers without doing much for the art"; LAT "splendid … likely to be a strong contender in the upcoming Academy Awards in virtually all categories"; WP "a perfectly stodgy and unimaginative movie … dramatically the work never comes alive"; TT "plods wearily through the story"; S&S "dreary"; MFB "wordy, repetitive and dull"). Unexpectedly, the film's director, Globe winner Charles Jarrott, did not receive a nomination. Jarrott's exclusion essentially ruled the film out of Best Picture contention. In the previous fifteen years, the Academy had given the Best Picture and Best Director prizes to different films only twice. More significantly, the last film to win Best Picture when its director had been overlooked was *Grand Hotel* in 1931/32.

Also cited for the Best Picture Oscar without a nomination for its director was the musical *Hello, Dolly!*, starring Barbra Streisand and directed by previous Best Actor nominee Gene Kelly (NYT "it doesn't really work"; LAT "it is grand, it is spectacular, it is sentimental"; WP "a lively, pretty, entertaining show"; V "warm-hearted and splashy extravaganza, harmlessly hyperbolic").

The year's fourth biggest box office hit, *Butch Cassidy and the Sundance Kid*, was in contention for both prizes but was considered too commercial for the Academy's top award (NYT "very funny in a strict contemporary way [but] you keep seeing signs of another, better film behind gags and effects"; LAT "a writer's triumph of a movie… a literate and sophisticated comedy"; CT "a frequently funny, sometimes hilarious film"; WP "no American film of the year has been as carefully written and exquisitely mounted, but in the long run its extraordinary for an absence of drama and common humanity"; V "lighthearted"; S&S "cool, engaging, superb").

In contrast, *Midnight Cowboy*, also nominated for both awards, was considered not commercial enough. The drama about male prostitutes in New York City had been given an X-rating (NYT "superior", "ultimately a moving experience"; LAT "an invariably moving study of unlikely friendship"; CT "at times invigoratingly funny, at others despairingly sad"; V "sometimes amusing but essentially sordid"; S&S "sporadically well observed"; FQ "very moving").

For his handling of *Midnight Cowboy*, John Schlesinger won the Directors Guild of America award, which had been indicative of both the Best Director and Best Picture winners for many years. However, the previous year's break in this tradition combined with the X-rating resulted in many observers being unable to confidently predict a winner.

On Oscar night, *Z* won the Oscar for Best Foreign-Language Film. The Best Picture Academy Award, however, was won by *Midnight Cowboy*. It remains the only X-rated film to have won the top Oscar. *Midnight Cowboy* also triumphed at the BAFTAs in London. A year later, *Butch Cassidy and the Sundance Kid* collected the Best Film BAFTA as well.

1969

BEST DIRECTOR

ACADEMY AWARDS
Constantin Costa-Gavras for *Z*
George Roy Hill for *Butch Cassidy and the Sundance Kid*
Arthur Penn for *Alice's Restaurant*
Sydney Pollack for *They Shoot Horses, Don't They?*
• John Schlesinger for *Midnight Cowboy*

GOLDEN GLOBE AWARDS
• Charles Jarrott – *Anne of the Thousand Days*
Gene Kelly – *Hello, Dolly!*
Stanley Kramer – *The Secret of Santa Vittoria*
Sydney Pollack – *They Shoot Horses, Don't They?*
John Schlesinger – *Midnight Cowboy*

DIRECTORS GUILD AWARD
Constantin Costa-Gavras – *Z*
George Roy Hill
– *Butch Cassidy and the Sundance Kid*
Dennis Hopper – *Easy Rider*
Sydney Pollack
– *They Shoot Horses Don't They?*
• John Schlesinger
– *Midnight Cowboy*

BRITISH ACADEMY AWARDS
Richard Attenborough
– *Oh! What a Lovely War*
Ken Russell – *Women in Love*
• John Schlesinger
– *Midnight Cowboy*
Peter Yates – *Bullitt*

NEW YORK – Constantin Costa-Gavras – *Z*
BOARD OF REVIEW – Alfred Hitchcock – *Topaz*
NATIONAL SOCIETY – François Truffaut – *Baisers Volés (Stolen Kisses)*

On 29 December 1969, Constantin Costa-Gavras was honoured in New York for his French-language political drama *Z* (NYT "has mastered his art"; CT "continually picks up the pace just before it begins to lag … [directed with] intelligence and purpose"; Obs "brilliantly written and directed"). British actor Richard Attenborough finished as runner-up for his directorial debut, *Oh! What a Lovely War* (NYT "a dazzling directorial debut"; WP "triumphantly polished"; S&S "a triumph").

Three days later veteran British film-maker Alfred Hitchcock was named Best Director by the National Board of Review for his espionage thriller *Topaz* (NYT "a movie of beautifully composed sequences, full of surface tensions, ironies, absurdities"; LAT "bravura displays of the fabled Hitchcock technique, replete with dazzling camera movements and acute imagery … remarkable"; WP "polished"; S&S "spellbindingly well made")

On 5 January 1970, Costa-Gavras finished as runner-up for the National Society of Film Critics accolade behind Frenchman François Truffaut for *Baisers Volés (Stolen Kisses)* (NYT "Truffaut is the star of the film"; LAT "carefully constructed, yet it retains a considerable air of spontaneity and immediate invention").

When the nominees for the Golden Globe were announced two weeks later, all four of these contenders were overlooked. The Hollywood Foreign Press Association instead short-listed: Charles Jarrott for the historical drama *Anne of the Thousand Days* (LAT "steadfastly traditional, absolutely devoid of gimmickry … the direction of Charles Jarrott is unobtrusive to the point of invisibility"; WP "Jarrott leaves a lot of empty space on that Panavision screen, but when he tries to fill the frame with extras, he doesn't know how to use them collectively or individually … the whole thing is embarrassing"; MFB "has done nothing to add filmic flow to an essentially statis concept"); Gene Kelly, a previous Best Actor Globe nominee, for the musical *Hello, Dolly!* (NYT "acts like a caretaker of a big, valuable property … [has] added nothing to the heritage of the musical"); Stanley Kramer for the comedy *The Secret of Santa Vittoria* (NYT "there's not one affecting, surprising or spontaneous moment … it's possible to see the interior mechanics of conventional movie-making in everything from its crowd scenes to an interior love scene"; LAT "a tour de force … the professionalism and the gloss are very high indeed"); Sydney Pollack for *They Shoot Horses, Don't They?* (NYT "by far the best thing that Pollack has ever directed"; LAT "heavy-handed"); and John Schlesinger for *Midnight Cowboy* (LAT "as an exercise in film-making, 'Midnight Cowboy' is dazzling"; WP "whenever Schlesinger attempts to enhance the material, he simply messes it up [while] whenever the direction is virtually invisible, the actors take over and play this rich, dirty, sentimental story for all it's worth"). When the Globes were presented on 2 February, it was Jarrott who emerged victorious.

Despite his win, Jarrott was not even a finalist for the Directors Guild of America award, presented nearly two weeks later. The winner was another English director: Schlesinger for *Midnight Cowboy*, the controversial X-rated drama about two New York City male prostitutes which was Schlesinger's first American film. Schlesinger had previously been unsuccessfully nominated for the award in 1965. Also in contention for the DGA prize were: New York honoree Costa-Gavras; Globe nominee Pollack; George Roy Hill for the hit

Western comedy *Butch Cassidy and the Sundance Kid* (NYT "there are some bothersome technical things about the movie"; CT "responsible for the strengths and weaknesses of the film … unable to give Butch and the Kid the depth of character given to Bonnie and Clyde, Hill has unfortunately elected to try to make the original look silly"); and actor-director Dennis Hopper for the popular hippie road movie *Easy Rider* (TT "clearly a talented director").

Two days after the DGA presentation, the Academy announced the Oscar nominees. Globe (Drama) winner *Anne of the Thousand Days* topped the list of contenders with ten nominations, but in a major shock, Jarrott was not among the Best Director candidates. He was the fourth Globe winner, and the second in as many years, to be shut-out of Oscar consideration. Globe nominee Kramer was also overlooked, possibly having undermined his chances in an interview for the Chicago Tribune in the lead up to the release of *The Secret of Santa Vittoria*. "There's too much emphasis on winning [Oscars]," he told Norma Lee Browning, "What the hell, it's only a temporary piece of crockery."

Also absent from the Oscar line-up were: New York runner-up Attenborough; NBR champ Hitchcock; NSFC winner Truffaut; Globe nominee Kelly, despite a Best Picture nod for his film; seventy-one-year old veteran Henry Hathaway for the Western *True Grit*, for which John Wayne won the Best Actor Oscar (NYT "Hathaway's clear-eyed, no-nonsense approach to movie-making has never been more effective, since he simply refuses to take the time to acknowledge the sentimentality in which the movie is really awash"; LAT "there were occasional uncertainties of tone, moments at which the film couldn't be sure whether it as an ordinary western or something quite special"; WP "clumsy and conventional … as a storyteller, Hathaway has been too lazy and haphazard … slipshod craftsmanship"); Bob Fosse for *Sweet Charity* (NYT "despite attempts to utilize the film form, the movie alternates between the painfully literal and the self-consciously cinematic"; LAT "nothing less than a masterpiece of comedic choreography"; WP "Fosse's eye is so bad that we never get the luxury of seeing if his staging and choreography are decent"; V "brilliant directorial debut"; S&S "as director he pulls constantly against himself, undermining his own meticulous [choreography] by inserting choppy efforts at mise en scene"; MFB "despite the exciting New York locations, several fine performances and the magnificent precision of the choreography, one is left with the impression of several splendid but essentially disjointed scenes connected only by formal editing devices"); Frank Perry for *Last Summer* (NYT "indulges the cast at the expense of the picture [which is marred by] technical imperfections [and] some resistible, fancy camera movements"; LAT "unable to conceal from us that [the movie] is in fact a created work, whose characters are propelled by a script and are actors acting … [a] failure of directorial restraint"; V "sensitive direction"); Lindsay Anderson for the Palme d'Or winner *if…* (LAT

"Anderson's artistic control falters but there is still such cinematic skill at hand"; WP "as a work of craftsmanship, [it] is one of the slickest and most accomplished English films of recent years … [yet] Anderson's style is not really original or innovative, but cinematically literate, a smart assimilation of various sources and styles"); Sam Peckinpah for *The Wild Bunch* (LAT "brilliantly made"; WP "the astonishing thing about Peckinpah is that he rarely lets up … [he] keeps sustaining and complicating the action even after he's got us running for cover … he's also extraordinarily good at characterizing the kind of men who embody violence"; CT "maintains a careful discipline"); and Sergio Leone for *Once Upon a Time in the West* (LAT "Leone is a master of the expressive gesture"; MFB "the film has considerable flair [but is] deliberately ponderous").

Instead the Academy nominated: Costa-Gavras, Pollack and Hill, each for the first time; Schlesinger for a second time; and, for a third occasion, Arthur Penn for *Alice's Restaurant* (LAT "[at times] studied and self-conscious"; CT "brilliant … marvelous technique"; S&S "brilliant"). The inclusion of Costa-Gavras marked the seventh time in a decade that the Academy had nominated the director of a foreign-language film.

On Oscar night, the DGA reclaimed its status as a reliable Oscar indicator following the previous year's shock upset. The winner of the Best Director Academy Award was Schlesinger. He was the fourth Englishman in a decade to win the Oscar. Schlesinger triumphed again at the British Academy Awards in a surprise win over the highly-favoured Attenborough. The BAFTA the following year was won by Hill for *Butch Cassidy and the Sundance Kid.*

Two years later, Schlesinger received a third Oscar nomination, for the British drama *Sunday, Bloody Sunday*.

1969

BEST ACTRESS

ACADEMY AWARDS
Geneviève Bujold as 'Anne Boleyn' in *Anne of the Thousand Days*
Jane Fonda as 'Gloria Betty' in *They Shoot Horses, Don't They?*
Liza Minnelli as 'Pookie' in *The Sterile Cuckoo*
Jean Simmons as 'Georgie Elgin' in *The Happy Ending*
• Maggie Smith as 'Miss Jean Brodie' in *The Prime of Miss Jean Brodie*

GOLDEN GLOBE AWARDS
(Drama)
• Geneviève Bujold – *Anne of the Thousand Days*
Jane Fonda – *They Shoot Horses, Don't They?*
Liza Minnelli – *The Sterile Cuckoo*
Jean Simmons – *The Happy Ending*
Maggie Smith – *The Prime of Miss Jean Brodie*

(Comedy/Musical)
Ingrid Bergman – *Cactus Flower*
Dyan Cannon – *Bob & Carol & Ted & Alice*
Kim Darby – *Generation*
• Patty Duke – *Me, Natalie*
Mia Farrow – *John and Mary*
Shirley MacLaine – *Sweet Charity*
Anna Magnani – *The Secret of Santa Vittoria*
Barbra Streisand – *Hello, Dolly!*

BRITISH ACADEMY AWARDS
Mia Farrow – *John and Mary* and *Rosemary's Baby* and *Secret Ceremony*
Glenda Jackson – *Women in Love*
• Maggie Smith – *The Prime of Miss Jean Brodie*
Barbra Streisand – *Funny Girl* and *Hello, Dolly!*
Mary Wimbush – *Oh! What a Lovely War*

NEW YORK – Jane Fonda – *They Shoot Horses, Don't They?*
BOARD OF REVIEW – Geraldine Page – *Trilogy*
NATIONAL SOCIETY – Vanessa Redgrave – *Isadora*

"So far this year, there hasn't been a single female performance of any real size to qualify for the Oscar," Joyce Haber reported in the Los Angeles Times in late September. "United Artists noticed this fact and its execs flew out to the coast to see a cut of Richard Brooks' 'The Happy Ending'. They were mightily impressed by Jean Simmons … 'Ending' was scheduled for release in 1970. Michel LeGrand doesn't start scoring until early next month! But U.A. asked Brooks to rush 'Ending' out for December to make Miss Simmons eligible for this year's Oscar." When the movie screened late in the year, critics were similarly impressed with Simmons' turn as the unhappily married woman in *The Happy Ending*. In the Los Angeles Times, Charles Champlin raved, "Richard Brooks' 'The Happy Ending' brings us one of the year's best and most moving performances: the portrayal by his wife, Jean Simmons, of a wife falling to pieces because her marriage has become an empty and undemanding ritual of habit and social duty … stunning … a performance of shattering intensity and importance [that is] full of truthful observation". Other critics concurred (V "moving, emotionally-wringing"; MFB "Simmons' performance just about holds together a tottering framework and almost makes the dialogue sound as though it wasn't scribbled on the backs of old envelopes"). When the film opened in the United Kingdom some months later, after the Academy Awards had been presented, The Times called her performance "splendid" and opined that she "should have got the Oscar". United Artists' expedited release strategy paid off when Simmons received nominations for both the Golden Globe (Drama) and the Academy Award.

The frontrunners for the Best Actress Oscar, however, were both daughters of previous Oscar contenders: Jane Fonda, the daughter of previous Best Actor nominee Henry Fonda; and Liza Minnelli, the daughter of previous Best Actress nominee Judy Garland and previous Best Director winner Vincente Minnelli.

Thirty-two-year old Fonda received her first nomination from the Academy for playing a competitor in a 1930s dance marathon in *They Shoot Horses, Don't They?* (NYT "fine"; LAT "[an] excellent, flamboyantly theatrical performance"; V "gives the film a personal focus and an emotionally gripping power"). The role was a break-through for Fonda after comic and sex-object roles, such as those in *Barefoot in the Park*, *Cat Ballou* and *Barbarella.* Previously nominated for the Golden Globe (Comedy/Musical) three times, *They Shoot Horses, Don't They?* saw Fonda short-listed for the Globe (Drama) for the first time.

The role of the neurotic college student in *The Sterile Cuckoo* was Minnelli's first starring role (NYT "one of the most appealing performances of the season, a triumph"; LAT "one of the year's most memorable and affecting star turns, a performance which quickly hypnotizes us into forgetting that it is indeed a performance and convinces us we are looking in on real life … emerges full-blown as a major acting talent"; CT "she never lets up in a performance that has more wisecracks than 30 minutes with Henny Youngman and it is because of this that Pookie smothers, rather than engages, your heart"; WP "rather effective – it seems inevitable that she'll win an Oscar nomination"; FQ "brilliant"; MFB "entirely compelling"). Life magazine praised the twenty-three-year old for "a performance which is so funny, so moving, so perfectly crafted and realized that it should win her an Academy Award". Only months after her mother's death, Minnelli was nominated for the first time.

The other two Oscar candidates had also been Globe (Drama) nominees. It was the first time the Academy exactly replicated the Globe (Drama) field without a change. French Canadian Geneviève Bujold was included for her portrayal of Anne Boleyn in *Anne of the Thousand Days* (NYT "a constantly delightful surprise"; LAT "emerges as a dazzling new star"; MFB "displays charm and a confident attack which will certainly make a star of her"). Maggie Smith, meanwhile, received her second nomination for portraying an unconventional teacher at a girls' school in 1930s Edinburgh in *The Prime of Miss Jean Brodie*, a role had been played by previous nominee Vanessa Redgrave in London and by Zoe Caldwell on Broadway (NYT "extraordinary", "a display of controlled, funny, elegant theatricality", "simply great … the kind of performance that not only has meaning within the context of the movie, but also can be consciously enjoyed as the work of an individual, fully developed intelligence exercising its talents for the sheer joy of it … a staggering amalgam of counter pointed moods, switches in voice levels and obliquely stated emotions, all of which are precisely right"; LAT "Smith gives us one of the superior screen performances – an inevitable Academy Award nomination next year if the Oscar is going to continue to mean anything at all"; WP "witty and touching"; CT "a one-woman lesson in acting"; V "a triumph" and a "tour de force"; TT "splendid … both funny and touching"; S&S "brings the heroine with her consciously theatrical gestures and trite romantic fantasies vividly to life"; FQ "extraordinary" and "commanding").

Overlooked for consideration were: Shirley MacLaine in *Sweet Charity* (NYT "never succeeds … MacLaine can sometimes by very comic, but she is a dull, shapeless dancer, an ordinary singer and an actress incapable of registering – outwardly – contradictory, funny internal anxieties"; LAT "MacLaine brings off superbly the rather peculiar challenge that a musical presents: to do a singing and dancing performance which is a slice of art rather than a slice of life, yet also to create a character who has some validity and identifiability as a creature who could exist in real life … MacLaine's finest hour"; WP "she's working too hard at effects that should come quietly and easily"; V her "finest and most versatile screen performance to date"; TT "charming"; S&S "splendidly funny and touching … MacLaine's creation is irresistible, carrying the film over its stylistic flurries"; MFB "performs the role with her customary galvanic kookiness and self-parodying waifishness"); Ali MacGraw in her film debut in *Goodbye, Columbus* (NYT "she is, for most of the film, exactly the right mixture of innocence and guile"; LAT "by any persuasion one of the most welcome newcomers in a long time"; WP "interesting"); Shirley Knight in *The Rain People* (NYT "although it deals with several minor characters, the movie never takes its attention away from Shirley Knight … a detailed and deliberate [performance]"; LAT "superbly acted"; V "a striking performance"); and Ingrid

Bergman in *Cactus Flower* (NYT "delightful"; LAT "she's not really well cast, being ill-prepared to be convincing as a widely-ignored spinster"; CT "in the end, it is Miss Bergman alone who makes 'Cactus Flower' worth tolerating"; WP "would be more convincing if her performance were less anxious"; S&S "nicely acted").

The New York Film Critics' Circle named Fonda as Best Actress while the National Board of Review named Geraldine Page for her performance in the made-for-television film 'Trilogy'. Following the re-editing and re-release of *Isadora*, the National Society of Film Critics honoured Vanessa Redgrave, who had been an Oscar nominee for her portrayal the previous year.

The Globe (Drama) was won by Bujold, but her victory did not make her the Oscar favourite. For the previous ten years in a row the Globe (Drama) winner had been nominated for the Oscar, only to go home empty-handed. In the Comedy/Musical category the surprise winner was previous supporting Oscar winner Patty Duke for *Me, Natalie* (NYT "mostly [the film is] just gags, delivered abrasively by Miss Duke, who is even less effective when registering pathos"; LAT "she is awfully, awfully good – funny in the wry, self-deprecating way the role demands, touching in her sense of loneliness, beautiful as she begins to bloom"; CT "winningly combines self-deprecating humor and a smarmless, sad sensitivity"). Many pundits had been expecting a win for Barbra Streisand in *Hello, Dolly!* (NYT "Streisand's obvious youth and real sexuality obliterated any sense of nostalgia in the 'Hello, Dolly!' number and add a curious ambiguity to other aspects of the role … [she is] circling around the role and finding laughs occasionally, but never quite committing herself to it"; LAT "superb … the performance is entirely and uniquely her own"; WP "the fascinating thing about Miss Streisand in this new film is that we want more of her even though we can sense that she's probably too young, both chronologically and emotionally, for this particular role").

On Oscar night, neither Fonda nor Minnelli, nor Globe winner Bujold, won the Oscar. The winner was Smith. The following day Variety commented "an actress who wasn't considered a prime contender won her Best Actress Oscar in a triumph of artistry." Observers opined that Smith's chances had been helped by her acclaimed stage performances in Los Angeles with the touring National Theatre of Britain during the voting period. Smith also won the BAFTA for *The Prime of Miss Jean Brodie*. In a unique situation resulting from different release dates on either side of the Atlantic, Smith won the British Academy Award over a field that included both the previous year's Best Actress Oscar winner and the following year's Best Actress Oscar winner.

Within a decade, Smith won another Oscar as Best Supporting Actress, while Fonda and Minnelli both won Best Actress statuettes.

1969

BEST ACTOR

ACADEMY AWARDS
Richard Burton as 'King Henry VIII of England' in *Anne of the Thousand Days*
Dustin Hoffman as 'Enrico Rizzo' in *Midnight Cowboy*
Peter O'Toole as 'Arthur Chipping' in *Goodbye, Mr Chips*
Jon Voight as 'Joe Buck' in *Midnight Cowboy*
• John Wayne as 'Reuben "Rooster" Cogburn'' in *True Grit*

GOLDEN GLOBE AWARDS
(Drama)
Alan Arkin – *Popi*
Richard Burton – *Anne of the Thousand Days*
Dustin Hoffman – *Midnight Cowboy*
Jon Voight – *Midnight Cowboy*
• John Wayne – *True Grit*

(Comedy/Musical)
Dustin Hoffman – *John and Mary*
Lee Marvin – *Paint Your Wagon*
Steve McQueen – *The Reivers*
• Peter O'Toole – *Goodbye, Mr Chips*
Anthony Quinn – *The Secret of Santa Vittoria*

BRITISH ACADEMY AWARDS
Alan Bates – *Women in Love*
• Dustin Hoffman – *John and Mary* and ***Midnight Cowboy***
Walter Matthau – *Hello, Dolly!* and *The Secret Life of an American Wife*
Nicol Williamson – *Inadmissible Evidence*

NEW YORK – Jon Voight – *Midnight Cowboy*
BOARD OF REVIEW – Peter O'Toole – *Goodbye, Mr Chips*
NATIONAL SOCIETY – Jon Voight – *Midnight Cowboy*

Frenchman Jean-Louis Trintignant won the Best Actor prize at the Cannes Film Festival for his performance as the government investigator in *Z* (NYT "excellent"; CT "consistently fine"; MFB "well conveyed" in a "subdued, quietly authoritative performance"). Although the film was embraced by American critics and earned five Oscar nominations, including Best Picture, Trintignant was overlooked for the year's other Best Actor accolades, as was his co-star, Yves Montand as the assassinated doctor (NYT "excellent").

Also passed over for consideration for any of the annual prizes were both Jean-Pierre Léaud for *Baisers Volés (Stolen Kisses)* (NYT "quite marvelous") and Malcolm McDowell for *if...* (NYT "especially good"; CT "played brilliantly").

The early frontrunners for Best Actor honours in the United States were Dustin Hoffman and Jon Voight in *Midnight Cowboy*, which was released in late May. Hoffman and Voight played two male prostitutes in New York City, one bitter and seriously ill, the other naive and romantic. The film offered a marked change of pace for Hoffman, who had become a star two years earlier in *The Graduate* (NYT "fine", "superior"; LAT "creates a character so whole, so convincing, so singular"; CT "tremendous"; WP "touching"; S&S "superb and largely unsentimental … establishes himself as a fine character actor"; MFB "beautifully observed"), and was a launching pad for Voight in his first major role (NYT "superior"; LAT "powerfully persuasive"; CT "tremendous … convincingly vulnerable"; WP "extraordinary"; MFV "convincing").

On 4 July 1969, John Wayne, who at sixty-two years of age was a beloved national legend, entered Best Actor contention when he earned some of the best reviews of his career as an ageing marshal with an eye-patch in the Western *True Grit* (NYT "a triumph" in "the best role of his career", "superb"; LAT "plays a role which sits like a crown atop his 40 years of playing John Wayne … no one else in Hollywood could have played it at all, and Wayne plays it with a stirrups-to-battered-Stetson authority which is gorgeous to watch"; CT "a sharp reminder that every once in a while John Wayne is able to play someone other than John Wayne … proves that he is also able to make a right proper Rooster"; WP "fine"; V "effective"; TT "a vintage presentation of the John Wayne we have always known").

Late in the year, in a musical remake of *Goodbye, Mr Chips*, Peter O'Toole won acclaim for his performance as schoolteacher Arthur Chipping, the part for which Robert Donat had won the Best Actor Oscar in 1939 (NYT "restrained, affectingly comic", "has never been better"; V "curious lack of warmth" but "demonstrates his seemingly limitless range"; S&S "skilful"; MFB "realistic").

Finally, in late December, Richard Burton entered the race in the historical drama *Anne of the Thousand Days*, which was given an Oscar qualifying run ahead of its general release the following year. Like O'Toole, Burton portrayed the same character for which an actor had previously won an Oscar: King Henry VIII (NYT "in excellent form"; LAT "one of his best performances in a notable career"; V "sensitive, vivid and arresting"; TT "unchanging"; MFB "Burton's Henry profits from the actor's personal magnetism and authoritative voice, though it is a monotonous performance, written and played all on one note"). Charles Laughton had won Best Actor in 1932/33 for playing the sixteenth century monarch in *The Private Life of Henry VIII*. Interestingly, Rex Harrison, another previous Best Actor Oscar winner, had played the role of the king in the original Broadway production of *Anne of the Thousand Days*.

1969

When the New York Film Critics Circle gathered at the end of the year, the stars of *Midnight Cowboy* dominated the Best Actor vote, with Voight eventually outpolling Hoffman for the award. Placing a distant third was Robert Redford as an Olympic skier in *The Downhill Racer* (NYT "performs well"; LAT "creates a laconic but complex character … a thoroughly realized characterization, devoid of all the sporting cliches").

The National Society of Film Critics also honoured Voight, while the National Board of Review selected O'Toole.

At the Golden Globe awards, Wayne, the sentimental favourite, won the Best Actor (Drama) award ahead of Burton, Hoffman, Voight, and Alan Arkin in *Popi* (NYT "an extraordinarily fine and winning performance … spontaneous and fluid as quicksilver, this definitive portrait of a lonely, stubborn underdog is funny, pathetic, admirable and real" "; LAT "superb … the triumph at last is just about all Arkin's").

In the Comedy/Musical category O'Toole collected his third Globe. He had won in the Drama category in 1964 and 1968 for playing King Henry II in *Becket* and *The Lion in Winter*. Among the other nominees was Anthony Quinn for his work in *The Secret of Santa Vittoria* (LAT "Quinn gives one of the bellowing, stomping, thrashing, gesticulating performances which must be the envy and despair of actors confined to conveying flaccid neuroses"). Contrasting his work in *Midnight Cowboy*, Hoffman was also nominated for the romantic comedy *John and Mary* (NYT "gives a performance by combining his mannerisms and the stooped strut of an over-age Holden Caulfield"; LAT "could hardly be better … a low-keyed and naturalistic performance").

While Cannes honouree Trintignant was overlooked for the Oscar, the five other main contenders were all included. Voight earned his first nod and Hoffman was mentioned for the second time in three years. O'Toole made the list for the fourth time and for the second year in a row, while Burton was recognised for a sixth time. The favourite, however, was Wayne.

Twenty years after he was first considered for the Best Actor Oscar, and nearly a decade after the disappointment of being overlooked for *The Alamo*, Wayne won the Academy Award as Best Actor at his second (and final) nomination. "Wow," he said as he stood before the Academy with his statuette, "If I had known that, I would have put that eyepatch on thirty-five years earlier."

Although he was eligible for the award, Wayne was not nominated for the Best Actor BAFTA. The British Academy instead honoured one the unsuccessful Oscar nominees. Hoffman was named for *John and Mary* in addition to *Midnight Cowboy*. The following year the BAFTA was won by Redford for three films including *Butch Cassidy and the Sundance Kid* and *The Downhill Racer*.

1969

BEST SUPPORTING ACTRESS

ACADEMY AWARDS
Cathy Burns as 'Rhoda' *in Last Summer*
Dyan Cannon as 'Alice Henderson' in *Bob & Carol & Ted & Alice*
• Goldie Hawn as 'Toni Simmons' in *Cactus Flower*
Sylvia Miles as 'Cass' in *Midnight Cowboy*
Susannah York as 'Alice LeBlanc' in *They Shoot Horses, Don't They?*

GOLDEN GLOBE AWARDS
• Goldie Hawn – *Cactus Flower*
Marianne McAndrew – *Hello, Dolly!*
Siân Phillips – *Goodbye, Mr Chips*
Brenda Vaccaro – *Midnight Cowboy*
Susannah York – *They Shoot Horses, Don't They?*

BRITISH ACADEMY AWARDS
Peggy Ashcroft – *Three Into Two Won't Go*
Pamela Franklin – *The Prime of Miss Jean Brodie*
• Celia Johnson – *The Prime of Miss Jean Brodie*

NEW YORK – Dyan Cannon – *Bob & Carol & Ted & Alice*
BOARD OF REVIEW – Pamela Franklin – *The Prime of Miss Jean Brodie*
NATIONAL SOCIETY – Siân Phillips – *Goodbye, Mr Chips* and **Delphine Seyrig – *Baisers Volés (Stolen Kisses)***

Siân Phillips won the National Society of Film Critics Best Supporting Actress award for her performance as the friend of the schoolteacher's wife in the musical remake of *Goodbye, Mr Chips*, in which the title character was played by her then husband, Peter O'Toole (NYT "never quite fits"; V "steals every scene she's in"). Even though Phillips subsequently received a Golden Globe nomination, the Academy overlooked her.

Sharing the NSFC prize with Phillips, and also overlooked for Oscar recognition, was Delphine Seyrig in François Truffaut's *Baisers Volés (Stolen Kisses)* (LAT "marvelously, maturely sexy").

Oscar voters also by-passed the winner of the National Board of Review award, Pamela Franklin, who played one of the students in *The Prime of Miss Jean Brodie* (NYT "excellent"; LAT "remarkable"; S&S "more than holds [her] own" opposite Maggie Smith). Franklin was nominated for the BAFTA but lost the accolade to her co-star Celia Johnson for her performance as the headmistress

(NYT "superb"; LAT "the revelation in the supporting roles is undoubtedly Celia Johnson"; V "comes off magnificently in a performance likely to be remembered"). A previous Best Actress Oscar nominee, Johnson was also passed over for the Academy Award.

Also absent from the Academy's list of nominees were: both BAFTA Best Actress nominee Mary Wimbush (V "moving") and Maggie Smith (NYT "stunning", "superb"; CT "her song, in which she is transformed from a chorine into war's harlot, should also win her an Academy Award nomination") in *Oh! What a Lovely War*; BAFTA nominee Peggy Ashcroft as the wife's mother in *Three Into Two Won't Go* (NYT "[a] nice supplementary performance"; LAT "gives an enormously moving characterization"; WP "the star of the show"; V "expertly essayed"); Patricia Quinn in *Alice's Restaurant* (NYT "marvelous", "beautifully played"; LAT "outstanding"); Judy Thomas in *The Wedding Party* (NYT "with her shy, nasal whine, a girl named Judy Thomas all but steals it"); Nan Martin in *Goodbye, Columbus* (NYT "very nice"; LAT "I particularly admired Nan Martin as the girl's mother"); and Karen Black in *Easy Rider* (LAT "desperately fine").

The Oscar candidates were all first-time nominees: Cathy Burns as an awkward adolescent cruelly victimised by her peers in *Last Summer* (NYT "vivid", "[her] one long monologue is too good, and it is so calculated that it stops the movie cold"; LAT "astonishingly talented … [her] long soliloquy is at first unbearably moving, but it goes on and on and becomes a performance we applaud for craft, not conviction"; V "touching"; FQ "superb"); Dyan Cannon in *Bob & Carol & Ted & Alice* (NYT "decently performed … delivers one of the film's really genuine moments"; LAT "remarkable"; CT "that [Cannon] is able to make us care about what happens to her [character] is a special achievement"; WP "an incredible embodiment of the 'square' virtues and vices"; V "superb … proves to be an expert comedienne"; S&S "excellent"); Goldie Hawn as the young mistress of a dentist in *Cactus Flower* (NYT "beautifully holding her own with the two veteran stars but also enhancing the content and flavour of the movie"; LAT "the pleasantest discovery … does marvelous vocal somersaults, all of which could get out of hand into ham awfully fast"; WP "charming and original"; V "a credible screen debut"; TT "really fresh and appealing"; S&S "nicely acted"; MFB "wholly enchanting"); Sylvia Miles as a middle-aged woman who picks up a cowboy hustler outside her posh New York apartment in *Midnight Cowboy* (NYT "especially good"; LAT "impressive"); and Susannah York as a contestant in a 1930s marathon dance who suffers a breakdown in *They Shoot Horses, Don't They?* (NYT "fine"; LAT "[an] excellent, flamboyantly theatrical performance"; V "powerful, moving"; FQ her "often brilliant performance is particularly astonishing").

1969

The favourite for the Oscar was Cannon, who had won the inaugural New York Film Critic's Circle Best Supporting Actress prize ahead of Burns and who had been a nominee at the Golden Globes in the Best Actress (Comedy/Musical) category. The darkhorse, meanwhile, was thought to be Miles.

At the Academy Awards ceremony, however, Golden Globe winner Hawn took home the golden statuette in a result which The New York Times described the following day as "a surprise". Hawn was best known for her stint as a regular on the television comedy series 'Laugh-In'. A year later, Hawn was one of the unsuccessful nominees for the Best Actress BAFTA for her performance. The British Academy Award for Best Supporting Actress that year was won by York for her performance in *They Shoot Horses, Don't They?*.

In 1980, Hawn earned a Best Actress nomination for *Private Benjamin.* In 2000, her daughter, Kate Hudson, was nominated for the Best Supporting Actress statuette for *Almost Famous*.

1969

BEST SUPPORTING ACTOR

ACADEMY AWARDS
Rupert Crosse as 'Ned McCaslin' in *The Reivers*
Elliott Gould as 'Ted Henderson' in *Bob & Carol & Ted & Alice*
Jack Nicholson as 'George Hanson' in *Easy Rider*
Anthony Quayle as 'Cardinal Wolsey' in *Anne of the Thousand Days*
• Gig Young as 'Rocky' in *They Shoot Horses, Don't They?*

GOLDEN GLOBE AWARDS
Red Buttons – *They Shoot Horses, Don't They?*
Jack Nicholson – *Easy Rider*
Anthony Quayle – *Anne of the Thousand Days*
Mitch Vogel – *The Reivers*
• Gig Young – *They Shoot Horses, Don't They?*

BRITISH ACADEMY AWARDS
Jack Klugman – *Goodbye, Columbus*
Jack Nicholson – *Easy Rider*
• Laurence Olivier – *Oh! What a Lovely War*
Robert Vaughn – *Bullitt*

NEW YORK – Jack Nicholson – *Easy Rider*
BOARD OF REVIEW – Philippe Noiret – *Topaz*
NATIONAL SOCIETY – Jack Nicholson – *Easy Rider*

The film sensation of the year was Jack Nicholson as the alcoholic lawyer who befriends the hippie heroes in *Easy Rider*, a part he got only at the last minute as a replacement for Rip Torn (NYT "Nicholson is so good that Easy Rider never recovers from his loss"; LAT "Nicholson's performance, creating a man who reeks of bourbon and failure but who is also richly funny and endlessly sympathetic, is one of the consummate pieces of screen acting … will haunt all of us who have seen the picture"; V "excellent"; S&S "brilliantly witty performance"; FQ "superbly played"; MFB "brilliantly and endearingly played"). The thirty-two-year old became a star overnight and won the inaugural New York Film Critics Circle Best Supporting Actor award as well as the National Society of Film Critics honour. Nicholson was nominated for the Globe, the BAFTA and the Oscar (each for the first time), but was outpolled for all three prizes.

1969

The winner of the Globe and the Oscar was Gig Young, for his portrayal of the emcee of the dance marathon in *They Shoot Horses, Don't They?* (NYT "fine"; LAT "[an] excellent, flamboyantly theatrical performance"; FQ "performance has depth and control"; MFB "superb"). Nominated for the Academy Award twice before in the 1950s, the fifty-six-year old had been the favourite for the Oscar in the lead up to the ceremony. As Life magazine commented, "if he doesn't get an Academy Award for his portrayal of human devastation, there is no justice."

Also nominated for the Oscar were: New York prize runner-up Elliott Gould as a lawyer involved in partner-swapping in the sex comedy *Bob & Carol & Ted & Alice* (NYT "decently performed … very funny"; LAT "creates and sustains a marvelously funny character, larger than life but never unlifelike"; CT "outstanding"; WP "an incredible embodiment of the 'square' virtues and vices"; S&S "excellent"); Anthony Quayle in *Anne of the Thousand Days* (LAT "admirably fleshed out"); and Rupert Crosse in the family comedy *The Reivers* (LAT "a fine discovery"; WP "[the] campaign under way to secure an Oscar nomination for Rupert Crosse [is] an excellent idea"). Crosse was only the second African-American man nominated for an Oscar in the acting categories, and the first named for the supporting prize. Gould, meanwhile, was the subject of some media attention during the season following his recent separation from his wife, the previous year's Best Actress winner, Barbra Streisand.

The most surprising omission from the Oscar list was Henry Fonda as the ruthless gunfighter in *Once Upon a Time in the West* (LAT "in fine fettle"; CT "excellent").

Also overlooked were: National Board of Review winner Philippe Noiret in *Topaz* (LAT "[a] thoroughly satisfying performance"; MFB "beautifully observed"); Jacques Perrin as the reporter in *Z* (NYT "excellent"); John Colicos as Cromwell in *Anne of the Thousand Days* (V "gripping"; MFB "reveals a striking screen personality"); child actor Mitch Vogel in *The Reivers* (NYT "played with relaxed stoicism"; LAT "good"); Mark Dignam as Polonius in *Hamlet* (NYT "very fine"); Jack Klugman in *Goodbye, Columbus* (NYT "very nice"; V "rates a big hand"); James Broderick in *Alice's Restaurant* (NYT "marvelous", "beautifully played"; LAT "outstanding"); Michael Lonsdale in *Baisers Volés (Stolen Kisses)* (NYT "pricelessly funny"); and Noel Coward for his final screen performance as the imprisoned crime boss in *The Italian Job* (LAT "in good form"; WP "the role seems to have been invented just to give Noel Coward something to do"; Obs "an inexplicable performance"). Robert Stephens, the husband of Best Actress Oscar winner Maggie Smith, was also passed over in *The Prime of Miss Jean Brodie*, the film for which Smith collected a golden statuette on Oscar night (LAT "marvelous').

1970

BEST PICTURE

ACADEMY AWARDS

Airport
(Hunter, Universal, 137 mins, 5 Mar 1970, $45.2m, 10 noms)
Five Easy Pieces
(BBS, Columbia, 96 mins, 12 Sep 1970, 4 noms)
Love Story
(Paramount, 99 mins, 16 Dec 1970, $48.7m / gr:$106.4, 7 noms)
*M*A*S*H*
(Aspen, Twentieth Century-Fox, 116 mins, 25 Jan 1970, $36.7m / gr:$73.2m, 5 noms)
• *Patton*
(Twentieth Century-Fox, 170 mins, 25 Jan 1970, $28.1m, 10 noms)

GOLDEN GLOBE AWARDS

(Drama)
Airport
Five Easy Pieces
I Never Sang for My Father
• *Love Story*
Patton

(Comedy/Musical)
Darling Lili
Diary of a Mad Housewife
Lovers and Other Strangers
• *M*A*S*H*
Scrooge

BRITISH ACADEMY AWARDS

• *Butch Cassidy and the Sundance Kid*
Kes
*M*A*S*H*
Ryan's Daughter

NEW YORK – *Five Easy Pieces*
BOARD OF REVIEW – *Patton*
NATIONAL SOCIETY – *M*A*S*H*

Box office success had an enormous impact on the Best Picture category at the Academy Awards. The year's top three commercial hits were all nominated for the Oscar. Also included was another hugely popular film that had been released late in the year and would subsequently finish as the box office champion of 1971. The only candidate in the field not to have been a smash hit with the public had entered into contention courtesy of the New York Film Critics Circle prize.

The year's dominant box office release was *Airport*, a disaster drama about the various incidents that occur at a major airport on a winter's night and their impact on the people involved. Directed by George Seaton, the film boasted an all-star cast headed by Burt Lancaster and including Dean Martin, George Kennedy, Helen Hayes, Jean Seberg, Jacqueline Bisset, Van Heflin and Maureen Stapleton. The film attained huge commercial success and a slew of Oscar nomination (ten in total, including Best Picture) despite some savage reviews. The New York Times critic Vincent Canby described it as "an immensely silly film" with "underdeveloped plot complications" and "some really idiotic dialogue," but acknowledged that "it will probably entertain millions of people." At the end of the year, the newspaper listed *Airport* as one of the year's ten worst films. Other critics were equally harsh (LAT "half the audience will wonder why they don't make movies like 'Airport' anymore and the other half will understand why … keeps its characters cardboard-simple … takes a lot of disbelieving … [but] the hokum is outrageous enough to be good fun"; CT "it's a long and tortuous road to the applause [with] dialogue that ranks among the silliest in memory and a labored plot that tells you everything twice … a horrendous success"; WP "a lousy movie … derivative … everything is utterly predictable"; MFB "corny is really the only word for this unbelievably old-fashioned look at the modern phenomenon of an international airport").

The year's second biggest hit was Robert Altman's *M*A*S*H*, an irreverent black comedy centred on the lives of people stationed at an army hospital during the Korean War. Unlike *Airport*, the popularity of *M*A*S*H* followed a strong response from critics. At the Cannes Film Festival, Altman's comedy had become the third American film to win the Palme d'Or (the last had been William Wyler's *Friendly Persuasion* in 1957). Upon its release in the United States, The New York Times called it "fascinating", "impudent, bold, and often very funny." At the end of the year, the newspaper labelled it as "the one unequivocably funny film of the year" and included it on its list of the year's ten best films – the only one of the five Best Picture Oscar nominees to be cited. There was similar praise from other sources (LAT "a rough, unique and stunning work"; CT "a disturbing, yet bright, black comedy … a collection of riotous and bittersweet episodes"; V "frequently funny"; MFB "wildly, irreverently, scabrously, blasphemously funny"). The Academy nominated *M*A*S*H* for five Oscars, including Best Picture and Best Director.

A very different war film finished the year in third place at the box office: *Patton*, a three-hour long biopic of General George S. Patton, one of the great US military leaders in the Second World War. Initial concerns about the appeal of the film in an atmosphere of growing anti-establishment sentiment, driven by America's involvement in the war in Vietnam, were quickly dispelled as audiences responded to the film's anti-war message and embraced George C. Scott's acclaimed portrayal of the radical war hero. Critics were also enthusiastic (NYT "both fascinating and appalling"; LAT "a remarkable and complex movie … we could hardly ask for a rounder or deeper understanding of an extraordinarily complicated and contradictory human being … engrossing – a most unconventional war movie"; CT "a step forward in film biography but repetitive"; V "one hell of a war picture, perhaps one of the most remarkable of its type ever made"; TT "a chilling demonstration of the brutality of war"). *Patton* equalled the ten nominations received by *Airport*, including nods for Best Picture and Best Director.

The most unexpected commercial hit, however, was *Love Story*, a romantic tragedy which opened in mid-December and quickly dominated the box office during the Oscar voting period. Critics were divided over the film (NYT "beautiful and romantic"; LAT "will be an enormous success … revives a glorious Hollywood tradition: the movie whose concluding minutes are observed amidst a swelling chorus of sniffles"; CT "a return to tearful melodrama … disappointed with the depth of character portrayal … and love by fiat doesn't work well in film"; WP "once one has conceded 'Love Story' its popularity and profits, there isn't much left … sentimental … there is scarcely a character or situation or line in the story that rings true or emotion honestly experienced and expressed"; V "excellent"; S&S "schmaltz"; MFB "absurd"). Oscar voters nonetheless mentioned it in seven categories, including Best Picture.

The remaining Best Picture Oscar nominee was *Five Easy Pieces*, a small character study starring Jack Nicholson as a man who returns to his family after an absence of several years (NYT "I'm not sure how 'Five Easy Pieces' will seem in retrospect – perhaps not all that good … a film that takes small risks and provides small returns"; LAT "[a] flawless piece of contemporary American portraiture"; WP "a clever and absorbing picture"; V "absorbing ... one of the top-quality entries of the year"; TT "excellent"; S&S "fascinating"; MFB "impressive"). Ironically, while *Five Easy Pieces* did not feature on the annual New York Times list of the year's ten best movies, the film's Oscar chances were initiated by its selection as the Best Picture of the year by the New York Film Critics' Circle. Since the east coast circle had begun handing out prizes in 1935, every Best Picture winner had gone on to receive a nomination for the Academy's top prize. *Five Easy Pieces* received four Oscar nominations, including Best Picture.

The Academy, however, were not the only group to embrace these commercial successes. *M*A*S*H* followed its win in Cannes with a Best Picture accolade from the National Society of Film Critics and a third placing in the voting by the New York critics. *Patton*, meanwhile, was the Best Picture choice of the National Board of Review. Furthermore, the Academy's short-list replicated the list of Golden Globe (Drama) nominees with one of the candidates dropped in favour of the Globe (Comedy/Musical) winner. The Hollywood Foreign Press Association had chosen to honour *Love Story* (which won a record-equalling five Globes) and *M*A*S*H* with the Best Picture accolades.

1970

The only Globe (Drama) nominee not considered for the Oscar was *I Never Sang for My Father*, a family drama which The New York Times had included, alongside *Airport*, as one of the year's ten worst releases (V "lacking a clear point of view").

In choosing such popular fare as *Airport* and *Love Story*, the HFPA and the Academy both overlooked: *Women in Love*, which had been a BAFTA nominee the previous year (NYT "intelligent [and] intensely romantic … about as sensuous as anything you've probably ever seen in a film"; LAT "an outstanding film … extremely impressive and moving"; CT "an important poetical expression of film art"); Ingmar Bergman's *En Passion (The Passion of Anna)*, which was the New York runner-up (NYT "superior", "beautiful"; LAT "[an] enthralling and finally overwhelming work of genius … great art"; V "deceptively deep drama"); Federico Fellini's *Satyricon* (NYT "[a] triumph … magnificently realised", "unforgettable" but "not an easy or pleasant movie"; LAT "a major work by one of the few true masters the film form has yet had"; WP "an artistic chore … tedious, grotesque"; S&S "should be impossible, utterly indigestible, but paradoxically it is not … magnificent"); the race-relations satire *The Landlord* (NYT "a wondrously wise, sad and hilarious comedy … with some of the sharpest, funniest dialogue in a long time"; LAT "often a scathingly funny movie … very good and moving"; WP "easily the funniest and most entertaining new film of the summer"); *Scrooge* (LAT "a spirit-raising, soul-satisfying, memory-warming delight … one of the best pieces of news for the family since the invention of toys"; V "a most delightful film in every way"; S&S "cheerless"); *Ma Nuit chez Maud (My Night at Maud's)* (LAT "the most blissfully retrograde movie in years", "demanding [yet] fascinating"; CT "one of the year's finest films … sets a standard for quietly intelligent dialog"); *Tristana* (NYT "a marveously complex, funny and vigorously moral movie"; LAT "a cool, controlled but powerful study"; S&S "brilliant"; SMH "melodramatic … easy viewing"); and *L'Enfant Sauvage (The Wild Child)* (NYT "a lovely, pure film … it may be a classic"; LAT "extraordinary and absorbing"; CT "I frequently was fascinated by its spareness"; WP "rare and profoundly gratifying experience, an emotionally honest and heartening heartbreaker").

Also by-passed by the Academy were several highly-anticipated films that met with mixed or poor critical reactions such as: David Lean's *Ryan's Daughter* (NYT "boring … the art it represents belongs to that school of very classy calendar art supported by airlines, insurance corporations and a few enlightened barber shops. It doesn't transfigure the world. It embalms it."; LAT "there is so much to be impressed by, including the scenery, that it is a hard disappointment to find so little to be moved by and so much to be bored by"; CT "poor casting, heavy-handed direction that becomes comical during the big love scene and empty-headed characters make David Lean's 'Ryan's Daughter' an epic disappointment"; V "a brilliant enigma ... [its] overlength seems to magnify some weaknesses"; TT a "spectacular disappointment" … "without heart or brains" that is "too bad even to be funny"); Mike Nichols' *Catch-22* (NYT "the best American film I've seen this year … as close to being an epic human comedy as Hollywood as ever made"; LAT "awfully good, and also a disappointment: chilly brilliant at its best but flawed at last by its detachment"; WP "ambitious [but] over-calculated [and] leaves me cold"; V "extreme disappointment"; TT "intermittently splendid ... [but the] marvellous parts do not add up to a marvellous whole"); *Darling Lili*, starring Julie Andrews (NYT "a pure if not perfect comedy … it is big, long, overproduced, but it has a lot of perverse charm and real cinematic beauty"; LAT "painful to see so painstaking and fantastically costly an enterprise mounted on so flimsy and indeed questionable a story premise, and executed with so little certainty as to whether the tone of the piece was to be pure romance, broad farce, suspense, melodrama or musical comedy … turns out to be a little of each and not enough of any"; CT "a waste of talent and money"; WP "too big and fancy to be enjoyable in a lighthearted, inconsequential way and too trifling to justify a running time of 136 minutes and all the costly, extravagant window dressing … too much décor in the place of sufficient story and personality"; TT "disappointing", "[a] misfire"; MFB "self-consciously inflated"); the Western comedy *Little Big Man*, starring Dustin Hoffman (NYT "tries to cover too much ground [and] often it is not terribly funny … both in spite of and because of these failings – is an important movie"; LAT "a densely packed, episodic, daring, uneven but unrepentant gallop through the winning of the West … great hunks of the movie could be hacked away without weakening the surging narrative thrust"; CT "an example of what an epic film should be … enchanting"; WP "a great opportunity that, unfortunately, hasn't been transformed into a great movie"; V "rambling"); and the comedy *The Out-of-Towners* (NYT "fails so insistently that it sees a conscious exercise in dulled insights and missed opportunities … may rank as technically the sloppiest as well as the most witlessly uncomfortable movie for some time"; LAT "probably the unfunniest Neil Simon work yet on the screen … a one-joke script and it is not entirely clear on whom the joke is"; CT "predictable [with] ludicrous dialogue"; MFB "the film is flawed by its shapelessness … manages to be hilarious and a little tedious at the same time").

On Oscar night, the Academy honoured *Patton* with the Best Picture statuette. By the end of the year, however, *Love Story* had become the third most commercially successful film ever released, while over the course of the rest of the decade three sequels to *Airport* were released and *M*A*S*H* inspired one of the longest-running and most acclaimed television series in history.

1970

BEST DIRECTOR

ACADEMY AWARDS
Robert Altman for *M*A*S*H*
Federico Fellini for *Satyricon*
Arthur Hiller for *Love Story*
Ken Russell for *Women in Love*
• Franklin J. Schaffner for *Patton*

GOLDEN GLOBE AWARDS
Robert Altman – *M*A*S*H*
• Arthur Hiller – *Love Story*
Bob Rafelson – *Five Easy Pieces*
Ken Russell – *Women in Love*
Franklin J. Schaffner – *Patton*

DIRECTORS GUILD AWARD
Robert Altman – *M*A*S*H*
Arthur Hiller – *Love Story*
David Lean – *Ryan's Daughter*
Bob Rafelson – *Five Easy Pieces*
• Franklin J. Schaffner – *Patton*

BRITISH ACADEMY AWARDS
Robert Altman – *M*A*S*H*
• George Roy Hill – *Butch Cassidy and the Sundance Kid*
David Lean – *Ryan's Daughter*
Ken Loach – *Kes*

NEW YORK – Bob Rafelson – *Five Easy Pieces*
BOARD OF REVIEW – François Truffaut – *L'Enfant Sauvage (The Wild Child)*
NATIONAL SOCIETY – Ingmar Bergman – *En Passion (The Passion of Anna)*

The National Society of Film Critics named Ingmar Bergman as Best Director for *En Passion (The Passion of Anna)* (LAT "work of genius … Bergman stays in complete control of his material"; S&S "it's blatant artifice, but the effect is brilliantly naturalistic"). It was the third time in four years that the group had honoured him. The National Board of Review, meanwhile, gave its Best Director prize to François Truffaut for *L'Enfant Sauvage (The Wild Child)* (LAT "cool, precise, almost documentary-like"; CT "an exercise in cinematic discipline … masterfully directed"; WP "Truffaut's direction is remarkably observant and straightforward and tactful"). Neither director, however, was considered for the Directors Guild of America award, the Golden Globe or the Oscar.

1970

Also overlooked for all the major US and UK prizes were: Luis Buñuel for *Tristana* (NYT "quintessential Buñuel"; WP "masterfully nonchalant"; SMH "in no way reminiscent of the many sided questionings and innovative form of earlier Buñuel work"); Erich Rohmer for *Ma Nuit chez Maud (My Night at Maud's)* (LAT "faultless direction"); Hal Ashby for *The Landlord* (LAT "Ashby, with his free-wheeling crispness of style and superbly theatrical disciplining of rich color, is a man of extraordinary acuity"); and Ronald Neame for *Scrooge* (NYT "has directed the movie with all of the delicacy possible after a small story has been turned into a comparatively large, conventional musical").

Despite a savage response from critics for his highly-anticipated *Ryan's Daughter*, previous winner David Lean received nominations from the DGA and the British Academy (CT "heavy-handed direction that becomes comical during the big love scene"). He did not, however, make the Oscar short-list.

In New York, the winner was Bob Rafelson, one of the new wave of young American directors whose style was greatly influenced by recent European cinema. He won for his second feature, the character study *Five Easy Pieces* (LAT "extraordinarily skillful"; V "well-directed"). Rafelson was nominated for both the DGA prize and the Globe, but was a shock omission from the list of Oscar nominees. He was the second New York Film Critics Circle Best Director prizewinner in three years to be snubbed by the Academy.

Short-listed by the Academy instead were: Robert Altman for *M*A*S*H* (LAT "sustains a breathtaking pace and an improvisational and documentary feeling … [the film] seems to have a life of its own … remarkable"); New York runner-up Federico Fellini for *Satyricon* (NYT "the quintessential Fellini film, a magical mystery tour"; LAT "a tour de force"; WP "[he is] stereotyping his direction"); Globe winner Arthur Hiller for *Love Story* (NYT "has framed what is essentially a two-character story of undergraduate love with such seeming simplicity that nothing confuses the basic situation"; LAT "has achieved an enveloping atmosphere of warmth and affection"; WP "now clumsy, now obvious"); Ken Russell for *Women in Love* (NYT "sometimes gets carried away with his lyric camera, but he shoots, for the most part, directly, letting the scenes play themselves without editorial comment by the camera"; CT "creates an extraordinary visual melody"; WP "[his] style is flamboyant and picturesque [but] glossy, overemphatic [and] dramatically incoherent"); and DGA winner Franklin J. Schaffner for *Patton* (NYT "superior"; LAT "Schaffner's considerable skill with actors makes even the vignettes of the mighty seem something more than excerpts from son-et-lumiere tableau"; WP "a great scenic tour de force … Schaffner's talent for panoramic composition is sweeping and beautiful"; V "excellent"; MFB "Schaffner's achievement is considerable").

On Oscar night, Schaffner became the twenty-first DGA winner in more then two decades to receive the Best Director statuette.

1970

BEST ACTRESS

ACADEMY AWARDS
Jane Alexander as 'Eleanor Bachman' in *The Great White Hope*
• Glenda Jackson as 'Gudrun Brangwen' in *Women in Love*
Ali MacGraw as 'Jenny Cavilleri' in *Love Story*
Sarah Miles as 'Rosy Ryan' in *Ryan's Daughter*
Carrie Snodgress as 'Tina Balser' in *Diary of a Mad Housewife*

GOLDEN GLOBE AWARDS
(Drama)
Faye Dunaway – *Puzzle of a Downfall Child*
Glenda Jackson – *Women in Love*
• Ali MacGraw – *Love Story*
Melina Mercouri – *A Promise at Dawn*
Sarah Miles – *Ryan's Daughter*

(Comedy/Musical)
Julie Andrews – *Darling Lili*
Sandy Dennis – *The Out-of-Towners*
Angela Lansbury – *Something for Everyone*
• Carrie Snodgress – *Diary of a Mad Housewife*
Barbra Streisand – *The Owl and the Pussycat*

BRITISH ACADEMY AWARDS
Jane Fonda – *They Shoot Horses, Don't They?*
Goldie Hawn – *Cactus Flower* and *There's a Girl in My Soup*
Sarah Miles – *Ryan's Daughter*
• Katharine Ross – *Butch Cassidy and the Sundance Kid* and *Tell Them Willie Boy is Here*

NEW YORK – Glenda Jackson – *Women in Love*
BOARD OF REVIEW – Glenda Jackson – *Women in Love*
NATIONAL SOCIETY – Glenda Jackson – *Women in Love*

For the first time since 1932/33, all the candidates for the Best Actress Oscar were first-time nominees.

Jane Alexander and Carrie Snodgress were mentioned for their film debuts as, respectively, the white lover of a black boxing champion in *The Great White Hope*, a role she had originated on Broadway (NYT "an initially charming performance by Jane Alexander who is eventually defeated by the hysterics of the script"; LAT "has her moments"; V "good"; FQ "through her performance there are only flickers of warmth and sensitivity"; MFB "a fine essay in sustained understatement"; SMH "the finest of performances") and as the wife in *Diary of a Mad Housewife* (NYT "will surely receive the critical praise she deeply deserves", "played with enormously fetching awkwardness", "takes top honors"; CT "a major new film talent … very much in control"; S&S "subtle").

Also nominated were two English actresses who were among the brightest stars of the new wave of British cinema: Glenda Jackson as a sexually liberated artist in *Women in Love*, a performance for which she had been a BAFTA nominee the previous year (NYT "stand out", "vivid"; LAT "very high quality"; CT "sensational … unusually rich"), and Sarah Miles as the adulterous, young Irish wife of a schoolteacher in *Ryan's Daughter* (LAT "Miles' performance is awfully good, quiet, sensitive and strong"; CT "only two characters have any substance and the credit for the performances goes to the actors. Both Mills and Miles have unusual control of their bodies").

Propelled by the huge box office success of her film, the final nominee was former fashion model Ali MacGraw. The wife of Paramount Vice-President Robert Evans, MacGraw was mentioned for her second film performance as the dying music student in *Love Story* (NYT "lovely"; LAT "simply extraordinarily fine … a lovely portrayal, not likely to be soon forgotten"; CT "does not fulfil the promise of her debut in 'Goodbye, Columbus'"; WP "a performance that only makes sense if one decides that it's satirical … MacGraw wears a permanently smug expression and fails to temper the vain, emotionally bullying tone of the dialogue … the performance is so heavy and wrong-headed that the emotional balance of the material turns upside-down"; V "standout").

The three major critics' groups all gave their Best Actress prizes to Jackson, who became the early favourite for the Academy Award. At the Golden Globes, however, she was surprisingly outpolled by MacGraw, whose film had opened only days before the critics had cast their ballots. With *Love Story* dominating the North American box office, the charismatic MacGraw became a media sensation. Observers began to speculate whether the tide of popularity would carry the young American to a victory on Oscar night as well.

The other surprise at the Globes was the victory of unknown newcomer Snodgress over four stars, among them three previous Oscar winners: Julie Andrews as a German spy in *Darling Lili* (NYT "perfect", "immensely funny"; LAT "has never looked better, warmer or more emotionally mature, nor has she sounded better … [but] she projects a richness which is wasted here"; CT "the film's few bright moments belong to Miss Andrews … a complete entertainer, and tho she is center stage for nearly the entire film, one never tires of her pure voice and intelligent acting"; V "Andrews' best moments are her singing sequences"; TT "shows a well-developed comic sense"); Sandy Dennis as the wife in *The Out-of-Towners* (NYT "Dennis exercises, or has had imposed upon her, exceptional self-effacing restraint"; LAT "plays the wife with a lovely and unmannered calm … it is one of her best performances"; V "superb"; MFB "unusually restrained"); Angela Lansbury in *Something for Everyone* (NYT "Lansbury, instead of reading her lines, is inclined to belt them"; LAT "reminding us again what a dazzling performer she is in even the most difficult of circumstances … she's someone for everyone, and that's something"; CT "marvelous", "outstanding"; WP "funny and invigorating"); and Barbra Streisand in *The Owl and the Pussycat* (NYT "[her] performance is mostly cold and edgy and aggressive and loud"; LAT "Streisand gets right inside Doris but ends up bursting through the confines of the character … she's terrific [but] impossible to believe"; CT "too shrill"; WP "astonishing in a non-singing role").

In addition to all the unsuccessful Globe (Comedy/Musical) nominees, the Academy overlooked: both Bibi Andersson and Liv Ullmann (second runner-up for the New York critics' prize) for *En Passion (The Passion of Anna)* (NYT both "superb", "perfectly performed"; V "exemplary"); Globe nominee Faye Dunaway as an unhappy fashion model, in *Puzzle of a Downfall Child* (NYT "creates a character of such lovely, tentative lucidity that to be with her is worth a whole movie"; LAT "creates a striking portrait"; MFB "the frailty of the central character comes through in Faye Dunaway's edgy, tentative style"; CT "handles many of the longer scenes with great skill"); Globe nominee Melina Mercouri as the mother in *A Promise at Dawn* (NYT "less than magnificent and far from brilliant, she is nevertheless perpetually active and endlessly expressive"; MFB "dominates, nay overpowers the film, giving an operatic performance"); Eva Marie Saint in *Loving* (NYT "wonderful"; LAT "[a] detailed and moving performance"); and Catherine Deneuve in *Tristana* (NYT "never before has her beauty seemed more precise and enigmatic").

On Oscar night, MacGraw became the twelfth consecutive Globe (Drama) winner to be nominated for the Oscar only to go home empty-handed. Instead, the statuette went to Jackson who was not in attendance at the Dorothy Chandler Pavilion on Oscar night and learned of her victory in a phone call from Bette Davis. "I hadn't expected the best actress award would go to a British actress this year, since Maggie Smith won it last year," she confessed at a press conference, "But I couldn't help hoping just a little. I was honestly surprised to find how pleased I was to have won. I didn't think I would feel such a thrill." Although happy to have won, Jackson admitted she would give the Oscar to her mother. "I've never been much a person for memorabilia. I don't keep playbills or photographs. Anyway, she is better at dusting than I am."

At the BAFTAs in London, Miles was favoured to win for *Ryan's Daughter*, but the award went to Katharine Ross, whose performance in *Butch Cassidy and the Sundance Kid* had not even earned a nomination from the Academy in Hollywood the previous year.

1970

BEST ACTOR

ACADEMY AWARDS
Melvyn Douglas as 'Tom Garrison' in *I Never Sang for My Father*
James Earl Jones as 'Jack Jefferson' in *The Great White Hope*
Jack Nicholson as 'Robert Eroica Dupea' in *Five Easy Pieces*
Ryan O'Neal as 'Oliver Barrett IV' in *Love Story*
• George C. Scott as 'Gen. George S. Patton' in *Patton*

GOLDEN GLOBE AWARDS
(Drama)
Melvyn Douglas
– *I Never Sang for My Father*
James Earl Jones
– *The Great White Hope*
Jack Nicholson – *Five Easy Pieces*
Ryan O'Neal – *Love Story*
• George C. Scott – *Patton*

(Comedy/Musical)
Richard Benjamin
– *Diary of a Mad Housewife*
• Albert Finney – *Scrooge*
Elliot Gould – *M*A*S*H*
Jack Lemmon
– *The Out-of-Towners*
Donald Sutherland – *M*A*S*H*

BRITISH ACADEMY AWARDS
Elliot Gould – *Bob & Carol & Ted & Alice*
Paul Newman – *Butch Cassidy and the Sundance Kid*
• Robert Redford – *Butch Cassidy and the Sundance Kid* and ***The Downhill Racer*** and ***Tell Them Willie Boy is Here***
George C. Scott – *Patton*

NEW YORK – George C. Scott – *Patton*
BOARD OF REVIEW – George C. Scott – *Patton*
NATIONAL SOCIETY – George C. Scott – *Patton*

For the first time, all five Best Actor (Drama) Golden Globe nominees were short-listed for the Oscar. The previous year the Academy had exactly matched the Globe (Drama) nominees for Best Actress for the first time.

Previous Best Supporting Actor Oscar winner, Melvyn Douglas, earned a second nomination from the Academy for his role as the elderly father in *I Never Sang for My Father* (NYT "performs with the kind of professional sufficiency one expects"; LAT "has a terrifying authenticity"; V "superb", "outstanding"; S&S "superb"; FQ "brutal" and yet "poignantly vulnerable"; MFB "the performance of his life"). James Earl Jones became the second African American considered for the Best Actor Oscar for reprising his stage role as a world champion heavyweight boxer in *The Great White Hope* (NYT "the film contains a performance that makes the windy, otherwise empty movie seem inhabited, if not by life, at least by art … Jones is marvellous to watch, combining heroic physical presence, technique and a completely mysterious way of projecting intelligence … commands attention"; LAT "magnificent … Jones is intensely vital, truly larger than life"; CT "magnificent", "outstanding … one of the year's two or three finest acting performances; V "an eye-riveting experience"; S&S "a full-blooded performance"; FQ "a loud, unmodulated, devouring performance"; MFB "outstanding"; SMH "stands out, unforgettably … every muscle tells a story"). Jack Nicholson received his second nod (and first in the lead category) as the man who returns to his family after a long absence in *Five Easy Pieces* (NYT "good"; LAT "a portrayal which is exhilarating to watch … a complex, full-range portrait"; V "a remarkably varied and daring exploration of a complex character, equally convincing in its manic and sober aspects"; TT "complex and subtle"; G "superb"; S&S "splendid, unassuming"; MFB "an impressive and observant performance"; SMH "every minute is a joy … communicated with minimum of effort and maximum of effect"). Ryan O'Neal was something of a surprise inclusion as the young Harvard law student in love with a dying girl in the box office smash *Love Story* (NYT "lovely"; LAT "simply extraordinarily fine … handles the dangerous and difficult scenes of heavy emotion with a restraint which underscores rather than overstates these emotions … a first-rate job and further enlivens this year's Best Actor race"; CT "gives the best performance of his career … tender enough to make the pain he feels seem real"; V "[a] personal triumph"). George C. Scott completed the ballot as the eponymous World War Two US General in *Patton* (NYT "continuously entertaining and, occasionally, very appealing"; LAT "one of the great and unforgettable screen characterizations … what is most impressive about [his performance] is its wholeness, its balance and restraint"; CT "an acting tour de force"; WP "a great acting tour de force … a very sophisticated performance"; V "outstanding"; TT "wonderfully controlled"; MFB "so totally immersed in his part that he almost makes one believe he is the man himself").

Scott had declined his second Oscar nomination in 1961 stating that he was opposed to the idea of comparing actors' performances and making them compete for prizes. Nearly a decade later, his stance had not altered. His outspokenness about the Academy created some confusion as to whether or not he really was the Oscar frontrunner, despite the fact that he had received all three critics' prizes and the Golden Globe. Observers speculated whether the award might not be won by either Douglas or Nicholson, who finished second and third, respectively, in the New York critics' voting. In London, for example, The Times declared its support for Nicholson saying, "if he does not get this year's Oscar the selectors want their heads examined."

1970

On Oscar night, the announcement of the Best Actor category was the most anticipated moment of the evening and there was thunderous applause when Goldie Hawn opened the envelope and exclaimed, "Oh, my God! The winner is George C. Scott!" The statuette was accepted by the producer of *Patton*, Frank McCarthy. Scott became the first person to win a clean sweep of the five major American accolades. He missed out on the BAFTA, however, outpolled by Robert Redford for his performances in three films, all of which had been eligible for Oscar consideration in 1969.

By matching the five Globe (Drama) nominees, the Academy overlooked the five Globe (Comedy/Musical) candidates: winner Albert Finney in *Scrooge* (NYT "marvellously hokey", "the movie belongs to Mr Finney"; LAT "belongs wholly and unforgettably to Albert Finney … catches all the classical cartoon comedy in Scrooge's scowling miserliness and all the jumping joyousness of his conversion to kindliness … gives him something like depth, and makes his progress from hater to lover gradual"; CT "[a] masterful performance … you will be startled by the totality of Finney's transformation … [he] takes full control of the film"; WP "makes his Scrooge a triumph of methodical, applied technique, rather than wit or fancy"; V "remarkable ... a professional high-water mark"); Richard Benjamin in *Diary of a Mad Housewife* (NYT "broad but believable"); Jack Lemmon in *The Out-of-Towners* (NYT "I can't fault Lemmon's performance; I simply can't see the reason for it"; LAT "he has brought off a particular characterization with all the skill anyone could ask for. It is simply, I think, that the characterization wanted better synchronizing with the thrust of the story"; CT "it is precisely those moments when he goes into an unpredictable, free-form, fast burn that he is a delight to watch"; V "superb"; MFB "gives his now familiar characterisation"); and the two stars of *M*A*S*H*, Donald Sutherland (NYT "a very elaborate performance" which "occasionally becomes annoying"; LAT "shows again what a strong and versatile actor he is") and Elliott Gould (NYT "marvelous"; LAT "extends the triumph he made in 'Bob & Carol'"). Gould had also been praised for *Getting Straight* (NYT "brilliant").

Also passed over for consideration were: both Alan Bates (NYT "vivid"; LAT "awfully good"; CT "fine") and Oliver Reed (NYT "fine"; LAT "awfully good") in *Women in Love*; Jason Robards in *The Ballad of Cable Hogue* (NYT "splendid"; LAT "a vivid performance, by all odds the best of his recent screen outings"; CT "[a] flawless performance … able to be both as tough and compassionate as his character"; WP "not quite convincing"; V "excellent"); Dustin Hoffman in *Little Big Man* (NYT "fine"; LAT "creating a character different from any he has done before, in a performance which could have been blindingly vivid and showy – and which now and again is – but which in the crucial quiet moments has an almost self-effacing quietness which is perfect";

CT "very good"; WP "isn't wholly successful … he's temperamentally wrong, a rather too intelligent and reticent actor for this particular archetype"); Alan Arkin in *Catch-22* (NYT "marvelous … funny and heroic"; LAT "self-effacing … a little more bravura would have been nice"); Beau Bridges in *The Landlord* (NYT "appealingly played"; LAT "brings off a difficult task"; WP "I don't think anyone would be quite as good in the central role as Bridges … a graceful, reassuring presence"); George Segal in *Loving* (NYT "I cannot happily imagine the film without him"; LAT "portrayed with pinpoint accuracy ... authentic … [a] detailed and moving performance"); Leonard Frey as the guest of honour in *Boys in the Band* (NYT "excellent without disturbing the ensemble"; LAT "assured … managed to retain a considerable believability"; CT "steals the show … always in control dramatically … his acidic delivery is brilliant"); Tony Lo Bianco in *The Honeymoon Killers* (NYT "Lo Bianco, with slightly too much profile and a characterization that suggests an immensely humanized early Bela Lugosi, is brilliant"; LAT "alternately tragic and comic, tender and sinister"; WP "very well played"); David Bradley in *Kes* (NYT "superb"; V "brilliantly played"; MFB "the children, and especially David Bradley as Billy, live their parts with total belief"); Max von Sydow in *En Passion (The Passion of Anna)* (NYT "splendidly played", "superb"; CT plays "with intensity and vitality"; V "exemplary"); Marcello Mastroianni in *Leo the Last* (NYT "a performance of great, self-effacing intelligence"; LAT "Mastroianni excites considerable sympathy, not as the character so much but as an actor trying to invest an unbelievable character with a kind of grimacing credibility"); and Richard Harris as Cromwell in *Cromwell* (LAT "this has been a year of masterful performances by actors and one of the finest is Richard Harris' as Oliver Cromwell"; V "[a] powerhouse performance"; TT "magnetic"; MFB "Harris is encouraged to play at, and often beyond, the full pitch of his vocal power; within its own terms it is a performance of vitality, but as a serious study of Cromwell is it simply absurd").

The morning after the Oscar ceremony, Scott was filming *The Hospital* at the Metropolitan Hospital in New York. Arriving on location he told reporters he was "frankly surprised to get the award, but I have no feeling about it one way or another." He said he knew nothing about a plan to send the statuette to the George S. Patton Jr. Museum in Fort Knox, Kentucky but said, "it sounds like a good idea." Despite his controversial opinions about the Oscars, the Academy nominated Scott as Best Actor again the following year for his performance in *The Hospital*.

1970

BEST SUPPORTING ACTRESS

ACADEMY AWARDS
Karen Black as 'Rayette Dipesto' in *Five Easy Pieces*
Lee Grant as 'Mrs Enders' in *The Landlord*
• Helen Hayes as 'Ada Quonsett' in *Airport*
Sally Kellerman as 'Maj. "Hot Lips" Houlihan' in *M*A*S*H*
Maureen Stapleton as 'Inez Guerrero' in *Airport*

GOLDEN GLOBE AWARDS
• Karen Black – *Five Easy Pieces*
Tina Chen – *The Hawaiians*
Lee Grant – *The Landlord*
Sally Kellerman – *M*A*S*H*
• Maureen Stapleton – *Airport*

BRITISH ACADEMY AWARDS
Evin Crowley – *Ryan's Daughter*
Estelle Parsons – *Watermelon Man*
Maureen Stapleton – *Airport*
• Susannah York – *They Shoot Horses, Don't They?*

NEW YORK – Karen Black – *Five Easy Pieces*
BOARD OF REVIEW – Karen Black – *Five Easy Pieces*
NATIONAL SOCIETY – Lois Smith – *Five Easy Pieces*

For *Five Easy Pieces*, Karen Black and Lois Smith seemed certain to receive Academy Award nominations. Smith won the National Society of Film Critics prize (NYT "good"; V "a marvelously brave and complex performance"), while in New York, Black finished runner-up for the Best Actress prize before being selected as Best Supporting Actress (NYT "good … [a] sustained characterization"; WP "endearingly played"; TT "beautifully unsentimentalised"; G "superb"). Black also won the National Board of Review award and was co-winner of the Golden Globe.

Sharing the Globe was Maureen Stapleton as the frightened wife in *Airport*, a role which Variety said she "transforms into an Academy Award calibre supporting role" and won praise from other critics (LAT "all-too-real anguish").

The Academy recognised Stapleton, as well as her co-star, Helen Hayes. Thirty-eight years after winning Best Actress, Hayes earned a second nod as an elderly stowaway (NYT "plays the stowaway with such outrageous abandon you believe she must have honestly thought it would be her last performance"; LAT "enchanting scene stealing ham"; V "a memorable character study"). Oscar voters also cited Black, but overlooked Smith in favour of the once blacklisted Lee Grant as the wealthy mother in *The Landlord* (NYT "devastatingly comic"; LAT "the characterization by Miss Grant is delicious"; WP "exceptionally good … the comic sensation of the show"; V "excellent"; S&S "memorable") and Sally Kellerman in *M*A*S*H* (NYT "marvelous"; LAT "nicely amusing").

In addition to Smith, two other glaring omissions from the list of Oscar nominees were Diana Sands and Tina Chen. While Lee Grant was recognised for her work in the same film, Sands was by-passed for her turn as the unfaithful wife in *The Landlord* (NYT "wonderfully honest"). Despite a Golden Globe nomination, meanwhile, Chen was snubbed for her performance as the matriarch in *The Hawaiians* (NYT "she is not remarkable"; LAT "impressive … the role spans a wide stretch of time and Miss Chen moves across it very well"; CT "[a] truly outstanding performance … her growth in character from a scared mouse to a strong but sympathetic grand lady is most remarkable").

Among those also passed over for consideration were: New York Film Critics Circle runner-up Françoise Fabian in *Ma Nuit chez Maud (My Night at Maud's)* (LAT "convincing and captivating"; CT "could hardly be better"); Edith Evans as The Spirit of Christmas Past in *Scrooge*; Diana Rigg as Portia in *Julius Caesar* (NYT "excellent"); Mary Jane Higby as the Albany widow in *The Honeymoon Killers* (NYT deserves "special praise"; LAT "well-played"; WP "well-played"); Glenna Forster-Jones as the African girl in *Leo the Last* (NYT "superb"; LAT "impressive"); Jane Carr in *Something for Everyone* (LAT "marvelously obese and adenoidal as the sex-starved and scheming daughter"; CT "the real scene-grabber"); Stella Stevens in *The Ballad of Cable Hogue* (NYT "it is Stella Stevens, at last in a role good enough for her, who most wonderfully sustains and enlightens the action"; LAT "a very expert comedienne who is able to be both stylish and sympathetic in her richly make-believe role"; CT "surprisingly competent"; WP "wonderfully touching"); Eleanor Bron in *Women in Love* (LAT "excellent"); and both Dorothy Stickney as the wife (NYT "performs with the kind of professional sufficiency one expects"; LAT "excellent"; V "superb", "excellent"; S&S "good") and previous winner Estelle Parsons as the daughter (NYT "left me cheerless"; V "superb", "outstanding") in *I Never Sang for My Father*. Parsons was also overlooked for her Globe nominated performance in *Watermelon Man* (CT "poorly played").

The frontrunners for the statuette were Black and Kellerman. In an upset, however, the sentimental winner was Hayes. She was the first person to win Oscars for acting in both the lead and supporting categories.

1970

BEST SUPPORTING ACTOR

ACADEMY AWARDS
Richard Castellano as 'Frank Vecchio' in *Lovers and Other Strangers*
Dan George as 'Old Lodge Skins' in *Little Big Man*
Gene Hackman as 'Gene Garrison' in *I Never Sang for My Father*
John Marley as 'Phil Cavilleri' in *Love Story*
• John Mills as 'Michael' in *Ryan's Daughter*

GOLDEN GLOBE AWARDS
Dan George – *Little Big Man*
Trevor Howard – *Ryan's Daughter*
George Kennedy – *Airport*
John Marley – *Love Story*
• John Mills – *Ryan's Daughter*

BRITISH ACADEMY AWARDS
Bernard Cribbins – *The Railway Children*
John Mills – *Ryan's Daughter*
• Colin Welland – *Kes*
Gig Young – *They Shoot Horses, Don't They?*

NEW YORK – Dan George – *Little Big Man*
BOARD OF REVIEW – Frank Langella – *Diary of a Mad Housewife* and ***The Twelve Chairs***
NATIONAL SOCIETY – Dan George – *Little Big Man*

Canadian Dan George, the first Native American nominated for an Oscar in the acting categories, was the Oscar favourite for playing the title character's Cheyenne grandfather in *Little Big Man* (CT "the most satisfying part of [the film]"; WP "appealing"; V "outstanding"; S&S "magnificent", "extraordinary"). He had easily won the New York Film Critics Circle prize and also received the National Society of Film Critics award.

The National Board of Review choice, however, was not an Oscar candidate. Academy voters overlooked Frank Langella for both *Diary of a Mad Housewife* (NYT "a beautifully complex charactization … nothing short of brilliant"; LAT "[has] created a fascinating character"; V "excellent") and *The Twelve Chairs* (LAT "miscast here and emerges as neither very evil, animated or funny"; CT "has a thankless role as a quasinarrator and manages to stay out of the way with grace"; WP "doesn't seem to embody what he should").

The other nominees were: Richard Castellano in *Lovers and Other Strangers* (NYT "plays the bridegroom's father with superb, befuddled, heavy-set delicacy and solemn good humor … [he] very nearly steals the film"; CT "Castellano's performance is one of the year's finest"; MFB "manages the transition from comedy to seriousness with skill"); Gene Hackman as the son in *I Never Sang for My Father* (NYT "left me cheerless"; LAT "impressive"; V "superb"; FQ "plays with great sensitivity, but no sentimentality"; MFB "beautiful support"); John Marley as the father of the dying heroine in *Love Story* (LAT "his relatively brief appearances on the screen are apt to move you as few moments you'll see all year"; CT "fine"; V "excellent"); and John Mills as the deformed mute in *Ryan's Daughter* (LAT "you had best set aside one of the Best Supporting Actor nominations for Mills right now … he is brilliantly effective, with an eloquence words could not improve on … superb in one of those roles which submerge the actor himself totally and leave only his craft showing"; CT "compelling"); V "a technical tour de force ... but overdrawn").

Overlooked were: previous Best Actor Oscar winner Alec Guinness as both King Charles I in *Cromwell* (LAT "a superb supporting performance"; V "formidable and unforgettable"; TT "a cunning, cumulative performance"; G "consistently interesting"; MFB "success in conveying both [the king's] sincerity and his obstinate deviousness") and as Jacob Marley in *Scrooge* (CT "a bit of a disappointment"; V "superb"); New York runner-up Paul Mazursky in *Alex in Wonderland* (NYT "beautifully played"; LAT "amusing"); previous winner Karl Malden in *Patton* (LAT "excellent … the part, inevitably, is pretty idealized, but Malden gives it warmth"; CT "superb … deserves special recognition for his role"; WP "bland"; MFB "neatly observed"); Trevor Howard in *Ryan's Daughter* (LAT "in a role which could have gone to bellowing caricature all to easily, makes the rumpled and gravy-stained padre a genuine human being"; V "assured"); Ray Milland in *Love Story* (LAT "a touching and understated performance"; CT "fine"); both Anthony Hopkins (LAT "excellent"; V "excellent") and Ralph Richardson (LAT "excellent"; V "outstanding"; MFB "splendid") in *The Looking Glass War*; both Tom Skerritt (LAT "excellent") and Robert Duvall (LAT "impressive once again") in *M*A*S*H*; Antonio Aguilar as the Mexican general in *The Undefeated* (NYT "excellent"); and Pat Hingle in *Bloody Mama* (NYT "Academy Awards have been given away for far lesser efforts"; V "outstanding").

The upset winner on Oscar night was Mills, who had already been a surprise victor at the Golden Globes. Mills did not repeat his win at the British Academy Awards, however. The BAFTA was won by a contender by-passed for Oscar consideration: Colin Welland as the schoolteacher in *Kes* (NYT "superb", "truly memorable").

1971

BEST PICTURE

ACADEMY AWARDS

A Clockwork Orange
(Hawk Films, Warner Bros., 137 mins, 2 Feb 1972, 4 noms)
Fiddler on the Roof
(Mirisch-Cartier, United Artists, 181 mins, 3 Dec 1971, $38.2m / gr:$50.0m, 8 noms)
• ***The French Connection***
(D'Antoni, Twentieth Century-Fox, 104 mins, 9 Oct 1971, $26.3m, 8 noms)
The Last Picture Show
(BBS, Columbia, BW 118 mins, 5 Oct 1971, 8 noms)
Nicholas and Alexandra
(Horizon, Columbia, 183 mins, 15 Dec 1971, 6 noms)

GOLDEN GLOBE AWARDS

(Drama)
A Clockwork Orange
• ***The French Connection***
The Last Picture Show
Mary, Queen of Scots
Summer of '42

(Comedy/Musical)
The Boy Friend
• ***Fiddler on the Roof***
Kotch
A New Leaf
Plaza Suite

BRITISH ACADEMY AWARDS

Death in Venice
The Go-Between
• ***Sunday, Bloody Sunday***
Taking Off

NEW YORK – ***A Clockwork Orange***
BOARD OF REVIEW – ***Macbeth***
NATIONAL SOCIETY – ***Le Genou de Clair (Claire's Knee)***

The winner of the Palme d'Or at the Cannes Film Festival was the British period drama *The Go-Between*, a prestigious drama which had been entered into competition only after director Joseph Losey arranged for its distribution rights to be purchased by Columbia. "M-G-M thought 'The Go-Between' was a worthless film," he explained to Mel Gussow of The New York Times. "They wanted to dump it. They planned to open it April 7 in Beverly Hills and forget it. They didn't want to show it at the Cannes Film Festival." It was the second British film in three years to win the coveted prize and it was praised at the time of its victory by The Times in London as "a film which in the planning stage nobody seemed to think would work and which yet had come off triumphantly." With a few notable exceptions, critics on both sides of the Atlantic lauded the movie when it was released later in the year (NYT "one of the loveliest, and one of the most perfectly formed, set and acted films we're likely to see this year"; LAT "one of the year's handsomest and most romantic pieces of movie-making"; CT "one of the year's most finely made and satisfying motion pictures"; WP "undeniably an interesting, high-class project, but I think it's also a high-class disappointment"; V "fascinating and charming"; S&S "masterly").

Another acclaimed release debuting at Cannes was *Death in Venice*, Italian director Luchino Visconti's version of Thomas Mann's novella about a gay artist's infatuation with a beautiful adolescent youth (NYT "the movie becomes, eventually, an elegant bore, full of rather lovely things on the periphery"; LAT "handsome, dazzling", "very demanding"; CT "a marvel of the cinematic art"; WP "tortuously slow going, but there are incidental pleasures and points of interest along the way"; V "has a compelling fascination and elegance"; TT "very beautiful"; SMH "has flaws … [but] it is impelling as a fanciful and fantastic study").

Both of these films were nominated as Best Film by the British Academy, alongside *Taking Off*, the first American film by Czech director Milos Forman which had shared the Jury Prize at Cannes (NYT "both touching and extremely funny … not a major movie experience but it is a charming one"; CT "very funny"; WP "a remarkably adroit and pleasurable satiric comedy"; V "very amusing"; MFB "in its best moments [it is] irresistibly funny") and John Schlesinger's *Sunday, Bloody Sunday*, a ground-breaking drama about a bisexual love-triangle involving a gay doctor, written by New Yorker film critic Penelope Gilliatt (NYT "fascinating … so good it will become one of those movies by which others are judged."; LAT "beyond any question the most perfectly executed and profoundly moving film I have seen in a very long time … a stunning work of art"; CT "a very mature movie"; WP "unusually intelligent, absorbing"; TT "remarkable ... scene by scene the film is a continuing triumph of observation"; S&S "a beautifully disciplined work"). The New York Times subsequently included the film as one of the year's ten best while in London it won a clean sweep of the top four BAFTAs: Best Film, Best Director, Best Actor and Best Actress.

Astonishingly, none of these films were seriously considered for the various Best Picture accolades in the United States. In the voting by the New York Film Critics Circle, *Sunday, Bloody Sunday* finished fourth. At the Academy Awards, Schlesinger's drama received nominations for Actor, Actress, Director and Screenplay, but was a glaring omission from the top category. The films that finished ahead of Schlesinger's drama in the top three places in the New York voting were, however, all nominated by the Academy.

1971

The winner in New York, with a total of 31 points, was *A Clockwork Orange*, Stanley Kubrick's extremely controversial vision of a Britain in the near future terrorized by gangs of violent young men (NYT "brilliant, a tour de force of extraordinary images, music, words and feelings ... it dazzles the senses and the mind"; LAT "violent, crude, cold, profoundly gloomy, now and again blackly funny, and as a piece of movie-making, alternately dazzling and curiously static and overlong … brilliant but disappointing … remote [but] genuinely thought-provoking"; V "a brilliant nightmare"; S&S "ingenious, inventive, exuberant"). It was the second X-rated film to be nominated for the Best Picture Oscar in three years.

The New York runner-up, finishing with 24 points was *The Last Picture Show*, Peter Bogdanovich's highly personal drama about the inhabitants of a decaying American town in the 1950s (NYT "the best American film of the year"; LAT "an exceptional and original work"; S&S "brilliantly understated"). It was the first black-and-white film nominated for the Academy's major prize since 1966.

Placed third in New York was *The French Connection*, a police drama with ambitious car chase sequences that were a huge hit with audiences (NYT "a film of almost incredible suspense"; LAT "a slam-bang, suspenseful, plain-spoken, sardonically funny, furiously paced melodrama [which is also] thought-provoking"; WP "an undeniably sensational movie").

The other two films short-listed for consideration by Oscar voters were the musical *Fiddler on the Roof*, which had divided critics but nonetheless became the second biggest commercial success of 1972 (NYT "a well-meant, if literalized, adaptation [and] not a grossly bad movie, but it left me untouched"; NYer "absolutely smashing"; LAT "a superior piece of entertainment … a thrilling and satisfying experience"; CT "a sumptuous entertainment laden with happiness and tears and taste"; WP "a great film … greatly moving, an extraordinarily powerful emotional experience … it should sweep next April's Academy Awards"; V "a powerhouse attraction"; TT "three hours of pure schmaltz") and *Nicholas and Alexandra*, a lavish historical drama about the last Tsar of Russia, directed by the previous year's Best Director Oscar winner, Franklin J. Schaffner (NYT "much less than a great movie"; V "a film of exquisite taste"; LAT "one of those movies which brings history alive with a clarity, a fidelity and an immediacy that make it understandable and unforgettable … a marvelous rarity"; S&S "disappointing").

In addition to the acclaimed BAFTA nominees, the Academy overlooked several other notable releases, including: *McCabe and Mrs Miller*, an unusual Western directed by Robert Altman and starring Warren Beatty and Julie Christie (LAT "powerfully good [but] also self-consciously stylized and artful and coolly clinical"; CT "a brilliant film"; WP "haunting … a glowing, original romantic classic … almost inexpressively moving"); the thriller *Klute*, for which Jane Fonda won the Best Actress statuette (WP "an unusually intelligent and engrossing murder melodrama … an unconventional, complex character study"; G "a first-class psychological tour de force"; S&S "astonishing"; FQ "compelling and alive and exhilarating"); the black comedy *The Hospital* (NYT "very serious, very funny"; LAT "works very well indeed"; CT "confused"; WP "thoroughly enjoyable"); and *The Panic in Needle Park* (NYT "burdened with a sometimes ridiculous screenplay"; LAT "a very nearly perfect piece of movie making … harrowing in its unflinching look at the addict world [but] can be admired as a piece of art"; CT "neither an especially interesting drama nor an effective anti-drug film"; WP "whatever social value [the film] aspired to is effectively canceled by its lack of dramatic interest … feels both interminable and unconvincing"; V "outstanding", "a total triumph", "compelling and vivid").

Among the acclaimed foreign productions snubbed by Oscar voters were: Roman Polanski's *Macbeth*, which had won the top prize from the National Board of Review (NYT "I can imagine a much better 'Macbeth'"; LAT "a very spare, straightforward film … neither stagy, not arty but sinewy … a noteworthy if esoteric achievement"); *Le Genou de Clair (Claire's Knee)*, the National Society of Film Critics prizewinner (NYT "comes very close to being a perfect movie of its kind … so funny and so moving, so immaculately realized, that almost any ordinary attempt to describe it must in some way diminish it"; CT "a supremely intelligent film"; WP "I think the picture is being generally overrated"; TT "a lovely film"); Bernardo Bertolucci's *Il Conformista (The Conformist)* (NYT "superior … is flawed, perhaps, but those very flaws may make it"; LAT "dazzling … fascinating"; CT "much more of a show than a story"; WP "an extraordinarily beautiful and spellbinding movie"; S&S "superbly realised"); and the 1970 British family film *The Railway Children* (NYT "perfectly lovely"; LAT "the warmest, sunniest, most preposterously good-hearted movie to come chuffing along since I can't remember when … charming, sentimental family entertainment"; WP "a very pretty and often charming picture"; S&S "engaging").

The Academy also ignored three films that had received poor or mixed reviews, and yet had been recognised with Globe nominations as Best Picture: the nostalgic drama *Summer of '42* (NYT "a little too perfect"; LAT "[I] disbelieved the movie almost from start to finish … it played to me as a concoction, drawn from literary or screen conventions rather than from the remembered truth of someone's life"; CT "only acceptable as an emotional and intellectual marshmallow"; WP "a romanticized version of growing up"; V "[a] mixed achievement"; MFB "so bathed in the moony mists of nostalgia that if fails to achieve any reality"); *Plaza Suite*, an adaptation of Neil Simon's popular comedy, starring Walter Matthau (NYT "aggressively tiresome"; LAT "a bright, diverting comedy"; CT "one of the most diverting films of the year"; WP "obnoxious ... what was amusing on the stage looks stiff and unfunny on the screen"); and the historical drama *Mary, Queen of Scots* (NYT "an exceptionally loveless, passionless costume drama ... solemn, well-groomed and dumb"; LAT "traditional ... a model of clarity and craftsmanship"; CT "stumbles"; WP "the sort of stodgy, plodding costume movie that cries out to be passed over"). While it had an Oscar qualifying run in Los Angeles, *Mary, Queen of Scots* didn't go into general release in North America until March 1972 which may have hindered its Oscar chances. The Washington Post's Gary Arnold observed, "in Universal, [the film] also has the least active of major film distributors when it comes to the art of film promotion."

Leading the list of nominees, each with eight mentions, were *Fiddler on the Roof*, *The French Connection* and *The Last Picture Show*. At the Golden Globe awards *Fiddler on the Roof* won the award for Best Comedy or Musical, while *The French Connection* was chosen as Best Drama.

Heading into the Oscar ceremony, *The French Connection* was the clear frontrunner for the Academy Award. While it tied for the most nominations with *Fiddler on the Roof* and *The Last Picture Show*, it had claimed both the Golden Globe (Drama) and the Directors Guild of America prize in the lead up to the Oscars. On the big night, it won four statuettes including Best Picture, Best Director and Best Actor for Gene Hackman. A few years later Hackman reprised his role in a sequel, *The French Connection II*, directed by John Frankenheimer. The film received moderate praise but no Oscar nominations.

At the following year's British Academy Awards, *A Clockwork Orange*, *The French Connection* and *The Last Picture Show* were all included in the Best Film category. The winner, however, was *Cabaret*, the musical drama which had been bested for that year's Best Picture Oscar by *The Godfather*.

1971

BEST DIRECTOR

ACADEMY AWARDS
Peter Bogdanovich for *The Last Picture Show*
• William Friedkin for *The French Connection*
Norman Jewison for *Fiddler on the Roof*
Stanley Kubrick for *A Clockwork Orange*
John Schlesinger for *Sunday, Bloody Sunday*

GOLDEN GLOBE AWARDS
Peter Bogdanovich – *The Last Picture Show*
• William Friedkin – *The French Connection*
Norman Jewison – *Fiddler on the Roof*
Stanley Kubrick – *A Clockwork Orange*
Robert Mulligan – *Summer of '42*

DIRECTORS GUILD AWARD
Peter Bogdanovich – *The Last Picture Show*
• William Friedkin – *The French Connection*
Stanley Kubrick – *A Clockwork Orange*
Robert Mulligan – *Summer of '42*
John Schlesinger – *Sunday, Bloody Sunday*

BRITISH ACADEMY AWARDS
Milos Forman – *Taking Off*
Joseph Losey – *The Go-Between*
• John Schlesinger – *Sunday, Bloody Sunday*
Luchino Visconti – *Death in Venice*

NEW YORK – Stanley Kubrick – *A Clockwork Orange*
BOARD OF REVIEW – Ken Russell – *The Boy Friend* and *The Devils*
NATIONAL SOCIETY – Bernardo Bertolucci – *Il Conformista (The Conformist)*

At the start of the annual film awards season, the previous two year's Oscar winners both seemed likely to contest the Best Director category at the Academy Awards once again, Franklin J. Schaffner for *Nicholas and Alexandra* (LAT "once again shows his ability to handle very large resources and effects without ever being overwhelmed by them or losing the personal dimension … film-making of a high order, solid and sensitive"; S&S "the saddest failure is Schaffner's inability to find a real centre for the film") and John Schlesinger for *Sunday, Bloody Sunday* (LAT "perfectly executed … extraordinary skill with which the theme has been particularized … as impeccably cut as a diamond"; CT "imaginatively directed"; WP "accomplished … Schlesinger's direction has never been better"). In the end, however, Schaffner was overlooked (although *Nicholas and Alexandra* was nominated as Best Picture). Schlesinger made the list for a third time (although *Sunday, Bloody Sunday* was left out of consideration for the top award).

Perhaps unsurprisingly given the reviews in major newspapers and journals, Academy members also baulked at nominating Ken Russell, the National Board of Review's unexpected choice for Best Director, for either of the films for which he received his accolade: the musical *The Boy Friend* (CT "as usual, the Russell canvas is bright, colourful and crowded. His only failure – and it is a considerable one – is a confused editing of three story lines"; WP "calling the lion's share of attention to himself, inflating [Sandy] Wilson's conception … and destroying the charm by making the original theatrical milieu ugly and salacious … the wrongheadedness and vulgarity are typically Russell") and the drama *The Devils* (NYT "as writer and director [he] has simplified and reduced the complexity of the drama to the dimensions of that most boring kind of Pop art"; WP "offers the gruesome spectacle of Ken Russell going overboard again"; MFB "not surprisingly, the actors can make little headway against the director's persistent comic-strip overstatement").

Also passed over were: National Society of Film Critics winner Bernardo Bertolucci for *Il Conformista (The Conformist)* (NYT "there are excesses in the film, but they are balanced by scenes of such unusual beauty and vitality that I couldn't care less"; LAT "superb control of the potentially melodramatic material"; CT "often visually compelling, but more often intellectually tired"; WP "has a grand style that seems effortless … [his] sense of imagery is lush, his colors rich and warming, his camera movement and cutting unusually supple"); Directors Guild of America and Golden Globe nominee Robert Mulligan for *Summer of '42* (WP "there is a mood that comes through … [but] a cinema cliche"; MFB "misfires"); Alan J. Pakula for *Klute* (LAT "visually stunning, full of surprises, bewildering and suspenseful, faultless in its timing"; WP "first-rate"; V "craftsmanly direction"; G "clearly someone to be reckoned with"; MFB "brilliant"); Robert Altman for *McCabe and Mrs Miller* (NYT "unsuccessful"; CT "Altman's craft is visible ... [he] is clearly a master"; WP "Altman doesn't suffocate the emotions with lugubrious pathos or overscaled, grandiloquent direction … [has] a loose, improvisatory, impressionistic technique of storytelling and characterization"); Joseph Losey for *The Go-Between* (LAT "Losey recreates the rich and orderly world of Edwardian England with a profusion of detail and a deep-reaching fidelity wonderful to see … [and] once again [he] collaborates marvelously well with playwright Harold Pinter"; CT "Losey's strength is technical precision and an unerring eye"); Milos

Forman for the comedy *Taking Off* (NYT "artfully constructed"); and, perhaps most notably, Luchino Visconti for *Death in Venice* (NYT "Visconti overdoes everything in the film"; LAT "cannot deny its awesome visual splendors, long a Visconti trademark"; CT "superbly done … one of the rare films justifying the conviction that the camera is a master key in the hands of a master"; WP "Visconti seems masterful at manipulating crowds and décor and helpless at clarifying the main point of the story"; MFB "Visconti eloquently and unostentatiously renders the novel's sense of impending doom").

The Academy did, however, recognise Stanley Kubrick, winner of his second accolade from the New York Film Critics Circle for *A Clockwork Orange* (NYT "it is always Kubrick's picture … even more technically interesting than '2001'"; LAT "impressively conveys tomorrow's world … uncompromising singularity and great if intermittent technical achievement"; V "masterful") and Peter Bogdanovich, the runner-up in the voting by the New York critics for *The Last Picture Show* (LAT "extremely impressive"; CT "[displays] obvious control of the medium"; WP "exceedingly well-made"). The margin had been 38 points to 21 with Bertolucci and Friedkin placed third and fourth respectively. Oscar voters also short-listed Norman Jewison for the musical *Fiddler on the Roof* (LAT "has been done not only with such artistry but also with such evident love"; WP "has extended and concentrated its dramatic force on the screen [and] emerged as a masterful director").

It was William Friedkin, however, who emerged as the frontrunner for the Oscar for the police drama *The French Connection* (LAT "as good a job as I've seen in a good while"; CT "paces his film at a speed that doesn't, on first viewing, give one a chance to pick up holes in the script"; WP "terrifically proficient direction"). In the lead up to the Oscars, Friedkin collected both the DGA honour and the Globe. On Oscar night, he added a golden statuette to his collection of trophies. Friedkin was nominated again two years later, for *The Exorcist*.

In London, meanwhile, Schlesinger collected his second BAFTA in four years. The following year, Bogdanovich, Friedkin and Kubrick were each in contention for the BAFTA, but were all bested by that year's Oscar winner.

1971

BEST ACTRESS

ACADEMY AWARDS
Julie Christie as 'Mrs Constance Miller' in *McCabe and Mrs Miller*
• Jane Fonda as 'Bree Daniels' in *Klute*
Glenda Jackson as 'Alex Greville' in *Sunday, Bloody Sunday*
Vanessa Redgrave as 'Mary, Queen of Scots' in *Mary, Queen of Scots*
Janet Suzman as 'Tzarina Alexandra of Russia' in *Nicholas and Alexandra*

GOLDEN GLOBE AWARDS
(Drama)
Dyan Cannon – *Such Good Friends*
• Jane Fonda – *Klute*
Glenda Jackson
– *Sunday, Bloody Sunday*
Vanessa Redgrave
– *Mary, Queen of Scots*
Jessica Walter – *Play Misty for Me*

(Comedy/Musical)
Sandy Duncan – *Star-Spangled Girl*
Ruth Gordon – *Harold and Maude*
Angela Lansbury
– *Bedknobs and Broomsticks*
Elaine May – *A New Leaf*
• Twiggy – *The Boy Friend*

BRITISH ACADEMY AWARDS
Lynn Carlin – *Taking Off*
Julie Christie – *The Go-Between*
Jane Fonda – *Klute*
• Glenda Jackson – *Sunday, Bloody Sunday*
Nanette Newman – *The Raging Moon (Long Ago, Tomorrow)*

NEW YORK – Jane Fonda – *Klute*
BOARD OF REVIEW – Irene Papas – *The Trojan Women*
NATIONAL SOCIETY – Jane Fonda – *Klute*

The organisers of the 44th Annual Academy Awards viewed the Best Actress category with some concern. Two actresses known for their controversial and outspoken political beliefs were major contenders for the statuette.

Jane Fonda had become the early Oscar frontrunner when *Klute* opened in June. As a New York prostitute stalked by a homicidal psychopath, Life magazine commented that she "emerges as probably the finest screen actress of her generation with a mercurial, subtly shaded and altogether fascinating performance" and other leading critics concurred (NYT "generally successful"; LAT "her finest performance yet"; CT "[a] fine performance"; WP "played brilliantly ... absolutely convincing ... [a] vivid and coherent and affecting performance"; V the film's "only rewarding element"; TT "perfect"; G "has never been better"; S&S "stunning", "superb"; FQ "mesmerizing"). Despite her anti-Vietnam War activism, Fonda won both the New York Film Critics Circle award (for the second time) and the National Society of Film Critics accolade, and received her second Best Actress Oscar nomination in just three years. Included alongside her despite her equally outspoken views about Vietnam was Vanessa Redgrave as the title character in *Mary, Queen of Scots* (LAT "deserves to be remembered come Oscar nomination time"; WP "surprisingly unremarkable, neither moving nor romantically exciting ... I was expecting Miss Redgrave to bring more force of personality to the character than she has"; V "played very well").

Two previous winners were also recognised, each for the second time: Julie Christie as the opium-addicted brothel madam in *McCabe and Mrs Miller* (LAT "gives one of the best performances of her career"; WP "a ravish, highstrung performance"; V "excellent"; S&S "never quite sheds her 'star' quality"); and Glenda Jackson as the career woman involved in a love triangle in *Sunday, Bloody Sunday* (NYT "superb"; LAT "marvelously fine ... Jackson is asked to be far less flamboyant than usual and she creates a totally recognizable, intelligent, aware modern woman"; CT "well-acted"; WP "too strong ... it's a constant struggle to believe in Miss Jackson ... [her] presence is peculiarly discordant, but it isn't uninteresting"; TT "it is hard to imagine how [she] could be improved on"; MFB "beautifully modulated performance"; S&S "convincing and vulnerable"). The Oscar chances of both women were further enhanced by their appearances in other projects – Christie as the aristocrat in *The Go-Between* (NYT "splendid"; LAT "interesting"; WP "strikes one as confusing rather than duplicitous") and Jackson as Queen Elizabeth I in *Mary, Queen of Scots* (NYT "a good deal of intensity"; LAT "deserves to be remembered come Oscar nomination time"; WP "makes the picture at least arguably worth seeing").

The only first-time candidate for the Oscar was South African-born actress Janet Suzman as the last Tsarina of Russia in the epic *Nicholas and Alexandra* (NYT "immensely effective"; LAT "played with spectacular skill"; V "just right"). Suzman was the only one of the short-listed actresses to have been mentioned for a performance in a Best Picture nominee.

Despite their positive reviews, the nominations of Christie and Suzman were nonetheless something of a surprise as neither had been candidates for the Golden Globe (Drama) nor featured prominently in the voting for any of the critics' prizes. Christie and Suzman were short-listed ahead of: National Board of Review prizewinner Irene Papas in *The Trojan Women* (NYT "commands attention"; LAT "of the women involved, only Irene Papas as Helen of Troy really gives the impression of being on home ground"); New York prize runner-up Gena Rowlands in *Minnie and Moskowitz* (NYT "most appealing [in a] quite special" performance; LAT "vivid and unforgettable … Rowlands is plain marvelous"; CT "cannot be faulted"; S&S "adroit"; MFB "superbly played"); NSFC prize runner-up Bibi Andersson in *Beröringen (The Touch)* (NYT "charming and affecting"; S&S "her finely gauged portrait of the gradual onset of paranoia, conveyed with the delicacy of an eye movement or the pursuing of just the corner of the mouth, has a subtlety that almost defeats [Ingmar] Bergman at his own game"; MFB "[a] magical performance … her characterisation of a shallow woman suddenly prey to deep emotions is faultless"); and Globe (Comedy/Musical) winner Twiggy in *The Boy Friend* (NYT "succeeds beyond all expectations"; CT "she plays to good effect").

Also overlooked were: Shirley MacLaine in *Desperate Characters*, for which she'd finished third in the voting by the New York critics (NYT "I have nothing but admiration"; LAT "fascinating … more impressive than I have ever seen her, acting with an intensity, intelligence and maturity which erases even the dimmest trace of the charming kook who came among us years ago"; WP "she pitches right in by keeping her natural warmth and humor out of sight"); Globe nominee Jessica Walter in *Play Misty for Me* (LAT "a sharp-edged, properly nervy portrayal of bright but pathetically destructive girl"; CT "outstanding"; V "superior"); Globe nominee Elaine May in *A New Leaf*, which she had also written and directed (NYT "as honestly appealing as she is funny"; LAT "costars in it dizzyingly well"; CT "marvelous"); Cannes Film Festival Best Actress winner Kitty Winn in *The Panic in Needle Park* (NYT "I liked all the performances except, I'm afraid, the award-winning one of Miss Winn, who produces more facial expressions – literally – than the rest of the cast put together"; LAT "authentic and sympathetic, ranking with the best performances of the year"; WP "a dull, languishing, anxiously smiling routine"; V "a smash"; S&S "over-calculated"); Lynn Carlin as the mother in *Taking Off* (NYT "very funny"; V "excellent"); and BAFTA nominee Nanette Newman in *The Raging Moon (Long Ago, Tomorrow)* (NYT "tender"; LAT "extremely affecting").

With the other major contenders for the critics' prizes and the winner of the Globe (Comedy/Musical) all excluded, Fonda was the strong favourite for the Academy Award over a field of four non-Americans.

On Oscar night, there was no surprise when Walter Matthau opened the envelope and announced Fonda had won. Her victory ended the drought for the winners of the Globe (Drama). She was the first actress to collect both awards since 1958. Fears of a controversial speech from Fonda, meanwhile, did not eventuate. Instead the actress simply told the audience, "There's a great deal to say, but I'm not going to say it tonight. I just want to thank you very much."

At the BAFTAs, Oscar nominees Christie (for *The Go-Between*), Fonda and Jackson were again among the candidates. In a different outcome, however, it was Jackson who triumphed.

1971

BEST ACTOR

ACADEMY AWARDS
Peter Finch as 'Dr Daniel Hirsh' in *Sunday, Bloody Sunday*
• Gene Hackman as 'Jimmy "Popeye" Doyle' in *The French Connection*
Walter Matthau as 'Joseph P Kotcher' in *Kotch*
George C. Scott as 'Dr Herbert Bock' in *The Hospital*
Topol as 'Tevye' in *Fiddler on the Roof*

GOLDEN GLOBE AWARDS
(Drama)
Peter Finch – *Sunday, Bloody Sunday*
• Gene Hackman – *The French Connection*
Malcolm McDowell – *A Clockwork Orange*
Jack Nicholson – *Carnal Knowledge*
George C. Scott – *The Hospital*

(Comedy/Musical)
Bud Cort – *Harold and Maude*
Dean Jones – *Million Dollar Duck*
Walter Matthau – *Kotch*
• Topol – *Fiddler on the Roof*
Gene Wilder – *Willy Wonka and the Chocolate Factory*

BRITISH ACADEMY AWARDS
Dirk Bogarde – *Death in Venice*
• Peter Finch – *Sunday, Bloody Sunday*
Albert Finney – *Gumshoe*
Dustin Hoffman – *Little Big Man*

NEW YORK – Gene Hackman – *The French Connection*
BOARD OF REVIEW – Gene Hackman – *The French Connection*
NATIONAL SOCIETY – Peter Finch – *Sunday, Bloody Sunday*

The New York Film Critics Circle vote for Best Actor was topped by three acclaimed performances by the stars of three of the year's most lauded films. The winner, with 31 points, was Gene Hackman as a New York narcotics detective in *The French Connection* (NYT "one of the most successful [characterizations] of his career"; LAT "creates an often unflattering credibility which is powerful indeed"; CT "realism is what Hackman achieves"; WP "riveting … [but] even as a 'turn' the performance is a little too squalid and frenetic for its own good"; V "believable"; S&S a "coldly malevolent portrait"; MFB "extremely convincing"). The runner-up, with 25 points, was Australian-born Peter Finch as a gay doctor involved in a love triangle in the English drama *Sunday, Bloody Sunday* (NYT "beautifully acted … the best thing he's done in years"; LAT "marvelously fine … a performance which almost certainly entitles him to whatever nominations are going"; CT "well-acted"; WP "superb … appears to fit into every aspect of his role with an uncanny verisimilitude"; TT "it is hard to imagine how [he] could be improved on"; MFB "[a] beautifully modulated performance"; S&S "convincing and vulnerable"). Finishing in third place with 16 points, was young Englishman Malcolm McDowell as the leader of a gang of vicious rapists in *A Clockwork Orange* (NYT "splendid"; LAT "well-played").

The day after the vote by the east coast circle, the National Society of Film Critics held its annual ballot. The group by-passed New York champ Hackman entirely, handing its prize to Finch ahead of McDowell by 33 points to 17. A week later, however, Hackman emerged victorious again with the award from the National Board of Review.

All three actors were short-listed for the Golden Globe (Drama) along with Jack Nicholson as a sex-obsessed college student in *Carnal Knowledge* (NYT "almost spectacularly right"; LAT "excellent … turns in some powerful moments [and] keeps us believing"; V "excellent"; S&S "remains a mannered actor giving a star performance"; MFB "makes a strong impact – but he is an indulgent actor") and the previous year's winner George C. Scott as a disillusioned doctor in *The Hospital* (NYT "excellent"; LAT "[the film] works because of another potent and irresistible star-actor performance by George C. Scott, who once again will be hard to ignore in the Oscar stakes … just plain marvelous, dominating the screen and giving us a beautiful character portrayal"; CT "particularly successful"; V "dominates every scene").

Among the nominees in the Comedy/Musical category were: Walter Matthau as a man who resists his family's plans to place him in a retirement village in *Kotch* (LAT "a splendid and salty performance"; CT "Matthau's performance of a feisty old man with mannerisms to match his age isn't sufficient to sustain a feature film"; WP "thoroughly unconvincing … perhaps the low point of his screen career, artistically speaking"; V "outstanding"; S&S "magnificent"; MFB "superbly observed"); Israeli actor Topol for reprising his London stage role as Tevye in *Fiddler on the Roof* (NYT "miscast", "amounts to a kind of theatrical blasphemy"; LAT "[a] marvelous and quickening presence … plays Tevye with a rich-voiced maturity and a beguiling charm that is deeply satisfying to watch"; CT "a continuing delight"; WP "marvelous … creates a full-bodied patriarchal image ... astonishing"; MFB "a triumph"); and Gene Wilder in *Willy Wonka and the Chocolate Factory* (NYT "quite appealling"; LAT "[a] wonderfully sly, subtle and beguiling performance"; S&S "faultless"; MFB "leaves the rest of the cast standing").

In early February, Hackman repeated his New York victory over Finch and McDowell and collected the Globe (Drama). The other prize was won by Topol.

1971

A fortnight after the Globe ceremony, on 22 February 1972, the Academy announced its list of nominees. Both Globe champions were mentioned: Hackman for the third time in five years, and Topol (who had been chosen for the film ahead of Zero Mostel, the originator of the role on Broadway) for the first (and only) time. Also making the list for the first time was New York runner-up Finch. Despite controversially refusing the Best Actor Oscar the previous year, Scott was also cited, for a fourth time. In a surprise, the final nominee was previous Best Supporting Actor winner, Matthau. The most glaring omission from the Oscar field was McDowell.

Other notable omissions included: Alan Bates in *The Go-Between* (NYT "splendid"; LAT "interesting"); Michael Jayston in *Nicholas and Alexandra* (NYT "immensely effective"; LAT "played with spectacular skill"); Dustin Hoffman in *Straw Dogs* (LAT "first-rate"; WP "alternately nervous and ingenuous and it's impossible to tell if we're supposed to be watching a coward, a cuckold or Everyman-when-threatened"; Time "superbly real"); Kirk Douglas in *A Gunfight* (NYT "laconic and forceful"; LAT performed "expertly"); Henry Fonda in *Sometimes a Great Notion* (NYT "[a] lovely performance"; LAT "turns in his most vivid performance in quite some time"); Al Pacino in *The Panic in Needle Park* (NYT "an exceptionally successful starring debut"; LAT "authentic and sympathetic, ranking with the best performances of the year"; WP "gives it a nice try"; V "terrific", "terribly effective"; S&S "over-calculated"); James Stewart in *Fools Parade* (NYT "the movie belongs to James Stewart, who has never been more wonderful"); Albert Finney in *Gumshoe* (NYT "very funny"; V "brilliant"; S&S "a superlative performance"); Buck Henry as the father in *Taking Off* (NT "very funny"; V "excellent"); and Dirk Bogarde in *Death in Venice* (NYT "the movie is spectacularly decorated by Dirk Bogarde's performance"; LAT "Bogarde once again demonstrates his remarkable gift for self-effacement and for working deeply within to create this tragic figure"; CT "perfection"; WP "Bogarde's quivering lip-quavering chin performance is simply wretched and tiresome"; V "subtle and moving", "compelling"; TT "remarkable", "very distinguished"; FQ "valiant"; MFB "excellent"; SMH "[he] is Mahler to the life").

Perhaps unsurprisingly given the film's non-mainstream nature, the Academy also ignored the performance of Richard Roundtree in *Shaft* which is now acknowledged as a ground-breaking role in American cinema (LAT "makes a commanding screen debut"; MFB "[an] excellent, edgy performance").

The favourite for the Academy Award was Hackman, and on Oscar night he received the Best Actor statuette.

Both Finch and Hackman won Best Actor awards from the British Academy for their performances: Finch in 1971, and Hackman the following year.

1971

BEST SUPPORTING ACTRESS

ACADEMY AWARDS
Ann-Margret as 'Bobbie' in *Carnal Knowledge*
Ellen Burstyn as 'Lois Farrow' in *The Last Picture Show*
Barbara Harris as 'Allison Densmore' in *Who is Harry Kellerman and Why is He Saying Those Terrible Things About Me?*
• Cloris Leachman as 'Ruth Popper' in *The Last Picture Show*
Margaret Leighton as 'Mrs Maudsley' in *The Go-Between*

GOLDEN GLOBE AWARDS
• Ann-Margret – *Carnal Knowledge*
Ellen Burstyn – *The Last Picture Show*
Cloris Leachman – *The Last Picture Show*
Diana Rigg – *The Hospital*
Maureen Stapleton – *Plaza Suite*

BRITISH ACADEMY AWARDS
Jane Asher – *Deep End*
Georgia Brown – *The Raging Moon (Long Ago, Tomorrow)*
Georgia Engel – *Taking Off*
• Margaret Leighton – *The Go-Between*

NEW YORK – Ellen Burstyn – *The Last Picture Show*
BOARD OF REVIEW – Cloris Leachman – *The Last Picture Show*
NATIONAL SOCIETY – Ellen Burstyn – *The Last Picture Show*

In reviews of *The Last Picture Show*, critics praised both Ellen Burstyn as the mother of a teenage girl (LAT "moving"; CT "excellent"; V "excellent") and Cloris Leachman as the neglected wife of a football coach (LAT "a fine piece of acting"; CT "excellent"; S&S "miraculously alternating between a creased despair with a glowing radiance"; MFB "outstanding"). The two actresses cleaned up the critics' awards. Burstyn won the New York Film Critics Circle and National Society of Film Critics awards and Leachman finished runner-up in New York and won the National Board of Review prize. Both were nominated for the Golden Globe, but the winner was Ann-Margret, who took home the trophy for her performance as a model in *Carnal Knowledge* (NYT "attains a perfect balance between the character's desperation, her aggressiveness and her surprising simplicity"; LAT "outstanding … very sympathetic indeed"; V "excellent"; TT "beautifully acted"; S&S "[an] incandescent performance … she plays the hesitant blank Bobbie with a truthfulness which seems to owe as much to instinct as to art"; MFB "well done").

The Academy nominated all three of these actresses for the Best Supporting Actress Oscar along with Barbara Harris as an aspiring singer in *Who is Harry Kellerman and Why is He Saying Those Terrible Things About Me?* (LAT "a brief but unforgettable performance which will be hard to overlook when the list of Best Supporting Actresses is drawn next time … infinitely endearing"; WP "[a] performance that lifts the film temporarily out of the doldrums") and Margaret Leighton in *The Go-Between* (NYT "splendid"; LAT "forceful"; V "impressive"; MFB "Leighton's Mrs Maudsley turns the most anodyne formalities into devastating innuendo"). All the nominees were first-time Oscar candidates.

With Burstyn and Leachman expected to split the vote, observers predicted a victory for Ann-Margret. The Oscar winner, however, was Leachman, who also had a supporting role on 'The Mary Tyler Moore Show' at the time.

In London, Leighton won the Best Supporting Actress BAFTA. The following year the same award was won by Leachman. Among the other nominees was Eileen Brennan who was also cited for her performance in *The Last Picture Show*.

The Academy overlooked: both Globe nominee Diana Rigg as a patient's daughter (NYT "excellent"; LAT "she is no match for Scott"; V "effective") and Nancy Marchand as the nurse (LAT "handsomely done"; V "excellent") in *The Hospital*; Globe nominee Maureen Stapleton in *Plaza Suite* (LAT "mixes comedy and pathos in a strong and very affecting performance"; CT "superb"; WP "pretentious"; G "superb"); BAFTA nominee Georgia Engel as the best friend in *Taking Off*; Candice Bergen in *Carnal Knowledge* (NYT "almost spectacularly right"; LAT "[an] outstanding characterization"; S&S "with [her character's] disappearance, the balance of the film is overthrown"); Jane Alexander in *A Gunfight* (NYT "an excellent performance"; V "excellent"); Irene Worth as Goneril in *King Lear* (NYT "fine … special mention must be made"; LAT "excellent … [a] classic study in female malevolence"); and Molly Picon as the old match-maker in *Fiddler on the Roof* (NYT "the single most touching performance in the film … she is excessive and outrageous and very dear"; LAT "Picon seems to me to be doing her own thing, a performance colourful in its own terms if never fully integrated with the ensemble. But colourful it is").

1971

BEST SUPPORTING ACTOR

ACADEMY AWARDS
Jeff Bridges as 'Duane Jackson' in *The Last Picture Show*
Leonard Frey as 'Motel' in *Fiddler on the Roof*
Richard Jaeckel as 'Joe Ben Stamper' in *Sometimes a Great Notion*
• Ben Johnson as 'Sam the Lion' in *The Last Picture Show*
Roy Scheider as 'Buddy Russo' in *The French Connection*

GOLDEN GLOBE AWARDS
Tom Baker – *Nicholas and Alexandra*
Art Garfunkel – *Carnal Knowledge*
• Ben Johnson – *The Last Picture Show*
Paul Mann – *Fiddler on the Roof*
Jan-Michael Vincent – *Going Home*

BRITISH ACADEMY AWARDS
• Edward Fox – *The Go-Between*
Michael Gough – *The Go-Between*
Ian Hendry – *Get Carter*
John Hurt – *10 Rillington Place*

NEW YORK – Ben Johnson – *The Last Picture Show*
BOARD OF REVIEW – Ben Johnson – *The Last Picture Show*
NATIONAL SOCIETY – Bruce Dern – *Drive, He Said*

Fifty-three-year old character actor Ben Johnson won an Oscar, a Globe, a BAFTA, and both the New York and National Board of Review awards as an old-timer in *The Last Picture Show* (LAT "moving"; CT "excellent"; V "moving"; MFB "outstanding"). Interestingly, his wins all came over distinctly different fields of contenders.

At the Oscars, Johnson out-polled: his twenty-two-year old co-star Jeff Bridges (LAT "awfully good"; CT "excellent"; WP "admirable"); Leonard Frey as the tailor in *Fiddler on the Roof* (NYT "fine"; LAT "gently comical"; CT "outstanding"); Richard Jaeckel in *Sometimes a Great Notion* (NYT "[a] lovely performance"; LAT "[a] solid performance"; V "touching"); and Roy Scheider as a cop in *The French Connection* (LAT "creates an often unflattering credibility which is powerful indeed"; V "believable").

The other Globe nominees, however, were: Tom Baker as Rasputin in *Nicholas and Alexandra* (NYT "how can one criticize Tom Baker's Rasputin?

… very good"; LAT "Rasputin, who has been a caricature in the popular imagination for years, becomes a credible personality in Tom Baker's fascinating performance"; V "deserves credit for making the controversial character just that and not the frequent caricature, and for believably conveying its spellbinding fascination without resorting to facile over-playing"); singer-turned-actor Art Garfunkel in *Carnal Knowledge* (NYT "almost spectacularly right"; LAT "excellent … a first-rate portrayal"; V "extremely capable"; S&S "gives such a beautiful performance, the embodiment of candour, anxiety and moral sweetness"); Paul Mann in *Fiddler on the Roof* (LAT "performs handsomely"); and Jan-Michael Vincent in *Going Home* (NYT "unfortunately, Jan-Michael Vincent is impossible as the son, admittedly an impossible role that requires the actor to be simultaneously appealing and psychotic"; LAT "fully credible and very involving … [has a] magnetic yet vulnerable intensity").

In the voting by the New York Film Critics Circle, meanwhile, Johnson had narrowly claimed the award ahead of Warren Oates in both *The Hired Hand* (WP "fine"; MFB "excellent") and *Two-Lane Blacktop* (NYT "the most interesting person in the film"; LAT "Oates, giving the performance of his career as a man feeling strong intimations of mortality, easily dominates and thus throws the picture off balance"). Alan Webb had finished in third place for his performance as the Duke of Gloucester in *King Lear* (NYT "fine … special mention must be made"; LAT "excellent"; WP "one is drawn to Webb immediately").

As *The Last Picture Show* wasn't released in the United Kingdom until the following year, Johnson's Best Supporting Actor BAFTA win came in 1972. Among those short-listed for the BAFTA was Max Adrian for his performance as the provincial director in *The Boy Friend* (WP "played with hectic ugliness"). Adrian was another whose work had been overlooked by the Academy, as well as the Hollywood Foreign Press Association and major critics' groups, during the 1971 awards season.

Nominated for the British Academy Award in 1971 were actors who each were overlooked for the Oscar: Edward Fox (NYT "splendid"; MFB "admirable") and Michael Gough (NYT "splendid") in *The Go-Between*; Ian Hendry in *Get Carter* (LAT "just the right touch of cool villainy"); and John Hurt in *10 Rillington Place* (LAT "effective [and] especially touching"; CT "fine work"; WP "[an] intelligent performance"; V "remarkably subtle and fascinating"; MFB "Hurt makes Evans pathetically red-eyed and hangdog, and compels total belief"). The winner was Fox.

While Fox and Gough received recognition in London, the performance of English youth Dominic Guard in *The Go-Between* was overlooked for awards consideration entirely on both sides of the Atlantic (NYT "played with lovely comic candor"; LAT "remarkably fine"; S&S "convincing").

1972

BEST PICTURE

ACADEMY AWARDS

Cabaret
(ABC, Allied Artists, 124 mins, 13 Feb 1972, $10.8m / gr:$42.7m, 10 noms)
Deliverance
(Warner Bros., 109 mins, 31 Jul 1972, $22.6m, 3 noms)
• *The Godfather*
(Ruddy, Paramount, 175 mins, 15 Mar 1972, $86.6m, 10 noms)
Sounder
(Radnitz, Mattel, Twentieth Century-Fox, 105 mins, 24 Sep 1972, 4 noms)
Utvandrarna (The Emigrants)
(Svensk Filmindustri, Warner Bros., 148 mins, 24 Sep 1972, 4 noms)

GOLDEN GLOBE AWARDS

(Drama)
Deliverance
Frenzy
• *The Godfather*
The Poseidon Adventure
Sleuth

(Comedy/Musical)
1776
Avanti!
Butterflies are Free
• *Cabaret*
Travels with My Aunt

BRITISH ACADEMY AWARDS

• *Cabaret*
A Clockwork Orange
The French Connection
The Last Picture Show

NEW YORK – *Viskningor och Rop (Cries and Whispers)*
BOARD OF REVIEW – *Cabaret*
NATIONAL SOCIETY – *La Charme Discret de la Bourgeoisie (The Discreet Charm of the Bourgeoisie)*

Francis Ford Coppola's three-hour Mafia crime epic *The Godfather*, an adaptation of Mario Puzo's best-selling novel, was the overwhelming favourite for the Best Picture Academy Award (NYT "one of the most brutal and moving chronicles of American life ever designed within the limits of popular entertainment", "superb" and "truly exciting"; LAT "marvelously well cast and acted … swift and theatrical … an instant classic"; WP "an extraordinary achievement: a new classic … the best gangster movie ever made … it will take some kind of movie to prevent 'The Godfather' from dominating next year's

Academy Awards"; V "overlong" and "occasionally confusing", "never so gripping as to be superior screen drama"). Released early in the year (in the month prior to the Oscar ceremony honouring the previous year's movies), *The Godfather* had taken in three times more at the box office than any of the year's other releases. It subsequently became the most commercially successful film of all time. Coppola's epic was the runner-up for the New York Film Critics Circle's Best Picture accolade and collected a record-equalling five Golden Globes, including Best Picture (Drama) and Best Director. Coppola was also named Best Director by the Directors Guild of America. When the Academy Award nominations were announced, *The Godfather* garnered eleven mentions in nine categories, although this tally was subsequently reduced to ten nominations in eight categories when Nino Rota was removed from the Best Music (Original Score) category after it was determined that he had drawn substantially on his score for the 1957 Italian film, *Fortunella.*

The only other serious contender for Oscar glory was also released early in the year: Bob Fosse's *Cabaret*, a film version of the Broadway musical by Kander and Ebb (NYT "one of those immensely gratifying imperfect works in which from beginning to end you can literally feel a movie coming to life … extraordinary"; LAT "the most thrilling [musical] I have ever seen, the most adult, the most intelligent, the most surpassingly artful in its joining of cinema, drama and music … engrossing and uncompromising, a work which is as electrifying as high art must always be"; CT "one of the truly fine movie musicals in recent years"; WP "imaginative, exhilarating"; V "heart-warming and disturbingly thought-provoking"; TT "remarkable and rewarding"; S&S "disappointing"; MFB "stylish, sophisticated entertainment"). *Cabaret* finished fifth in the voting by the New York critics, was named Best Picture by the National Board of Review and won the Globe for Best Picture (Comedy/Musical).

The remaining Oscar nominees were: John Boorman's survival adventure *Deliverance* (NYT "the most stunning piece of moviemaking released this year"; LAT "an engrossing adventure … at the level of brute physical action [it] is an absolutely first-rate piece of movie-making [but] is least successful when it is trying to be most thoughtful"; CT "superb"; WP "a distinctive and gripping piece of work"; V "uncompromising"; S&S "although 'Deliverance' walks a precarious tightrope, it manages not to overbalance"; MFB "works so magnificently … a taut, exciting thriller"); Martin Ritt's drama *Sounder* (LAT "it is almost impossible to watch the movie without being moved to tears"; CT "deserving of the highest acclaim"; WP "remarkably touching and heartening"; V "outstanding"; TT "a minor classic"; Obs "heart-warming yet largely unsentimental"); and *Utvandrarna (The Emigrants)*, a Swedish historical epic about migration to the United States (NYT "a stately, pictorially romantic chronicle"; LAT "a surpassing piece of film-making and a powerful recapturing of a great tide in history, brought alive in immediate human terms … unforgettable"; WP "one of the most beautiful epic films ever made … visually marvelous and dramatically compelling"; V "a movie of rare beauty"; TT "inexorably gloomy but intimate epic"; S&S "visually striking, but too cool and distant to be more than marginally engrossing"; MFB "extremely disappointing"). *Utvandrarna*, one of the previous year's Best Foreign-Language Film nominees, was only the third foreign-language film short-listed for the Best Picture Oscar. Its sequel, *Nybyggarna (The New Land)*, was simultaneously nominated for the Best Foreign-Language Film Oscar.

Among the notable absentees from the Academy's major prize short-list were: National Society of Film Critics winner *La Charme Discret de la Bourgeoisie (The Discreet Charm of the Bourgeoisie)* (NYT "brilliant", "extraordinarily funny and perfectly acted"; LAT "[a] gleaming triumph [and] a joy to watch"; TT a "masterpiece"; S&S "savage and blisteringly funny"); *Sleuth* (NYT "a great deal of fun"; LAT "a rich, rich, rich creation [and] a showcase for high-style acting"; CT "entertaining [and] deserving of the highest acclaim"; TT "very effective"); Alfred Hitchcock's *Frenzy* (NYT "immensely entertaining"; LAT "Hitchcock's best picture in years"; CT "grand entertainment"; WP "decidedly pedestrian"; V "a first-rate melodrama"; S&S "remarkable"); and the 1971 French comedy *Trafic (Traffic)* (NYT "terrific [and] splendidly funny" as well as "a work of extraordinary art"; S&S "disappointing ... sporadically funny").

The New York Film Critics Circle winner, Ingmar Bergman's *Viskningor och Rop (Cries and Whispers)* was not eligible for Oscar consideration until it received a qualifying run in a Los Angeles cinema the following year.

Many observers predicted a sweeping victory for *The Godfather*. However, on the night, it looked as if the overwhelming favourite was going to be entirely shut-out. The night's biggest upset was the naming of Fosse as Best Director. His win brought *Cabaret*'s tally to seven statuettes. *The Godfather*, at that stage in the evening, had won none. In the latter part of the ceremony, however, *The Godfather* won Best Adapted Screenplay for Coppola and Puzo as well as Best Actor for Marlon Brando. In the penultimate category, Liza Minnelli collected Best Actress for *Cabaret*. When Clint Eastwood opened the evening's final envelope, the winner of the Best Picture Oscar was *The Godfather*. Coppola's crime drama won three statuettes. *Cabaret* won eight, setting a new record Oscar haul for a film not also named Best Picture.

At the British Academy Awards, Fosse's musical was named Best Film. *The Godfather*, surprisingly, was not even a nominee.

1972

BEST DIRECTOR

ACADEMY AWARDS
John Boorman for *Deliverance*
Francis Ford Coppola for *The Godfather*
• Bob Fosse for *Cabaret*
Joseph L. Mankiewicz for *Sleuth*
Jan Troell for *Utvandrarna (The Emigrants)*

GOLDEN GLOBE AWARDS
John Boorman – *Deliverance*
• Francis Ford Coppola – *The Godfather*
Bob Fosse – *Cabaret*
Alfred Hitchcock – *Frenzy*
Billy Wilder – *Avanti!*

DIRECTORS GUILD AWARD
John Boorman – *Deliverance*
• Francis Ford Coppola – *The Godfather*
Bob Fosse – *Cabaret*
George Roy Hill – *The Slaughterhouse Five*
Martin Ritt – *Sounder*

BRITISH ACADEMY AWARDS
Peter Bogdanovich – *The Last Picture Show*
• Bob Fosse – *Cabaret*
William Friedkin – *The French Connection*
Stanley Kubrick – *A Clockwork Orange*

NEW YORK – Ingmar Bergman – *Viskningor och Rop (Cries and Whispers)*
BOARD OF REVIEW – Bob Fosse – *Cabaret*
NATIONAL SOCIETY – Luis Buñuel – *La Charme Discret de la Bourgeoisie (The Discreet Charm of the Bourgeoisie)*

The New York Film Critics Circle gave their Best Director prize to Ingmar Bergman, the Swedish director whom the National Society of Film Critics had already honoured three times over the previous four years. Bergman's film, *Viskningor och Rop (Cries and Whispers)* was not, however, eligible for Oscar consideration until the following year.

The NSFC winner and New York second runner-up Luis Buñuel, meanwhile, seemed unlikely to be considered by the Academy Award despite acclaim for his handling of the French film *La Charme Discret de la Bourgeoisie (The Discreet Charm of the Bourgeoisie)* (NYT "has never been more fully in control of his talents, as a filmmaker, a moralist, social critic and humorist"; LAT "[a] honed and gleaming triumph"). A newspaper quoted him as saying, "Nothing would disgust me more, morally, than receiving an Oscar. Nothing in the world would make me go accept it. I wouldn't have it in my home!" He later called the report, "a full twisting of facts" and that he'd merely said, "At my age, I don't care about prizes." Although Buñuel ultimately did not feature in the Best Director category, his film won the statuette for Best Foreign-Language Film.

Eight other directors had been considered by the New York critics. The runner-up had been Francis Ford Coppola for *The Godfather* (LAT "the consistency of texture is an index of Coppola's skillful control … [has] brought off an assured and richly detailed piece of movie storytelling on a massive scale"; WP "[his] control of both the visual design and the dramatic substance is almost flawless"; S&S "expert direction"). Finishing jointly in fourth place were Bob Fosse for the musical *Cabaret* (NYT "Fosse makes mistakes, partly because his camera is a more potent instrument than he realizes, but he also makes discoveries"; LAT "exquisitely sculpted … artful in its joining of cinema, drama and music ... [Fosse] here proves what an extraordinarily inventive film-maker he is"; CT "the movie version has got what the stage play desperately needed: direction … Fosse, better known as a choreographer, gets the credit for making 'Cabaret' one of the truly great movie musicals in recent years"; WP "Fosse is exceptionally good with dramatic scenes [and his] dramatic sensibility seems to heighten his brilliance as a director of musical sequences"; TT "brilliant"; G "Fosse's own sharp sense of style adds to the magic") and Jan Troell for the Swedish historical drama *Utvandrarna (The Emigrants)* (NYT "carefully detailed ... to his credit, Mr Troell tries to keep his melodrama small"; LAT "eloquent and stunning work [by] a remarkable talent"; WP "succeeds with epic material in a way that few directors ever have").

Also receiving votes from the New York circle were: Alfred Hitchcock for the thriller *Frenzy* (NYT "in dazzling, lucid form … other directors make movies *about* passion. Hitchcock makes his *with* passion, which is why watching 'Frenzy' is like riding a roller coaster in total darkness"; LAT "exquisitely timed … does have all the marks of work by a master at his craft and at his most assured"; CT "technical excellence"; WP "still sufficiently skillful and assured to produce an entertaining thriller"); Martin Ritt for the drama *Sounder* (NYT "something of a problem … he seems to strive for classical plainness, but to succeed only in being ordinary"; LAT "sure and subtle control"; WP "achieves a very hard-earned simplicity and intensity of feeling … in the long run his reserved, unemphatic style pays off"; V "masterful direction"); actor-writer-director Elaine May for the comedy *The Heartbreak Kid* (NYT "behind the laughs there is a real understanding of character – which is something that, I suspect, can be attributed to Miss May"; V "deft"); and John Boorman for the survival drama *Deliverance* (NYT "Boorman's understanding of the sheer kinaesthetic power of film gives 'Deliverance' a sensuous immediacy … the only star is the director"; CT "Boorman is really the star of the movie, as much as any director this year"; WP "Boorman looks like the wrong talent for this material whenever there's an extended dramatic sequence or whenever one begins to crave a little coherence, a little sense of proportion"; S&S "brilliant").

Surprisingly, Jacques Tati did not feature in the voting by the circle despite acclaim for *Trafic (Traffic)* (NYT "the very special work of a filmmaker with a unique gift for visual comedy"; TT "superb").

The Hollywood Foreign Press Association and Directors Guild of America both selected four of the New York contenders and one ring-in for their awards, although their exact choices differed. Nominated for both accolades were: Boorman, Coppola and Fosse. The remaining candidates for the Globe were Hitchcock and previous winner Billy Wilder for *Avanti!* (LAT "handsomely mounted [but flawed by] needless and interminable length"; S&S "Wilder films an astonishingly high proportion of it in long shot, the images offhandedly composed"). The other two guild award finalists, meanwhile, were Ritt and George Roy Hill for *The Slaughterhouse Five* (NYT "Hill's achievement is in transferring to film the author's ebullient senses of humor and chaos"; CT "does not always maintain the sharp edge of the tragicomedy present in the novel"; WP "keeps straining for greatness … what Hill neglects to do is involve the paying customer. His picture is full of ambitious efforts, but none of them take hold emotionally"; V "mechanically slick, dramatically sterile"; S&S "plays safe").

From both these fields Coppola emerged the winner. This double victory, combined with the New York prize, made him the strong favourite for the Academy Award. Over the past twenty-three years the DGA winner had also claimed the Oscar twenty-two times, and the only guild champ to not have also won the Academy Award had failed to collect the Globe.

When the DGA result was declared, the Oscar nominees had already been announced. Like the HFPA and the DGA before it, the Academy nominated four New York contenders and a ring-in. Boorman, Coppola, Fosse and Troell were all mentioned for the first time. Surprisingly, the fifth nominee was previous winner Joseph L. Mankiewicz for *Sleuth* (LAT "is most at home with notably literate material and superlative actors"; S&S "smoothly directed").

At the 45th Annual Academy Awards, *Cabaret* won more Oscars than any other film. Among this tally of eight statuettes was the Best Director Oscar for Fosse, whose victory over Coppola was a major shock. It was only the second time that the Academy had selected a different winner from the Guild. The two men were both in contention for the Oscar again in 1974 and 1979.

In London, the British Academy also presented its Best Director accolade to Fosse. Coppola had not even been nominated.

1972

BEST ACTRESS

ACADEMY AWARDS
• Liza Minnelli as 'Sally Bowles' in *Cabaret*
Diana Ross as 'Billie Holiday' in *Lady Sings the Blues*
Maggie Smith as 'Aunt Augusta' in *Travels with My Aunt*
Cicely Tyson as 'Rebecca Morgan' in *Sounder*
Liv Ullmann as 'Kristina' in *Utvandrarna (The Emigrants)*

GOLDEN GLOBE AWARDS
(Drama)
Diana Ross – *Lady Sings the Blues*
Cicely Tyson – *Sounder*
• Liv Ullmann – *Utvandrarna (The Emigrants)*
Trish Van Devere – *One is a Lonely Number*
Tuesday Weld – *Play It as It Lays*
Joanne Woodward – *The Effect of Gamma Rays On Man-In-the-Moon Marigolds*

(Comedy/Musical)
Carol Burnett – *Pete 'n' Tillie*
Goldie Hawn – *Butterflies are Free*
Juliet Mills – *Avanti!*
• Liza Minnelli – *Cabaret*
Maggie Smith – *Travels with My Aunt*

BRITISH ACADEMY AWARDS
Stéphane Audran – *The Butcher*
Anne Bancroft – *Young Winston*
• Liza Minnelli – *Cabaret*
Dorothy Tutin – *Savage Messiah*

NEW YORK – Liv Ullmann – *Utvandrarna (The Emigrants)* and ***Viskningor och Rop (Cries and Whispers)***
BOARD OF REVIEW – Cicely Tyson – *Sounder*
NATIONAL SOCIETY – Cicely Tyson – *Sounder*

For her performance as a woman struggling to provide for her family during the Depression in *Sounder*, Cicely Tyson earned rave reviews from critics and won the Best Actress accolades from both the National Board of Review and the National Society of Film Critics (NYT "expert ... seems to understand that part of screen acting is keeping secrets from the camera, and she does suggest a range of personality beneath and beyond the ambitions of this film"; LAT "engaging, strong and credible ... inspiring to watch"; CT "strong"; WP "quite extraordinary ... she doesn't get a 'big' scene in any formal sense, but she's such a charged and intelligent presence, so splendidly in tune with the character she plays, that you can't take your eyes off her … [she will be] formidable competition for the year's best actress Academy Award"; V "terrific"; TT "faultless"; Obs "outstanding"; S&S "excellent"). She was the first African-American woman to receive Best Actress honours from any of the major awards groups.

Tyson also finished as the runner-up for the Best Actress award in New York. The overwhelming winner, however, with 38 points to Tyson's 14, was Norwegian actress Liv Ullmann. She was honoured for two performances: as a Swedish farmer's wife reluctantly migrating to America in *Utvandrarna (The Emigrants)* (NYT "[her performance has] a kind of spontaneous truth, in look and gesture"; LAT "unforgettable") and as one of three sisters in Ingmar Bergman's *Viskningor och Rop (Cries and Whispers).*

For the former of these portrayals, Ullmann also outpolled Tyson to win the Golden Globe (Drama). Unusually, there were four rather than just three other nominees: singer-turned-actress Diana Ross as the alcoholic singer Billie Holiday in the otherwise poorly reviewed biopic *Lady Sings the Blues* (NYT "how is it possible for a movie that is otherwise so dreadful to contain such a singularly attractive performance in the title role?"; LAT "achieves now and again an amazing likeness to the lady with the white flowers in her hair … and in some of the songs she also reproduces, with startling fidelity, that wistful, plaintive, wounded child quietness which made Billie Holliday heartbreaking to hear … but the exciting surprise is not that Miss Ross sings well; it is that she acts with terrific charm and very impressive intensity … it is one of the truly fine screen performances, full of power and pathos and enormously engaging and sympathetic"; CT "[the film] is a failure [but is still] entertaining because of an old-fashioned *grand dame* performance by Diana Ross … [she] frequently touches the great lady's fragile, sweet and blousy tone while also paying attention to her unique phrasing"; V "particularly effective"; TT "a remarkably impressive and mature performance"; S&S "does a nice job"; MFB "remarkable"); Trish Van Devere as a young divorcee in *One is a Lonely Number* (NYT "beautifully played"; LAT "both ingratiating and convincing"; V "projects a credible warmth and depth of character"; MFB "sensitive"); Tuesday Weld as a neglected wife in *Play It as It Lays* (NYT "beautifully performed"; WP "doesn't project anything in the role, and she also looks wrong"; V "fine"); and Joanne Woodward as the reclusive mother of two girls in the drama *The Effect of Gamma Rays on Man-In-the-Moon Marigolds*, a film directed by her husband, previous Best Actor Oscar nominee Paul Newman (NYT "at times I had the feeling that Miss Woodward was auditioning for the role of Sadie Thompson"; LAT "an all-stops-out performance [but] she seems miscast, never seeming truly vulnerable and always seeming slightly superior to [her character]"; WP "intense and energetic"; V "brilliant"; S&S "virtuoso performance").

Three of these six Globe (Drama) nominees were recognised by the Academy: Ullmann, Ross and Tyson, all mentioned for the first time. The inclusion of both Ross and Tyson marked the first time that two African-Americans had been nominated in the same acting category at the Oscars.

The remaining Oscar nominees were Globe Comedy/Musical winner Liza Minnelli (her second nod) as a cabaret star in early 1930s Germany in Bob Fosse's musical drama *Cabaret* (NYT "she is sometimes wrong in the details of her role, but so magnificently right for the film as a whole that I should prefer not to imagine it without her … she moves and sings with a strength, warmth, intelligence, and sensitivity to nuance that virtually transfixes the screen"; LAT "gives a remarkable star turn"; CT "uneven"; WP "establishing herself as the early heavy favourite for next year's Academy Award in a vibrant, appealing, versatile impersonation"; TT "a bright new star"; G "a magnificent performer, [but] she isn't really a Sally Bowles par excellence, yet the performance still works because of her personality"; S&S "stridently effective"; MFB "excellent") and previous winner Maggie Smith (her third mention) as an eccentric elderly aunt in *Travels with My Aunt*, a role that she inherited following the withdrawal of Katharine Hepburn (NYT "seems to have surrounded her character rather than to have inhabited it … caricature rather than personality"; LAT "should bring fresh honors to Miss Smith … convincing"; WP "disconcerting … seems both insistent and tentative, an uneasy combination for sure"; V "thoroughly delightful"; TT a "tour de force"; Obs "looks marvellous [but the film's] faults stem, I'm afraid, almost entirely from Maggie Smith's performance … works conscientiously to convince us that she is a 70-year-old [but] in concentrating so hard on externals Miss Smith has sacrificed a quality central to Graham Greene's heroine and usually very much a part of her own performance, an irresistible charm"; S&S "tiringly metallic performance"; MFB "[an] irritatingly mannered and monotonous performance").

The short-listing of Smith was considered a surprise by many. In a review of *The Effect of Gamma Rays on Man-In-the-Moon Marigolds*, Gary Arnold wrote in The Washington Post, "The film's commercial chances would have been enhanced if Miss Woodward had been nominated for an Academy Award. Many people expected she would be, and heaven knows she would have made a more sensible candidate than Maggie Smith, whose performance in 'Travels with My Aunt' was downright painful. Perhaps the inescapable nastiness of the role kept Miss Woodward, strong as she is, out of the finals this year."

In addition to the exclusion of Woodward along with Globe (Drama) nominees Van Devere and Weld, Oscar voters also by-passed: previous winner Barbra Streisand in the screwball comedy *What's Up, Doc?* (NYT "although she never lets us forget the power than seems always to be held in uncertain check, she is surprisingly appealing, more truly comic than she's ever before been on film"; LAT "takes charge here as elsewhere … has a vivid comedic style"; S&S "plays the spirit of subversive irresponsibility to some wickedly witty but dubiously effective extremes"); previous Best Supporting Actress winner Goldie Hawn as the woman who falls in love with a young, blind singer in *Butterflies are Free* (WP "she works too hard"; V "funny and touching, is a delight throughout"; MFB "the film's main pleasure lies in the playing of Goldie Hawn: in what is probably her best part to date, she subtly sketches in Jill's feckless qualities, at the same time hinting at something deeper underneath"); Cannes Film Festival Best Actress honoree Susannah York as a woman with a fragmenting personality in *Images* (NYT "Miss York confined mainly to sly petulance and a few yowls, has done better"; LAT "York dominates events, of course, and she is scary and sympathetic equally, and exciting to watch"; WP "Miss York's attempts to handle the three men in her exploding psyche look peculiarly facetious"); Carol Burnett in *Pete 'n' Tillie* (NYT "she is grand"; LAT "at some distance from her persona as a television comedienne … extremely affecting"); previous winner Anne Bancroft as Lady Randolph Churchill in *Young Winston* (WP "Bancroft's role is not an enviable one … I'm not sure anyone could shine in this rather uptight and conventional conception of [Lady Randolph]"; V "stunning"); and Olga Bellin as the abandoned pregnant woman in *Tomorrow* (NYT "has to talk too much"; LAT "immensely poignant").

Following her win at the Globes, and her film's tally of ten nominations, Minnelli was the overwhelming favourite for the Academy Award.

On Oscar night, Rock Hudson opened the envelope to announce that Minnelli had won the statuette. "Thank you for giving me this award," she told the audience, "You've made me very happy." Her win came fourteen years after her father, Vincente Minnelli, had received the Best Director award for the musical *Gigi* and eighteen years after her late mother, Judy Garland, had narrowly missed claiming the Best Actress Oscar for her performance in the musical *A Star is Born*. Minnelli was triumphant again at the BAFTAs.

The month following the Academy Awards ceremony, the jury at the 1973 Cannes Film Festival awarded its Best Actress honour to Joanne Woodward for her performance in *The Effect of Gamma Rays on Man-In-the-Moon Marigolds*.

1972

BEST ACTOR

ACADEMY AWARDS
• Marlon Brando as 'Don Vito Corleone' in *The Godfather*
Michael Caine as 'Milo Tindle' in *Sleuth*
Peter O'Toole as 'Jack, 14th Earl of Gurney' in *The Ruling Class*
Laurence Olivier as 'Andrew Wyke' in *Sleuth*
Paul Winfield as 'Nathan Lee Morgan' in *Sounder*

GOLDEN GLOBE AWARDS
(Drama)
• Marlon Brando – *The Godfather*
Michael Caine – *Sleuth*
Laurence Olivier – *Sleuth*
Al Pacino – *The Godfather*
Jon Voight – *Deliverance*

(Comedy/Musical)
Edward Albert – *Butterflies are Free*
Charles Grodin – *The Heartbreak Kid*
• Jack Lemmon – *Avanti!*
Walter Matthau – *Pete 'n' Tillie*
Peter O'Toole – *The Man of La Mancha*

BRITISH ACADEMY AWARDS
Marlon Brando – *The Godfather* and *The Nightcomers*
• Gene Hackman – *The French Connection* and *The Poseidon Adventure*
George C. Scott – *The Hospital* and *They Might Be Giants*
Robert Shaw – *Young Winston*

NEW YORK – Laurence Olivier – *Sleuth*
BOARD OF REVIEW – Peter O'Toole – *The Man of La Mancha* and *The Ruling Class*
NATIONAL SOCIETY – Al Pacino – *The Godfather*

After the first round of voting by the New York Film Critics Circle, Stacy Keach lead the Best Actor ballot with 20 points for his performance as a boxer in John Huston's *Fat City* (LAT "a very, very fine and effecting performance"; WP "Keach really seems inexpressive to a fault ... I found it shockingly easy to forget that Keach was in the movie ... [a] good stage actor who lacks screen presence ... his performance is simply dull and unimaginative").

Following on 17 points was Marlon Brando as the head of a Mafia family in Francis Ford Coppola's epic *The Godfather* (NYT "his performance sets the pitch for the entire production ... immensely moving"; LAT "gives a performance which is at once a tour de force and so economical that it seems to be understated … so natural, so charming, so totally the character, rather than the actor acting, that you can only be astonished"; WP "his performance is typically daring … as so often the case, Brando gradually wins one over to his conceptions and becomes more affecting as the movie goes along"; V "truly remarkable" in a "tour de force"; S&S "outstanding"; MFB "effortlessly authoritative").

After further rounds of voting, however, neither man emerged victorious. The accolade went to Laurence Olivier for a third time. He ultimately won with 30 points for his portrayal of a mystery writer in *Sleuth* (NYT "to witness Olivier at work in 'Sleuth' is to behold a one-man revue of theatrical excesses – all marvelous", "hugely funny and extravagant"; LAT "it's no surprise to find Olivier making such artful vocal magic ... vividly energetic and enjoyable"; CT "gives the burlesque performance of his career"; V "outstanding"). Brando finished as the runner-up, trailing by just three points. In third place, with 20 points, was James Mason as a school professor in *Child's Play* (NYT "fine … gives [the film] unexpected dimension"; LAT "intense … Mason's performance, in its power and also in its subtle shifting, ranks with the best portrayals in his long, impressive career. It stays in the memory"; MFB "gives his usual reliable performance").

Fourth in the final voting by the New York circle was Peter O'Toole as an eccentric earl who believes that he is Jesus Christ in *The Ruling Class* (NYT "splendid"; LAT "the likes of O'Toole's scenery-chewing has not been seen in years. He stammers, he perspires, he has epileptic fits, he rants and raves, flits and dances, shivers and stares, grins and grimaces. It is all, I'm afraid, like a graduation exercise at a second-rate drama academy and I find it impossible to watch without squirming in embarrassment"; CT "O'Toole is reason enough to [watch]"; WP "at his worst"; TT "flamboyant"; MFB "gloriously encapsulating and outdoing his every neurotic role"). O'Toole was honoured by the National Board of Review for this performance and also his turn in the musical *The Man of La Mancha* (NYT "especially fine", "funny, gentle and affecting"; LAT "has tremendous dignity and authority and possesses a touching vulnerability and eloquence, but his indubitable Britishness alongside his Italianate costars makes him seem as if he's doing a reprise of 'Goodbye, Mr Chips'"; WP "until the death scene, when O'Toole strikes a couple of sympathetic chords, it seems like a hideously misbegotten performance – a Quixote without nobility or pathos"; TT "marvelous").

The National Society of Film Critics, meanwhile, selected Brando's co-star in *The Godfather*, Al Pacino, for his performance as the Mafia boss' sensitive and educated younger son (LAT "seems to change from within even as we watch"; WP "'The Godfather' is Michael's story and Pacino's film … manages to convey the essential, tragic moral change [in his character]"; V "outstanding";

S&S "outstanding"; MFB "portrayed with finely calculated intensity …. almost, but not quite, he steals the film from Brando").

Both Brando and Pacino were nominated for the Golden Globe (Drama) as were: Olivier and his co-star in *Sleuth*, Michael Caine (NYT "perfect"; LAT "[a] pleasure to discover Caine as an actor of such range and agility, giving as good as he gets from the preeminent actor of the English stage"; V "sensational"; MFB "adequate but uninspired"); and Jon Voight as one of the men on a doomed canoe expedition in *Deliverance* (NYT "extraordinary"; LAT "proves again what a versatile actor he is"; WP "I found Voight's performance, as both conceived and executed, one of the most incomprehensible I've ever seen").

O'Toole was nominated for the Globe (Comedy/Musical) for *The Man of La Mancha*. Among the other nominees was Edward Albert as the young blind man in *Butterflies are Free* (LAT "has the innocence, the intelligence and the ingratiating openness that the part calls for and it seemed to me that he brought off very well indeed the harder-than-it looks job"; WP "quite engaging and competent"; MFB "likeably eloquent if a little self-conscious at times"). His father, Eddie Albert, was overlooked for the Best Supporting Actor Globe for the comedy *The Heartbreak Kid* but was nominated by the Academy. Another of the nominees was Walter Matthau in *Pete 'n' Tillie* (NYT "has given weightier performances but none more disarming"; LAT "I would like to say a few words in almost limitless praise of Walter Matthau"; WP "funny, ingratiating"). The winner, however, was Jack Lemmon in Billy Wilder's *Avanti!* (LAT "the central performance by Jack Lemmon is deplorably misguided"; MFB "creates a splendidly grating, ulcer-prone persona").

The Globe (Drama), meanwhile, was won by Brando. It was his second trophy from the Hollywood Foreign Press Association following his win for *On the Waterfront* in 1954.

Among those overlooked for the Globe, and subsequently the Oscar as well, were: Robert Redford as an aspiring politician in *The Candidate* (NYT "[his] best performance to date"; LAT "Redford's own performance is almost too easy to take for granted, it is so right and natural. But in fact, it may well be the best thing he has ever done"; CT "a winning performance"; WP "when Redford persists in his cutesy, ingenuous act he seems either misguided or unperceptive … one doesn't believe for a minute"; V "a virtuoso performance"); Gene Hackman as the religious man in the hit disaster film *The Poseidon Adv*enture (NYT "fairly convincing"; LAT "another fine performance"; CT "does what he can with a fatuous role"); Robert Duvall as the handyman in *Tomorrow* (NYT "such a good actor that he seems entirely different from one film to the next"; LAT "another richly developed characterization"); Max von Sydow as an immigrant farmer in *Utvandrarna (The Emigrants)* (LAT "unforgettable"); and French comic actor-director Jacques Tati in *Trafic (Traffic)* (TT "superb").

1972

The Academy nominated both Brando and Pacino, but not both as Best Actor. Previous winner Brando earned his sixth Best Actor nod, while Pacino was mentioned (for the first time) in the secondary category. Co-stars Caine and Olivier were both included as Best Actor, for the second and eighth time respectively. Globe winner Lemmon was overlooked, but O'Toole was recognised for a fifth time for his role in *The Ruling Class*. Surprisingly, the final nominee was African-American Paul Winfield. Despite strong reviews for his performance as a man jailed for stealing food for his family during the Depression in *Sounder*, Winfield had been by-passed throughout the awards season (NYT "expert"; CT "makes the movie go"; WP "seems to be overdoing the hearty, virile, laughing father"; V "terrific"; TT "faultless"; S&S "excellent").

During the Oscar voting the profile of Brando, already a strong favourite for the Academy Award, was increased even further with the release of Bernardo Bertolucci's *Last Tango in Paris*. Critics raved about his portrayal of an ageing businessman involved with a young woman, and his nude scenes made him the subject of widespread discussion. In 1973, he would receive both Oscar and BAFTA nominations as Best Actor for his performance.

As Oscar night approached, however, speculation began to mount as to whether Brando would attend the ceremony. He told the Hollywood Foreign Press Association that he would not attend the Globes because of "a singular lack of honor in this country today."

While there was no proxy to collect Brando's Golden Globe, there was a stand-in when the absent actor was named Best Actor by the Academy for the second time. A young woman called Sacheen Littlefeather, a Native American civil rights activist and actress, appeared on the stage and politely refused to accept the statuette explaining that Brando wanted to protest Hollywood's negative portrayal of Native Americans. It was the second time in three years that the Best Actor Oscar had been refused by the winner.

Brando's actions were roundly criticised in the media and many in Hollywood. "My own reaction is that he has no guts," declared Daniel Taradash, the President of the Academy. "If he had any class, he would have come down here and said it himself." Reporter Norma Lee Browning in the Chicago Tribune, meanwhile, said "Brando's hijacking of the Oscar lectern [was a] gutless caper, the epitome of bad taste [which] has not only hurt his cause but himself as well [since] his peers will probably think twice before ever voting him another Oscar." Over the subsequent years, however, Brando's stance and the dignity with which Littlefeather spoke have been an inspiration for others.

Brando was nominated for the BAFTA for *The Godfather*, but was outpolled by the previous year's Oscar winner, Gene Hackman, for his performances in both *The French Connection* and *The Poseidon Adventure*.

1972

BEST SUPPORTING ACTRESS

ACADEMY AWARDS
Jeannie Berlin as 'Lila Kolodny Cantrow' in *The Heartbreak Kid*
• Eileen Heckart as 'Mrs Baker' in *Butterflies are Free*
Geraldine Page as 'Gertrude' in *Pete 'n' Tillie*
Susan Tyrrell as 'Oma' in *Fat City*
Shelley Winters as 'Belle Rosen' in *The Poseidon Adventure*

GOLDEN GLOBE AWARDS
Marisa Berenson – *Cabaret*
Jeannie Berlin – *The Heartbreak Kid*
Helena Kallianiotes – *Kansas City Bomber*
Geraldine Page – *Pete 'n' Tillie*
• Shelley Winters – *The Poseidon Adventure*

BRITISH ACADEMY AWARDS
Marisa Berenson – *Cabaret*
Eileen Brennan – *The Last Picture Show*
• Cloris Leachman – *The Last Picture Show*
Shelley Winters – *The Poseidon Adventure*

NEW YORK – Jeannie Berlin – *The Heartbreak Kid*
BOARD OF REVIEW – Marisa Berenson – *Cabaret*
NATIONAL SOCIETY – Jeannie Berlin – *The Heartbreak Kid*

Jeannie Berlin was the Oscar frontrunner for playing a woman deserted by her husband on their honeymoon, in *The Heartbreak Kid*, a film directed by her mother, Elaine May (NYT "great performing"; LAT "extraordinary … brings off a hugely difficult comedy assignment with great style"; V "a natural comedienne of fine talent"; S&S "played with admirably undignified gusto"; FQ "splendid"). Berlin easily won the New York Film Critics Circle award on the first ballot, and also received the National Society of Film Critics prize.

The main challenger for the statuette was Golden Globe champ and two-time previous Oscar winner Shelley Winters as an overweight, former swimming champion in the disaster film *The Poseidon Adventure* (NYT "touching"; LAT "Winters is trapped in the cliches"; CT "steals the show"; V "outstanding").

The other nominees were: Eileen Heckart as a blind musician's possessive mother in *Butterflies are Free*, a part she had played on stage in London and New York (LAT "terrific – amusing when her words are etched with acid, winning when her guard is down"; WP "first-rate"; MFB "Heckart's mother is convincingly obtuse"); Geraldine Page (her fifth nod) as the matchmaker in *Pete 'n' Tillie* (NYT "the funniest thing we have seen on film all year"; LAT "marvelous to watch, suggesting more with a flutter of fingers than most actresses can manage in soliloquies"); and New York runner-up Susan Tyrrell as a boxer's drunken girlfriend in *Fat City* (NYT "one of the year's two or three most exciting performances"; LAT "dazzling … extravagantly histrionic, but you feel that the performance is part of the character, rather than a way of impersonating the character. She gives enormous vitality to the movie"; CT "considerably overplayed from the start"; WP "really overdoes the blubbery, whiney, argumentative bad-drunk routine … she's not in the least touching"; V "effective"; S&S "immaculate control of timing"; MFB "harrowingly authentic [in a] tearful, whisky-voiced performance").

The glaring omission from the list was National Board of Review winner Marisa Berenson in *Cabaret* (NYT "very fine"; LAT "first-rate"; V "excellent"). For her performance, Berenson was both a Globe and BAFTA nominee.

Also overlooked were: Janet MacLachlan as the teacher in *Sounder* (NYT "expert [and] interesting"; WP "strong"); Vivien Merchant in *Frenzy* (NYT "marvelous"; S&S "superb"); Madeline Kahn in *What's Up, Doc?* (NYT "superb … just about walks off with the movie"; LAT "[a] standout"; MFB "stands out from an already impressive supporting cast"); and Nell Potts in *The Effect of Gamma Rays on Man-In-the-Moon Marigolds*, a film starring her mother, Joanne Woodward, and directed by her father, Paul Newman (NYT "only Nell Potts is allowed to perform at something like a reasonable pace … a lovely, solemn performance").

Pundits seemed to view the race as a contest between critics' choice Berlin and Globe winner Winters, who already had two Best Supporting Actress statuettes on her mantelpiece. In an upset on Oscar night, the winner was Heckart.

At the British Academy Awards, Berenson and Winters were both outpolled by the previous year's Oscar winner, Cloris Leachman in *The Last Picture Show*.

1972

BEST SUPPORTING ACTOR

ACADEMY AWARDS
Eddie Albert as 'Mr Dwayne Corcoran' in *The Heartbreak Kid*
James Caan as 'Sonny Corleone' in *The Godfather*
Robert Duvall as 'Tom Hagen' in *The Godfather*
• Joel Grey as 'The Master of Ceremonies' in *Cabaret*
Al Pacino as 'Michael Corleone' in *The Godfather*

GOLDEN GLOBE AWARDS
James Caan – *The Godfather*
James Coco – *The Man of La Mancha*
• Joel Grey – *Cabaret*
Alec McCowen – *Travels with My Aunt*
Clive Revill – *Avanti!*

BRITISH ACADEMY AWARDS
Max Adrian – *The Boy Friend*
Robert Duvall – *The Godfather*
• Ben Johnson – *The Last Picture Show*
Ralph Richardson – *Lady Caroline Lamb*

NEW YORK – Robert Duvall – *The Godfather*
BOARD OF REVIEW – Joel Grey – *Cabaret* and **Al Pacino – *The Godfather***
NATIONAL SOCIETY – Joel Grey – *Cabaret* and **Eddie Albert – *The Heartbreak Kid***

As the malevolent emcee of a 1930s Berlin nightclub in *Cabaret*, a role that he had originated on Broadway six years earlier, Joel Grey won both the Golden Globe and the Oscar (NYT "a superbly refined caricature", "an impeccably stylized performance", "excellent"; LAT "first-rate"; CT "plays the emcee to the kitsch hilt"; WP "spellbinding"; TT "absolutely right"; G "goes through his routines with a sharpness of timing and a bounding attack that could scarcely be bettered … where his numbers are good, he makes them excellent; where they are excellent, he almost literally stops the show"). Grey also received accolades from the National Board of Review and the National Society of Film Critics, both of which he shared.

The other NBR winner was Al Pacino as the educated younger son of a Mafia boss in *The Godfather* (LAT "seems to change from within even as we watch";

WP "'The Godfather' is Michael's story and Pacino's film ... manages to convey the essential, tragic moral change [in his character]"; V "outstanding"; S&S "outstanding"; MFB "portrayed with finely calculated intensity .... almost, but not quite, he steals the film from Brando"). Eddie Albert was the other recipient of the NSFC honour as the wealthy father of a seductive beauty in *The Heartbreak Kid* (NYT "superbly comic", "steals what he can of the film"; V "scores"). At the Globes, Pacino was nominated in the Best Actor (Drama) category and Albert was overlooked altogether. Both men, however, received Oscar nominations alongside Grey. Albert was also the runner-up in the voting by the New York Film Critics Circle.

The other Oscar candidates were Pacino's co-stars in *The Godfather*: James Caan as the headstrong eldest son (LAT "excellent [and] terrifically effective"; MFB "excellent") and Robert Duvall as the family lawyer (LAT "very strong"; MFB "excellent"). Caan had been the only member of the film's cast nominated for the supporting Globe, while Duvall had been the winner of the New York plaudit. It was the fourth time that three actors from the same film had been mentioned in the same category.

Overlooked for consideration were: Robert Shaw, who placed third in the voting by the New York circle, for his turn as Lord Randolph Churchill in *Young Winston* (NYT "powerful"; CT "it works well [and] credit for that must be shared by Robert Shaw"; V "outstanding"; S&S "Shaw's performance is the film's strong card, commanding in its first half"); Alec McCowen both in *Travels with My Aunt* (NYT "does marvelous things as Henry"; LAT "politely underplays"; WP "a most ingratiating performance"; TT "quietly but emphatically steals so many scenes"; Obs "the real triumph [of the film] ... a beautifully judged performance"; S&S "admirable") and *Frenzy* (NYT "marvelous"); Clive Revill in *Avanti!* (NYT "a fine job"; V "the standout"); Ned Beatty for his debut in *Deliverance* (NYT "excellent"; LAT "excellent"; V "outstanding"); Kevin Hooks for his debut as the eldest son in *Sounder* (NYT "rather expert"; LAT "fine ... Hooks as the boy thrust toward manhood is the boy, not an actor"; CT "played with uncommon maturity"; V "excellent"; TT "faultless"); and BAFTA nominee Ralph Richardson as King George IV in *Lady Caroline Lamb* (LAT "the acting is splendid in a grand and florid way"; WP "makes a superfluous appearance in [a] stupidly written cameo").

1973

BEST PICTURE

ACADEMY AWARDS

American Graffiti
(Lucasfilm, Universal, 110 mins, 1 Aug 1973, $25.1m / gr:$115.0m, 5 noms)
The Exorcist
(Warner Bros., 122 mins, 26 Dec 1973, $66.3m / gr:$165.0m, 10 noms)
• ***The Sting***
(Phillips, Universal, 129 mins, 22 Dec 1973, $72.2m / gr:$156.0m, 10 noms)
A Touch of Class
(Brut, Avco Embassy, 105 mins, 22 Jun 1973, gr:$18.3m, 5 noms)
Visknigor och Rop (Cries and Whispers)
(Svenska Filminstitutet, New World, 106 mins, 22 Dec 1972, 5 noms)

GOLDEN GLOBE AWARDS

(Drama)
Cinderella Liberty
The Day of the Jackal
• ***The Exorcist***
Last Tango in Paris
Save the Tiger
Serpico

(Comedy/Musical)
• ***American Graffiti***
Jesus Christ Superstar
Paper Moon
Tom Sawyer
A Touch of Class

BRITISH ACADEMY AWARDS

The Day of the Jackal
Don't Look Now
La Charme Discret de la Bourgeoisie (The Discreet Charm of the Bourgeoisie)
• ***La Nuit Américaine (Day for Night)***

NEW YORK – *La Nuit Américaine (Day for Night)*
BOARD OF REVIEW – *The Sting*
NATIONAL SOCIETY – *La Nuit Américaine (Day for Night)*

"What the Devil Happened to The Exorcist's Oscar?" asked a headline in The New York Times on 5 May 1974. In the article that followed, Foster Hirsch commented, "'The Exorcist' was cheated. It ought to have won the Oscar that went to 'The Sting'." He described the film as "powerful", "riveting and compelling" and speculated, "in conspicuously bypassing William Friedkin's thriller, did the Academy choose safe entertainment, wholesome fun over wicked horror-show titillation?" The Chicago Tribune's Gene Siskel certainly thought so. "The Academy's choice of 'The Sting' as best picture marked a reward for the kind of conventional entertainment Hollywood regularly turned out in the years before hard-core skin flicks and kung-fu," he wrote the day after the ceremony.

The Exorcist and *The Sting* were the only serious contenders for the Best Picture Academy Award. They were released within four days of one another in late December, both to mixed reviews. They dominated the box office, each earning over three times as much as their competition, to finish with similar grosses as the top two films of 1974. During the awards season, both received prestigious Best Picture awards, and they topped the list of Oscar contenders, each honoured with ten nominations. Although almost inseparable on all these counts, the two films contrasted dramatically in both content and style.

Reuniting *Butch Cassidy and the Sundance Kid* director George Roy Hill with the hit comedy's two stars, Paul Newman and Robert Redford, *The Sting* was a light-hearted film about two small-time Chicago con-men. Critics praised it as escapist entertainment but few initially regarded it as a major Oscar contender (NYT "it looks and sound like a musical comedy from which the songs have been removed … but the film is so good-natured, so obviously aware of everything it's up to, even its own picturesque frauds, that I opt to go along with it … one forgives its unrelenting efforts to charm"; LAT "an unalloyed delight … pure entertainment"; WP "a clever, suspenseful, enjoyable charade … good, escapist fun [but] by no stretch of the imagination a work of art"; TT "unabashed, light-hearted entertainment"; S&S "it overdoes things [but] is a charmer, no doubt about that"; MFB "thoroughly old-fashioned"). It was thus a huge surprise when the National Board of Review named *The Sting* as Best Picture just two days after it had been released (and two days before the release of *The Exorcist*). At the very end of the year, *The Sting* was notably absent from The New York Times list of the twenty best films of the year and did not feature in the voting for Best Picture by the New York Film Critics Circle. When the Golden Globe nominations were announced, neither the film nor Hill were even mentioned for the major awards. *The Sting*, however, was hugely popular and inspired a revival of Scott Joplin's ragtime music.

By contrast, *The Exorcist* was a dark and confronting horror thriller about a young adolescent girl possessed by the Devil and the Catholic priests that battle to free her (NYT "elegant occultist claptrap [which is] a practically impossible film to sit through", "establishes a new low for grotesque special effects"; LAT "a genuinely shocking movie … [has] ferocious strength … a movie landmark"; CT "[a] remarkable film … thru technical virtuosity at every artistic level, [it] becomes more than a shocking movie: a film with a strong, positive force. I loved it."; WP "a proficient shocker … appallingly effective [but] appallingly worthless beneath the surface"; V "powerful"; SMH "a spectacle … suspenseful, well-acted"). The film was directed by William Friedkin, who had helmed the

Best Picture Oscar-winner from two years earlier, *The French Connection.* The film divided critics and was condemned by conservative leaders and some religious groups, but was enormously popular. At the Golden Globes, it received the awards for Best Picture (Drama) and Best Director.

On Oscar night, the dark and controversial horror film received just two statuettes: for Best Adapted Screenplay and Best Sound. The light-comedy crime caper triumphed with seven Oscars, including Best Picture. *The Sting* was the first film produced by Universal to claim the Academy's top honour since *All Quiet on the Western Front* in 1929/30. Both movies yielded sequels over the coming years, none of which were considered by the Academy.

The contest between *The Exorcist* and *The Sting* overshadowed the other three Best Picture Oscar nominees: George Lucas' nostalgic *American Graffiti,* which was the runner-up in New York and won the Globe for Best Comedy/Musical (NYT "easily the best movie so far this year … a lasting work of art", "very good ... funny, tough, unsentimental"; LAT "profoundly affecting … one of the most important American films of the year"; WP "an inspired sentimental journey … perhaps a minor work of art, but it's an extraordinarily harmonious and appealing work"; V "first-rate Americana"; SMH "positively reeks of nostalgia"); the romantic comedy *A Touch of Class* (NYT "a very patchy movie - enormously funny in bits and pieces and sometimes downright dumb"; CT "raucous at best, contrived silliness at worst"; WP "agreeably breezy and funny for about the first 30 or 40 minutes [but then] collapses"; V "sensational"; TT "a leaden and oddly disastrous example of what happens when you shoot for high comedy and miss"; MFB "a waste of two considerable talents"); and Ingmar Bergman's *Viskningor och Rop (Cries and Whispers),* winner of the National Board of Review Best Foreign-Language Film prize and the New York Film Critics Circle Best Picture accolade for the previous year (NYT "magnificent, moving and very mysterious … it stands alone and it reduces almost everything else you're likely to see this season to the size of a small cinder"; LAT "[a] truly overwhelming film … exhilarating as great art always is"; WP "a masterpiece … one can't help being fascinated … a visually imposing and spellbinding piece of work"; V "an emotionally draining tour de force"; S&S "stunning"; MFB "flawlessly acted").

In The Washington Post, Gary Arnold lamented the "marked decline in both dramatic material and overall quality" from the previous year's Best Picture line-up. The inclusion of *A Touch of Class* he wrote was particularly "difficult to comprehend" ahead of more deserving candidates such as: *Nybyggarna (The New Land),* the sequel to the 1972 Best Picture Oscar nominee, *Utvandrarna (The Emigrants)* (NYT "a shattering film", "no less than a masterly exercise in film-making", "lovely and moving"; LAT "one of the most impressive films of this year, and any year, a towering work with few parallels in the whole archive of the movies … incredibly moving"; CT "breathtaking … a brilliant historical film"; WP "stirring and engrossing"); the violent drama *Mean Streets* (NYT "a tough, vivid melodrama … unequivocally first class"; LAT "harrowing, intense, gruelling even, 'Mean Streets' is an unqualified triumph"; WP "unrelenting, breathless, and definitely on the brilliant side … moves with an energy that is frightening"; S&S "amazingly intense", "remarkable"); the low-budget melodrama *Walking Tall*, which became the year's unexpected word-of-mouth box office hit (LAT "devastating", "powerful", "deeply involving"; WP "a movie you'll never forget … the film could certainly be better in many respects [and yet it] could scarcely be more vivid and powerful"); and the police corruption drama *Serpico* (NYT "galvanizing and disquieting"; LAT "one of the year's best-crafted and most engrossing and disturbing movies"; CT "curiously, the film's singularity of purpose is both its principal strength and weakness"; WP "an engrossing and frequently forceful melodrama"; V "excellent").

Other notable films overlooked for consideration were: Globe nominee *Last Tango in Paris* (NYT "most affecting when it's most ambiguous, cross-breeding tragic melodrama with elegant satire [but then] goes so surprisingly banal that [nothing] can make it seem as important as we want it to be"; WP "falls far short of becoming a quintessential drama of sexual conflict, but it is a quintessential art movie"; TT "falls some way short of greatness"); Globe and BAFTA nominee *The Day of the Jackal* (LAT "overwhelming … wholly an entertainment, a movie of plot rather than of character or political significance"; CT "a superior adventure movie … vivid, sustained suspense"; WP "peculiarly neutral, noncommittal entertainment: moderately absorbing but not in the least exciting or intense"); the popular historical romance drama *The Way We Were* (NYT "claptrap"; LAT "persuasive and involving"; CT "has moments of genuine affection [but] credibility [is] stretched beyond belief"; WP "ponderous"; V "talky, redundant and moody"; SMG "gets lost"); the thriller *Don't Look Now* (NYT "possibly the most subtle and sophisticated horror film ever made … profoundly unsettling"; LAT "overmannered and artificial"; CT "see it at least twice"); and Jacques Tati's 1967 French comedy *Playtime* (NYT "nothing less than a brilliant film", "[one of] the greatest screen comedies of all time" and "Tati's most brilliant film"; WP "his films reflect a particular comic temperament and that temperament is gentle and contemplative rather than sassy or boisterous [and this is] his best movie to date").

The winner of the New York critics' Best Picture accolade, François Truffaut's *La Nuit Américaine (Day for Night)* won the Best Film BAFTA and the Oscar for Best Foreign-Language Film. It was not, however, eligible for Oscar consideration in other categories until the following year, at which time it received three nominations, including Best Director and Best Supporting Actress, but was overlooked for Best Picture.

1973

BEST DIRECTOR

ACADEMY AWARDS
Ingmar Bergman for *Visknningor och Rop (Cries and Whispers)*
Bernardo Bertolucci for *Last Tango in Paris*
William Friedkin for *The Exorcist*
• George Roy Hill for *The Sting*
George Lucas for *American Graffiti*

GOLDEN GLOBE AWARDS
Bernardo Bertolucci – *Last Tango in Paris*
Peter Bogdanovich – *Paper Moon*
• William Friedkin – *The Exorcist*
George Lucas – *American Graffiti*
Fred Zinnemann – *The Day of the Jackal*

DIRECTORS GUILD AWARD
Bernardo Bertolucci
– *Last Tango in Paris*
William Friedkin – *The Exorcist*
• George Roy Hill – *The Sting*
George Lucas – *American Graffiti*
Sidney Lumet – *Serpico*

BRITISH ACADEMY AWARDS
Luis Buñuel
– *La Charme Discret de la Bourgeoisie (The Discreet Charm of the Bourgeoisie)*
Nicolas Roeg – *Don't Look Now*
• François Truffaut
– *La Nuit Américaine (Day for Night)*
Fred Zinnemann
– *The Day of the Jackal*

NEW YORK – François Truffaut – *La Nuit Américaine (Day for Night)*
BOARD OF REVIEW – Ingmar Bergman – *Visknningor och Rop (Cries and Whispers)*
NATIONAL SOCIETY – François Truffaut – *La Nuit Américaine (Day for Night)*

The National Board of Review gave their Best Director award to Ingmar Bergman for his Swedish drama *Visknningor och Rop (Cries and Whispers)* (NYT "focus so sharp"; LAT "a surpassing example of the film-maker's art, the best film Bergman has done in many years and a masterwork likely to be watched for years"; WP "powerfully expressive"; V "impeccable direction"; S&S

"stunning"). In doing so, they followed the example of the New York Film Critics Circle who had named Bergman as Best Director the previous year for his handling of the same film.

The New York critics, meanwhile, honoured François Truffaut for *La Nuit Américaine (Day for Night)*, a French-language film about a director's efforts to film a poorly-written romance. Truffaut also won his second Best Director prize from the National Society of Film Critics. He was not, however, eligible for Oscar consideration until the following year.

While the critics' groups honoured foreigners for non-American films, the frontrunners for the main awards in Hollywood were a trio of American film-makers for local projects. William Friedkin, who had won the Best Director Oscar two years earlier for *The French Connection*, was a strong contender with the controversial, but popular horror film, *The Exorcist* (NYT "is not unintelligently put together"; CT "brilliantly achieved … technical virtuosity at every artistic level"; WP "an extremely adroit technician … [the film] is impeccably composed and edited and there's no use denying the immediate, visceral impact Friedkin gets into the most shocking bits"). George Roy Hill was in contention for the light-hearted caper *The Sting* (NYT "all a little too much, but excess is an essential part of the film's style"; LAT "quality Hollywood craftsmanship … not for a second does Hill allow the pace to lag"; CT "[the film] has obviously been made with loving care [and it] has the technical craftsmanship of Hollywood's golden era"; WP "the film has a graceful, unhurried storytelling rhythm … Hill's calm, trim, mellow style of direction [is] a distinct joy … Hill's direction is a model of wit and economy"; V "outstanding direction"). And finally, George Lucas was in the running for *American Graffiti*, a semi-autobiographical coming-of-age drama that had unexpectedly finished as the year's tenth biggest box office hit (NYT "his work with the actors in 'American Graffiti' is a revelation"; LAT "masterfully executed … a considerable technical achievement"; CT "well-made"; V "a truly masterful job"; SMH "formless [and] shamelessly self-indulgent").

Both Friedkin and Lucas were nominated for the Golden Globe, along with: Bernardo Bertolucci for *Last Tango in Paris* (NYT "magnificently rich"); Peter Bogdanovich for *Paper Moon* (CT "displays a talent for revitalizing the morality and visual style of films long past"; WP "Bogdanovich, extraordinarily capable with the straight-forward material of 'The Last Picture Show' appears to strain and miscalculate"); and previous winner Fred Zinnemann for the thriller *The Day of the Jackal* (LAT "awesomely detailed … what is overwhelming about the movie is the care Zinnemann has expended on very detail … the triumph of Zinnemann's work is that the suspense is sustained despite the length [of the film]"; CT "the film's vivid, sustained suspense [is] an achievement … Zinnemann's method is worth noting"; WP "exemplary"; MFB "has lost none of his sense of how to diagram an action sequence"). In the end, it was Friedkin who took home the Globe as Best Director for the second time in three years.

The Academy nominated Friedkin and Hill, each for the second time. Critics' winner Bergman and Globe nominees Bertolucci and Lucas were also mentioned, all for the first time.

Four of the Oscar nominees were also finalists for the Directors Guild of America honour: Bertolucci, Friedkin (for the second time), Hill (for the third time and second consecutive year) and Lucas. Instead of Bergman, the guild short-listed Sidney Lumet (for the fourth time) for *Serpico* (NYT "[the film] is galvanizing because of the tremendous intensity that Mr Lumet brings to this sort of subject"; LAT "one of the year's best-crafted movies"; V "adept").

Overlooked for consideration for the various Best Director accolades were: Jan Troell for *Nybyggarna (The New Land)* (NYT "a masterly exercise in film-making"; LAT "a singular personal triumph for Troell"; WP "has a uniquely beautiful and liberating movie vision ... has mastered the difficult but transcendent technique of rendering epic story material intimately"); New York runner-up Constantin Costa-Gavras for *État de siège (State of Siege)* (NYT "Costa-Gavras's techniques [creates suspense] by a lot of breathless cross-cutting, by the continual use of the zoom lens in or out, by the kind of shrewd pacing tricks that are the movie equivalents of the way sensational stories are presented in tabloid newspapers"; LAT "notably competent"; WP "peculiarly didactic ... never succeeds"; MFB "Costa-Gavras is unable to resist the opportunist tricks of the skilled exponent of political melodrama"); Martin Scorsese for *Mean Streets* (NYT "the look, language and performances are so accurate, so unselfconscious, so directly evocative"; LAT "'Mean Streets' unfolds with the inevitability and power of a classic tragedy ... Scorsese makes a wealth of incident and detail endlessly revealing"; WP "Scorsese's brilliance lies not in telling a memorable story but in conveying environment, in evoking in us the same sense of confinement and urban peril [as his characters]"); Nicolas Roeg for *Don't Look Now* (NYT "succeeds in transforming the pulp material into a richly evocative personal vision of the possibilities of evil"; S&S "puts Nicolas Roeg right at the top as a film-maker"); and Jacques Tati for the 1967 comedy *Playtime* (NYT "Tati's use of sound in 'Playtime' is extraordinarily funny"; WP "Tati's comic vision is peculiarly mellow and appealing").

On 16 March 1974, the DGA announced that Hill was the winner of its annual accolade. The choice was something of a surprise and the victory made Hill the Oscar favourite. The Academy Award had been presented to the DGA winner twenty-two times over the past twenty-four years, and yet Hill had not even been a nominee for the other traditional Oscar indicator, the Globe.

On the night, *The Sting* easily bettered *The Exorcist*. The film won seven statuettes, including Best Picture and Best Director for Hill.

1973

BEST ACTRESS

ACADEMY AWARDS
Ellen Burstyn as 'Mrs MacNeil' in *The Exorcist*
• Glenda Jackson as 'Vicki Allessio' in *A Touch of Class*
Marsha Mason as 'Maggie Paul' in *Cinderella Liberty*
Barbra Streisand as 'Katie Morosky' in *The Way We Were*
Joanne Woodward as 'Rita Walden' in *Summer Wishes, Winter Dreams*

GOLDEN GLOBE AWARDS
(Drama)
Ellen Burstyn – *The Exorcist*
• Marsha Mason – *Cinderella Liberty*
Barbra Streisand – *The Way We Were*
Elizabeth Taylor – *Ash Wednesday*
Joanne Woodward – *Summer Wishes, Winter Dreams*

(Comedy/Musical)
Yvonne Elliman – *Jesus Christ Superstar*
• Glenda Jackson – *A Touch of Class*
Cloris Leachman – *Charley and the Angel*
Tatum O'Neal – *Paper Moon*
Liv Ullmann – *40 Carats*

BRITISH ACADEMY AWARDS
• Stéphane Audran – *La Charme Discret de la Bourgeoisie (The Discreet Charm of the Bourgeoisie)* and *Juste Avant la Nuit (Just Before Nightfall)*
Julie Christie – *Don't Look Now*
Glenda Jackson – *A Touch of Class*
Diana Ross – *Lady Sings the Blues*

NEW YORK – Joanne Woodward – *Summer Wishes, Winter Dreams*
BOARD OF REVIEW – Liv Ullmann – *Nybyggarna (The New Land)*
NATIONAL SOCIETY – Liv Ullmann – *Nybyggarna (The New Land)*

Just three years after she won the Best Actress Oscar for her role in the drama *Women in Love*, Glenda Jackson won a second statuette as a divorcee embarking on a new romance in the comedy *A Touch of Class* (NYT "extremely funny"; WP "it's novel and enjoyable to see Glenda Jackson in a romantic comedy role"; V "outstanding"; MFB "Jackson is not equipped for lightness … miscast"). She was the only nominee not in attendance at the ceremony, and triumphed over four Americans who had been mentioned for performances in dramatic roles.

Jackson's win, however, should not have been a complete surprise. In the lead up to the Oscars (where she had been nominated for the third time in four years), she had won the Golden Globe (Comedy/Musical) and had only very narrowly been outpolled for the Best Actress award in New York (she lost by just two points). She was also a nominee for the Best Actress BAFTA in London. Jackson also had the benefit of a contrasting role that year in the period drama *Bequest to the Nation (The Nelson Affair)* (NYT "rather fun to watch … an all-stops-out performance"; LAT "a razzling-dazzling fireworks display"; V "another manifestation of her diversified range").

The Best Actress Academy Award had been considered a three-way contest between the Globe (Drama) champ and two previous Oscar winners.

As a woman having a mid-life crisis in *Summer Wishes, Winter Dreams*, previous winner Joanne Woodward won her second New York Film Critics Circle prize and earned her third Oscar nomination (NYT "the moments of vulnerability just aren't convincing"; LAT "[a] careful and evolving characterization … subtle and affecting"; V "first-rate"; TT "accurate and excellent"). Earlier in the year she had been honoured at the Cannes Film Festival for a performance in *The Effect of Gamma Rays on Man-In-the-Moon Marigolds* which Academy voters had overlooked the previous year.

Previous winner Barbra Streisand received her second mention as a political activist in *The Way We Were* (NYT "she's not really an actress … she's an impersonator [and] when the impersonation fits the contours of the public personality the performance can be effective as it is for a short space of time [here, but her] performance goes wrong when the story follows the now-married couple to post-war Hollywood"; LAT "wonderfully well-acted … has never been better, playing a role close to her own tough-minded and singular self, but playing it with restraint to create a character rather than a performance and letting the vulnerability show through"; WP "one feels drawn to [her]"; V shows "superior dramatic versatility"; TT "tends to act rather a lot"; MFB "superb").

Both Woodward and Streisand, however, were outpolled for the Globe (Drama) by Marsha Mason, who had come to prominence with her performance as a warm-hearted hooker, with an illegitimate child of mixed ethnicity, who befriends a sailor in *Cinderella Liberty* (NYT "so good that you wish the script were equal to [her]"; LAT "stunningly acted … plays the hooker with a kind of documentary fervor … not less than marvelous"; WP "provides a glaring showcase for Mason's distinctive strengths and weaknesses"; V "superb"). The Academy short-listed Mason for the first time.

The fifth nominee for the Oscar was Ellen Burstyn as the mother in the horror film *The Exorcist* (LAT "her portrayal of a woman driven to the edge by events beyond reckoning is stark and strong"; WP "an oddly unattractive interpretation – shrill and irritable"; V "a fine performance"; SMH "well-acted").

1973

The most glaring omission from the list of Oscar nominees was Norwegian actress Liv Ullmann. "Looking at the best actress nominees," wrote Gary Arnold in The Washington Post, "you're haunted by the thought that the most imaginative performances of the year by Liv Ullmann in 'The New Land' and '40 Carats' weren't even nominated". Ullman was named Best Actress by both the National Board of Review and the National Society of Film Critics for the second time (each group had chosen her as Best Actress in 1968) for her portrayal of a homesick Swedish emigrant in the nineteenth century in *Nybyggarna (The New Land)* (NYT "[a] carefully nuanced performance"; LAT "[a] dazzling performance"; WP "remarkable … [her] performance is especially striking ... there's no wasted emotion in her acting … a glorious performance"). She received a Golden Globe (Comedy/Musical) nomination, meanwhile, for playing a New York divorcee pursued by a much younger man in the English-language comedy *40 Carats* (NYT "utterly lost … she is, I suspect, constitutionally incapable of dealing with this sort of nonsense"; LAT "makes the heroine not merely sympathetic but thoroughly believable"; CT "[the film] works and is funny because of the performance of Liv Ullmann"; WP "brings a wonderful economy and precision of expression"; MFB "the thanklessness of the part is only compounded by Miss Ullmann's inability to handle light comedy"). Ullmann was also eligible for Oscar consideration for the other performance for which she had been cited by the east coast circle in 1972: as one of the sisters in Ingmar Bergman's *Viskningor och Rop (Cries and Whispers)* (LAT "another astonishing portrayal"; S&S "flawlessly acted").

Also by-passed for the Oscar were: BAFTA nominee Julie Christie in *Don't Look Now* (NYT "excellent"; LAT "intense"; MFB "striking"); Sarah Miles in *The Hireling* (NYT "a calm, intelligent performance"; V "splendid"); Claire Bloom reprising her West End and Broadway performance as Nora in *A Doll's House* (NYT "evolves with the play itself"; LAT "thrilling … polished into an admirable naturalness and subtlety … remarkable and effective"; CT "beautiful"; MFB "gives an intelligent reading of the part"); Lili Darvas for her final film performance in the 1971 Hungarian film *Szerelem (Love)* (NYT "splendid"; WP "striking"); both 1972 National Society runner-up Harriet Andersson (LAT "[with] a soul-deep conviction which appears to transcend the craft of acting, Harriet Andersson conveys the sense of real anguish so tellingly that it is impossible not to be moved") and BAFTA Best Supporting Actress nominee Ingrid Thulin (LAT "bursting out of repression with shrieks of rage and despair, brings off moments which link Bergman's landed gentry with the agonies of Greek tragedy") in *Viskningor och Rop (Cries and Whispers)*; and Lotte Tarp as an emotionally-disturbed woman in the Danish drama *Farlige Kys (Dangerous Kisses)* (V "her performance is low-keyed but brutally effective").

1973

BEST ACTOR

ACADEMY AWARDS
Marlon Brando as 'Paul' in *Last Tango in Paris*
• Jack Lemmon as 'Harry Stoner' in *Save the Tiger*
Jack Nicholson as 'Billy L. Buddusky SMI' in *The Last Detail*
Al Pacino as 'Frank Serpico' in *Serpico*
Robert Redford as 'Johnny Hooker' in *The Sting*

GOLDEN GLOBE AWARDS
(Drama)
Robert Blake – *Electra Glide in Blue*
Jack Lemmon – *Save the Tiger*
Steve McQueen – *Papillon*
Jack Nicholson – *The Last Detail*
• Al Pacino – *Serpico*

(Comedy/Musical)
Carl Anderson – *Jesus Christ Superstar*
Richard Dreyfuss – *American Graffiti*
Ted Neeley – *Jesus Christ Superstar*
Ryan O'Neal – *Paper Moon*
• George Segal – *A Touch of Class*

BRITISH ACADEMY AWARDS
Marlon Brando – *Last Tango in Paris*
• Walter Matthau – *Charley Varrick* and *Pete 'n' Tillie*
Laurence Olivier – *Sleuth*
Donald Sutherland – *Don't Look Now* and *Steelyard Blues*

NEW YORK – Marlon Brando – *Last Tango in Paris*
BOARD OF REVIEW – Al Pacino – *Serpico* and Robert Ryan – *The Iceman Cometh*
NATIONAL SOCIETY – Marlon Brando – *Last Tango in Paris*

A year after winning his second Best Actor Oscar, Marlon Brando was honoured by the New York Film Critics Circle (for the second time) for his turn as a man involved with a younger woman in *Last Tango in Paris* (NYT a "courageous performance … has pulled out all the stops without fear of looking absurd"; WP "attempts to fill out the character with bits of his own experience and with the force of his personality, and he's often fascinating to watch, amusing or brilliantly intense in isolated scenes [but] those isolated moments don't add up to a whole, comprehensible character … I was not convinced"; TT "a performance of shattering intensity"; MFB "[a] magnificent achievement"). Brando was also named Best Actor by the National Society of Film Critics.

The runner-up in the east coast critics' vote (falling 5 points short, with 33 to Brando's tally of 38) was Al Pacino as a young police officer fighting to expose corruption in *Serpico* (NYT "splendid"; LAT "his portrait ranges from easy charm to bitter humor to tenderness to raging frustration. It is a complex and evolving portrait, and Pacino brings it off with a remarkable economy"; WP "the film seems to hang together emotionally on Pacino's performance ... [he] convinces"; V "outstanding"). Two weeks before the New York vote, Pacino had been honoured by the National Board of Review, sharing the accolade with the late Robert Ryan for his supporting performance in *The Iceman Cometh* (NYT "almost unbearably affecting to watch ... his finest hours as a superb craftsman ... heartbreakingly fine"; CT "particularly fine"; V "amazing").

When the Golden Globe nominations were announced, the day after the announcement of the New York honourees, Brando was a notable absentee from the Best Actor (Drama) category. Pacino ultimately won the trophy ahead of a field that included: Jack Lemmon in *Save the Tiger* (NYT "very good"; LAT "stunning ... [an] extraordinarily affecting and sensitive portrayal ... it is much the best thing Lemmon has ever done"; CT "played with commendable passion"; V "powerful", "will garner a heap of praise for his performance"; TT "very fine indeed"; MFB "Lemmon's performance is a marvellously creased and furrowed replica of middle-aged bewilderment, but becomes gradually less affecting"); Steve McQueen in *Papillon* (LAT "does give a persuasive performance of Oscar proportions"; CT "the publicity mill is grinding out the idea that McQueen will be nominated for an Academy Award. If that happens the nomination will represent another triumph for the grovel-and-wince school of acting ... [his] character becomes dreadfully tiring"; WP "works hard with obvious sincerity, but the character has no radiance or charisma"; V "outstanding"); and Jack Nicholson in *The Last Detail* (NYT "remarkably good", "by far the best thing he's ever done"; MFB "a scene-stealing performance").

The winner of the Best Actor (Comedy/Musical) Globe was George Segal in *A Touch of Class* (NYT "extremely funny"; WP "his performance struck me as hectic and strained"; V "outstanding", "superb"; MFB "finely judges the balance between comedy and sexuality"). Among the other nominees were Richard Dreyfuss as one of the high-school graduates in *American Graffiti* (NYT "marvelous"; LAT "gives the character a roundness which is partly expressed, partly implied by remarkable powers of implication"; WP "unusually convincing") and Ryan O'Neal as a con-man selling bibles during the Depression in *Paper Moon* (NYT "first-class ... moves easily between his roles as star and as straight-man for Tatum [O'Neal]"; CT "continually reminds us that 'Paper Moon' is just a movie, and a Hollywood production at that"; WP "his performance has no style or authority"; S&S "accomplished").

1973

When the Academy announced the Oscar nominees three weeks after the Globe ceremony, Brando appeared on the list of contenders for a seventh time and second consecutive year. Also in contention were: Globe winner Pacino; previous Best Supporting Actor winner Lemmon; Nicholson; and, in a major surprise, Robert Redford as one of the two Chicago con-men in *The Sting* (LAT "in top form"; WP "sharp and appealing"; S&S "in fine form"). Redford had also starred in the hit romantic drama *The Way We Were*. Surprisingly, Globe winner Segal was overlooked, despite nominations for his film and co-star, as was Globe nominee McQueen despite a strong campaign.

Also by-passed were: Paul Newman in *The Sting* (LAT "in top form"; WP "sharp and appealing … Newman is the unchallenged crowd pleaser [of the film] … a tough act to follow"; S&S "in fine form"); previous winner Fredric March in his final film, *The Iceman Cometh* (NYT "superb"; CT "particularly fine"; V "superb"); James Caan as the sailor involved with a prostitute in *Cinderella Liberty* (NYT "fine"; LAT "marvelous … gives another of his sensitive portrayals of men blessed with good hearts rather than strong intellects"; WP "there's not much for Caan to do except act inoffensive"; V "outstanding"); Fred Williamson as a gangster in otherwise poorly-reviewed *Black Caesar* (NYT "imposing"; LAT "[the film] suggests its fast-rising star Fred Williamson possesses the emotional range and stamina to sustain a large-scale role [but] alas, he's working in a vacuum"; V "outstanding"); both Harvey Keitel (NYT "unselfconscious"; WP "tremendously strong") and Robert De Niro (NYT "a spectacular performance"; WP "tremendously strong"; V "outstanding"; S&S "pulls it off triumphantly … goes beyond technique … his performance hardly seems like acting at all, but rather like some sort of super-naturalistic presence") in *Mean Streets*; Max von Sydow in *Nybyggarna (The New Land)* (NYT "[a] carefully nuanced performance"; LAT "[a] dazzling performance"; WP "remarkable"); Joe Don Baker in *Walking Tall* (LAT "highly ingratiating – and can move you to tears"; WP "he is at once 'real' and forceful … effective"); Rip Torn in *Payday* (NYT "he virtually disappears into the role"; LAT "convincing"); BAFTA nominee Donald Sutherland in *Don't Look Now* (NYT "excellent"; LAT "intense"; MFB "striking"); and Sean Connery as a detective investigating a series of rapes in *The Offence* (NYT a "startling performance … has a depth of feeling that will amaze").

On Oscar night, the Best Actor statuette went to the sentimental favourite: Jack Lemmon. The winner of the Best Supporting Actor statuette in 1955, Lemmon was the first man to win Oscars in both lead and support categories.

In 1974, unsuccessful Oscar nominee Jack Nicholson won Best Actor prizes at the British Academy Awards and the Cannes Film Festival for his performance in *The Last Detail*.

1973

BEST SUPPORTING ACTRESS

ACADEMY AWARDS
Linda Blair as 'Regan MacNeil' in *The Exorcist*
Candy Clark as 'Debbie' in *American Graffiti*
Madeline Kahn as 'Trixie Delight' in *Paper Moon*
• Tatum O'Neal as 'Addie Loggins' in *Paper Moon*
Sylvia Sidney as 'Rita's mother' in *Summer Wishes, Winter Dreams*

GOLDEN GLOBE AWARDS
• Linda Blair – *The Exorcist*
Valentina Cortese – *La Nuit Américaine (Day for Night)*
Madeline Kahn – *Paper Moon*
Kate Reid – *A Delicate Balance*
Sylvia Sidney – *Summer Wishes, Winter Dreams*

BRITISH ACADEMY AWARDS
• Valentina Cortese – *La Nuit Américaine (Day for Night)*
Rosemary Leach – *That'll Be the Day*
Delphine Seyrig – *The Day of the Jackal*
Ingrid Thulin – *Viskningor Och Rop (Cries and Whispers)*

NEW YORK – Valentina Cortese – *La Nuit Américaine (Day for Night)*
BOARD OF REVIEW – Sylvia Sidney – *Summer Wishes, Winter Dreams*
NATIONAL SOCIETY – Valentina Cortese – *La Nuit Américaine (Day for Night)*

For *La Nuit Américaine (Day for Night)*, Valentina Cortese won the BAFTA and both New York Film Critics Circle and National Society of Film Critics awards. She was not in Oscar contention, however, until 1974.

The Globe winner was fourteen-year-old Linda Blair as the girl possessed by the Devil in *The Exorcist* (LAT "played with endearing innocence then with frightening unrecognizability"; WP "the most effective performer in the film"; SMH "well-acted"). Blair's chances of repeating her win, however, were undermined when it was revealed that her voice in the 'possession' sequences had been dubbed, without credit, by previous Oscar winner Mercedes McCambridge.

Claiming the Oscar was an even younger nominee: ten-year old Tatum O'Neal, the daughter of previous Best Actor nominee, Ryan O'Neal, with whom she co-starred (in a leading role) as a con-man's daughter in *Paper Moon* (NYT "first-class"; LAT "robustly endearing [and] she certainly commandeers every moment … she is just plain marvelous"; CT "beguiling"; WP "I expected to be more affected by Tatum O'Neal than I was. In fact, the keenest disappointment for me was the lack of anything original or moving in her performance ... she's a surprisingly reserved screen presence, subdued and self-conscious"; V "outstanding"; TT "played with devastating assurance, faultless skill and the reticence of great clowning"; S&S "accomplished").

In addition to Blair, the nominees outpolled for the Oscar were: Madeline Kahn in *Paper Moon* (NYT "I also very much liked Madeline Kahn's very broad characterization as a carnival kootch girl"; LAT "excellent"; WP "a grotesquely overplayed performance"; V "excellent"); Candy Clark in *American Graffiti* (NYT "marvelous"; LAT "makes the dumb blonde more than a stereotype"; WP "makes a lasting, delightful impression"); and National Board of Review winner Sylvia Sidney in *Summer Wishes, Winter Dreams*, her first film role in seventeen years (LAT "a smashing, sharp-tongued and salty portrayal"; V "first-rate").

Overlooked by the Academy were: Vivien Merchant in both *The Offence* (NYT "beautifully played"; MFB "seems curiously subdued") and *The Homecoming*, for which she was a BAFTA nominee in 1976 (NYT "outstanding"; LAT "the level of acting [by the six cast members] is spectacularly high … it is possible to be enthralled by the quality of the performances"; WP "impeccable"); Diana Rigg in *Theatre of Blood* (NYT "funny and legitimately moving"; LAT "delightful"); Anna Massey in *A Doll's House* (NYT "fine"; LAT "conveys a quiet strength born of ill-use by the world and does it with an admirable soft-voiced underplaying"; CT "superb"; V "outstanding"); Helen Mirren in *O, Lucky Man!* (NYT "superb", marvelous"); Cindy Williams in *American Graffiti* (NYT "marvelous"); both Laurie Heineman (LAT "stunning"; V "excellent") and Patricia Smith (LAT "stunning"; V "excellent") in *Save the Tiger*; Brenda Benet as the call girl in *Walking Tall* (LAT "topnotch"; WP "[a] striking performer … stunning"); previous winner Celeste Holm as Aunt Polly in the musical *Tom Sawyer* (NYT "fine", "lovely"; LAT "an extremely compassionate and touching performance"; V "sensational", "a personal triumph"; MFB "excellent"); and Margaret Leighton as Lady Nelson in *Bequest to the Nation (The Nelson Affair)* (LAT "achieves an intimate portrait, sharp but life-sized"; V "smashing", "outstanding").

1973

BEST SUPPORTING ACTOR

ACADEMY AWARDS
Vincent Gardenia as 'Dutch Schnell' in *Bang the Drum Slowly*
Jack Gilford as 'Phil Greene' in *Save the Tiger*
• John Houseman as 'Prof. Kingsfield' in *The Paper Chase*
Jason Miller as 'Father Karras' in *The Exorcist*
Randy Quaid as 'Laurence M. Meadows SN' in *The Last Detail*

GOLDEN GLOBE AWARDS
Martin Balsam – *Summer Wishes, Winter Dreams*
Jack Gilford – *Save the Tiger*
• John Houseman – *The Paper Chase*
Randy Quaid – *The Last Detail*
Max von Sydow – *The Exorcist*

BRITISH ACADEMY AWARDS
Ian Bannen – *The Offence*
Denholm Elliott – *A Doll's House*
Michael Lonsdale – *The Day of the Jackal*
• Arthur Lowe – *O, Lucky Man!*

NEW YORK – Robert De Niro – *Bang the Drum Slowly*
BOARD OF REVIEW – John Houseman – *The Paper Chase*
NATIONAL SOCIETY – Robert De Niro – *Bang the Drum Slowly*

When James Mason withdrew from the role of a Harvard law professor in *The Paper Chase*, he was replaced by a seventy-year old veteran Hollywood producer who had never previously had a credited role in a feature film: John Houseman (V "outstanding"). His debut performance won Houseman the National Board of Review award, the Golden Globe and the Oscar. It also saw him finish as the runner-up for the New York Film Critics Circle accolade.

The only other strong contender, surprisingly, was overlooked for the Oscar (as he was for the Globe). As a simple-minded baseball player in *Bang the Drum Slowly*, Robert De Niro won both the New York and National Society of Film Critics accolades (LAT "ingratiating"; V "very good"). One of the actors considered ahead of De Niro was his co-star, Vincent Gardenia, who played the team manager (NYT "plays Dutch with a belligerent comic diligence that should constitute any director's dream performance"; LAT "deserves to be remembered at Oscar nomination time"; CT "hilarious"; WP "[a] weirdly oversized performance").

Also nominated were: Jack Gilford in *Save the Tiger* (NYT "very good"; LAT "stunning ... played with dour and sympathetic naturalism"; V "outstanding"); playwright Jason Miller as one of the priests in *The Exorcist* (LAT "a darkly forceful performance"; CT "brilliant acting"; WP "adequate, though never precisely magnetic"; SMH "well-acted"); and Randy Quaid as a young sailor being escorted to the stockade in *The Last Detail* (NYT "marvelous"; MFB "excellent").

In addition to De Niro, Oscar voters by-passed: co-stars Ralph Richardson (LAT "gives one of his ablest and most restrained portrayals"; V "outstanding"), BAFTA nominee Denholm Elliott (LAT "sensationally effective"; CT "superb"; V "excellent") and Anthony Hopkins (NYT "brilliant"; LAT "sensationally effective"; CT "beautifully played") in *A Doll's House*; co-stars Jeff Bridges (LAT "sensational"; V "brilliant"), Moses Gunn (NYT "superb") and the late Robert Ryan (NYT "almost unbearably affecting to watch ... his finest hours as a superb craftsman ... heartbreakingly fine"; CT "particularly fine"; V "amazing") in *The Iceman Cometh*; both BAFTA nominee Ian Bannen (NYT "fine"; MFB "brings off a minor tour de force with his depiction of bewildered, tormented hysteria") and Trevor Howard (NYT "beautifully played"; MFB "seems curiously subdued") in *The Offence*; BAFTA nominee Arthur Lowe in *O, Lucky Man!* (NYT "superb", "marvelous"); Ian Holm in *The Homecoming* (NYT "outstanding"; LAT "mesmerizing"; WP "impeccable"); William Hansen in *Save the Tiger* (V "superb"); Henry Gibson in *The Long Goodbye* (CT "Gibson plays a villain so well that one's mind cannot accept that it is really Gibson"; V "excellent"); BAFTA nominee Michael Lonsdale as the police commissioner in *The Day of the Jackal* (V "excellent"); Globe nominee Martin Balsam in *Summer Wishes, Winter Dreams* (V "first-rate") and Robert Shaw in the Best Picture Academy Award winner *The Sting* (LAT "in top form"; CT "[a] pleasure"; V "brilliant").

1974

BEST PICTURE

ACADEMY AWARDS

Chinatown
(Evans, Paramount, 131 mins, 22 June 1974, $8.4m, 11 noms)

The Conversation
(Directors Co, Paramount, 113 mins, 7 Apr 1974, 3 noms)

• *The Godfather Part II*
(Coppola, Paramount, 200 mins, 12 Dec 1974, $30.6m / gr:$57.3m, 11 noms)

Lenny
(Worth, United Artists, BW 111 mins, 10 Nov 1974, 6 noms)

The Towering Inferno
(Irwin Allen, Twentieth Century-Fox, Warner Bros., 165 mins, 20 Dec 1974, $55.0m / gr:$116.0m, 8 noms)

GOLDEN GLOBE AWARDS

(Drama)
• *Chinatown*
The Conversation
Earthquake
The Godfather Part II
A Woman Under the Influence

(Comedy/Musical)
The Front Page
Harry and Tonto
The Little Prince
• *The Longest Yard*
The Three Musketeers

BRITISH ACADEMY AWARDS

Chinatown
• *Lacombe, Lucien*
The Last Detail
Murder on the Orient Express

NEW YORK – *Amarcord*
BOARD OF REVIEW – *The Conversation*
NATIONAL SOCIETY – *Scener ur ett Äktenskap (Scenes from a Marriage)*

Two of the year's highly-anticipated Oscar contenders, each a big-budget adaptation of a revered piece of American literature, both turned out to be major disappointments when released in the first half of the year.

In March, *The Great Gatsby*, an adaptation of F. Scott Fitzgerald's celebrated novel, was described by Vincent Canby in The New York Times as "lifeless" and "ponderous." Directed by Jack Clayton from a script by Francis Ford Coppola, and starring Robert Redford and Mia Farrow, the film managed modest box office success despite almost universally negative reviews (LAT "interminable"; WP "a fiasco … has a lot of inept, embarrassing work"). Any hopes of awards seasons glory beyond accolades for production design were dashed. "Victim of its own publicity overkill, 'The Great Gatsby' has become the movie to hate" explained Foster Hirsch in The New York Times two months after the film's release, "Slaughtered by the critics … the picture has been dismissed as a desecration of a great American novel; it's been damned as insensitive, numbingly reverential, ludicrously miscast, stultifyingly dull".

Two months later, most critics were equally scathing about Peter Bogdanovich's *Daisy Miller*, starring Cybill Shepherd as Henry James' naive heroine (NYT "something of a triumph for everyone concerned", "works amazingly well"; LAT "a partial success"; CT "a casting error upsets [what] might have been a small jewel [of a film]"; WP "bumptious"; V "a dud"; MFB "a literary adaptation which reveals a fine contempt for literary subtlety"). While the support of both critics Vincent Canby and Nora Sayre saw *Daisy Miller* appear on The New York Times list of the year's ten best releases, its Oscar chances had by then been long obliterated.

The early frontrunner for the Best Picture Academy Award was Roman Polanski's detective drama *Chinatown* (LAT "the finest American film of the year"; CT "tedious from beginning to just before the end"; WP "pretty snazzy entertainment, certainly the most stylish and engrossing detective melodrama in years"; V "outstanding"; Obs "the kind of film the critical fraternity will be inclined to overrate"; S&S "immediately involving"; MFB "a solid, many-layered detective puzzle").

Francis Ford Coppola's *The Conversation*, a drama about a surveillance expert, also earned strong reviews and took out the Palme d'Or at the Cannes Film Festival (NYT "extremely grim", "haunting"; LAT "stunning … seems to work on every level … a powerful and important picture"; CT "a distinguished film"; WP "flawed [but] an unusually intriguing and impressive work"; V "superb"; HRp "a film of triumphant style and overwhelming passion"; S&S "remarkably ambitious … a first-rate psychological portrait … a triumph"; MFB "fascinating … an unqualified success").

Towards the end of the year, critics praised both John Cassavetes' *A Woman Under the Influence* (NYT "extremely compelling … a thoughtful film that does prompt serious discussion"; LAT "as private and unyielding a statement of the film-maker's truth as I think the medium presently allows, and it is no small achievement"; CT "invigorating"; WP "protracted, dithering and ultimately pointless") and the feminist drama *Alice Doesn't Live Here Anymore* (NYT "[a] riveting, entertaining movie"; LAT "seemingly uncertain whether to be a stylized and updated revision of the romantic comedy mode of the late '30s or a rough-and-tumble piece of social realism flavored with bitter comedy"; WP "not so much a good movie – that is, a fully conscious, accomplished and satisfying piece of work – as a touchstone"). Audiences, meanwhile, rushed to see two all-star studio blockbusters: *Murder on the Orient Express*, an adaptation of the classic Agatha Christie mystery novel (NYT "elaborate and witty"; LAT "the purest of pure escapist entertainment … a special delight"; CT "suspenseful escapist entertainment … superbly slick, stylishly done"; WP "an attractive, likeable entertainment") and the disaster film *The Towering Inferno* (NYT "this year's best end-of-the-world movie"; LAT "engrossing … does it extraordinarily well, with style and flair and continuously growing suspense and drama. It is almost impossible to withhold belief and concern"; CT "fails to develop any interest in its characters … every minute of its excessive 165 minutes is a stunt not a story … a technical achievement more concerned with special effects than with people"; WP "a sensational piece of commercial entertainment [with] ingenious, exciting action sequences … a triumph of sustained excitement").

Several foreign-language films also entered into contention for the year's Best Picture accolades late in the year: Ingmar Bergman's *Scener ur ett Äktenskap (Scenes from a Marriage)* (NYT "a movie of such extraordinary intimacy", "a superb film"; WP "may come as something of a disappointment … has a rambling, equivocal air"; V "somewhat flawed but still fascinating"; FQ "emotional dynamite"); Louis Malle's *Lacombe, Lucien* (NYT "uncompromising", "provocative"; LAT "an exquisitely realized masterpiece … an impassioned film of infinite grace … in every way a major work"; CT "a troubling film, one filled with memorable performances and a visual excellence in sunlight and darkness"; WP "an intelligent and compelling piece of work"; TT "satisfying and absorbing"; S&S "tantalising, but wholly satisfying"); and two films directed by Lina Wertmüller, *Film d'Amour e d'Anarchia (Love and Anarchy)* (NYT "passionate and stirring"; LAT "superbly evocative"; CT "a visually stunning and freshly acted mix of sex, politics and strong characters"; WP "a rather hysterical mixture of romantic and political melodrama") and the farce *Mimi Metallurgico Ferito Nell'onore (The Seduction of Mimi)* (NYT "one of the best films of this season"; CT "unsatisfying").

The most anticipated film of the year, however, was released in December: *The Godfather Part II*, Francis Ford Coppola's epic sequel to the biggest box office hit of all time which two years earlier had been named Best Picture by the Academy. Surprisingly, Vincent Canby dismissed the film in The New York Times as "not a sequel in any engaging way ... it's not really much of anything". He lamented the film's "failed aspirations" and "earnest confusions" calling it a "mess" and a "fractured epic" and concluded that it "doesn't illuminate or enrich the original film" but instead merely "recalls how much better [the] original film was. The movie was a notable absentee from the newspaper's annual list of the year's best productions. The reaction among leading film critics ranged from qualified enthusiasm to similar disappointment (LAT "the creative, aesthetic success of this long enterprise is also, I think, on the heroic side … [it] is quieter, less propulsive, less furiously violent [but] it is compellingly watchable"; CT "at times the vision is as beautiful, as harrowing and as exciting as the original … 'The Godfather Part II' may be the second best gangster movie ever made"; WP "imposing but essentially superfluous … exquisite and impressive as it often looks, fails to provide a fresh narrative, a fresh concept or fresh revelations … more redundant than essential"; V "excellent"; S&S "its most obvious limitation is that it essentially tells us nothing new"; MFB "it is a good deal less effective [than the original], partly because the narrative line is rather too involved for its own good and because the film doesn't really stand up on its own").

The first major list of critics' prizewinners was announced on Christmas Day: the National Board of Review named Cannes winner *The Conversation* as the year's Best Picture. Five days later, the New York Film Critics Circle gave their top accolade to *Amarcord* (which had been named Best Foreign-Language Film by the NBR). Bergman's *Scener ur ett Äktenskap* finished as runner-up followed by the two Coppola films with *Chinatown* trailing in fifth position in the voting. On 5 January 1975, the National Society of Film Critics chose *Scener ur ett Äktenskap* as Best Picture.

Four days later the Hollywood Foreign Press Association included both Coppola films in the list of candidates for the Golden Globe (Drama) along with *Chinatown* and *A Woman Under the Influence*. In the Comedy/Musical category, the acclaimed road trip movie *Harry and Tonto* (LAT "sentimental, enjoyable and firmly optimistic"; CT "extremely funny"; WP "an unusually mellow and affectionate film … has real merit and significance"; MFB "sustained low-key sententiousness") and a new screen version of *The Front Page* (NYT "extremely funny"; LAT "sparkling dialogue, vivid performances, a surefire plot and a splendid evocation of a colorful era add up to a lusty, zesty entertainment of wide appeal"; CT "isn't as funny as it should be … the pace of the picture is much too slow"; WP "messy and misbegotten [although] it has some entertaining qualities") were among the nominees, but the lauded box office flop *Claudine* was a surprise omission (NYT "the best American comedy of the year"; LAT "an engrossing and effective movie"; WP "a fitfully effective, structurally ramshackle comedy-drama"; V "outstanding").

Also unrecognised by the HFPA, and subsequently ignored by the Academy as well, were Robert Altman's *Thieves Like Us* (NYT "engaging, sharply observed"; LAT "affecting", "demanding and subtle, a seductive reverie of a film"; CT "breaks no new ground"; WP "disappointing") and Terrence Malick's *Badlands* (NYT "cool, sometimes brilliant … a most important and exciting film"; CT "compelling"; WP "bad … [an] empty, alienating art movie … a perfunctory, heavily stylized chase melodrama"). At the end of January, the

Globes were won by *Chinatown* and *The Longest Yard* (NYT "a terrible picture"; LAT "popular entertainment at its rousing best … both clever and unsubtle"; CT "old-fashioned"; WP "a deplorable-enjoyable movie").

Both *Claudine* and *Harry and Tonto* appeared on the annual New York Times list of the year's ten best movies along with *Amarcord, Lacombe, Lucien* and *Scener ur ett Äktenskap*. In a major surprise, however, neither of the Coppola dramas nor *Chinatown* made the list. While the rival top ten list published in Time magazine, did feature *Chinatown* and both *The Conversation* and *The Godfather Part II*, Bergman's acclaimed *Scener ur ett Äktenskap* was notable by its absence. *Amarcord* and Wertmüller's *Mimi Metallurgico Ferito Nell'onore* were selected by Time instead. Interestingly, the only American film to appear on both lists was *Badlands*.

In late January, controversy erupted when the Academy announced that NSFC winner and New York runner-up *Scener ur ett Äktenskap* was ineligible for Oscar consideration because of an Academy by-law stating films adapted from a television programme must be screened in cinemas in the same year. Bergman's drama had been screened in Sweden as six hour-long episodes in 1973. Outraged observers pointed to other cases in which the rule had not been invoked, but the Academy stood firm.

Fellini's *Amarcord* was also out of contention. The film was the official Italian entry for the Academy Award for Best Foreign-Language Film and the Academy's out-dated rules meant it would be disqualified from the category if it went into general release in Los Angeles in the same year. Consequently, while the film had been screened in dozens of cities across the United States and contested, and won, several major critics' prizes, it would not be eligible for the Best Picture and Best Director Oscars until the next year, following a delayed release in Los Angeles.

Leading the Oscar field were *Chinatown* and *The Godfather Part II*, each with eleven nominations, including nods for Best Picture. Coppola's other drama, *The Conversation*, also received a Best Picture nomination. In a surprise, given its generally poor reviews, the biopic *Lenny* was also short-listed for the top statuette (NYT "one-fourth brilliant" but the remainder is "just more description"; LAT "severe, earnest, uncompromising, very strong and ultimately very depressing … an unreservedly admirable film, artful and imaginative"; WP "curiously solemn, reverential, evasive"; V "excellent", "a landmark contemporary biographical drama"; Sp "there is so much that is fascinatingly wrong-headed in this beautifully-made production that I hardly know where to grasp it to tear it apart. And it surely must be torn apart"). Completing the ballot was *The Towering Inferno*. "The nomination of 'The Towering Inferno' in the Oscar best picture category has produced surprisingly few outcries," reported Charles Champlin in the Los Angeles Times. "The Barnum & Bailey approach to film-making often irritates the chamber music crowd, metaphorically speaking. But what the picking of 'The Towering Inferno' seems to applaud is not box-office success as such but spectacular craftsmanship that thrills, or ought to thrill, anyone who loves the motion picture form whatever its content."

Notably absent from the list of Best Picture Oscar nominees was François Truffaut's *La Nuit Américaine (Day for Night)*, which the previous year had won the Oscar as Best Foreign-Language Film and had been named Best Picture by the New York critics, the NBR and the British Academy (NYT "an exhilarating comedy", "hilarious, wise and moving"; LAT "[this] homage to the movies and all those who make them is beyond question the warmest, liveliest, funniest, slyest, most revealing and most deeply affectionate ever paid … a masterpiece … one of the most sheerly enjoyable movies of any year"; CT "a wonderfully tender story [and] a special movie"; WP "a pleasant, enjoyable anecdotal movie"; TT "enjoyable", "funny, thoughtful, oddly elegiac"; S&S "brilliant"; MFB "sentimental").

On Oscar night, *Chinatown* did not manage to overshadow *The Godfather Part II* the way that *Cabaret* had eclipsed the victory of *The Godfather* two years earlier. Polanski's drama won just one statuette. Coppola's sequel received six, including Best Director and Best Picture.

At the British Academy Awards, Malle's *Lacombe, Lucien*, overlooked in Hollywood, won the Best Film award. A year later, the British Academy honoured another film by-passed for the 1974 Best Picture Oscar: *Alice Doesn't Live Here Anymore*. Surprisingly, *The Godfather Part II* was not even among the BAFTA nominees.

1974

BEST DIRECTOR

ACADEMY AWARDS
John Cassavetes for *A Woman Under the Influence*
• Francis Ford Coppola for *The Godfather Part II*
Bob Fosse for *Lenny*
Roman Polanski for *Chinatown*
François Truffaut for *La Nuit Américaine (Day for Night)*

GOLDEN GLOBE AWARDS
John Cassavetes – *A Woman Under the Influence*
Francis Ford Coppola – *The Conversation*
Francis Ford Coppola – *The Godfather Part II*
Bob Fosse – *Lenny*
• Roman Polanski – *Chinatown*

DIRECTORS GUILD AWARD
Francis Ford Coppola
– *The Conversation*
• Francis Ford Coppola
– *The Godfather Part II*
Bob Fosse – *Lenny*
Sidney Lumet
– *Murder on the Orient Express*
Roman Polanski – *Chinatown*

BRITISH ACADEMY AWARDS
Francis Ford Coppola
– *The Conversation*
Sidney Lumet
– *Murder on the Orient Express*
Louis Malle – *Lacombe, Lucien*
• Roman Polanski – *Chinatown*

NEW YORK – Federico Fellini – *Amarcord*
BOARD OF REVIEW – Francis Ford Coppola – *The Conversation*
NATIONAL SOCIETY – Francis Ford Coppola – *The Conversation* and
The Godfather Part II

Two years after he had was dramatically outpolled on Oscar night, Francis Ford Coppola was once again the overwhelming favourite for the year's Best Director honours. The only question over his chances was the possibility of him receiving a double nomination, thus splitting his own vote and handing victory to another nominee.

Both the Hollywood Foreign Press Association and the Directors Guild of America named Coppola twice – a separate nomination for each of the two films for which he had earlier won the National Board of Review and National Society of Film Critics awards, *The Conversation* (NYT "some of the action drags –

perhaps because the style is so muted, so deliberately dry and cool"; LAT "dynamite"; CT "the story is well told, and it is tricky [but it] takes a back seat to the film's disturbingly somber mood"; WP "visually beautiful, aurally striking, interestingly conceived [but suffers from] the draggingly slow pace at which it is directed") and *The Godfather Part II* (NYT "[a] mess … much of the time it's next to impossible to figure out who's doing what to whom, not, I suspect, because its mode is ambiguity, but because it's been cut and edited in what looks to have been desperation"; CT "[at times] he succeeds … but he often fails"; WP "by failing to discover a new dramatic approach to his subject, Coppola places himself in the curious position of directing an epic homage to his own movie … comes dangerously close to self-parody"; V "superbly directed"; MFB "drives its narrative along with the same exhilarating skill"). Coppola lost the Globe, but claimed the Guild honour for the second time in three years. At the Oscars, Coppola was not in competition with himself. He received his second Best Director nomination for *The Godfather Part II.*

Also nominated for a second time was the director who had unexpectedly won the Oscar ahead of Coppola in 1972: Bob Fosse for *Lenny* (NYT "inhibited"; CT "trying very hard to achieve a realistic look [but] it's all very obvious [and] by reaching so hard for realism, Fosse only underscores his failure"; WP "the film is exceptionally well made in its own severely limited, stylized and misleading terms. Fosse has a tight rein on the conception and every facet of the production").

This year, however, Coppola's main challenger was considered to be Globe winner Roman Polanski for *Chinatown* (LAT "carefully calculated and accelerating pace [and a] demonstration of a medium mastered … [his] control is sure throughout"; CT "the majority of the problems are to be found in Polanski's direction … artificially overcomposed [and the] pacing is dreadfully slow"; WP "Polanski's smooth, lucid direction achieves exactly the right tone, pace and tensions … assured").

Completing the short-list were both John Cassavetes, a former nominee in the acting and writing categories, for *A Woman Under the Influence*, for which his wife Gena Rowlands was nominated as Best Actress (LAT "the power, the intensity, the depth of the revelations Cassavetes and his two principal collaborators give us about love and marriage justify the raw and unprettied heft of the film"; WP "Cassavetes' method of directing remains strained and inarticulate") and François Truffaut for *La Nuit Américaine (Day for Night)* (LAT "the tone of 'Day for Night' is lightly amusing, a kind of dramatized documentary about the spinning of dreams. But beyond the affection is something sharper and stronger"; CT "mixing genuine emotion with a farcical film story, Truffaut has made one of his finest films in years").

1974

Overlooked for consideration were: Martin Scorsese for *Alice Doesn't Live Here Anymore* (LAT "keeps the whole film solidly rooted in a world of all-too-real bars"; WP "the direction is unfocused and often self-contradictory"); Robert Altman for *Thieves Like Us* (NYT "a perfectly integrated work"; LAT "affirms [his] place in the front ranks of American directors"; CT "he has a natural talent for telling a story effortlessly; there are passages of 'Thieves Like Us' that 'read' like good, popular novels in both speed and clarity of image"; WP "flawless [but] in a meaningless, dramatically counter-productive sense"); Louis Malle for *Lacombe, Lucien* (LAT "has achieved a new maturity and complexity ... there is throughout [the film] a sense of rightness, a feeling that Malle has fully elucidated every moment ... a triumph of subtle, revealing nuances and details"; V "expertly directed"); Terrence Malick for his feature directorial debut, *Badlands* (NYT "one may legitimately debate the validity of Malick's vision, but not, I think, his immense talent"; LAT "there is simply no doubt of his technical command of the medium, his creative powers and cool intelligence"; CT "to watch 'Badlands' is to immediately recognize the skill of its director"); Lina Wertmüller for *Film d'Amour e d'Anarchia (Love and Anarchy)* (NYT "solidly professional"; LAT "rigorously, exquisitely structured, 'Love and Anarchy' is in its movement and every gesture gloriously operatic, superbly evocative and splendidly sensual"; CT "dazzles ... visually stunning"; WP "resorts to hectic, hambone techniques"); and John Berry for *Claudine* (LAT "he has evoked performances from everyone which extract the full angry voltage from the script"; V "directed superbly").

The New York prizewinner, Federico Fellini for *Amarcord*, was not eligible for Oscar consideration until the following year.

On Oscar night, as expected, Coppola won the Best Director Academy Award. He also won his third statuette in the writing categories. His father, Carmine Coppola, won an Oscar in the music categories, but his sister, Talia Shire was an unsuccessful nominee for Best Supporting Actress.

In London, Polanski received the BAFTA ahead of a field of nominees that included Coppola for *The Conversation*. At the British Academy Awards the following year, *The Godfather Part II* did not even earn Coppola a nomination.

1974

BEST ACTRESS

ACADEMY AWARDS
• **Ellen Burstyn as 'Alice Hyatt' in *Alice Doesn't Live Here Anymore***
Diahann Carroll as 'Claudine Price' in *Claudine*
Faye Dunaway as 'Evelyn Mulwray' in *Chinatown*
Valerie Perrine as 'Honey Bruce' in *Lenny*
Gena Rowlands as 'Mabel Longhetti' in *A Woman Under the Influence*

GOLDEN GLOBE AWARDS
(Drama)
Ellen Burstyn
– *Alice Doesn't Live Here Anymore*
Faye Dunaway – *Chinatown*
Valerie Perrine – *Lenny*
• **Gena Rowlands**
– *A Woman Under the Influence*
Liv Ullmann
– *Scener ur ett Äktenskap*
(Scenes from a Marriage)

(Comedy/Musical)
Lucille Ball – *Mame*
Diahann Carroll – *Claudine*
Helen Hayes – *Herbie Rides Again*
Cloris Leachman
– *Young Frankenstein*
• **Raquel Welch**
– *The Three Musketeers*

BRITISH ACADEMY AWARDS
Faye Dunaway – *Chinatown*
Barbra Streisand – *The Way We Were*
Cicely Tyson – *The Autobiography of Miss Jane Pittman*
• **Joanne Woodward – *Summer Wishes, Winter Dreams***

NEW YORK – Liv Ullmann – *Scener ur ett Äktenskap (Scenes from a Marriage)*
BOARD OF REVIEW – Gena Rowlands – *A Woman Under the Influence*
NATIONAL SOCIETY – Liv Ullmann – *Scener ur ett Äktenskap (Scenes from a Marriage)*

"There is not one false or faulted instant in the playing of Liv Ullmann," said The Times in its review of Ingmar Bergman's drama *Scener ur ett Äktenskap (Scenes from a Marriage)*. The New York Times commented "Ullmann again establishes herself as one of the most fascinating actresses of our time." Most critics concurred (NYT "an astonishing and triumphant performance"; LAT "simply astonishing … unforgettable"; WP "we're interested in Liv Ullmann at the expense of the character she portrays"; V "superb"). At the end of the year

1974

Ullmann was named Best Actress by the New York Film Critics Circle for the second time in three years and by the National Society of Film Critics for the second consecutive year and for the third time in seven years. She was also a strong contender for the National Board of Review award (which she had won twice before) and was a nominee for the Golden Globe (Drama) which she had won in 1972. Ullmann seemed certain to receive her second Best Actress Oscar nomination in three years and claim the statuette.

In a major shock, however, the Academy cited a rule that stated that any film that had originated from television would not qualify for Oscar consideration unless it was screened in cinemas in the same year. As *Scener ur ett Äktenskap* had first been shown as a six-part television series in Sweden in 1973, it was suddenly declared ineligible. The announcement was met with considerable outcry by Academy members and film critics. Many pleaded with the Board of Governors to reverse their decision. A letter appeared in the Los Angeles Times requesting that Ullmann's performance be allowed to compete for the Oscar, signed by several actresses, including the two seen as most likely to benefit from Ullmann's exclusion. Even though observers pointed to past cases in which the Academy had failed to enforce the clause in the rules, the Academy refused to back down. Ullmann was out of contention.

Instead the Academy nominated: Ellen Burstyn (her third nomination and her second consecutive mention for Best Actress) as a middle-aged mother trying to fulfil her dream of becoming a singer in *Alice Doesn't Live Here Anymore* (NYT "Miss Burstyn never misses the eccentric beat that distinguishes [the role] … Burstyn is terrific"; LAT "[a] highly charged and sympathetic portrayal… high among the year's best work"; WP "seems to be overacting in a large percentage of her scenes … exaggerated and abrupt"; V "wonderfully good"); Diahann Carroll as a woman trying to raise six children on welfare in the comedy *Claudine*, a role she inherited from the terminally ill Diana Sands (NYT "the beauty of this performance is in the force of her toughness and wit … even when the dialogue gets cute [her] characterization retains an intensity that gives the movie a basic no-nonsense toughness"; LAT "convincing and touching"; WP "valiant but not really satisfying … perfectly sincere and competent"; V "sensational"; MFB "beautifully played"; SMH "superbly spontaneous"); Faye Dunaway (her second nod) as the femme fatale in *Chinatown* (NYT "good"; LAT "begins as the fairly standard femme perhaps fatale, but finally lets us see convincingly the torment behind the cool, and she is touching indeed"; CT "Dunaway's mannered, nervous tics turn you away not from her character, but from the way she is playing that character"; WP "Dunaway's appearance is rather hideously stylized … one wonders if she's been victimized by vampires – but this is her first decent performance in several films"; Obs "Nicholson and Polanski between them seem to be intent on getting a passionate/hysterical performance from Miss Dunaway"); Valerie Perrine as the drug-addicted wife of stand-up comic Lenny Bruce in the biopic *Lenny* (NYT "immensely effective in individual scenes but the character remains a cipher"; LAT "conscientious and impressive … [has not previously done anything] to prepare us for the power and depth of her portrayal … the year has not yet produced a more assured and affecting piece of acting … the nominating Academy will almost surely acknowledge"; V "a sensational performance"; WP "her performance isn't all that exceptional"); and Gena Rowlands (her first nomination) as a woman suffering a nervous breakdown in *A Woman Under the Influence*, a film directed by her husband, John Cassavetes, who also received a nomination (NYT "an extraordinary characterization"; LAT "the most overpowering, gut-knotting, achingly believable and beautifully sympathetic portrayal I have watched in a very long time … the triumph for this actress is that what we watch are not skyrocketing histrionics, a tragedienne chewing the scenery and her menfolk with equal flair, but the dazed, lost, frightened confusions of a vibrant, high-strung woman"; CT "first-rate [and] something rare … absolutely riveting; she doesn't make one false move"; WP "works like a demon to make Mabel distinctive, but she never succeeds in making her believable … one of the busiest performances I've ever seen"; V a "tour de force"; S&S "one of the most resplendently kooky performances in years"; MFB "strong"). Burstyn, Carroll and Rowlands had all signed the letter to the Los Angeles Times. The nomination of Perrine, meanwhile, followed a strong campaign by United Artists to have her mentioned for the Best Actress prize; she had been named Best Supporting Actress by the New York critics and the NBR.

Overlooked for consideration were: Shelley Duvall in *Thieves Like Us* (NYT "beautifully played", "quite special"; LAT "enormously appealing and vulnerable"; WP "her acting technique and ranges are still severely limited, but she'd make a lasting impression if there were simply more of her and more to her"); Sissy Spacek in *Badlands* (NYT "splendid"; LAT "perfect"; CT "excellently played"); Globe nominee Lucille Ball in *Mame* (NYT "has some great moments"; LAT "strangely inappropriate"; WP "echoes of Rosalind Russell's fast-moving, fast-talking Auntie Mame kept coming back over Lucy's faltering, stationary line readings"; V "great").

Unsurprisingly, Academy members ignored the critically savaged performances of Mia Farrow in *The Great Gatsby* (NYT "immense, courageous work … she's not afraid to make Daisy unlikeable … Farrow plays a rich woman not from the outside, as a comedy of manners caricature, but from the character's own point of view"; LAT "makes Daisy credible enough"; WP "dreadful"; V "excellent") and Cybill Shepherd in *Daisy Miller* (NYT "she catches the gaiety and the directness of Daisy"; CT "she is not equal to the task … positively embarrassing ... she seems hopelessly out of place"; WP "there's bad acting and bad acting, and Cybill Shepherd sets an excruciating new standard ... her connotations are all wrong"; V "miscast"; MFB "[a] conspicuously disastrous performance").

Rowlands had been the runner-up to Ullmann for the New York accolade, and had been named Best Actress by the NBR. As a result, when she won the Globe (Drama) she became the frontrunner for the Academy Award. The winner, however, was Burstyn for *Alice Doesn't Live Here Anymore*, a film that she had fought to have made.

It is impossible to know who would have won the Oscar if Ullmann had been among the nominees, but it is worth noting that at the following year's British Academy Awards, Ullmann, Burstyn and Perrine (by then a Cannes Film Festival winner as Best Actress for her performance in *Lenny*) were all nominated for Best Actress, along with Anne Bancroft in *Prisoner of Second Avenue*. As in Hollywood, the winner was Burstyn.

1974

BEST ACTOR

ACADEMY AWARDS
• **Art Carney as 'Harry Coombs' in *Harry and Tonto***
Albert Finney as 'Hercule Poirot' in *Murder on the Orient Express*
Dustin Hoffman as 'Lenny Bruce' in *Lenny*
Jack Nicholson as 'J.J. Gittes' in *Chinatown*
Al Pacino as 'Michael Corleone' in *The Godfather Part II*

GOLDEN GLOBE AWARDS
(Drama)
James Caan – *The Gambler*
Gene Hackman – *The Conversation*
Dustin Hoffman – *Lenny*
• **Jack Nicholson – *Chinatown***
Al Pacino – *The Godfather Part II*

(Comedy/Musical)
• **Art Carney – *Harry and Tonto***
James Earl Jones – *Claudine*
Jack Lemmon – *The Front Page*
Walter Matthau – *The Front Page*
Burt Reynolds – *The Longest Yard*

BRITISH ACADEMY AWARDS
Albert Finney – *Murder on the Orient Express*
Gene Hackman – *The Conversation*
• **Jack Nicholson – *The Last Detail***
Al Pacino – *Serpico*

NEW YORK – Jack Nicholson – *Chinatown* and *The Last Detail*
BOARD OF REVIEW – Gene Hackman – *The Conversation*
NATIONAL SOCIETY – Jack Nicholson – *Chinatown* and *The Last Detail*

The New York Daily News described Jack Nicholson as "a sure bet" to win an Oscar at his fourth nomination in six years for playing a 1930s private investigator in *Chinatown* (NYT "good"; LAT "another masterful, individual and engrossing characterization"; CT "miscast … seems uncomfortable in this role"; WP "[an] expert performance … a triumph"; V "excellent"; Obs "the best impersonation of a private detective we have had in some time … [he] is just right"). Along with his Oscar-nominated turn in *The Last Detail* from the previous year, his performance in *Chinatown* won Nicholson the Best Actor honours from both the New York Film Critics Circle and the National Society of Film Critics. It was his third and second prize from each group, respectively. Nicholson won the Golden Globe for Best Actor (Drama) for *Chinatown* and seemed certain to win the Oscar when New York runner-up and National Board of Review champ, Gene Hackman, was overlooked by the Academy for his role as a surveillance expert in Francis Ford Coppola's *The Conversation* (NYT "an impressive portrayal", "superb [and] fascinating"; LAT "ranks in its understated and internalized way with the very best roles he has yet done"; CT "superior … a marvelously controlled performance"; WP "it is really a pretty juicy part, and in the hands of an actor with more than one facial expression, could have been memorable. As it is Hackman plays Hackman, sullen, morose and unappealing"; TT "seems able to transform his whole physique into the character"; MFB "wholly persuasive").

On Oscar night, however, the upset winner was fifty-five-year old Art Carney as a seventy-two-year old widower who hitch-hikes across America with his cat in *Harry and Tonto* (NYT "Carney maintains a quiet dignity and resilience throughout, though he has to address too many of his lines to a cat"; LAT "playing with a warm and understated authority"; CT "gives the character of Harry equal amounts of guts and intelligence"; WP "[a] beautifully discreet performance"; V "excellent"). Carney had been considered Nicholson's only challenger following his win in the Comedy/Musical category at the Globes. He was a popular character actor, known for his Broadway appearances and television work. He had originated Jack Lemmon's role in 'The Odd Couple' on Broadway, and won several Emmys for his supporting role in the television series 'The Honeymooners'. The Oscar brought Carney a series of significant roles, notably in *The Late Show*, for which he won the 1977 National Society of Film Critics Best Actor award (but not a second nomination from the Academy).

None of the other three Oscar nominees attended the ceremony. They were: Albert Finney (his second nod) as Agatha Christie's iconic Belgian detective Hercule Poirot in *Murder on the Orient Express* (NYT "extraordinary … it's a performance of exaggeration which is fun to watch both for the goals achieved and the risks taken"; LAT "he is formidable, merveilleux and a bloody delight"; CT "his is a performance worth its stuffing"; WP "[an] undeniable stellar performance [which] makes the picture actively worth seeing … Finney successfully dominates the show and holds it together … Finney succeeds in disarming you"; V "outstanding"; MFB "a succulent tour de force of disguise"); Dustin Hoffman (his third mention) as stand-up comic Lenny Bruce in *Lenny* (NYT "brilliantly acted"; LAT "conscientious and impressive"; CT "tries hard to capture the man, but he doesn't look right … he can't hide his own warmth from us"; WP "doing his earnest and occasionally touching best to overcome the year's most frustrating example of miscasting"; V "at or near his best"; Sp "played with enormous charm"); and Al Pacino for reprising the role of Michael Corleone, in *The Godfather Part II* (NYT "Pacino, so fine the first time out, goes through the film looking glum"; LAT "yet another outstanding portrayal"; CT "standout"; WP "powerfully impersonated once more … a forceful portrayal … you can't take your eyes off Pacino, and when he explodes you damn well vibrate, but he's still repeating himself … it's no longer a new, surprising portrayal"; V "outstanding"; MFB "good in a rather monotonous way").

Overlooked for the Oscar were: 1973 Cannes honoree Giancarlo Giannini as the farmer in Lina Wertmüller's *Film d'Amour e d'Anarchia (Love and Anarchy)* (NYT "shaded"; LAT "accomplished artistry"; CT "striking"); James Earl Jones in *Claudine* (NYT "by far the best thing Mr Jones has ever done in films … even when the dialogue gets cute [his] characterization retains an intensity that gives the movie a basic no-nonsense toughness"; LAT "is once again a superlative performer"; WP "a playful, winning performance"; V "sensational"; MFB "beautifully played"); both Globe nominee Jack Lemmon (NYT "marvelous"; LAT "vivid"; CT "the glory that is Lemmon talking on a telephone and screwing up his face as if he were sucking on a citrus"; WP "adequate") and Globe nominee Walter Matthau (NYT "marvelous"; LAT "glorious"; WP "sharper and funnier" than his co-star) in *The Front Page*; Robert Redford in *The Great Gatsby* (NYT "miscast"; LAT "it is not easy to accept him as the poor boy who has clawed his ruthless way to the wealth all for the love of a girl … yet Redford creates a character of ambiguity if not deep mystery"; WP "dreadful … awkward, stilted"; V "excellent"; MFB "bland"); Peter Falk in *A Woman Under the Influence* (NYT "a rousing performance"; LAT "creates one of the most complex and contradictory portraits in his career"; CT "fine"; MFB "strong"); Globe nominee James Caan in *The Gambler* (NYT "generally convincing"; LAT "a hypnotically absorbing performance, at once charming and dismaying, by James Caan who must certainly have an Academy Award nomination for it"; WP "achieves a superficial degree of intensity … strong, if essentially futile"; V "excellent"); Keith Carradine in *Thieves Like Us* (NYT "beautifully played"; LAT "enormously appealing and vulnerable"); Martin Sheen in *Badlands* (NYT "splendid"; LAT "perfect"; CT "excellently played"); Jean-Paul Belmondo in *Stavisky* (NYT "at his best … has all the authority and gaiety of the man" ;V "excellent"); and Pierre Blaise as the teenage farm boy in *Lacombe, Lucien* (LAT "a performance of Bresson-like gravity and totality"; CT "memorable"; WP "his authenticity is impressively realized"; V "remarkable").

Erland Josephson was ruled out of contention when the Academy declared Ingmar Bergman's *Scener ur ett Äktenskap (Scenes from a Marriage)* to be ineligible for Oscar consideration because it had been shown on Swedish television the previous year (NYT a "complex performance"; LAT "simply astonishing"; TT "there is not one false or faulted instant in the playing of Erland Josephson").

1974

BEST SUPPORTING ACTRESS

ACADEMY AWARDS
• Ingrid Bergman as 'Greta Ohlsson' in *Murder on the Orient Express*
Valentina Cortese as 'Severine' in *La Nuit Américaine (Day for Night)*
Madeline Kahn as 'Lili von Shtupp' in *Blazing Saddles*
Diane Ladd as 'Flo' in *Alice Doesn't Live Here Anymore*
Talia Shire as 'Connie Corleone' in *The Godfather Part II*

GOLDEN GLOBE AWARDS
Bea Arthur – *Mame*
• Karen Black – *The Great Gatsby*
Jennifer Jones – *The Towering Inferno*
Madeline Kahn – *Young Frankenstein*
Diane Ladd – *Alice Doesn't Live Here Anymore*

BRITISH ACADEMY AWARDS
• Ingrid Bergman – *Murder on the Orient Express*
Sylvia Sidney – *Summer Wishes, Winter Dreams*
Sylvia Syms – *The Tamarind Seed*
Cindy Williams – *American Graffiti*

NEW YORK – Valerie Perrine – *Lenny*
BOARD OF REVIEW – Valerie Perrine – *Lenny*
NATIONAL SOCIETY – Bibi Andersson – *Scener ur ett Äktenskap (Scenes from a Marriage)*

In 1973 Valentina Cortese earned critical acclaim and acting prizes on both sides of the Atlantic for her performance as a fading movie star in the French satire *La Nuit Américaine (Day for Night)* (NYT "superb", "hugely funny and hugely affecting"; LAT "impeccable … Cortese's salty performance has been justly honored by critics' groups"; CT "played beautifully"; WP "wonderfully flamboyant"; V "remarkable"; TT "beautifully acted"). She won the Golden Globe, the BAFTA and the New York Film Critics Circle and National Society of Film Critics awards.

The following year Cortese was a strong contender for the Best Supporting Actress Oscar, especially with both the critics' winners out of contention. New York and National Board of Review winner Valerie Perrine was included by Academy members in the Best Actress category for her performance in *Lenny*, while New York runner-up and NSFC winner Bibi Andersson was excluded when the Academy ruled that *Scener ur ett Äktenskap (Scenes from a Marriage)* was ineligible for Oscar consideration because it had screened as a mini-series on Swedish television during the previous calendar year (TT "played with shattering brilliance").

Nominated for the Oscar alongside Cortese were: previous two-time Best Actress Oscar winner Ingrid Bergman (her sixth nomination) in the all-star murder mystery thriller *Murder on the Orient Express* (LAT "unforgettable [in] a cameo to be especially unforgotten at nomination time"; WP "[an] undeniable stellar performance [which] makes the picture actively worth seeing … [a] brief but triumphant portrait"; MFB "the signal success in the casting"); Madeline Kahn (her second consecutive and final nod) as a saloon singer in the Western spoof *Blazing Saddles* (NYT "does a marvellously unkind take-off on Marlene Dietrich"; LAT "doing a maliciously exact counterfeit of Marlene Deitrich"; WP "ponderous"; V "simply terrific"; S&S "show-stopping"; MFB "an amazing tour de force"); Diane Ladd as a waitress in the drama *Alice Doesn't Live Here Anymore*, for which she won the BAFTA the following year (NYT "splendidly played"; LAT "wonderful … high among the year's best work"; WP "seems right on target"; V "excellent"); and Talia Shire, the sister of Best Director winner Francis Ford Coppola, in *The Godfather Part II* (WP "makes a vivid impression").

Overlooked were: Golden Globe winner Karen Black in *The Great Gatsby* (NYT "good as the camera allows … her major scene, when she tearfully describes her first meeting with Tom, has been shot in such a tight close-up it almost destroys the actress with visual italics"; LAT "makes the most of it"); Geraldine Fitzgerald in *Harry and Tonto* (NYT "played with batty precision"; LAT "unforgettably good"); Aurore Clément in *Lacombe, Lucien* (NYT "superb"); both Mildred Natwick (NYT "very good indeed"; CT "[a] fully realized characterization"; V "excellent"; S&S "as the film progresses one becomes increasingly grateful for the quiet authority of Mildred Natwick's Mrs Costello, suggesting more of [Henry] James' world in single lines than the remainder of the film in all its exertions") and Eileen Brennan (NYT "very good indeed"; V "outstanding") in *Daisy Miller*; BAFTA nominee Sylvia Syms in *The Tamarind Seed* (NYT "not at all bad"; LAT "marvelous … Syms is dazzlingly nasty"; V "impressive"); and Globe nominee Bea Arthur in *Mame* (TT "performs alchemical feats with her material").

On Oscar night, Bergman unexpectedly won her third award. In her acceptance speech, she called Cortese's portrayal "the most beautiful performance" of the year.

1974

BEST SUPPORTING ACTOR

ACADEMY AWARDS
Fred Astaire as 'Harlee Clairborne' in *The Towering Inferno*
Jeff Bridges as 'Lightfoot' in *Thunderbolt and Lightfoot*
• Robert De Niro as 'Vito Corleone' in *The Godfather Part II*
Michael V. Gazzo as 'Frank Pentangeli' in *The Godfather Part II*
Lee Strasberg as 'Hyman Roth' in *The Godfather Part II*

GOLDEN GLOBE AWARDS
Eddie Albert – *The Longest Yard*
• Fred Astaire – *The Towering Inferno*
Bruce Dern – *The Great Gatsby*
John Huston – *Chinatown*
Sam Waterston – *The Great Gatsby*

BRITISH ACADEMY AWARDS
Adam Faith – *Stardust*
• John Gielgud – *Murder on the Orient Express*
John Huston – *Chinatown*
Randy Quaid – *The Last Detail*

NEW YORK – Charles Boyer – *Stavisky*
BOARD OF REVIEW – Holger Löwenadler – *Lacombe, Lucien*
NATIONAL SOCIETY – Holger Löwenadler – *Lacombe, Lucien*

Thirty-four years after his former dance partner Ginger Rogers had won an Oscar, seventy-six-year old Fred Astaire won the Golden Globe and earned his first ever Academy Award nomination for his performance as a con-artist in the all-star blockbuster *The Towering Inferno* (LAT "outstanding"; V "excellent"). He seemed certain to collect the statuette.

In a huge upset, however, the Oscar was won by Robert De Niro for his mostly foreign-language performance as the young Vito Corleone, the character portrayed by Marlon Brando in an Oscar-winning performance two years earlier, in *The Godfather Part II* (NYT "played with a fascinating, reserved passion by Robert De Niro until the shadow of Brando's earlier performance falls over it and turns it into what amounts to an impersonation"; LAT "a sensational performance ... does an amazing job of preparing us for the Brando we remember"; CT "fine"; WP "does an intelligent job as the young Vito, but the role is so haunted and inhibited by what Brando did as the older Vito that it seems basically redundant … it doesn't deepen or enrich our apprehension of the original character"; V "excellent"; MFB "splendid ... suggests that he might have given Brando more than a run for his money"). De Niro had been the runner-up for the New York Film Critics Circle award.

Also nominated were: playwright Michael V. Gazzo (NYT "superb"; LAT "vivid"; WP "a marvelous performance"; MFB "brilliant") and Actors' Studio teacher Lee Strasberg (NYT "an extraordinarily effective screen debut … the dominant performance of the picture ... fascinating"; LAT "a vivid portrait"; CT "played over a wide range"; WP "impressive"; MFB "good in a rather monotonous way") in *The Godfather Part II*; and, unexpectedly, Jeff Bridges in *Thunderbolt and Lightfoot*, whose inclusion the New York Daily News could explain only as the result of "the steady barrage of ads promoting [his] performance" (NYT "disarming"; LAT "allows Bridges to draw upon those deep resources that have made him one of the most persuasive young actors on the screen today"; WP "acts up a storm").

The most surprising omissions from the Oscar short-list were Globe nominee Bruce Dern in *The Great Gatsby* (NYT "makes the character work despite the odds"; LAT "a fascinating portrait"; WP "the only actor likely to come out of this project with his reputation enhanced"; V "excellent"), previous Best Director winner and BAFTA nominee John Huston in *Chinatown* (NYT "good"; LAT "one of his best, strongest and least mannered roles"; CT "communicates a corruption more naked, more out-front evil, than contemporary crime"; Obs "superb") and eventual BAFTA winner John Gielgud as a valet in the popular, all-star murder mystery *Murder on the Orient Express* (CT "superb").

The two French-language performances singled out by the major critics' groups during the awards season were also missing from the Academy's list of nominees: National Board of Review and National Society of Film Critics winner Swedish actor Holger Löwenadler as the Jewish tailor in *Lacombe, Lucien* (NYT "superb"; LAT "commandingly played … dominates the film and gives it its moral center"; CT "memorable"; WP "a superb performance"; V "outstanding"); and New York Film Critics Circle winner and previous Best Actor Oscar nominee Charles Boyer as an aristocrat in *Stavisky* (NYT "effortlessly elegant … it's a treat to watch him playing with Mr Belmondo"; WP "makes a welcome appearance"; V "efficient").

Among those also overlooked were: John Cazale as both the weak, older brother in *The Godfather Part II*, a role he had also played in the original film two years earlier (LAT "a fine piece of acting"; CT "[a] standout … memorable"; WP "very fine"; MFB "brilliant") and as a wiretapper's assistant in *The Conversation* (NYT "a fine, nervy performance"; LAT "coolly right"); Allen Garfield as a boastful wiretapper in *The Conversation* (NYT "splendid"; CT "a fine supporting performance"; V "outstanding"); Sam Waterston in *The*

Great Gatsby (NYT "splendid ... beautifully played ... makes it all work"; LAT "almost completely wrong for the part"; V "excellent"); Harvey Keitel in *Alice Doesn't Live Here Anymore* (NYT "stunningly played"; LAT "splendid"; WP "contributes a fine supporting performance here"); David Wayne in *The Front Page* (LAT "a scene stealer"); Donald Pleasance in *The Black Windmill* (NYT "in his best form"; LAT "afforded a rewarding opportunity, playing to the hilt a prissy bureaucrat"); and Paul Sorvino in *The Gambler* (NYT "all of the other actors, with the exception of Paul Sorvino who plays a sympathetic bookie, seem defeated by the quality of the material"; LAT "gemlike"; V "outstanding").

At the British Academy Awards the following year, Astaire won the Best Supporting Actor BAFTA. Surprisingly, De Niro was not included among the nominees.

1975

BEST PICTURE

ACADEMY AWARDS

Barry Lyndon
(Hawk, Warner Bros., 184 mins, 18 Dec 1975, 7 noms)
Dog Day Afternoon
(Warner Bros., 124 mins, 21 Sep 1975, $22.5m, 6 noms)
Jaws
(Zanuck, Universal, 124 mins, 20 Jun 1975, $129.5m / gr:$260.0m, 4 noms)
Nashville
(Altman, Paramount, 159 mins, 13 Jun 1975, $9.0m, 5 noms)
• ***One Flew Over the Cuckoo's Nest***
(Fantasy, United Artists, 133 mins, 20 Nov 1975, $59.9m / gr:$112.0m, 9 noms)

GOLDEN GLOBE AWARDS

(Drama)
Barry Lyndon
Dog Day Afternoon
Jaws
Nashville
• ***One Flew Over the Cuckoo's Nest***

(Comedy/Musical)
Funny Lady
Return of the Pink Panther
Shampoo
• ***The Sunshine Boys***
Tommy

BRITISH ACADEMY AWARDS

• ***Alice Doesn't Live Here Anymore***
Barry Lyndon
Dog Day Afternoon
Jaws

NEW YORK – ***Nashville***
LOS ANGELES – ***Dog Day Afternoon*** and ***One Flew Over the Cuckoo's Nest***
BOARD OF REVIEW – ***Barry Lyndon*** and ***Nashville***
NATIONAL SOCIETY – ***Nashville***

In The New York Times, influential film critic Vincent Canby called Robert Altman's ensemble epic *Nashville* "the movie sensation that all other American movies this year will be measured against" and his colleagues offered similarly strong praise (NYT "original and free-flowing … extraordinary [and] fascinating … a film of enormous feeling"; LAT "a rollicking and vivid entertainment … amazingly varied … the most original and provocative American film in a very long time"; CT "a special motion picture ... very funny … deserves attention";

WP "stunning … a politically haunted work of art … it's one of the few American movies that lends itself to intelligent political comment … acquires unusually powerful and complex emotional reverberations"; Obs "a splendid movie"; MFB "intriguing … the most exciting commercial American movie in years"). Despite the critical acclaim, the public, however was unmoved and *Nashville* made less than $10 million.

In contrast, Steven Spielberg's *Jaws* became the most successful film ever, breaking the $100 million barrier in domestic rentals (NYT "entertaining"; LAT "a coarse-grained and exploitative work which depends on excess for its impact"; WP "a new classic of cinematic horror … one of the most exciting and satisfying thrillers ever made … should set the standard in its field for many years to come"; V "an artistic and commercial smash"). Despite its B-grade horror film content, it became a Best Picture contender on the back of critical acclaim and its unprecedented commercial success. Time magazine included the film on its annual list of the year's ten best releases.

Another box office hit was the comedy *Shampoo*, starring Warren Beatty and Julie Christie. The critical response, however, was mixed (NYT "the American comedy of the year … a witty, furtively revolutionary, foul-mouthed comedy-of-manners"; LAT "one of those movies likely to attract business because it is notorious rather than because it is admirable … almost too heavy-handedly a political picture"; CT "a good movie"; WP "a smart, racy sex comedy … a diverting and interesting piece of work"; V "the excellent creative components do not add up to a whole").

Among the most highly-anticipated releases of the year were the musicals *Funny Lady*, the sequel to *Funny Girl* with Barbra Streisand reprising her role as Fanny Brice, and *Tommy*, the film version of The Who's rock musical. Both were popular with cinemagoers. *Tommy* received a mixed reception from critics (NYT "virtually explodes with excitement on the screen … mad, funny, irreverent, passionately over-produced, very, very loud and full of the kind of magnificent physical energy that usually wrecks a movie"; LAT "an overwhelming, thunderous, almost continuously astonishing achievement, coherent and consistent from first frames to last"; CT "a disappointing, slap-dash pictorialisation"; WP "on screen it's just banal"; V "spectacular in nearly every way"; MFB "decidedly a mixed bag") while *Funny Lady* was largely slammed (NYT "as long as Miss Streisand is singing, 'Funny Lady' is superb entertainment, but the minute she stops the movie turns into a concrete soufflé. It's heavy and tasteless [and] bland … moments meant to be dramatic are embarrassingly bad"; LAT "a mature musical, supplying all the verve and color that goes with the form"; CT "[a] predictable extravaganza"; WP "lavish but uninspired … a joyless, mechanical Big Movie Musical"; MFB "a shoddy, joyless enterprise").

1975

Perhaps the most eagerly-awaited film of the year among cinephiles was Stanley Kubrick's three-hour adaptation of *Barry Lyndon* which entered cinemas in December on a massive wave of publicity. Critics were sharply divided and audiences underwhelmed (NYT "a leisurely, serious, witty, inordinately beautiful, premium-length screen adaptation … unique … so glorious to look at, so intelligent in its conception and execution, that one comes to respond to it on Kubrick's terms"; LAT "[a] disaster … intellectually, emotionally and dramatically hollow"; CT "surpassingly beautiful [and] most welcome … the kind of film made for viewing when you feel like curling up with a good movie"; V "a most elegant and handsome adaptation"; TT "marvellous"; S&S "not an easily approachable work"; MFB "Kubrick's most intensely human spectacle" but "blankly remote and unapproachable").

Outperforming these anticipated studio projects were two small, independent films that were hits with both critics and audiences: *Dog Day Afternoon* (NYT "funny [and] vivid"; LAT "so eccentric and original a work that it does not categorize easily ... engrossing and unpredictable"; CT "superb"; WP "gritty and gripping … a triumphant new classic of American movie naturalism … no other film of 1975 has generated as much dramatic passion and impact … the picture to beat for the next set of Oscars"; V "outstanding"; S&S "a movie of surprising wit, humour and understanding"); and Milos Forman's *One Flew Over the Cuckoo's Nest* (NYT "too schematic to be honestly moving"; LAT "overwhelming"; CT "a solid picture of entertainment"; WP "absorbing and frequently powerful … impressive and touching"; V "brilliant cinema"). The two films shared the inaugural Best Picture prize from the Los Angeles Film Critics Association

The National Board of Review's top prize was shared as well, with both *Barry Lyndon* and *Nashville* chosen. The New York Film Critics Circle and the National Society of Film Critics, meanwhile, honoured Altman's film.

The Golden Globe (Drama) list was comprised of these four critically lauded films and Spielberg's box office smash. *Nashville* led the field with a record nine nominations, but it was *One Flew Over the Cuckoo's Nest* that emerged the winner in the Drama category. In the other category, meanwhile, the highly-favoured *Shampoo* was outpolled by *The Sunshine Boys* (NYT "has a lot of attractive things to recommend it … [but] one keeps wanting it to be better"; WP "amusing"; V "extremely sensitive and lovable"; MFB "highly amusing").

In the Los Angeles Times, Charles Champlin predicted that the short–list for the Best Picture Oscar would mirror the Globe (Drama) category with one change – *The Sunshine Boys*, he said, would be short-listed in place of *Barry Lyndon*. Instead the Academy replicated the Globe (Drama) line-up exactly. The chances of *Jaws* taking home the statuette, however, were all but ruled out by the exclusion of Spielberg from the Best Director category. No film had won

Best Picture without having its director nominated since *Grand Hotel* in 1931/32. With more nominations than any other film, *One Flew Over the Cuckoo's Nest* was the favourite to win on Oscar night.

Overlooked for consideration were: Federico Fellini's *Amarcord*, the previous year's New York Film Critics Circle's Best Picture prizewinner and Best Foreign-Language Film Oscar winner (NYT "marvelous … a film of exhilarating beauty", "extravagantly funny"; LAT "entertaining, amusing and satisfying"; WP "a masterpiece … abundantly entertaining"; S&S "does not live up to hopes … simple and classical to the point of denial"; SMH "could be his greatest masterwork of all"); *The Day of the Locust* (NYT "fascinating"; LAT "remote, bloodless and untouching"; CT "overdoes itself"; WP "ultimately, the ordeal doesn't seem worth the expenditure of time, energy and money"; V "lack of clarity"; MFB "frustrating"); *The Passenger* (NYT "dazzling", "compelling", "stunning" and "fascinating"; LAT "a masterpiece of visual beauty and rigorous artistry that is as tantalizing as it is hypnotic"; WP "sterile and insufferable"; V "an excellent film spectacle"; G "a very remarkable film"); *Hearts of the West* (NYT "thoroughly delightful"; LAT "it is all pretty silly"); *The Man Who Would Be King* (NT "highly entertaining … great fun"; LAT "has energy and grandeur and if it misses a classic perfection, it is a vast-scale money's-worth of a movie"; WP "enjoyable", "absorbing and appealing"); and *L'Histoire d'Adèle H. (The Story of Adele H.)* (NYT "profoundly beautiful"; LAT "beautiful, romantic, creatively daring and ambitious, and interesting – but also forced and unaffecting"; WP "unusually authentic [but] easier to admire than like").

The Oscar chances of *Nashville* lengthened when it was overlooked by the British Academy. In contrast *Barry Lyndon*, *Dog Day Afternoon* and *Jaws* were all mentioned in London where Forman's film was not in contention (it was up for BAFTAs the following year). While Kubrick won for Best Director and Al Pacino won Best Actor for *Dog Day Afternoon*, the top prize went to *Alice Doesn't Live Here Anymore*, which had been overlooked for a Best Picture Oscar nomination the previous year.

In the early part of the Oscar ceremony, an upset seemed possible – *Barry Lyndon* won four awards from four nominations in the technical categories, while *One Flew Over the Cuckoo's Nest* came up empty-handed from as many chances. When the major awards were announced, however, Milos Forman's drama won Director, Adapted Screenplay, Actress and then Actor. By the time Audrey Hepburn opened the Best Picture envelope it was no surprise that *One Flew Over the Cuckoo's Nest* was the winner. It became the first film since 1935 to sweep the Oscars for Picture, Director, Actor and Actress. It completed the sweep again at the BAFTAs in London the following year.

1975

BEST DIRECTOR

ACADEMY AWARDS
Robert Altman for *Nashville*
Federico Fellini for *Amarcord*
• **Milos Forman for *One Flew Over the Cuckoo's Nest***
Stanley Kubrick for *Barry Lyndon*
Sidney Lumet for *Dog Day Afternoon*

GOLDEN GLOBE AWARDS
Robert Altman – *Nashville*
• **Milos Forman – *One Flew Over the Cuckoo's Nest***
Stanley Kubrick – *Barry Lyndon*
Sidney Lumet – *Dog Day Afternoon*
Steven Spielberg – *Jaws*

DIRECTORS GUILD AWARD
Robert Altman – *Nashville*
• **Milos Forman – *One Flew Over the Cuckoo's Nest***
Stanley Kubrick – *Barry Lyndon*
Sidney Lumet – *Dog Day Afternoon*
Steven Spielberg – *Jaws*

BRITISH ACADEMY AWARDS
• **Stanley Kubrick – *Barry Lyndon***
Sidney Lumet – *Dog Day Afternoon*
Martin Scorsese – *Alice Doesn't Live Here Anymore*
Steven Spielberg – *Jaws*

NEW YORK – Robert Altman – *Nashville*
LOS ANGELES – Sidney Lumet – *Dog Day Afternoon*
BOARD OF REVIEW – Robert Altman – *Nashville* and **Stanley Kubrick – *Barry Lyndon***
NATIONAL SOCIETY – Robert Altman – *Nashville*

"I can't believe it! They went for Fellini instead of me!" cried Steven Spielberg when the Oscar nominations for Best Director were announced. Later he explained, "It hurts because I feel it was a director's movie." In the second half of the year Spielberg's *Jaws* had unexpectedly become the most commercially successful film of all time. Critics attributed much of the film's success to the twenty-nine-year old's direction. Vincent Canby of The New York Times, for example, said the film had been "cleverly directed" and said that Spielberg "has so effectively spaced out the shocks that by the time we reach the spectacular final confrontation ... we totally accept the makebelieve on its own foolishly entertaining terms". Others concurred (LAT "a potent and well-made movie … [he] shows an uncommon flair for handling big action"; CT "the fear is artfully achieved"; WP "Spielberg's technique and ingenuity don't fail him at any crucial juncture … [his] sense of movement comes into play most impressively"; S&S "[the film's] singular financial performance is ultimately a matter of the craft of the film-makers involved … [it] is an extraordinarily well made entertainment … a landmark of modern cinematic engineering").

The omission of Spielberg from the Best Director short–list was a shock both because of the nomination of his film as Best Picture and because there had been such a consensus during the awards season about the contenders for the Best Director prize.

Critics had embraced both Robert Altman for the satirical *Nashville* (LAT "undoubtedly the best and most assured film Altman has yet made and the most consistently revealing of his unique and remarkable gifts as a film-maker … an extraordinary achievement [and] a dazzling effort … [the film] succeeds by its deceptively light hand"; CT "[a] remarkable achievement"; WP "[his] technique works splendidly"; Obs "the great achievement of 'Nashville' is that Altman has worked with his cast to produce a many-layered film in which patterns overlap, repeat, merge … it's the sheer richness of the film that makes it remarkable") and Stanley Kubrick for the epic literary adaptation *Barry Lyndon* (NYT "assured … Kubrick has pulled of something that's most original"; CT "thoroughly successful in achieving [his intentions]… technically, Kubrick's film is more than proficient: it's innovative"). They had shared the prize from the National Board of Review, while Altman had been given the edge over Kubrick by the New York Film Critics Circle and the National Society of Film Critics.

Also received positively by critics had been Sidney Lumet, who had won the Los Angeles Film Critics Association's inaugural prize for *Dog Day Afternoon* (LAT "in good hands"; CT "maintains a terrific, roller-coaster pace"; WP "[the script] has given Lumet a golden opportunity to direct from strength, combining his vivid feeling for big-city settings, characters and tensions with an equally vivid sense of theatricality"; V "film-making at its best"), and Czech director Milos Forman for *One Flew Over the Cuckoo's Nest* (WP "sustains a somber, realistic atmosphere").

These four and Spielberg had been the nominees for the Best Director Golden Globe and also the Directors Guild of America award (Forman was the winner on both occasions). Prior to the Oscar nominations it had been expected that once again the same five directors would be mentioned. It was thus a surprise when Spielberg, the only one on the Globe and Guild lists not to have won a prize, was overlooked in favour of the New York Film Critics Circle choice for Best Director the previous year: Federico Fellini for *Amarcord* (NYT "working in peak condition"; WP "appears to renew himself artistically"; S&S "does not seem to be interested in doing much with the basic material to transform it").

The snub to Spielberg was highlighted when he was nominated by the British Academy along with Kubrick, Lumet and Martin Scorsese for *Alice Doesn't Live Here Anymore* (a 1974 release in the US). In London, it was Altman who was overlooked (Forman was not in contention until the following year).

Also overlooked were: Ken Russell for *Tommy* (NYT "at long last the man and his method have found a nearly perfect match in subject material ... Mr Russell's style seems to liberate Mr Townshend's rock score and lyrics"; LAT "it was inevitable that Russell would one day find the material ideally suited to his fabulist's imagination, and in the rock opera 'Tommy', Russell has"; WP "Russell's draggy, heavily melodramatized scenario has the curious effect of weakening the original libretto"); Michelangelo Antonioni for *The Passenger* (NYT "a major achievement by one of the world's great film-makers"); previous winner John Schlesinger for *The Day of the Locust* (NYT "a film that took truly remarkable self-assurance to make"; LAT "the craftsmanship is faultless"; WP "impressively crafted"); previous winner John Huston for *The Man Who Would Be King* (WP "his directing style was once crisper and more energetic, but the film has enough humor, exotic atmosphere, love of character and colourful acting to remain absorbing and appealing"); and François Truffaut for *L'Histoire d'Adele H. (The Story of Adele H.)* (LAT "beautiful, creatively daring and ambitious – but also forced"; WP "a good example of the kind of rigorous, masterful film-making that's easier to admire than like"; S&S "under-directed").

At his fourth and final nomination, Fellini was considered a non–starter in the race for the Best Director Oscar. The favourite was Globe and DGA winner and first–time Oscar nominee Forman. The main challengers were believed to be critics' choice Altman at his second nomination and Kubrick, who was up for the award for the fourth (and final) time.

In the absence of Forman, Kubrick won the Best Director prize from the British Academy and in Hollywood it seemed for a while that he and his epic period film might cause a major upset at the Oscars. The first half of Academy Awards night belonged to *Barry Lyndon*, which won all four of the technical awards for which it was nominated. In contrast *One Flew Over the Cuckoo's Nest* collected none of the Oscars in the technical categories. When the films came head to head for the Best Director prize, however, the momentum shifted. William Wyler opened the envelope and named Milos Forman as Best Director. *Barry Lyndon* did not win another award that night. In contrast, *One Flew Over the Cuckoo's Nest* went on to sweep the rest of the Academy's top five prizes.

A year later in London, Forman won the BAFTA for Best Director for *One Flew Over the Cuckoo's Nest* as part of another sweep of the major trophies.

1975

BEST ACTRESS

ACADEMY AWARDS

Isabelle Adjani as 'Adèle Hugo' in *L'Histoire d'Adèle H. (The Story of Adele H.)*

Ann-Margret as 'Nora Walker Hobbs' in *Tommy*

• Louise Fletcher as 'Nurse Mildred Ratched' in *One Flew Over the Cuckoo's Nest*

Glenda Jackson as 'Hedda Gabler' in *Hedda*

Carol Kane as 'Gitl' in *Hester Street*

GOLDEN GLOBE AWARDS

(Drama)

Karen Black – *The Day of the Locust*

Faye Dunaway – *Three Days of the Condor*

• Louise Fletcher – *One Flew Over the Cuckoo's Nest*

Marilyn Hassett – *The Other Side of the Mountain*

Glenda Jackson – *Hedda*

(Comedy/Musical)

Julie Christie – *Shampoo*

Goldie Hawn – *Shampoo*

• Ann-Margret – *Tommy*

Liza Minnelli – *Lucky Lady*

Barbra Streisand – *Funny Lady*

BRITISH ACADEMY AWARDS

Anne Bancroft – *Prisoner of Second Avenue*

• Ellen Burstyn – *Alice Doesn't Live Here Anymore*

Valerie Perrine – *Lenny*

Liv Ullmann – *Scener ur ett Äktenskap (Scenes from a Marriage)*

NEW YORK – Isabelle Adjani – *L'Historie d'Adèle H. (The Story of Adele H.)*

LOS ANGELES – Florinda Bolkan – *Una Breve Vacanza (A Brief Vacation)*

BOARD OF REVIEW – Isabelle Adjani – *L'Historie d'Adèle H. (The Story of Adele H.)*

NATIONAL SOCIETY – Isabelle Adjani – *L'Historie d'Adèle H. (The Story of Adele H.)*

"Do Any of These Actresses Rate an Academy Award?" asked The New York Times just days before the announcement of the Oscar nominations. In the article that followed Judy Klemesrud wrote, "There are so few surefire candidates this year that the list may be downright embarrassing. Studios and producers have been flailing around trying to come up with somebody, anybody, to push for the award in trade paper ads". She speculated that the winner might be a relatively unknown actress, like Marilyn Hassett in *The Other Side of the Mountain.* While the film had been dismissed by most critics, Klemesrud reported that "film insiders say that she has a chance of winning the Oscar." She went on to note that "because of the dearth of Best Actress contenders, Louise Fletcher, who was acclaimed as the wretched Nurse Ratched in 'One Flew Over the Cuckoo's Nest' has been elevated from what, in any normal year, would be the supporting actress category, into a leading contender for Best Actress."

Klemesrud was not alone in her lack of enthusiasm. "You just look at the Best Actress list and your heart sinks," Village Voice film critic Molly Haskell told Klemesrud, "It really makes you realize the paucity of roles for women. Usually when a year has been miserable for women, there has always been at least one really good contender. But this year, no one stands out. There is nothing like Ellen Burstyn's performance in 'Alice Doesn't Live Here Anymore'."

Burstyn, the previous year's Best Actress winner, soon joined the public debate by appearing on television urging Academy members not to vote for Best Actress this year in protest of the lack of quality roles for women. Fletcher responded by saying that it would have been nicer if Burstyn had made her comments when she had been a nominee. Interestingly, Burstyn had been one of a group of distinguished actresses, including Anne Bancroft, Angela Lansbury and Geraldine Page, who had turned down Fletcher's role as Nurse Ratched.

At the end of the year, the critics groups strengthened the view that it was a weak year for leading actresses in Hollywood films by opting for two foreign performances. For her debut as the distraught youngest daughter of French novelist Victor Hugo in François Truffaut's period drama *L'Histoire d'Adèle H. (The Story of Adele H.)*, Isabelle Adjani won the prizes from the National Board of Review, the National Society of Film Critics and the New York Film Critics Circle (NYT "played with extraordinary grace … a lovely performance"; LAT "the role might have defeated anyone because the actress is asked to make the unbelievable believable [and] Adjani cannot do it"; CT "to my mind doesn't deserve the cascading praise showered upon her by the New York critics"; WP "[she is] in fairly precocious command of some largely untapped emotional resources [but] Truffaut's production is so dominated by mood and understatement that even the role of Adele remains curiously tempered"; V "[an] exemplary performance"). The Los Angeles Film Critics Association gave their inaugural award to Florinda Bolkan in *Una Breve Vacanza (A Brief Vacation)* (LAT "very affecting"; WP "a sympathetic performance … does an exceptional job of expressing the personality of this shy, affectionate, plodding and terribly pressured working class woman"; MFB "[a] sensitive performance"). Bolkan was also runner–up to Adjani for the New York award.

The Hollywood Foreign Press Association overlooked both performances. Instead the Golden Globe nominees were mainly established American actresses whose work had mostly garnered mixed or negative reviews from critics. The Comedy or Musical category included four Oscar winners: Barbra Streisand, for her reprisal of her Oscar–winning role as Fanny Brice in *Funny Lady* (NYT "superb"; LAT "she sings superbly [and] what I find most impressive and likeable about the performance is the softened, bittersweet maturity that Streisand lets us see"; CT "she doesn't disappoint"; WP "Streisand doesn't do anything to earn one's applause on this occasion: even her vocals are on the meager side … [she] is restrained by a suffocating star treatment … [an] aloof, unappealing performance"; V "outstanding", "sensational"; MFB "the impersonation is more wayward than before"); Liza Minnelli in *Lucky Lady* (NYT "Minnelli's Claire is neither funny nor sad but an actress trying like hell to convince you that she is [and] the more she tries, the worse she gets … [her] performance is a mistake"; LAT "the miscalculations begin with a wrong reading of what Liza Minnelli does well … it is a mishandling, or a miscasting, fatal to the [film]"; WP "in her efforts to come on tough and dirty, Minnelli begins looking anxious and sounding slightly confused"); and both Julie Christie (NYT "querulous and brittle; at moments, she squeals with anger … she and Mr Beatty perform together without any of the attractive tensions that seeped through 'McCabe and Mrs Miller'"; LAT "[a] sensitive and rounded performance … her drunken fury at the election party is a stunning revelation"; WP "chemistry seems to be supplanting characterization rather than enhancing it") and Goldie Hawn (NYT "has little to do but reproach Mr Beatty … her nimble sarcasm is wasted"; LAT "a mature and touching achievement for her"; WP "excellent") in *Shampoo*. The winner, however, was the fifth nominee: Ann-Margret for her role in the rock musical *Tommy* (NYT "extravagantly fine", "tough, vulgar, witty and game", "sensational"; LAT "what gives 'Tommy' much of its power is the intensity of the performances [and] Ann-Margret as the tarty mother proves that what she did in 'Carnal Knowledge' was not a onetime accident … a strong, remarkable and self-effacing portrayal"; WP "an often seriously florid performance, full of rolling eyes and flaring nostrils and clenched teeth"; V "most effective"; MFB makes "strenuous efforts to act the lines").

In the Drama category, Hassett was nominated for portraying paraplegic former skier Jill Kinmont in *The Other Side of the Mountain* (NYT "an extremely pretty, efficient young actress"; LAT "played well"; CT "conveys an enormous amount of warmth"; WP "she isn't particularly impressive … [she is] obviously sincere, but her emotional range and technique seem very limited").

Also nominated were: Karen Black in *The Day of the Locust* (NYT "only the figure of Karen Black softens the film with something like pathos"; LAT "just right"; CT "overplayed"; WP "the sight of Karen Black trotting out her shrill, overworked tart routine for the umpteenth time is not in the least alluring or edifying" "; S&S "performs well"); Faye Dunaway for her performance in a supporting role in *Three Days of the Condor* (LAT "vivid ... although she is portraying a fairly neurotic freelance photographer, comes off with an attractive warmth and flashes of humor in what is one of her most likable though least-demanding roles"); Louise Fletcher for her performance in a supporting role in *One Flew Over the Cuckoo's Nest* (NYT "more interestingly ambiguous than the character in Mr Kesey's novel"; CT "oozingly good ... she may have come up with the most surprisingly fine performance in the film"; WP "the characterization is perhaps too smooth and subdued to be dramatically satisfying but Fletcher reproduces a convincing note of social science self-righteousness"; V "excellent"; MFB "brilliant"); and previous winner Glenda Jackson for reprising her stage triumph in *Hedda* (NYT "lively ... this version of [the play] is all Miss Jackson's Hedda and, I must say, great fun to watch ... Jackson's technical virtuosity is particularly suited to a character like Hedda"; LAT "should bring two-time Academy Award-winner Glenda Jackson yet another try at Oscar ... [a] formidable, fully illuminated Hedda"; WP "strictly speaking, Jackson's performance defies credibility, but her Hedda is probably as diverting as it is dubious ... [nonetheless] she could win her third Oscar considering the caliber of the competition this year"; SMH "every nuance of speech and action becomes crystal clear in the hands of [a] talented performer like Jackson"). Runner–up for the Best Supporting Actress prize from the New York critics, Fletcher was in the most high–profile picture. Unsurprisingly, she won the Globe and subsequently entered the Oscar race as the favourite.

Nominated for the Oscar were the two Globe winners, the New York critics' choice and previous winner Jackson. Adjani was the youngest ever Best Actress nominee at just twenty years of age, while Jackson earned her fourth nod in six years. Despite her Globe nomination, Hassett was by-passed in favour of an equally unknown actress who had not previously been considered for any of the Best Actress accolades despite some of the year's best reviews: twenty-three-year old Carol Kane for *Hester Street* (NYT "extraordinary", "magnificent"; CT "turns what might have been an ordinary movie into something special ... she's so good she doesn't need dialog to be effective"). Notably none of the nominees were in Hollywood productions.

On Oscar night, it was Fletcher who emerged as the winner of the Best Actress statuette as *One Flew Over the Cuckoo's Nest*. She added the Best Actress BAFTA to her collection a year later but never again made the Academy's short-list.

1975

BEST ACTOR

ACADEMY AWARDS
Walter Matthau as 'Willy Clark' in *The Sunshine Boys*
• **Jack Nicholson as 'Randle Patrick McMurphy' in *One Flew Over the Cuckoo's Nest***
Al Pacino as 'Sonny Wortzik' in *Dog Day Afternoon*
Maximilian Schell as 'Arthur Goldman' in *The Man in the Glass Booth*
James Whitmore as 'President Harry S. Truman' in *Give 'Em Hell, Harry!*

GOLDEN GLOBE AWARDS
(Drama)
Gene Hackman – *The French Connection II*
• **Jack Nicholson – *One Flew Over the Cuckoo's Nest***
Al Pacino – *Dog Day Afternoon*
Maximilian Schell – *The Man in the Glass Booth*
James Whitmore – *Give 'Em Hell, Harry!*

(Comedy/Musical)
Warren Beatty – *Shampoo*
George Burns – *The Sunshine Boys*
James Caan – *Funny Lady*
• **Walter Matthau – *The Sunshine Boys***
Peter Sellers – *Return of the Pink Panther*

BRITISH ACADEMY AWARDS
Richard Dreyfuss – *Jaws*
Gene Hackman – *The French Connection II* and *Night Moves*
Dustin Hoffman – *Lenny*
• **Al Pacino – *The Godfather Part II* and *Dog Day Afternoon***

NEW YORK – Jack Nicholson – *One Flew Over the Cuckoo's Nest*
LOS ANGELES – Al Pacino – *Dog Day Afternoon*
BOARD OF REVIEW – Jack Nicholson – *One Flew Over the Cuckoo's Nest*
NATIONAL SOCIETY – Jack Nicholson – *One Flew Over the Cuckoo's Nest*

For the second year in a row Jack Nicholson was the favourite to win the Best Actor Oscar, this time for his portrayal of a mental patient in *One Flew Over the Cuckoo's Nest*, a role played on stage a dozen years earlier by former Best Actor nominee Kirk Douglas. For his performance, Nicholson earned his fifth Oscar nomination in just seven years and his third consecutive mention as Best Actor

(NYT "magnetic … the performance that gives direction to those of everyone else in the cast"; LAT "the finest of all the fine portrayals Nicholson has already given us … it is astounding to see how he can regulate the intelligence of the character he is playing … [a] matchless characterization"; WP "compelling … effective and involving"; V "outstanding"; MFB "brilliant").

Nicholson's Oscar chances were aided by the praise he'd also received for his turn as a disillusioned American television reporter in Michelangelo Antonioni's *The Passenger* (NYT "a role that [he] assumes with such grace and ease that one almost forgets he's an actor"; LAT "splendid … he is able to evoke enormous sympathy for this lost, drifting man"; WP "he's all wrong … [his] flashes of frustration seem to derive from his dilemma as an actor rather than the hero's presumed dissatisfaction with himself"; V "commanding and resourceful"; G "a splendidly personal performance … astonishing").

Also nominated as Best Actor for a third consecutive year, and equalling Marlon Brando's record four consecutive nominations in the acting categories, was Al Pacino for his portrayal of a gay man who holds up a bank in *Dog Day Afternoon* (NYT "brilliant", "beautifully acted"; LAT "Pacino's performance dominates the film and he gives another measure of his remarkable range"; CT "he displays so much energy he made me believe the unbelievable"; WP "a great performance … virtually assured of his fourth consecutive Oscar nomination, and this performance may be too legendary to deny … volatile, funny and profoundly moving"; V "terrific"; MFB "excellent").

In the lead up to the Oscars, Pacino was perceived as Nicholson's main challenger as the two men split the critics prizes between them. Nicholson was named Best Actor by the New York Film Critics Circle for the second year in a row (his third acting award from the group), becoming the first man to be so honoured. He was also given a second consecutive Best Actor award by the National Society of Film Critics as well as the prize from the National Board of Review. Demonstrating their independent-mindedness in their inaugural year, the Los Angeles Film Critics Association chose Pacino.

Both men were nominated for the Golden Globe (Drama), along with: Gene Hackman for reprising his 1971 Oscar–winning role in *The French Connection II* (LAT "a brilliant piece of acting … can an extension of an Oscar-honored achievement be honored a second time? There are not likely to be five better portrayals by December"; CT "overplayed"; G "could scarcely by better … it's first and foremost Hackman's film"); previous winner Maximilian Schell for *The Man in the Glass Booth* (NYT "Schell rants and colourfully carries on with all those sudden shifts of mood and pace that are supposed to make a role interesting to the actor and the public alike, but this performance makes one aware of little except surface mannerisms"; LAT "an authentic tour de force"; WP "Schell's style of acting is humourless and gruelling … [an] obviously hard-working, well-meaning performance"); and, in a surprise choice, James Whitmore for his portrayal of President Truman in a recording of his one–man stage show *Give 'Em Hell, Harry!* (NYT "Whitmore may suffer the disadvantage of playing a stage part on the screen, but it is a first-rate stage performance"; LAT "remarkable"; V a "tour de force", "outstanding"). Nicholson made history when he emerged as the winner from this field, becoming the first man to win back to back Globes as Best Actor (Drama).

A challenger for the Oscar emerged in the form of the winner of the Golden Globe in the Comedy or Musical category. Walter Matthau won for his performance in *The Sunshine Boys* (NYT "at the top of his most antisocial form ... is so good playing old men, we may never know when he finally becomes one"; CT "never convinced me … overacting … you can't help but know it's a performance"; WP "surprisingly funny and plausible"; V "outstanding"; MFB "occasionally goes uncomfortably over the top"). Matthau triumphed over a field that included Warren Beatty as the womanizing hairdresser in *Shampoo* (NYT "played with intense, exuberant self-absorption"; LAT "seems the most complicated and the most believable [in the cast]").

Matthau joined Nicholson and Pacino on the Oscar short–list along with Schell and Whitmore. For the first time, all five Best Actor nominees were previous Oscar nominees.

Noticeably absent from the Best Actor Oscar line-up was Ryan O'Neal for his performance in the Best Picture nominee *Barry Lyndon* (NYT "it's much more of an accomplished performance that he's likely to receive credit for"; CT "far more successful than you'd expect"; MFB "the presence of Ryan O'Neal is not a perverse casting against type, but essential to the way Kubrick has revised the character of Thackeray's swashbuckling braggart"). Also overlooked were both Michael Caine and Sean Connery in *The Man Who Would Be King* (LAT "the performance [of the two leads] rank with their very best work"; WP "a major share of the credits belongs to Connery and Caine, who bring enthusiasm, physical authority and rapport to their roles … vivid, extroverted playing") and both Roy Scheider (LAT "an intense performance"; WP "the most human, vulnerable character Scheider has ever played on the screen and his performance is excellent") and BAFTA nominee Richard Dreyfuss (NYT "comes across with wit and easy self-assurance … a lively, individual and sympathetic performance … comes off best [of the film's cast]") in *Jaws*.

Just prior to the Academy Awards, Pacino won the Best Actor prize from the British Academy. Nicholson's portrayal of McMurphy would not be in contention for the British awards until the following year. The BAFTA win, however, was not enough to propel Pacino to an Oscar upset. "I was surprised to win," said Nicholson after accepting his first Best Actor Academy Award, "because I was a favourite four times before."

1975

BEST SUPPORTING ACTRESS

ACADEMY AWARDS
Ronee Blakley as 'Barbara Jean' in *Nashville*
• Lee Grant as 'Felicia Carr' in *Shampoo*
Sylvia Miles as 'Jessie Florian' in *Farewell, My Lovely*
Lily Tomlin as 'Linnea Reese' in *Nashville*
Brenda Vaccaro as 'Linda Riggs' in *Once Is Not Enough*

GOLDEN GLOBE AWARDS
Ronee Blakley – *Nashville*
Geraldine Chaplin – *Nashville*
Lee Grant – *Shampoo*
Barbara Harris – *Nashville*
Lily Tomlin – *Nashville*
• Brenda Vaccaro – *Once Is Not Enough*

BRITISH ACADEMY AWARDS
Ronee Blakley – *Nashville*
Lelia Goldoni – *Alice Doesn't Live Here Anymore*
• Diane Ladd – *Alice Doesn't Live Here Anymore*
Gwen Welles – *Nashville*

NEW YORK – Lily Tomlin – *Nashville*
BOARD OF REVIEW – Ronee Blakley – *Nashville*
NATIONAL SOCIETY – Lily Tomlin – *Nashville*

The ensemble cast of Robert Altman's satire *Nashville* dominated the awards season with five actresses from the film receiving awards or nominations: Ronee Blakley in her feature film debut as a sensitive country singer (NYT "makes an enchanting debut [with] a delicate and funny performance"; LAT "[a] success"; WP "the most touching performer in the film"; Obs "excellent"); Geraldine Chaplin as a British radio reporter (NYT "the film's single miscalculation, so broad that [the role] nearly destroys every scene she barges through [and] I'm not at all sure it's [her] fault"; LAT "amusing"; WP "reveals an unexpected flair for comedy"; Obs "she has some good lines, but Chaplin plays them consistently over the top"); Barbara Harris as an aspiring singer-songwriter (LAT "she just about makes off with the film, adding another to her list of unforgettable presences"); Lily Tomlin in her feature film debut as a gospel singer and mother of two deaf children (NYT makes a spectacular dramatic debut"; LAT "very affecting"; WP "played with extraordinarily affecting restraint"); and Gwen Welles as a waitress with ambitions to be a singer (NYT "[a] superlative performance"; LAT "terrific").

In a role originally developed by, and intended for, Louise Fletcher, Tomlin won the New York Film Critics Circle and National Society of Film Critics prizes. The National Board of Review, meanwhile, gave their prize to Blakley, a former backup vocalist who had been writing songs for the character of singer Barbara Jean, and then got the part when Susan Anspach was forced to withdraw. Both received Golden Globe and Academy Award nominations. Blakley was also short-listed for her performance by the British Academy in London.

Chaplin and Harris joined Blakley and Tomlin on the Golden Globe list. Also mentioned were formerly-blacklisted actress Lee Grant as a bored wife in *Shampoo* (NYT "brings grace to a thankless part", "the film's only interesting performance"; LAT "Grant comes closest to being a stereotype … yet the actress' skill carries the part beyond jokey distortions and reveals the harder, sadder truths about fear of emptiness, fear of rejection, fear of aging"); and Brenda Vaccaro as a zany magazine editor in *Once Is Not Enough* (LAT "all but steals [the movie] … tears right into her part [and] breaks through the film's shiny surface with her comedic gifts"). Although Grant was favoured to take away the accolade, in a surprise result the winner was Vaccaro.

Globe nominees Blakley, Tomlin, Grant and Vaccaro all received Academy Award nominations. The fifth candidate was Sylvia Miles, who earned her second nod as an alcoholic mother in the remake of *Farewell, My Lovely* (NYT "Miles plays a role that seems an overdone cliché until you realize that she is doing it with such subtlety that her lost beauty keeps flickering back"; LAT "marvelous"; S&S "[a] lovely performance"). While Tomlin was considered the favourite, close competition from Blakley and a poor showing on Oscar night by *Nashville* may have accounted for the upset win by Grant. It was the crowning glory of her comeback after being blacklisted. She was nominated again for Best Supporting Actress the following year and later directed one of the 1986 Oscar nominees for Best Documentary (Feature).

Among those overlooked for awards season recognition were both Karen Black as a Grand Ole Opry star in *Nashville* (LAT "very good"); Blythe Danner in *Hearts of the West* (NYT "consistently well played"); Jenny Runacre as the guilt-ridden wife in *The Passenger* (LAT "exactly right"); Geraldine Page as an evangelist in *The Day of the Locust* (NYT "extraordinarily vivid"; CT "overplayed"); Jennie Linden in *Hedda* (NYT "fine … succeeds in uncovering the smugness beneath Mrs Elvsted's helplessness"); and Adriana Asti in *Una Breve Vacanza (A Brief Vacation)* (LAT "Asti, giving the performance of a lost lifetime, is unforgettable").

1975

BEST SUPPORTING ACTOR

ACADEMY AWARDS
• George Burns as 'Al Lewis' in *The Sunshine Boys*
Brad Dourif as 'Billy Bibbit' in *One Flew Over the Cuckoo's Nest*
Burgess Meredith as 'Harry Greener' in *The Day of the Locust*
Chris Sarandon as 'Leon Shermer' in *Dog Day Afternoon*
Jack Warden as 'Lester' in *Shampoo*

GOLDEN GLOBE AWARDS
• Richard Benjamin – *The Sunshine Boys*
John Cazale – *Dog Day Afternoon*
Charles Durning – *Dog Day Afternoon*
Henry Gibson – *Nashville*
Burgess Meredith – *The Day of the Locust*

BRITISH ACADEMY AWARDS
• Fred Astaire – *The Towering Inferno*
Martin Balsam – *The Taking of Pelham One, Two, Three*
Burgess Meredith – *The Day of the Locust*
Jack Warden – *Shampoo*

NEW YORK – Alan Arkin – *Hearts of the West*
BOARD OF REVIEW – Charles Durning – *Dog Day Afternoon*
NATIONAL SOCIETY – Henry Gibson – *Nashville*

The four major precursors to the Academy Award were won by four different actors. Astonishingly, not one of them was nominated for the Oscar.

The New York Film Critics Circle award was won by Alan Arkin as a film director in early Hollywood in the comedy *Hearts of the West* (NYT "delightful … consistently well played"; LAT "has a broad good time") while the National Society of Film Critics gave its prize to Henry Gibson in *Nashville* (NYT "[a] superlative performance"; LAT "sensational"; WP "a fairly inspired satirical portrayal … manages to endow Haven with considerable authority while conveying his awful unctuousness and egomania"; V "[the] highlight of this film"; TT "outstanding") and the National Board of Review chose Charles Durning as a level-headed cop in *Dog Day Afternoon* (LAT "gives a performance as vigorous as Pacino's own, and it works"; WP "a fine performance"). The Golden Globe, meanwhile, went to Richard Benjamin as the long-suffering nephew *in The Sunshine Boys* (WP "funny to watch").

1975

Of the five Golden Globe nominees, the Academy recognised only one: Burgess Meredith in *The Day of the Locust* (LAT "has a tour de force part and it is to be watched with enjoyment and admiration, not with conviction"; CT "overplayed ... [an] outsized grab for pathos"; WP "gives a lively performance"; S&S "performs well"). Also nominated were: Brad Dourif for his screen debut as the nervous youth in *One Flew Over the Cuckoo's Nest* (WP "impressive... does wonders with a role that ought to guarantee disaster ... Dourif was handed a melodramatic cliché, but he's made it human again"); Chris Sarandon for his film debut as a bank robber's gay lover in *Dog Day Afternoon* (NYT "just the right mixture of fear, dignity and silliness"; LAT "Sarandon, in one of the year's most difficult acting chores, makes the lover extravagantly hysterical but preserves the viewer's sympathy"; WP "extraordinary ... a dazzling movie debut"; MFC "excellent"); Jack Warden in *Shampoo* (NYT "the most exactly sketched and placed character"; LAT "takes a caricature of a figure, posturing and nearly ridiculous, and finds in it the truer dimensions ... plays here with a sort of increasing restraint which gives the character at last an odd and affecting dignity"; WP "excellent"; V "outstanding"); and eighty-year old George Burns for *The Sunshine Boys* (NYT "an astonishingly legitimate funny performance"; CT "a welcome treasure of silence in a too-loud film"; WP "seems every inch the character he plays"; V "outstanding"; MFB "an irresistibly funny portrait").

In addition to the four prizewinners, the members of the Academy overlooked: John Cazale as the accomplice in *Dog Day Afternoon* (LAT "art at its best"; CT "played with a haunting, sallow-cheeked silence"; WP "first-rate"); both Keith Carradine (NYT "[a] superlative performance") and Keenan Wynn (LAT "touching"; MFB "superbly self-contained") in *Nashville*; Robert Shaw as the shark hunter in *Jaws* (NYT "comes across with wit and easy self-assurance"; LAT "undeniably colorful"; CT "compelling"; WP "smashing"); Murray Melvin as an aristocrat's personal chaplain in *Barry Lyndon* (NYT "superb"; CT "the highest level of acting excellence"); Timothy West in *Hedda* (NYT "most effective"); Max von Sydow as a hitman in *Three Days of the Condor* (LAT "vivid ... is able to give a by-now clichéd figure a good measure of individuality"); and Christopher Plummer as Rudyard Kipling in *The Man Who Would Be King* (NYT "gives the film weight"; LAT "ranks with his very best work"; WP "contributes an expert impersonation").

The sentimental favourite among the five first–time nominees on Oscar night was Burns, the oldest man to that to date to be nominated in the acting categories. Burns had been among the Best Actor (Comedy/Musical) nominees at the Globes, but had been switched to the supporting category by the studio to avoid competing for an Oscar with co-star Walter Matthau. The ploy paid off. On Academy Awards night, Burns won the Oscar.

The following year in London, the British Academy honoured Dourif.

1976

BEST PICTURE

ACADEMY AWARDS

All the President's Men
(Wildwood, Warner Bros., 138 mins, 7 Apr 1976, $29.0m, 8 noms)
Bound for Glory
(United Artists, 147 mins, 5 Dec 1976, 6 noms)
Network
(Gottfried, Chayefsky, M-G-M, United Artists, 120 mins, 14 Nov 1976, 10 noms)
• ***Rocky***
(Chartoff-Winkler, United Artists, 119 mins, 21 Nov 1976, $56.2m / gr:$117.2m, 10 noms)
Taxi Driver
(Phillips/Scorsese, Columbia, 113 mins, 8 Feb 1976, $11.6m, 4 noms)

GOLDEN GLOBE AWARDS

(Drama)
All the President's Men
Bound for Glory
Network
• ***Rocky***
Voyage of the Damned

(Comedy/Musical)
Bugsy Malone
The Pink Panther Strikes Again
The Ritz
Silent Movie
• ***A Star is Born***

BRITISH ACADEMY AWARDS

All the President's Men
Bugsy Malone
• ***One Flew Over the Cuckoo's Nest***
Taxi Driver

NEW YORK – *All the President's Men*
LOS ANGELES – *Network* and *Rocky*
BOARD OF REVIEW – *All the President's Men*
NATIONAL SOCIETY – *All the President's Men*

Two films about journalists were the frontrunners for the year's various Best Picture accolades.

The early favourite (released in April) was *All the President's Men*, a dramatisation of the Watergate investigation by two Washington Post journalists (NYT "riveting … a spellbinding detective story ... and a vivid footnote to some contemporary American history … an unequivocal smash-hit"; LAT "a classic motion picture … quiet beyond anything else … engrossing"; CT "exciting"; WP "an absorbing movie that somehow fails to evolve into a rousing, dramatically satisfying movie as well"; S&S "painstaking and absorbing entertainment"; MFB "meticulous [and] understated").

The other main contender, released seven months later in November, was *Network*, a satire about an American television network (NYT "brilliantly, cruelly funny", "vivid and flashing"; LAT "[a] coruscating and corrosive assault on commercial television ... [a] persistent and intent piece of work ... has vitality and a provocative excitement that is forever rare"; CT "savagely funny"; WP "ostentatiously opinionated ... never formulates a convincing case ... a flawed movie"; S&S "a brilliant, shocking, corrosive satire").

The darkhorse, many observers felt, was Martin Scorsese's *Taxi Driver*, which had won the Palme d'Or at the Cannes Film Festival (NYT "compelling ... a vivid, galvanizing portrait"; CT "disturbing ... vivid and violent ... but much too much to stomach"; WP "a smoldering, ominous and profoundly upsetting character profile"; V "powerful").

In their second year, the Los Angeles Film Critics Association shifted their event to make their awards the first major accolades of the season. For the second time, they declared a tie for Best Picture. The winners were *Network* and, in a surprise, the small-budget drama *Rocky* (NYT "oversold [and] sentimental"; LAT "very, very special ... in one warming stroke it revives and restores the vital tradition of the low-cost and unpretentious movie"; WP "a transparent piece of inspirational hokum ... nevertheless it evolves into a peculiarly winning sort of derivative movie: a triumphantly warmed-over heartwarmer"; CT "a great movie? Hardly ... flatout schmaltzy ... likeable as it may be, 'Rocky' does have gaping flaws"; V "some genuinely strong emotional impact").

The day after the west coast critics' vote, the National Board of Review selected *All the President's Men* as Best Picture. The Los Angeles prizewinners, *Network* and *Rocky*, were placed second and third respectively. Scorsese's *Taxi Driver* did not feature in the group's top ten.

Early in the new year, *All the President's Men* consolidated its position as the Oscar frontrunner with Best Picture accolades from the New York Film Critics Circle and the National Society of Film Critics on consecutive days. It won the east coast critics' accolade 40 points to 26 over *Network* on the second ballot. In third place, with 18 points, was Lina Wertmüller's *Pasqualino Settebellezze (Seven Beauties)* (NYT "[an] ambitious work of almost shattering impact", "as often harrowing as it is boisterously funny", "an extraordinary achievement"; LAT "the kind of powerful, personal, social and political statement that is rare anywhere in film-making"; CT "tempestuous, operatic, and often burlesque"; WP "[an] ambitious, overreaching blow-out ... dreadful bombast"; MFB "a treasure-trove for hunters of significant allusions, but the exercise proves scarcely worth the trouble"). Finishing fourth in the New York voting and finishing runner-up for the NSFC honour was *Taxi Driver*.

1976

The Golden Globe (Drama) was considered the award that would clinch the Oscar momentum for *All the President's Men* or see it swing towards *Network*. They vied for the trophy against *Rocky*, the biopic *Bound for Glory* (NYT "has a number of very good things going for it … [but] doesn't have much of a screenplay"; LAT "one of this year's most admirable and triumphant surprises"; V "outstanding", "brilliant"; WP "the sort of picture Hollywood is perhaps best prepared to take pride in – and overrate"; S&S "sidesteps any attempt to get to the heart of the elusively beguiling folk-singer") and the much maligned historical drama *Voyage of the Damned* (NYT "alternately sluggish and hysterical", "clumsy, tasteless and self-righteous ... worse than merely boring"; LAT "fails to generate the full emotional impact inherent in the source material"; CT "sprawling … succeeds because of its truth and despite its form and dialog"; WP "makes a desultory shambles of a heartbreaking true story … in a word, lamentable"; V "sluggish"; MFB "yet another gargantuan epic that demonstrates the folly of relying for dramatic weight on a star-studded international cast"). In a major shock, however, neither of the frontrunners won the Globe, even though Lumet won Best Director for *Network*. Victorious on the night was *Rocky*, which suddenly seemed a distinct chance for an unlikely win at the Academy Awards.

Another film that emerged from the Globes as an unexpected Oscar contender was the second remake of *A Star is Born*, starring Barbra Streisand. The film won a record-equalling five Globes, including Best Picture (Comedy/Musical), even though it had divided critics and been cited by The New York Times as one of the year's ten worst films (NYT "light-weight"; LAT "it is not a very successful movie … rarely stops seeming manufactured … disappointingly uninvolving"; CT "a lumbering love story"; WP "[a] failure … could scarcely be more disenchanting"; V "a superlative remake"; MFB "has no coherence whatsoever ... hackneyed").

When the Oscar nominations were announced *Network* and *Rocky* led the field, each with ten nominations, including Best Picture and Best Director. Also earning recognition for both awards was *All the President's Men* with eight mentions. Included in the top category, but shut out of the Best Director contest, were *Bound for Glory* and *Taxi Driver*.

Overlooked for consideration were: Wertmüller's *Pasqualino Settebellezze*; Globe and BAFTA nominee *Bugsy Malone*, a gangster spoof with an all-child cast (NYT "wildly uneven but imaginative and stylish satire"; LAT "a rare, original, tuneful, lighthearted, uplifting, charming and preposterously innocent family film"; WP "a freakish embarrassment"; S&S "it deserves to do well … in its curious artificiality, 'Bugsy' has a delightful authenticity"; MFB "the total effect is captivating … an adult film for children made with much wit, much originality and no patronising sentiment"); *Next Stop, Greenwich Village* (NYT "a big disappointment … commonplace [and] second-rate"; LAT "beautifully conceived, textured and acted … it is very, very funny"; WP "engaging"; V "outstanding", "gentle and touching"); Los Angeles and Globe Best Foreign-Language Film winner, *Ansikte mot Ansikte (Face to Face)*, for which Ingmar Bergman was nominated as Best Director (NYT "beautiful, agonizing"; LAT "[an] intensely and intimately personal work [that] is greatly powerful and affecting"; CT "mechanical"; WP "emotionally evasive and philosophically platitudinous"; SMH "striking"); the French film *Cousin, Cousine*, a surprise box office hit (NYT "an exceptionally winning, wittily detailed comedy", "wise, gentle, supremely romantic"; LAT "engaging"; CT "charming"; MFB "charming and polished"); the Russian science fiction film *Solaris*, winner of the special jury prize at the 1972 Cannes Film Festival (NYT "[a] complex and sometimes very beautiful film"; LAT "[a] wondrously beautiful and astonishing masterpiece … a dazzlingly imaginative work of the highest order with awesome production values"; WP "special … it stimulates thought … eerie, almost haunted ... a slow, deliberate, almost languid film"); and Satyajit Ray's drama *Ashani Sanket (Distant Thunder)* which won Best Picture at the 1973 Berlin Film Festival and appeared on The New York Times' list of the top ten films of 1975 before finally receiving a cinematic release in Los Angeles in April 1976 (NYT "fine, elegiac … has the impact of an epic without seeming to mean to"; LAT "harrowing … as beautiful as it is stark"; WP "a luminous and humane film")

Unsurprisingly, the Academy also ignored the disastrous remake of *King Kong* (NYT "something to make you cringe with embarrassment").

Rocky became the Oscar favourite when its director, John G. Avildsen, won the Directors Guild of America prize ahead of Lumet and Pakula. During most of the Academy Awards ceremony, however, it seemed as if the Academy was going to snub the Globe winner. With the evening's final two awards yet to be announced, *Rocky* had received only one statuette: Best Film Editing. Its acclaimed rivals, however, had dominated the festivities, each winning four Oscars, and between them accounting for all the acting and writing trophies (*Network* was just the second film to win three awards in the acting categories, following *A Streetcar Named Desire* in 1951).

In a reflection of its eponymous under-dog hero's victory against the odds, however, *Rocky* claimed the evening's final Oscars for Best Director and Best Picture. The film eventually finished 1977 as the second biggest hit at the box office (behind George Lucas' science fiction blockbuster *Star Wars*).

All the President's Men, *Network*, *Rocky* and *Taxi Driver* all received Best Film nominations from the British Academy, but none received the organisation's top honour. In 1976, *All the President's Men* and *Taxi Driver* were outpolled by the previous year's Best Picture Oscar winner, *One Flew Over the Cuckoo's Nest*, while the following year *Network* and *Rocky* were eclipsed by *Annie Hall*, the winner of that year's Best Picture Academy Award.

1976

BEST DIRECTOR

ACADEMY AWARDS
• John G. Avildsen for *Rocky*
Ingmar Bergman for *Ansikte mot Ansikte (Face to Face)*
Sidney Lumet for *Network*
Alan J. Pakula for *All the President's Men*
Lina Wertmüller for *Pasqualino Settebellezze (Seven Beauties)*

GOLDEN GLOBE AWARDS
Hal Ashby – *Bound for Glory*
John G. Avildsen – *Rocky*
• Sidney Lumet – *Network*
Alan J. Pakula – *All the President's Men*
John Schlesinger – *Marathon Man*

DIRECTORS GUILD AWARD
• John G. Avildsen – *Rocky*
Sidney Lumet – *Network*
Alan J. Pakula – *All the President's Men*
Martin Scorsese – *Taxi Driver*
Lina Wertmüller – *Pasqualino Settebellezze (Seven Beauties)*

BRITISH ACADEMY AWARDS
• Milos Forman – *One Flew Over the Cuckoo's Nest*
Alan J. Pakula – *All the President's Men*
Alan Parker – *Bugsy Malone*
Martin Scorsese – *Taxi Driver*

NEW YORK – Alan J. Pakula – *All the President's Men*
LOS ANGELES – Sidney Lumet – *Network*
BOARD OF REVIEW – Alan J. Pakula – *All the President's Men*
NATIONAL SOCIETY – Martin Scorsese – *Taxi Driver*

The early Oscar frontrunner was Alan J. Pakula, the New York Film Critics Circle and National Board of Review winner as well as National Society of Film Critics runner-up for *All the President's Men* (NYT "much of the effectiveness of the movie is in its point of view … its strength is the virtually day-by-day record of the way Bernstein and Woodward conducted their investigations … beautifully detailed"; LAT "a superlative piece of movie making … [Pakula's] hallmark here as before is meticulous naturalism"; CT "Pakula's greatest achievement is the way he unobtrusively weaves outside events into [the] narrative of the reporters' story"; WP "exceptionally well-made … modest, careful, smooth craftsmanship [but] verges on being meticulous to a fault … [becomes] emotionally limiting … lacks an expansive vision and an elemental spark of showmanship and inspiration"; V "ingenious direction"; S&S "crisp dramatic counterpoint is part and parcel of the way he persistently restricts his canvas … simply but effectively boxes the audience in … compiling evidence with all the clipped allusiveness and atmospheric tension of classic mystery fiction"; MFB "Pakula has admirably opted for something closer to documentary ... meticulous [and] understated treatment").

His main challenger for the Academy's Best Director statuette, it initially seemed, was Sidney Lumet, who won in Los Angeles and finished fourth in New York for *Network* (LAT "the electric energy of Sidney Lumet's direction make the message indelible … but 'Network' for all its vitality and impact is still a rough-hewn movie"; CT "credit, too, to director Sidney Lumet … [he] tells Chayefsky's story unobtrusively"; WP "Lumet seems to be interpreting Chayefsky's manipulations and shouting matches in a mood of almost documentary earnestness, underling the obviousness"; V "outstanding").

Emerging as the darkhorse was National Society of Film Critics prizewinner Martin Scorsese for *Taxi Driver* (LAT "it has a muscle-tensing, skin-pricking, apprehensive suspense that builds from those first unsettling moments like an air-raid siren"; CT "Scorsese is in full control of his camera, even if the violence he plays with overpowers him"; WP "Scorsese's energy, visual flair and sensuous feeling for New York City locations give Schrader's original obsessions a compelling rhythm and atmospheric richness and resonance that they might never have had under any other director … superbly visualized"; V "excellent").

Lumet appeared to gain the edge with a win at the Golden Globes and a record seventh Directors Guild of America nomination, but John G. Avildsen unexpectedly became the favourite when he won the Guild honour for *Rocky* (NYT "none too decisive direction"; LAT "'Rocky' seems wonderfully guileless, but it is the innocence won of an artful sophistication crafty enough to conceal itself … Avildsen has learned how to do much with little … brilliantly orchestrated"; WP "a certain amount of unpretentiousness may be crucial to the picture's charm, but in the last analysis it needs a more attentive direction than John Avildsen has been able or willing to supply").

At the Academy Awards, the strong record of the DGA as an indicator of Oscar success was extended when Avildsen emerged with the statuette ahead of Pakula and Lumet. The other nominees were Ingmar Bergman for *Ansikte mot Ansikte (Face to Face)* (NYT "Bergman creates a stunning picture"; S&S "less artificial [than his previous films] … Bergman has allowed himself to be caught off-guard"; WP "skilful superficiality"; SMH "a very striking, startling and potent example of Bergman in top form") and Lina Wertmüller, who had placed third in the voting by the New York Film Critics Circle, for *Pasqualino Settebellezze (Seven Beauties)* (NYT "the work of a film maker at the peak of her energies, so full of ideas and images that she can afford to throw away moments that other, less talented directors would tediously emphasize"; LAT "she executes her grotesqueries and her savageries with flair, and her powers of bizarre invention are considerable"; CT "often heavy-handed"; WP "all too obvious"; MFB "simply works up a series of analogies"). Wertmüller was the first woman ever nominated for either the DGA accolade or the Best Director Oscar.

In addition to Scorsese, the Academy overlooked: Alfred Hitchcock for his final film, *Family Plot* (NYT "has the exhilarating effect of seeing a magic trick performed smoothly and effortlessly"; LAT "precisely paced [and] suspenseful"; WP "it's as if Hitchcock no longer knew the difference between vital and superfluous or redundant exposition and no longer possessed a command of visual shorthand"; V "masterfully controlled"; MFB "[the film's] implausibilities and illogicalities are flourished with such triumphant sleight of hand"); Brian De Palma for *Carrie* (NYT "cannily and stylishly constructed"; LAT "superior craftsmanship"; CT "the film builds to a fine climax through a set of strong performances and De Palma's aggressive camera movement"; WP "brilliantly directed … King's material seems to have provided De Palma with the opportunity to synthesize every aspect of his versatile, exciting filmmaking talent"); Andrei Tarkovsky for *Solaris* (NYT "its rhythm is slow [and] the sense of wonder that Mr Tarkovsky has created yields to a certain didacticism"; LAT "a dazzlingly imaginative work"); BAFTA nominee Alan Parker for his feature film directorial debut *Bugsy Malone* (NYT "remarkably successful"; WP "Parker cannot be trusted to take the saccharine out of his own confections"; S&S "few members of his young cast having acted before, Parker constructs and protects their performances through a remarkable editing pace … [and he] observes the detail of the gangster genre with affectionate accuracy"); and Satyajit Ray for his 1973 drama *Ashani Sanket (Distant Thunder)* (NYT "the work of a director who has learned the value of narrative economy"; LAT "Ray's imagery has always been striking, and never more so – or more elegantly stylized – than here"; WP "distinguished by the simplicity of feeling, the economy of expression and the generosity of spirit that have informed Ray's work from the beginning").

1976

BEST ACTRESS

ACADEMY AWARDS
Marie–Christine Barrault as 'Marthe' in *Cousin, Cousine*
• Faye Dunaway as 'Diana Christensen' in *Network*
Talia Shire as 'Adrian' in *Rocky*
Sissy Spacek as 'Carrie White' in *Carrie*
Liv Ullmann as 'Dr Jenny Isaksson' in *Ansikte mot Ansikte (Face to Face)*

GOLDEN GLOBE AWARDS
(Drama)
• Faye Dunaway – *Network*
Glenda Jackson – *The Incredible Sarah*
Sarah Miles – *The Sailor Who Fell from Grace with the Sea*
Talia Shire – *Rocky*
Liv Ullmann – *Ansikte mot Ansikte (Face to Face)*

(Comedy/Musical)
Jodie Foster – *Freaky Friday*
Barbara Harris – *Family Plot*
Barbara Harris – *Freaky Friday*
Goldie Hawn – *The Duchess and the Dirtwater Fox*
Rita Moreno – *The Ritz*
• Barbra Streisand – *A Star is Born*

BRITISH ACADEMY AWARDS
Lauren Bacall – *The Shootist*
• Louise Fletcher – *One Flew Over the Cuckoo's Nest*
Rita Moreno – *The Ritz*
Liv Ullmann – *Ansikte mot Ansikte (Face to Face)*

NEW YORK – Liv Ullmann – *Ansikte mot Ansikte (Face to Face)*
LOS ANGELES – Liv Ullmann – *Ansikte mot Ansikte (Face to Face)*
BOARD OF REVIEW – Liv Ullmann – *Ansikte mot Ansikte (Face to Face)*
NATIONAL SOCIETY – Sissy Spacek – *Carrie*

Two years after she had been controversially declared ineligible for Oscar consideration by the Academy, Norwegian actress Liv Ullmann was once again a strong contender for the year's Best Actress accolades for her performance as a psychiatrist suffering a nervous breakdown in Ingmar Bergman's *Ansikte mot Ansikte (Face to Face)* (NYT "gives a triumphant performance in what must be one of the greatest roles Bergman has ever written for a woman … nothing short of immense ... another tour de force ... magnificently played"; LAT "her performance has unutterably believable and soul-wrenching power … one of the truly fine film portrayals … demanding and devastating"; CT "Ullmann running through the emotional spectrum as only she can do"; WP "[a] tour de force"; V a "virtuoso performance"; TT "compelling and remarkably detailed"; S&S "Bergman rests nearly its entire weight on the performance by Liv Ullmann, who pulls all the stops out for what must have been exhausting scenes to play"; SMH "she is a tool to carry out Bergman's complicated project with magnificent control and intelligence"). The New York Film Critics Circle gave Ullmann their Best Actress award for the third time in just five years (by a margin of 41 points to 28). She also received a third prize in a decade from the National Board of Review as well as the plaudit from the Los Angeles Film Critics Association.

The only major critics' accolade that Ullmann did not collect was the Best Actress trophy from the National Society of Film Critics for which she polled third. The group had already honoured her three times over the previous decade. The NSFC winner was twenty-seven-year old Sissy Spacek in the horror film *Carrie* (NYT "a marvel ... she makes us perfectly aware that she is overacting, and yet she is very effective"; CT "[a] strong performance"; WP "beautifully portrayed … the dramatic revelation of the show … gives the fantastic narrative a consistently touching and believable human core … responds splendidly to every mood and transformation the role requires"; S&S "a fine performance"). Spacek polled third in the New York voting.

Despite these critics' accolades, most pundits considered the frontrunner for the Oscar to be Faye Dunaway as an ambitious television news executive in *Network* (NYT "Dunaway, in particular, is successful in making touching and funny, a woman of psychopathic ambition and lack of feeling"; LAT "cracklingly good … a cruel cartoon, well-played"; WP "as credible as anyone could possibly be"; V "excellent"; S&S "accomplished"). Dunaway had been runner-up for both the New York and NSFC prizes and won the Golden Globe (Drama) ahead of Ullmann. She received her third nomination from the Academy for her performance. In The Washington Post, Gary Arnold observed, "Dunaway, overdue for an Academy Award, is supposed to have it all sewed up on the strength of this vividly superficial performance. It seems a pity this role had to be what it is. For the record, the outstanding feature of her performance is Diana's busy-busy walk. It's a very amusing character 'signature': when we see Diana coming, we know she means business."

Also nominated for the Oscar were: critics' winners Ullmann (for the second time) and Spacek (for the first time); Marie–Christine Barrault in the French film *Cousin, Cousine* (NYT "very good"; LAT "a triumph"); and Talia Shire (her second nomination) as the girlfriend of a boxer in *Rocky* (NYT "comes off best [in the cast] … genuinely touching and funny … she's so good, in fact, that she almost gives weight to Mr Stallone's performance"; LAT "[an] intelligent, sensitive and touching performance"; WP "gets an extraordinary amount of expressive mileage out of the underwritten role of Adrian"; TT "brings her own conviction to the rather badly written role"). Shire's performance had been considered in the supporting category for much of the awards season. Although she had finished fourth in the New York critics' Best Actress voting, she won the circle's Best Supporting Actress award as well as the supporting plaudit from the NBR. She finished runner-up in the supporting category in the NSFC voting. The nominations of Barrault and Ullmann, meanwhile, marked the second time two foreign-language performances had been short-listed for the same statuette.

Even though she had received mixed-to-negative reviews, the most surprising omission from the category was arguably Globe (Comedy/Musical) champ and previous winner Barbra Streisand in the third version of *A Star is Born* (LAT "the movie is a Streisand concert in which the star is not so much born as canonized"; CT "made palatable by Streisand's superb singing [but she] isn't very convincing as the ingenue"; WP "there was probably no way to prevent Streisand from making a spectacle of her own performance … seems to be victimizing her talent by a peculiar form of pretension"; V "her finest screen work to date"; MFB "fails to convince"). Streisand was, however, nominated in the music categories and subsequently won the Oscar for Best Music (Song).

Also by-passed for consideration were: Globe nominee Glenda Jackson as Sarah Bernhardt in *The Incredible Sarah* (NYT "the only reason to put up with [this] disaster"; LAT "she is a sight worth seeing … her deep identification with the role she is playing overpowers the other elements"; V "excellent"; MFB "struggles"); Barbara Harris for her dual Globe-nominated performances as the mother in *Freaky Friday* (LAT "so special in her antic charm"; CT "a serviceable job with mediocre material"; MFB "delightful") and as a professional medium in *Family Plot* (NYT "hilarious"; LAT "the most extensive and appropriate movie role that [she] has yet had … splendidly assured"; CT "overacts"; WP "[the role] just allows her to indulge bad acting habits"; V "sensational"); BAFTA nominee Rita Moreno for reprising her Tony Award-winning performance as a talentless entertainer in *The Ritz* (NYT "comically incandescent"; LAT "flamboyantly entertaining and successful [in] a show-stopping creation ... hilarious but also sympathetic and in its zany way tender"; CT "top honors"; MFB "a consistent gum-chewing pleasure"); and BAFTA nominee Lauren Bacall in *The Shootist* (V "outstanding"; S&S "vibrant").

Ineligible for Oscar consideration was the performance of Rachel Roberts in *Alpha Beta*, a 1972 recording of her stage success, which had screened on British television two years earlier (NYT "extraordinary … she makes classic tragedy out of this row-house misery"; LAT "superb").

On Oscar night, Dunaway repeated her Globe victory and received the Oscar for Best Actress. She was outpolled for the BAFTA the following year, however, by that year's Oscar winner, Diane Keaton in *Annie Hall*.

1976

BEST ACTOR

ACADEMY AWARDS
Robert De Niro as 'Travis Bickle' in *Taxi Driver*
• Peter Finch as 'Howard Beale' in *Network*
Giancarlo Giannini as 'Pasquale Frafuso' in *Pasqualino Settebellezze (Seven Beauties)*
William Holden as 'Max Schumacher' in *Network*
Sylvester Stallone as 'Rocky Balboa' in *Rocky*

GOLDEN GLOBE AWARDS
(Drama)
David Carradine – *Bound for Glory*
Robert De Niro – *Taxi Driver*
• Peter Finch – *Network*
Dustin Hoffman – *Marathon Man*
Sylvester Stallone – *Rocky*

(Comedy/Musical)
Mel Brooks – *Silent Movie*
• Kris Kristofferson – *A Star is Born*
Peter Sellers – *The Pink Panther Strikes Again*
Jack Weston – *The Ritz*
Gene Wilder – *Silver Streak*

BRITISH ACADEMY AWARDS
Robert De Niro – *Taxi Driver*
Dustin Hoffman – *All the President's Men* and *Marathon Man*
Walter Matthau – *Bad News Bears* and *The Sunshine Boys*
• Jack Nicholson – *One Flew Over the Cuckoo's Nest*

NEW YORK – Robert De Niro – *Taxi Driver*
LOS ANGELES – Robert De Niro – *Taxi Driver*
BOARD OF REVIEW – David Carradine – *Bound for Glory*
NATIONAL SOCIETY – Robert De Niro – *Taxi Driver*

The overwhelming critics' choice for Best Actor was Robert De Niro. Two years after receiving the Best Supporting Actor Oscar, he was a serious contender in the lead performance category for his portrayal of a deranged New York cab driver in *Taxi Driver*. The New York Times called him "riveting" and "superb" while Variety said he was "terrific" in "a smash performance." Such raves were typical of the critical response (NYT "he manages to display both pathos and lethally dangerous charm … a performance that is effective as much for what Mr De Niro does as for how he does it. Acting of this sort is rare in films"; LAT "strong and convincing"; CT "first-rate, though always bordering on the heavy-handed"; WP "a flawless central performance … De Niro seems to possess an instinctive understanding of the desolate state of mind he's attempting to illustrate … [he] never overstates"; TT "a wonderful performance"; S&S "De Niro's best performance to date"; FQ "the film's most affecting element"). At the end of the year, De Niro convincingly won the New York Film Critics Circle prize (by 33 points to 19) and accolades from the Los Angeles Film Critics Association and the National Society of Film Critics.

The one major critics' honour that De Niro did not receive was the National Board of Review award, which was presented to David Carradine for his portrayal of folksinger Woody Guthrie in *Bound for Glory* (NYT "[a] dry, haunted performance"; LAT "[his] controlled and considered performance is an impressive achievement … an earnest and hardworking performance"; CT "is undone by the script … isn't that compelling"; WP "played with surprising canniness and authority … invests the character with enough selfishness and deviousness to keep the picture from caving in with sentimentality"; MFB "Carradine's extraordinary performance is a masterly exercise in studied simplicity"). Carradine had finished as the runner-up for the New York prize. In its review of *Bound for Glory*, The New York Times commented "Carradine's performance is almost the entire film" so it was something of a surprise when the film was nominated for Best Picture but Carradine, a Globe nominee, was overlooked for a Best Actor Oscar nomination.

Similarly, *All the President's Men* was short-listed for the top Oscar but both Dustin Hoffman and Robert Redford were by-passed (NYT "play their roles with the low-keyed, understated efficiency required"; LAT "one of the satisfactions of the film is that they do not do star turns. They are working actors acting the parts of working journalists with a rumpled, tie-askew believability"; CT "Hoffman is smashing … a performance that's invisible the first time you see it and riveting the second time … Redford doesn't give us a new character, just a variation on his dominant screen image"; WP "astute impersonations" in roles that "are not major acting challenges", "they shade the roles intelligently but they don't try to dominate the conception, which stresses methodology rather than characterization"; S&S "controlled edginess"; MFB "Hoffman's dazzling character impersonation and Redford's dazzling star persona"). Hoffman was also ignored for his turn as a man victimised by a former Nazi in *Marathon Man* (NYT "superior"; LAT "elegantly acted … Hoffman finds another character not quite like any he has done before … the performance could have gone wrong in several directions; it doesn't. It is watchable and hugely sympathetic"; WP "Hoffman's acting is flawless").

Perhaps the most surprising omission from the list, however, was previous winner John Wayne for his final screen role as an old gunfighter dying of cancer in *The Shootist* (LAT "Wayne naturally dominates with his larger-than-life presence yet reveals to us rare tenderness and vulnerability"; V "outstanding"; S&S "Wayne's performance is masterly").

Others overlooked by the Academy were: Golden Globe (Comedy/Musical) winner Kris Kristofferson in *A Star is Born* (LAT "Kristofferson's performance generally is alive and interesting and, toward the end, he generates considerable sympathy"; CT "more of a presence than an actor"; WP "Kristofferson is in miserable singing voice [and it's] a strain trying to accept the character as vaguely credible"; V "magnificent"; MFB "makes a far better impression [than his co-star]"); previous Best Supporting Actor Oscar winner Walter Matthau in the comedy *The Bad News Bears* (NYT "[a] rich interpretation"; LAT "makes his gloriously seedy coach an alternately outrageously hilarious, hard-driving, fair and even compassionate man"); and Philippe Noiret in *L'Horloger de Saint-Paul (The Clockmaker)* (NYT "[an] extraordinary performance ... a performance of the high calibre that we now take for granted from him"; LAT "extraordinary [and] powerful … an eloquent, commanding presence … one of those brilliant characterizations which seem to start from the soul and move out through the pores"; CT "beautifully played"; WP "[a] careful, restrained performance").

The performance of Albert Finney in *Alpha Beta*, a filmed version of his stage success, was ineligible having screened on British television two years earlier (NYT "extraordinary"; LAT "superb").

Nominated for the Oscar ahead of these contenders were: De Niro (his second nomination, and his first as Best Actor); Sylvester Stallone as an underdog boxer in *Rocky* (NYT "unconvincing", "[his performance is] the large hole at the center of the film … less a performance than an impersonation ... all superficial mannerisms and movements"; LAT "a once-in-a-lifetime coming together of man and material … makes Rocky colourful, not too bright and altogether heroic and engrossing"; CT "the story is carried along by Stallone's performance"; WP "brings a fresh personality and undeniable emotional conviction to his clichéd character … it's fun to witness such a personal, off-the-pace acting triumph"; TT "fascinating"); Giancarlo Giannini as a small-time con-artist in a German concentration camp in *Pasqualino Settebellezze (Seven Beauties)* (NYT "marvelously well-acted", "superb"; LAT "the mugging here reaches caricature"; CT "[the film] can be enjoyed for Giancarlo Giannini's leading performance … he's equally adept playing a clown and a lover … a good Everyman"); and both the late Peter Finch (his second nod) as a disillusioned and unstable television news anchor and previous winner William Holden (his third and final nomination) as a television news executive in *Network* (both LAT "cracklingly good"; V "excellent") .

In mid-January 1977, Finch suffered a fatal heart-attack while promoting the film for Oscar recognition, and although he posthumously won the Globe (Drama) and been nominated for the Oscar, observers believed that he and co-star Holden would split the *Network* vote between them and hand the statuette to one of the other nominees. The support for Holden was demonstrated by his third-place finish in the New York critics' voting (which took place prior to Finch's death). Oscar voters had never previously given an award to an actor posthumously, notably resisting sentiment and by-passing James Dean twice in the mid-1950s and Spencer Tracy for his final screen role in *Guess Who's Coming to Dinner* in 1967.

While the critics had embraced De Niro, the widely-tipped favourite for the Oscar was Stallone, who was only the third person nominated in the acting and writing categories in the same year. *Rocky* had received the same number of nominations as *Network*, and was the Best Picture frontrunner.

On Oscar night, however, sentiment prevailed. The Australian-born Finch became the first actor to win an Oscar posthumously. His statuette was accepted by the film's writer, Paddy Chayefsky, and Finch's Jamaican-born widow, Eletha, who told the audience: "I wish he were here tonight to be with us all. But since he is not here I will always cherish this for him."

At the British Academy Awards the following year, Finch was again triumphant, over a field of nominees that included both Holden and Stallone. It was his fifth BAFTA, a record tally at that time.

1976

BEST SUPPORTING ACTRESS

ACADEMY AWARDS
Jane Alexander as 'Book-keeper' in *All the President's Men*
Jodie Foster as 'Iris Steensman' in *Taxi Driver*
Lee Grant as 'Lili Rosen' in *Voyage of the Damned*
Piper Laurie as 'Margaret White' in *Carrie*
• Beatrice Straight as 'Louise Schumacher' in *Network*

GOLDEN GLOBE AWARDS
Lee Grant – *Voyage of the Damned*
Marthe Keller – *Marathon Man*
Piper Laurie – *Carrie*
Bernadette Peters – *Silent Movie*
• Katharine Ross – *Voyage of the Damned*
Shelley Winters – *Next Stop, Greenwich Village*

BRITISH ACADEMY AWARDS
Annette Crosbie – *The Slipper and the Rose*
• Jodie Foster – *Bugsy Malone* and *Taxi Driver*
Vivien Merchant – *The Homecoming*
Billie Whitelaw – *The Omen*

NEW YORK – Talia Shire – *Rocky*
BOARD OF REVIEW – Talia Shire – *Rocky*
NATIONAL SOCIETY – Jodie Foster – *Taxi Driver*

Talia Shire won the New York Film Critics Circle and National Board of Review awards for her performance in *Rocky*, but following a campaign by United Artists, was named in the Best Actress category at the Golden Globes and the Oscars.

As a result, the Oscar frontrunners were New York runner-up and National Society of Film Critics champ fourteen-year old Jodie Foster as a child prostitute in *Taxi Driver* (NYT "gritty, shocking ... an acting tour de force"; LAT "played with a stunning blend of innocence and world-weary wisdom … [she is] strong and convincing … remarkable"; CT "first-rate"; WP "very well played"; FQ "brings a scary precocity to her part") and Piper Laurie as the religious mother in *Carrie*, her first film role in fifteen years (NYT "finely controlled, full-throttle power"; LAT "truly terrifying"; CT "[a] strong performance"; WP "a strong-voiced, triumphant return to the screen"; V "played superbly").

1976

At the Globes, where Foster was an unexpected absentee (she was a nominee for Best Actress in a Comedy or Musical for *Freaky Friday*), the surprise winner was Katharine Ross whose performance in *Voyage of the Damned* had not been well received by critics (NYT "Ross, who looks like a Rose Bowl parade queen, is a joke as a humane Havana whore").

When the Oscar nominations were announced, Ross became the second Globe winner in three years to be overlooked. Short-listed ahead of her were: both Foster and Laurie; Jane Alexander as the informer in *All the President's Men* (NYT "moving"; LAT "outstanding"; MFB "plays perfectly"); the previous year's Best Supporting Actress Oscar winner Lee Grant in *Voyage of the Damned* (WP "mawkishly overripe … Lee Grant has secured another Oscar nomination by hacking her hair off"); and Beatrice Straight as the wife of an adulterous television executive in *Network* (LAT "crackling good"; V "excellent", "outstanding").

By-passed contenders included: Globe nominee Shelley Winters in *Next Stop, Greenwich Village* (NYT "funny at times [but] just as often she's stupefying"; LAT "now and again comes perilously close to being the stereotyped Jewish parent"; CT "the one big flaw in the film is Mazursky's reliance on the broad comedy of Shelley Winters as Lenny's Jewish mother"; WP "plays the role of a smothering, embarrassing mama with stupendous verve and authenticity"; V "one of the most superb characterizations of her career"); BAFTA nominee Annette Crosbie in the musical *The Slipper and the Rose* (NYT "excellent"; WP "consistently delightful"; MFB "the chief triumph [of the film] is Annette Crosbie's harassed Fairy Godmother"); and Melinda Dillon as the wife of folksinger Woodie Guthrie in *Bound for Glory* (NYT "fine support"; LAT "remarkable [and] sensationally real"; V "excellent").

On Oscar night, the surprise winner was Straight, who appeared in only two scenes of the film. "I'm the darkhorse and this was very unexpected," she told the audience.

At the BAFTAs, Foster won Best Supporting Actress for both *Taxi Driver* and *Bugsy Malone* (NYT "the star of the show ... superbly funny"; LAT "what 'Bugsy' has going for it are its ideas, a bright and wistfully engaging score and the ever-remarkable presence of Jodie Foster … [she] has little to say or do but does it eloquently, making her own raised eyebrow speak volumes"; WP "Foster's astonishing self-possession and emotional maturity set her miles apart histrionically"; V "outstanding"; S&S "brings a snake-like hunger to the film"). Surprisingly, among the other nominees was Vivien Merchant for her performance in the American Film Theatre's 1973 version of Harold Pinter's play *The Homecoming*. Oscar voters had overlooked her performance three years earlier.

1976

BEST SUPPORTING ACTOR

ACADEMY AWARDS
Ned Beatty as 'Arthur Jensen' in *Network*
Burgess Meredith as 'Mickey' in *Rocky*
Laurence Olivier as 'Szell' in *Marathon Man*
• Jason Robards as 'Ben Bradlee' in *All the President's Men*
Burt Young as 'Paulie' in *Rocky*

GOLDEN GLOBE AWARDS
Marty Feldman – *Silent Movie*
Ron Howard – *The Shootist*
• Laurence Olivier – *Marathon Man*
Jason Robards – *All the President's Men*
Oskar Werner – *Voyage of the Damned*

BRITISH ACADEMY AWARDS
Martin Balsam – *All the President's Men*
• Brad Dourif – *One Flew Over the Cuckoo's Nest*
Michael Hordern – *The Slipper and the Rose*
Jason Robards – *All the President's Men*

NEW YORK – Jason Robards – *All the President's Men*
BOARD OF REVIEW – Jason Robards – *All the President's Men*
NATIONAL SOCIETY – Jason Robards – *All the President's Men*

For his portrayal of Washington Post executive editor Ben Bradlee in *All the President's Men*, Jason Robards won a clean sweep of the three major critics' prizes and won the Best Supporting Actor Academy Award. "Jason Robards may be on screen for no more than ten minutes, but ten minutes of Ben Bradlee looms disproportionately large, since he's the most vivid and emphatic character on the premises," wrote Gary Arnold in The Washington Post before marvelling at "the sheer clarity of this impersonation" and declaring that "Robards has captured him to a T" (LAT "portrayed to laconic perfection"; WP "[an] astute impersonation"; V "excellent"; MFB "plays perfectly").

His main challenger for the critics' prizes was Harvey Keitel in *Taxi Driver*, who finished as the runner-up for the New York Film Critics Circle and National Board of Review accolades. Surprisingly, however, Keitel was overlooked for both the Golden Globe and the Oscar.

1976

The winner of the Globe was Laurence Olivier as a sadistic Nazi dentist in *Marathon Man* (NYT "[a] superb performance"; LAT "elegantly acted … Olivier ran his own risks, of being too villainous a villain, a caricature of evil"; CT "[the film] develops tension only when Olivier is on the screen … a credible enemy … if Paramount Pictures can finesse Olivier into the supporting actor category, he may walk away with his second Oscar"; WP "there's not a thing wrong with his performance"). The Academy nominated Olivier for a record-equalling ninth time.

Also in contention were Ned Beatty as the CEO of a television network in *Network* (NYT "beautifully played"; LAT "creates a dynamite cameo quite removed from his usual [portrayals]"; V "excellent") and both Burgess Meredith as the manager (NYT "effective"; LAT "a vivid characterization … but for its skill, it is still identifiable as a performance and the one element you would have wished changed for the purposes of the ensemble"; TT "knowingly expert") and Burt Young as the brother-in-law in *Rocky* (NYT "effective"; LAT "highest honors for the art that does not show itself as art").

Omitted from consideration were: Robert Duvall as a television network chief executive in *Network* (NYT "fine"; LAT "makes his hard-line professional executive believable if not sympathetic"); Peter Falk in the spoof *Murder by Death* (NYT "hilariously mugged … one of the principal joys of the film"; LAT "gives 'Murder by Death' its vitality and its funniest moments"; WP "impersonated brilliantly"); BAFTA nominee Michael Hordern as the king in the musical *The Slipper and the Rose* (NYT "excellent"; WP "consistently delightful"); both Globe nominee Oskar Werner (NYT "all right") and Max von Sydow (LAT "it is his fine and sensitive performance that gives the film its unity"; WP "with the admirable exception of Max von Sydow's Capt. Schroeder, the plummy roles get mawkishly overripe") in *Voyage of the Damned*; Harvey Keitel as a pimp in *Taxi Driver* (NYT "fine"; CT "first-rate"; WP "a marvelously vile, insinuating performance"); Fernando Rey as a concentration camp prisoner in *Pasqualino Settebellezze (Seven Beauties)* (NYT "especially effective"; LAT "elegant"); and both Hal Holbrook as Deep Throat (LAT "a fine study"; V "outstanding") and BAFTA nominee Martin Balsam as managing editor Howard Simons (WP "walks skillfully through a role that relays necessary pieces of exposition"; V "strong") in *All the President's Men.*

At the BAFTAs, Robards was among the candidates outpolled by Brad Dourif in *One Flew Over the Cuckoo's Nest.* Dourif had been an unsuccessful Oscar nominee the previous year.

A year after winning the Oscar, Robards won a second Best Supporting Actor statuette for portraying writer Dashiell Hammett in *Julia.*

1977

BEST PICTURE

ACADEMY AWARDS

• ***Annie Hall***

(Rollins-Joffe, United Artists, 93 mins, 20 Apr 1977, $19.0m, 5 noms)

The Goodbye Girl

(M-G-M, Warner Bros., 110 mins, 1 Dec 1977, $41.8m, 5 noms)

Julia

(Twentieth Century-Fox, 118 mins, 2 Oct 1977, $16.0m, 11 noms)

Star Wars

(Twentieth Century-Fox, 121 mins, 25 May 1977, $170.9m / gr:$322.7m, 10 noms)

The Turning Point

(Hera, Twentieth Century-Fox, 119 mins, 14 Nov 1977, $16.0m, 11 noms)

GOLDEN GLOBE AWARDS

(Drama)

Close Encounters of the Third Kind

I Never Promised You a Rose Garden

Julia

Star Wars

• ***The Turning Point***

(Comedy/Musical)

Annie Hall

• ***The Goodbye Girl***

High Anxiety

New York, New York

Saturday Night Fever

BRITISH ACADEMY AWARDS

• ***Annie Hall***

A Bridge Too Far

Network

Rocky

NEW YORK – *Annie Hall*

LOS ANGELES – *Star Wars*

BOARD OF REVIEW – *The Turning Point*

NATIONAL SOCIETY – *Annie Hall*

The Los Angeles Film Critics Association, the National Board of Review and the National Society of Film Critics all announced the winners of their annual film awards on the same day: 19 December 1977. Each group named a different film as Best Picture.

For the second year in a row the west coast circle selected a popular mainstream movie: George Lucas' science fiction blockbuster *Star Wars*, which at the time was the most commercially successful film ever made (NYT "the most elaborate, most expensive, most beautiful movie serial ever made"; LAT "the year's most razzle-dazzling family movie, an exuberant and technically astonishing space adventure"; CT "a fun picture … what places it a sizable cut above the routine is its spectacular visual effects"; WP "delightful … a new classic … a witty and exhilarating synthesis of themes and clichés … irresistible"; V "magnificent"; Time "the year's best movie"; TT "genuine escapism", a "triumph"; S&S "frequently exciting"; MFB "monumentally empty, based on not a single idea but a wealth of conceits … this flight into atavistic fantasy is undoubtedly successful on some levels, notably in its sheer narrative speed [but it] is less than half convincing").

The NBR chose *The Turning Point*, a drama about professional ballet, starring Shirley MacLaine and Anne Bancroft (NYT "entertaining"; LAT "a handsome, thoughtful, well-spoken and emotionally holding piece of stylish entertainment"; CT "refreshing", "multifaceted"; WP "'Star Wars' has a powerful force to contend in the 1977 Academy Awards race: 'The Turning Point', Herbert Ross' enormously appealing movie … vividly enacted"; V "one of the best films of this era ... an absolute triumph"; S&S "pure soap opera").

The NSFC, meanwhile, gave their top accolade to Woody Allen's romantic comedy *Annie Hall* (NYT "hilarious and moving"; CT "beneath the constant gag lines, there's something deadly serious and thoroughly tender about the picture"; WP "presentable and easy to take [but] a soft, fuzzy, mildly diverting letdown … superficial"; V "touching and hilarious", "terrific") by 43 points to 27 over Luis Buñuel's final project, *Cet Obscur Objet de Désir (That Obscure Object of Desire)* (NYT "triumphantly funny and wise"; LAT "a delight to watch … swift, sexy and hypnotically intriguing … a fascinating, original and beguiling piece of work"; WP "a masterpiece"; V "almost hypnotic"). Finishing in third place, with 21 points, was the science fiction drama *Close Encounters of the Third Kind* (NYT "spectacular", "stunning"; LAT "a magic act with dramatic interludes … thrilling … stays light on its legs, mystical and reverential but not solemn"; CT "very good … first-rate entertainment … [although] the middle could stand some rewriting, the film's final visual and emotional payoff is almost enough to warrant the incredible hype this picture has received from Columbia Pictures"; WP "exciting and ingratiating"; V "superb"; S&S "a combination of pixillated inspirational fantasy and heavy-footed uplifting religiosity [but] for all its hesitations and insufficiencies [it] is the first of the new breed of science fiction film which approaches the best in the literature, and effectively obliterates the faint, sterile traces of 'Star Wars'"; SMH "a big, expensive bore").

The same three films topped the vote by the New York Film Critics Circle two days later, and finished in the same order. *Annie Hall* won with 46 points, ahead of Bunuel's finale with 28 points and Spielberg's drama on 12 points.

All these films were mentioned for Golden Globes, although *Cet Obscur Objet de Désir* was mentioned only for the Best Foreign-Language Film award.

1977

Nominated in the Best Picture (Drama) category alongside *The Turning Point* and the two science fiction films were: *Julia*, Fred Zinnemann's dramatisation of playwright Lillian Hellman's friendship with an anti-fascist freedom fighter in the 1930s (NYT "well-meaning" but "lifeless"; LAT "gripping"; WP "illustrates how a gracefully made movie can slip away by failing to establish a firm dramatic footing … elegantly ephemeral"; V "superbly sensitive film", "most superior"; TT "a handsome, sincere and workmanlike film"); and *I Never Promised You a Rose Garden*, an adaptation of a novel about a schizophrenic teenager (NYT "carefully realized"; WP "places a premium on shock effects and mawkish reassurances at the price of the authenticity and hard-earned inspirational resolution that distinguished the novel").

Annie Hall was in consideration for the Best Picture (Comedy/Musical). Other nominees included the romantic comedy *The Goodbye Girl* (LAT "the best and most blissfully satisfying romantic comedy of the year and then some"; CT "charming [and] entertaining"; WP "satisfying … genuinely amusing"; SMH "witty, well-made") and the popular hit *Saturday Night Fever* (LAT "a smash … [a] thoroughly absorbing drama, at once poignant and pulsating and infectious … could turn into a potent sleeper and Oscar contender"; CT "very good … makes good moviemaking seem easy"; WP "quickly degenerates into an urban exploitation film").

In a surprise, both the Globe winners were films directed by Herbert Ross, the winner of the Best Director Globe. *The Turning Point* won in the Drama category, while in the Comedy/Musical category the winner was *The Goodbye Girl*. Both films received Best Picture nominations from the Academy.

Also nominated for the top Oscar were *Annie Hall*, *Julia* and *Star Wars*. With eleven nominations each, *Julia* and *The Turning Point* led the field of Oscar contenders with *Star Wars* trailing their tally by just one.

Overlooked for consideration were: *Close Encounters of the Third Kind*, for which Steven Spielberg earned a Best Director nod; *Equus* (NYT "this new 'Equus' is probably about as good as one can get on film"; LAT "a far richer, more fully dimensioned experience than it was on the stage"; WP "a hack film … badly botched … read the play"); *The Late Show* (NYT "wise and witty", "remarkably accomplished", "charming"; LAT "snugly satisfying … an artful and affectionate original, lively and enjoyable"; CT "a marvelous comedy"; WP "surprisingly satisfying entertainment"); *3 Women* (NYT "funny, moving", "a film of immediate emotional impact; LAT "nonchalantly sparkling from start to almost-finish but [with] a clatteringly unsuccessful end … its pat ending notwithstanding, '3 Women' is a vivid and original work"; WP "fascinating but elusive … a masterpiece-in-the-making that doesn't quite make it in the final analysis, a masterpiece that gets away"; V "impressive", "absorbing, moody and often compelling"; MFB "one of the most challenging movies to come out of

Hollywood recently [but] also one of the most disappointing"; S&S "belongs to that rare category of imaginative works which defy analysis"); *Handle with Care (Citizens Band)* (NYT "one of the funniest, wittiest, most refreshing, most American – in short, one of the best – films of the year", "a stunning composition"; LAT "a dandy entertainment … a successful topical comedy … bright, bouncy and hilarious"; CT "rather patronizing … much of its comedy is forced"); BAFTA nominee *A Bridge Too Far* (NYT "massive, shapeless, often unexpectedly moving, confusing, sad, vivid and very, very long ... leaves one exhausted instead of exhilarated"; LAT "not just admirable but astonishing: a war film both monumental in its scale and surprising in its subtlety … spectacular in the size and range of its effects, earnestly well-acted"; CT "[it] isn't a story; it's a parade of famous faces … more often tedious than glamorous ... action dwarfs personalities"; WP "an unusually conscientious and impressive war epic"); *Joseph Andrews*, the second adaptation of a Henry Fielding novel that Tony Richardson had directed, following his 1963 Best Picture Oscar winner *Tom Jones* (NYT "funny, stylish, infinitely cheerful"; LAT "works well"; WP "a very funny movie [although] sometimes tedious"; V "tired" and "ludicrous"); *Providence* (NYT "a lot of fuss and fake feathers about nothing … fatally empty"; LAT "seems to me as near to being a masterpiece as any I have seen in a long, long time … rich and ravishing … literate and often ribaldly funny … formidable and intimidating … all in all a film of extraordinary complexity"; WP "insufferable … a barren, enervating viewing experience"; V "striking", "an unusual visual tour de force"); *Roseland* (NYT "funny, moving, imaginative"; LAT "a masterpiece on an intimate scale … one of the year's best pictures … exquisitely nuanced [and] ineffably poignant"; WP "the movie works on the strength of its performances"); and *L'Homme Qui Aimait Les Femmes (The Man Who Loved Women)* (NYT a "sophisticated comedy"; LAT "sensitive and intelligent"; CT "[a] tender comedy … a measured, mature, gentle picture").

The Directors Guild of America named Woody Allen as Best Director, which made the New Yorker and his film the frontrunners for Academy honours. On Oscar night, *Annie Hall* became the first comedy to win the top statuette since *Tom Jones* in 1963. It won a total of four awards. The night's other big winner was *Star Wars*, which collected more Oscars than any other contender: six (plus an honorary award). The evening's biggest loser was *The Turning Point*. It became the most nominated film not to have received an award, with no success from its eleven nominations.

At the British Academy Awards, *Annie Hall* was named Best Film, ahead of a field of nominees that included the previous year's Oscar winner, *Rocky*. At the following year's BAFTA ceremony *Julia* triumphed over a field that included both *Close Encounters of the Third Kind* and *Star Wars*.

1977

BEST DIRECTOR

ACADEMY AWARDS
• Woody Allen for *Annie Hall*
George Lucas for *Star Wars*
Herbert Ross for *The Turning Point*
Steven Spielberg for *Close Encounters of the Third Kind*
Fred Zinnemann for *Julia*

GOLDEN GLOBE AWARDS
Woody Allen – *Annie Hall*
George Lucas – *Star Wars*
• Herbert Ross – *The Turning Point*
Steven Spielberg – *Close Encounters of the Third Kind*
Fred Zinnemann – *Julia*

DIRECTORS GUILD AWARD
• Woody Allen – *Annie Hall*
George Lucas – *Star Wars*
Herbert Ross – *The Turning Point*
Steven Spielberg – *Close Encounters of the Third Kind*
Fred Zinnemann – *Julia*

BRITISH ACADEMY AWARDS
• Woody Allen – *Annie Hall*
Richard Attenborough – *A Bridge Too Far*
John G. Avildsen – *Rocky*
Sidney Lumet – *Network*

NEW YORK – Woody Allen – *Annie Hall*
LOS ANGELES – Herbert Ross – *The Turning Point*
BOARD OF REVIEW – Luis Buñuel – *Cet Obscur Objet de Désir (That Obscure Object of Desire)*
NATIONAL SOCIETY – Luis Buñuel – *Cet Obscur Objet de Désir (That Obscure Object of Desire)*

The same three directors contested the awards from the New York Film Critics Circle and the National Society of Film Critics. By a narrow margin of just 35 points to 33, the east coast circle gave their plaudit to Woody Allen for the comedy *Annie Hall* (S&S "his technical and narrative assurance has reached a new level") ahead of Luis Buñuel for *Cet Obscur Objet de Désir (That Obscure Object of Desire)* (NYT "a work of such perfect control and precision … with an effortlessness matched by no other director today, Buñuel creates a vision of a world as logical as a theorem, as mysterious as a dream, and as funny as a vaudeville gag"; WP "elegant"). Finishing third on the ballot was Steven Spielberg for *Close Encounters of the Third Kind* with 14 points (LAT "marvelously clever"; CT "what [makes it a good movie] are writer-director Spielberg's sense of humor, his ability to surprise, and some absolutely stunning visual effects"). The NSFC vote resulted in a win for Buñuel (with 31 points) over Spielberg (with 25 points), who managed to gain a one point advantage over Allen.

On the same day as the NSFC vote, Buñuel also collected the National Board of Review prize for the second time in six years.

Outpolling these three directors for the accolade from the Los Angeles Film Critics Association was Herbert Ross for the ballet drama *The Turning Point* (LAT "it is vivid movie-making … Ross seems sure of himself, his actors and his camera"; V "sensational"). Demonstrating his ability to handle a variety of material, Ross also earned praise for directing the romantic comedy *The Goodbye Girl*, for which Richard Dreyfuss won the Best Actor Academy Award (LAT "sensitively directed"; WP "as one might have anticipated, Ross depicts this theatrical setting with a confident ironic touch … [he] gives Simon's material an admirable sense of pace and balance on the screen").

Ross was also victorious at the Golden Globe awards for his work on *The Turning Point* where the other nominees were: Allen; Spielberg; George Lucas for the box office sensation *Star Wars* (NYT "beautifully and cheerfully done … one of Mr Lucas's particular achievements is the manner in which he is able to recall the tackiness of the old comic strips and serials he loves without making a movie that is, itself, tacky"; LAT "remarkable professionalism"; CT "whenever the inanity of the entire enterprise begins to surface, [he] pulls out a striking visual trick"; WP "Lucas can draw upon a variety of action-movie sources with unfailing deftness and humor. He is in superlative command of his own movie-nurtured fantasy"; V "has succeeded brilliantly"); and previous winner Fred Zinnemann for the drama *Julia* (LAT "traditional craftsmanship [that is] satisfying … a movie in which you feel the director's control, and his sensitivity to character and relationships, his ability in equal measure to tell a story and to capture the emotions in potent situations"; WP "the crucial problem is that there's so little sense of urgency about anything the filmmakers do").

The Globe win appeared to be an excellent sign for Ross' Oscar chances when both the DGA and the Academy nominated the same five candidates for their Best Director honours. It was the sixth time that the Guild and Oscar contenders had matched (the last time being in 1967), and the first time ever that exactly the same field had been considered for the Oscar, Globe and DGA award. Ross' chances also seemed buoyed by the fact that *The Turning Point* was one of the two films with the most Oscar nominations (the other being Zinnemann's

Julia) and also by the inclusion of his other film, the comedy *The Goodbye Girl*, in the Best Picture category as well.

Notable omissions from these lists were: Buñuel, whose negative opinion of the Oscars was well known; Robert Altman for *3 Women* (LAT "Altman is identifiable anew as one of the most fluent, inventive, individual and magical film-makers"; WP "Altman has failed to dramatize [the threat to his characters] and its repercussions adequately"); Sidney Lumet for *Equus* (NYT "[had made] intelligent decisions [in adapting the play]"; LAT "superbly crafted"; WP "a great piece of theater has been turned into a hack film by a director who leaves nothing to our imagination … badly botched … Lumet's literal-minded approach appears to expose weaknesses obscured on the stage"; V "outstanding"; S&S "[his] realistic technique effectively nullifies the theatrical event"); Alain Resnais for *Providence* (LAT "sure and subtle"; V "elegant direction'); James Ivory for *Roseland* (LAT "impeccably crafted … what saves 'Roseland' from being obvious and easily sentimental is the very high quality of the writing [and] the sensitivity and compassion of Ivory's direction"; WP "seems to have the knack of getting his stars to transcend the banality of their roles"); and Ettore Scola for *Una Giornata Particolare (A Special Day)* (LAT "'A Special Day' also is a triumph for Mastroianni and for writer-director Ettore Scola"; WP "the basic problem is that Scola doesn't arrange things any more ingeniously, even after the awkward meeting … he slips into a sentimental stupor [and then] remains doggedly sentimental ... Scola appears to be stifling his own richest talents along with the actors'"; V "brilliant").

In something of a surprise, however, the DGA named Allen as the year's Best Director. As only two DGA winners since 1949 had not gone on to also collect the Oscar, the Guild accolade made Allen the favourite for the statuette. The factors that continued to give Ross hope of a win was that Allen had expressed complete disinterest in the Academy and the Oscars, and had also stated that he would not be attending the ceremony.

On Oscar night, however, Ross could not manage an upset. Neither could Lucas, whose film won more statuettes than any other that year. The Best Director winner was Allen. The comic actor-writer-director was also awarded the Best Screenplay Oscar.

In London, Allen received BAFTAs for both Best Director and Best Screenplay. During the awards season, he had also earned writing awards from the New York and Los Angeles critics, the NSFC and the Writers Guild of America.

1977

BEST ACTRESS

ACADEMY AWARDS
Anne Bancroft as 'Emma Jacklin' in *The Turning Point*
Jane Fonda as 'Lillian Hellman' in *Julia*
• Diane Keaton as 'Annie Hall' in *Annie Hall*
Shirley MacLaine as 'Deedee Rodgers' in *The Turning Point*
Marsha Mason as 'Paula McFadden' in *The Goodbye Girl*

GOLDEN GLOBE AWARDS
(Drama)
Anne Bancroft – *The Turning Point*
• Jane Fonda – *Julia*
Diane Keaton
– *Looking for Mr Goodbar*
Kathleen Quinlan
– *I Never Promised You a Rose Garden*
Gena Rowlands – *Opening Night*

(Comedy/Musical)
Sally Field – *Smokey and the Bandit*
• Diane Keaton – *Annie Hall*
• Marsha Mason – *The Goodbye Girl*
Liza Minnelli – *New York, New York*
Lily Tomlin – *The Late Show*

BRITISH ACADEMY AWARDS
Faye Dunaway – *Network*
Shelley Duvall – *3 Women*
• Diane Keaton – *Annie Hall*
Lily Tomlin – *The Late Show*

NEW YORK – Diane Keaton – *Annie Hall*
LOS ANGELES – Shelley Duvall – *3 Women*
BOARD OF REVIEW – Anne Bancroft – *The Turning Point*
NATIONAL SOCIETY – Diane Keaton – *Annie Hall*

"For the first time in a number of seasons, there will be some real competition at the end of the year for awards for best performances by leading actresses" commented Vincent Canby in The New York Times on 18 September 1977. Two years after the newspaper had famously bemoaned the lack of serious Best Actress Oscar contenders, Canby, in an article entitled 'Actresses Stage a Comeback', listed six notable performances that were worthy of the Academy's attention: Berlin Film Festival winner Lily Tomlin as the wacky woman in the comedy *The Late Show* (NYT "superb", "wild, unpredictable, funny and terrifically touching"; LAT "creates a comical character but stops well short of being a grotesque and in the end generates sympathy"; CT "Tomlin plays a variation on one of her high-energy, wacko nightclub characters, which is too intense for the big screen. You can see her working"; WP "an ingratiating screwball original"; V "topnotch performance", a "knockout"); Cannes Film Festival honoree Shelley Duvall as the object of a young girl's adoration in Robert Altman's *3 Women* (NYT "memorable ... as funny and moving as anything you're likely to see the rest of the year", "remarkable"; WP "appears to be acting with both range and technical facility … arresting and impassioned"; V "magnificent"; MFB "[an] enticingly precise performance"' S&S "part of the marvel of her performance is its spontaneity"); Geraldine Chaplin in the 1976 Spanish film *Cria Cuervos (Cria!) (Raise Ravens)* (NYT "excellent", "superb", "beautifully acted"; LAT "the most impressive acting achievement for her so far, brought off extremely well [in] a testingly dramatic role"; CT "hauntingly played"); Diane Keaton as a character loosely based on herself in the comedy *Annie Hall* (NYT "marvelous" in "the performance of a career", "[Allen's] camera finds beauty and emotional resources that somehow escape the notice of other directors"; WP "Keaton's acting is not so pleasing, but then about all she's asked to do is look and talk flustered"); Kathleen Quinlan as a teenager with schizophrenia in *I Never Promised You a Rose Garden* (NYT "a remarkably fine, contained performance … there are no mannerisms, no tricks", "a performance as notable for the excesses it avoids as for the honest and simplicity of what is achieved"; LAT "it is hard to think of a more fortunate choice to play the difficult central role than Kathleen Quinlan … a spectacular performance, which makes real the imaginary terrors of the mind"; CT "[a] fine performance … you can feel her pain and elation"; WP "undeniably a clever, eager, sincere young performer but for some reason she still fails to move me"; V "lends freshness and admirable reserve to a role that could have lapsed entirely into histrionic hysterics"; TT "well-acted"; MFB "excellent"); and Hanna Schygulla in the German film *Effi Briest* (NYT "superb", "stunning", "[a] delicate performance"; LAT "dazzling … Schygulla dominates the entire film").

While many of these performances merited an Oscar nomination, Canby concluded, there were a handful of highly-anticipated performances in films that had not yet been released, that he believed would dominate the Academy's list of candidates. These were: Jane Fonda as playwright Lillian Hellman in *Julia* (NYT "marvelous and true"; LAT "in her best portrayal since 'Klute', Fonda conveys with lovely detail the emergence of a sensitive, proud, thoughtful, creative woman"; WP "[an] intriguing, tensed-up performance … Fonda suggests the internal conflicts gnawing at a talented woman who craves self-assurance … [a] persuasive performance"; TT "conducts an interesting exploration of young Lillian's self-testing"; S&S "perfect"); both Anne Bancroft (LAT "she is dazzling to see, tough and vulnerable, wry and resilient, a woman of masks we are able to glimpse behind") and Shirley MacLaine (LAT "MacLaine has had nothing so rewarding to do in a long time and she is a terribly effective counterpoint to Bancroft"; CT "MacLaine is the one you'll remember from 'The Turning Point'. She is dead center in her portrayal of a woman who has turned a corner in life and suddenly feels lost"; V "magnificent ... will rank as one of MacLaine's career highlights") in *The Turning Point* (NYT "[both give] powerhouse performances"; LAT "the performances by Bancroft and MacLaine are stunning, and both are at Academy Award level"; WP "a joint Oscar for Bancroft and MacLaine would make perfect sense, because the characterizations are interdependent"); and Diane Keaton in a contrasting dramatic role as a woman whose sexual liberation has tragic consequences in *Looking for Mr Goodbar* (NYT "virtually the only reason to see [the film]"; LAT "a bold and beautiful performance … it was an acting challenge unsparing in its demands and her achievement is high among the year's finest"; CT "worth seeing, if only for Keaton … she's superb. What Keaton does is give balance to an overdrawn movie, humanity to a film full of caricatures … a performance with a full range of emotions, none of which ring false … she is believable when she is sunny and she is believable when she is mean"; WP "doesn't have enough power to embody Terry, whose intense, frighteningly neurotic dimensions expose the narrowness of her acting range, which doesn't rise above light, lovable neurosis"; V "excellent"; S&S "impressive").

"Want to make some money?" asked Gene Siskel in the Chicago Tribune when *Looking for Mr Goodbar* opened a month later, "Then get a bet down on Diane Keaton to win the 1977 best actress Oscar. Keaton is absolutely compelling in 'Looking For Mr Goodbar', even when the film is not."

When the Oscar nominations were announced, four of the nominees were contenders identified by Canby: MacLaine and Bancroft were both nominated for the fourth time; Fonda made the list for a third time; and Keaton was mentioned for the first time, receiving the nomination for her comic turn in *Annie Hall* rather than for her performance in the controversial *Looking for Mr Goodbar*. Completing the list was Marsha Mason (her second nod) as a single mother who becomes involved with a writer in *The Goodbye Girl*, a film written by her husband, Neil Simon (NYT "especially funny"; LAT "[the film] confirms that Marsha Mason is a fine actress, and a romantic comedienne of star quality"; WP "very nice … funny and touching"; V "great").

The most glaring omission by the Academy was Duvall in *3 Women*, who had added the Los Angeles Film Critics Association Best Actress accolade to her Cannes prize and had finished as the runner-up for both the New York Film Critics Circle accolade and the National Society of Film Critics honour. Her co-star, Sissy Spacek, controversially awarded the Best Supporting Actress prize by the New York Film Critics Circle for her performance, was also overlooked for a Best Actress nomination by members of the Academy (LAT "somehow invests the character with power of implication"; WP "gives Pinky an undercurrent of native wit and toughness even when she's behaving ingenuously … seems to be preparing the way for a quality of perception that Altman himself fails to give the character credit for"; V "excellent"; S&S "does not have the charm or the conviction to convey the rapturous engrossment, the predatory innocence which should prepare us for the changes which are to follow … there's exactly the wrong sort of calculation about her acting").

From Canby's list both Tomlin and Quinlan were also notable absentees, although both received Golden Globe nominations. Others overlooked were: Sophia Loren in *Una Giornata Particolare (A Special Day)* (NYT "movie acting at its best", an "acting tour de force", "magnificent"; LAT "makes a stunning comeback … her awesome beauty and abundant maternal warmth are given full range here in a very rich role … finally 'A Special Day' belongs to Sophia Loren"; WP "Loren and Mastroianni project screen personalities large and sympathetic enough to magnify the importance of the deliberately 'little' people they've been asked to impersonate"; V "[her] measured, natural performance [is] flawless"; S&S "[a] virtuoso performance"); Globe nominee Liza Minnelli in *New York, New York* (NYT "nor, eventually, does [the film] well serve Liza Minnelli"; LAT "[the two stars] give performances that have extraordinary intensity, consistency, depth, charm and pathos … does the best dramatic performance of her film career to date"; CT "a better singer than actress"; WP "seems to have been robbed of the chance to make a big splash"; V "the film belongs to her"); and Sally Field for both her work in the drama *Heroes* (NYT "a total delight"; LAT "splendid"; V "sensational" in a "triumph") and her Globe-nominated turn in the hit comedy *Smokey and the Bandit* (NYT "nicely played"; LAT "turns the extraordinary feat of being wistfully sweet, sympathetic and funny"; WP "endearing").

Keaton was the overwhelming favourite for the Oscar. She won both the New York and NSFC Best Actress awards and collected the Best Supporting Actress prize from the NBR. As well as winning Best Actress in New York for *Annie Hall*, she finished third in the voting for her work in *Looking for Mr Goodbar*. At the Golden Globes, Keaton was nominated for both Best Actress awards and triumphed in the Comedy/Musical category, sharing the trophy with Mason. In the Drama category, the winner was Fonda, who took home her second Globe.

On Oscar night, Keaton won the Academy Award for *Annie Hall*. Soon after she triumphed again in London, outpolling Faye Dunaway in *Network* (the previous year's Best Actress Oscar winner) and two of the most notable omissions from the Academy's list: Duvall and Tomlin. The following year Fonda won the BAFTA for her performance in *Julia* ahead of a field that included both Bancroft and Mason.

1977

BEST ACTOR

ACADEMY AWARDS
Woody Allen as 'Alvy Singer' in *Annie Hall*
Richard Burton as 'Dr Martin Dysart' in *Equus*
• Richard Dreyfuss as 'Elliot Garfield' in *The Goodbye Girl*
Marcello Mastroianni as 'Gabriele' in *Una Giornata Particolare (A Special Day)*
John Travolta as 'Tony Manero' in *Saturday Night Fever*

GOLDEN GLOBE AWARDS
(Drama)
• Richard Burton – *Equus*
Marcello Mastroianni – *Una Giornata Particolare (A Special Day)*
Al Pacino – *Bobby Deerfield*
Gregory Peck – *MacArthur*
Henry Winkler – *Heroes*

(Comedy/Musical)
Woody Allen – *Annie Hall*
Mel Brooks – *High Anxiety*
Robert De Niro – *New York, New York*
• Richard Dreyfuss – *The Goodbye Girl*
John Travolta – *Saturday Night Fever*

BRITISH ACADEMY AWARDS
Woody Allen – *Annie Hall*
• Peter Finch – *Network*
William Holden – *Network*
Sylvester Stallone – *Rocky*

NEW YORK – John Gielgud – *Providence*
LOS ANGELES – Richard Dreyfuss – *The Goodbye Girl*
BOARD OF REVIEW – John Travolta – *Saturday Night Fever*
NATIONAL SOCIETY – Art Carney – *The Late Show*

The year's major Best Actor accolades were split between a large number of actors with only the eventual Oscar winner claiming more than one prize.

The National Board of Review named John Travolta for his performance as a disco dancer in the popular *Saturday Night Fever* (NYT "Travolta is so earnestly in tune with the character that Tony becomes even more touching … [he] dances with a fine arrogance that follows naturally from the rest of his performance, and he has one solo number that stops the show", "deft and vibrant, and he never condescends to the character"; LAT "dazzling"; V "okay").

Travolta, a former television star, also finished third in the voting for the New York Film Critics Circle and National Society of Film Critics prizes.

The NSFC gave their accolade to Art Carney as an ageing private investigator out to avenge his partner's death in the comedy *The Late Show* (NYT "superb"; LAT "manages to invest the man with tremendous dignity and style"; CT "[a] flawless performance … Carney triumphs … [he] is effortless"; V "[a] topnotch performance", "terrific").

The Los Angeles Film Critics Association, meanwhile, honoured Richard Dreyfuss as an aspiring actor in *The Goodbye Girl* (LAT "the movie also confirms Richard Dreyfuss is an actor of star quality, able here to balance his histrionic flair with moments of affecting quiet, and a maturity to sober out the brashness"; CT "make no mistake about it, the very best thing about 'The Goodbye Girl' is the character of Elliot Garfield as played by Dreyfuss … very entertaining when [he] takes center stage"; WP "Dreyfuss makes Elliot a winning image of a dedicated, funny, live-wire actor … you want [the writer] to clear the deck faster so that his exceptional leading actor can have more room to operate"; V "his best screen performance to date ... great"). In his review of the comedy, The Washington Post's Gary Arnold declared, "if the role of Elliot doesn't lead to a long overdue first Oscar nomination for Dreyfus, I don't know what would."

The New York critics presented their plaudit to the NSFC runner-up, John Gielgud as a dying novelist in *Providence* (NYT "true feeling and intelligence"; LAT "a thrilling performance … there is the huge enjoyment of watching the consummate skill of Gielgud at work"; CT "a fine performance"; WP "superb", "has so much verbal authority that he even rises above a fairly loathsome character"; V "extraordinary"; TT "a portrait at once precise and human"; S&S "brilliant"; FQ "beautifully played"). Gielgud received 37 points, six more than runner-up Fernando Rey in Luis Buñuel's final film *Cet Obscur Objet de Désir (That Obscure Object of Desire)* (NYT "beautifully played"; WP "brings undeniable emotional conviction to his role and the rare affecting moments derive from his inherent dignity and courtliness").

Surprisingly, while many of these actors were considered for the Oscar, none were the favourite. As a psychiatrist who tries to understand a troubled youth's obsession with horses in *Equus*, a role originated on stage by Anthony Hopkins, Richard Burton won his first (and only) Golden Globe award as Best Actor (Drama) (NYT "beautifully, sometimes almost grandly acted", "dominates the movie", "the best Burton performance since 'Who's Afraid of Virginia Woolf'"; LAT "represents the finest work of Richard Burton since 'Who's Afraid of Virginia Woolf?' and he surely will be an Oscar contender … [a] tour de force"; WP "hogs the screen … Burton's very presence tends to accentuate the overbearing artificiality of the character's emotional conflicts … overblown delivery"; TT "[an] overemphatic but still impressive performance"). When he was subsequently nominated for the Oscar, many observers predicted that the Academy would finally honour the Welshman with the statuette for which he had been unsuccessfully nominated six times over the previous twenty-five years.

The nominees outpolled by Burton for the Globe were: Marcello Mastroianni as the troubled gay man in *Una Giornata Particolare (A Special Day)* (NYT "movie acting at its best", an "acting tour de force"; LAT "'A Special Day' is a triumph for Mastroianni … [he is] superb"; WP "Loren and Mastroianni project screen personalities large and sympathetic enough to magnify the importance of the deliberately 'little' people they've been asked to impersonate"; S&S "virtuoso performance"); Al Pacino as a Grand Prix race driver in the critically savaged *Bobby Deerfield* (LAT "catastrophically ill-suited [for the part] … he is quite unconvincing"; CT "appealing … [a] magnetic presence"; WP "the first landmark embarrassment of his career … screenwriter Alvin Sargent hasn't invented a context in which Pacino could act characteristically intense, vulnerable and impassioned without exposing himself to ridicule … excruciating"; V "excellent"; MFB "it is Al Pacino's perfectly measured and modulated performance, suggesting a mind struggling to absorb behaviour it cannot understand, that holds one's attention"); Gregory Peck as General Charles MacArthur in the biopic *MacArthur* (NYT "remarkably good … makes the characters disgracefuly appealing … the actor displays a wit that gives an edge to the performance and humanity to a character who it might well have been impossible to be around"; LAT "the role is probably the most difficult and demanding Peck has ever undertaken and it provides his most impressive appearance since his gentle lawyer in 'To Kill a Mockingbird'"; WP "resolutely sincere yet uninspired … Peck is too passive an actor to transform MacArthur's greatest oratorical moments into great scenes"); and television star Henry Winkler, in his first starring film role, as an unstable Vietnam veteran in *Heroes* (NYT "[a performance] that seems to be aggressively cute not because he's appealing, but because the will to please is so naked and the mannerisms are so unconnected to life. Television is creating a school of acting made up entirely of signals that evoke emotions less often than they label them"; LAT "[a] fine and watchable performance"; V "good though flawed"). Although many had believed that Peck's impersonation of MacArthur would receive an Oscar nomination as George C. Scott's portrayal of Patton had done seven years earlier, only Burton and Mastroianni were mentioned by the Academy from among the Globe (Drama) candidates. Peck later admitted that he was himself disappointed with the film which he felt had been rushed through production by a studio which lacked faith in the project.

Surprisingly, the other three Oscar finalists (each first-time candidates) were all nominees for the Globe (Comedy/Musical): Los Angeles winner Dreyfuss, who also collected the Globe; NBR winner Travolta; and Woody Allen as a stand-up comic in *Annie Hall*, a film which he also wrote and directed.

In addition to critics' prizewinners Gielgud and Carney, the Academy overlooked: Globe nominee Robert De Niro in Martin Scorsese's *New York, New York* (NYT "the movie can't keep up with him"; LAT "[the two stars] give performances that have extraordinary intensity, consistency, depth, charm and pathos … another confirmation of his versatility and dedication, most notably his self-effacing willingness to be actively unlovable"; CT "what kept me involved throughout the confusion was De Niro's performance … he is the most compelling actor in American film"; V "outstanding"); George C. Scott as a sculptor with three sons in *Islands in the Stream* (NYT "played with fine, disciplined intensity", "perfectly realised"; LAT "Scott's performance stands with his best, which is very, very good, and his mixture of arrogance and tenderness, sadness without self-pity, is impressive to watch"; CT "superior"; MFB "excellent"); Bruce Davison as a convicted child molestor brutally victimised by prison inmates in *Short Eyes* (NYT "stands out [in] a performance so intimate it's almost painful to watch"; LAT "impressive"; WP "delivered with riveting conviction … Davison transmits the distressing mixture of shame and uncontrollable desire in Davis' lines with a sincerity that intensifies the appalling candor and eloquence of the lines themselves … Davison's performance is astonishing, a genuinely shocking exposure of human weakness. It must have transfixed the company and jumped out at the rushes"; V a "standout"); Paul Le Mat in the independent comedy *Handle with Care (Citizens Band)* (NYT "extremely good"); and Charles Denner in *L'Homme Qui Aimait Les Femmes (The Man Who Loved Women)* (NYT "very, very funny").

On Oscar night, the highly-favoured Burton once more left empty-handed. The surprise winner was thirty-year old Dreyfuss for *The Goodbye Girl*. His win was probably helped by his starring role in the popular *Close Encounters of the Third Kind.* He joined Marlon Brando as the youngest Best Actor recipient to that date. Dreyfuss won again at the BAFTAs the following year, but it was not until 1995 that he received a second Oscar nomination. Burton never again made the Academy's list.

Dreyfuss was not, however, the only Best Actor nominee to receive awards on Oscar night. Woody Allen won the statuettes for Best Original Screenplay and Best Director.

1977

BEST SUPPORTING ACTRESS

ACADEMY AWARDS
Leslie Browne as 'Emilia Rodgers' in *The Turning Point*
Quinn Cummings as 'Lucy McFadden' in *The Goodbye Girl*
Melinda Dillon as 'Jillian Guiler' in *Close Encounters of the Third Kind*
• Vanessa Redgrave as 'Julia' in *Julia*
Tuesday Weld as 'Katherine Dunn' in *Looking for Mr Goodbar*

GOLDEN GLOBE AWARDS
Ann-Margret – *Joseph Andrews*
Joan Blondell – *Opening Night*
Leslie Browne – *The Turning Point*
Quinn Cummings – *The Goodbye Girl*
• Vanessa Redgrave – *Julia*
Lilia Skala – *Roseland*

BRITISH ACADEMY AWARDS
• Jenny Agutter – *Equus*
Geraldine Chaplin – *Welcome to L.A.*
Joan Plowright – *Equus*
Shelley Winters – *Next Stop, Greenwich Village*

NEW YORK – Sissy Spacek – *3 Women*
LOS ANGELES – Vanessa Redgrave – *Julia*
BOARD OF REVIEW – Diane Keaton – *Annie Hall*
NATIONAL SOCIETY – Ann Wedgeworth – *Handle with Care (Citizens Band)*

"She's going to be very interested to find out she was playing a supporting role!" one member of the New York Film Critics Circle was overheard commenting to a colleague when it was announced that Sissy Spacek had been selected by the group for its Best Supporting Actress award for her performance as the young woman who worships her co-worker in *3 Women* (NYT "both innocent and eerie"; LAT "Spacek somehow invests the character with power of implication, hints of a past that is not what we imagine it was, of deeds that may not bear close examination"; WP "Spacek gives Pinky an undercurrent of native wit and toughness even when she's behaving ingenuously … Spacek seems to be preparing the way for a quality of perception that Altman himself fails to give the character credit for"; V "excellent"; S&S "Spacek does not have the charm or the conviction to convey the rapturous engrossment, the predatory innocence which should prepare us for the changes which are to follow … there's exactly the wrong sort of calculation about her acting"). Many observers regarded Spacek as one of the two co-leads of the Altman film, although she did finish in third place in the Best Supporting Actress voting by the National Society of Film Critics as well.

The National Board of Review made a similarly surprising choice for Best Supporting Actress, selecting Diane Keaton for her performance in the romantic comedy *Annie Hall* (NYT "marvelous" in "the performance of a career", "[Allen's] camera finds beauty and emotional resources that somehow escape the notice of other directors"; WP "Keaton's acting is not so pleasing, but then about all she's asked to do is look and talk flustered"). Although several critics shared the observation by Gary Arnold in The Washington Post that despite the title, "the movie is not really about a girl named Annie Hall", Keaton was regarded as a leading actress at the other major awards season events, including the Academy Awards where she won the Best Actress statuette.

Runner-up to Spacey in New York, six points adrift of the winner's tally of 31 points, was Vanessa Redgrave for her portrayal of a 1930s anti-Fascist campaigner in *Julia* (NYT "marvelous and true"; LAT "a presence … the achievement is the more impressive for having had to be done so economically"; V "excellent" S&S "exactly portrayed"). Redgrave was the winner of the Los Angeles Film Critics Association prize and also collected the Golden Globe in the lead up to the Oscars. A previous nominee in the lead category, she was the strong favourite and collected the golden statuette.

Redgrave's victory came over four first-time nominees, three of whom had scarcely rated a mention from leading film critics when their films had been released: Leslie Browne as the teenage ballerina in *The Turning Point* (NYT "charmingly played"; LAT "a beguiling and wide-eyed performance … she seems incisively observed"; WP "Browne's performance – as dancer and actress – will prove a sublime revelation to moviegoers"); ten-year old Quinn Cummings as a daughter of a divorced couple in *The Goodbye Girl* (V "great"); Melinda Dillon as the mother of an abducted child in *Close Encounters of the Third Kind*; and Tuesday Weld as the elder sister in *Looking for Mr Goodbar* (V "great").

Notably absent from the list of Oscar nominees were both the honoree and runner-up in the NSFC voting: Ann Wedgeworth and Marcia Rodd, respectively, as the wives of a bigamous truck driver in the independent comedy *Handle with Care (Citizens Band)* (NYT "as rambunctiously, seriously funny as any actors I've seen in American film this year"; LAT "Rodd and Wedgeworth, for all their fine work, have perhaps never before been shown to such advantage on the screen").

Also by-passed were: Globe nominee Lilia Skala as a retired cook who once dreamed of opera stardom in the third section of *Roseland* (LAT "extraordinary [and] excellent … it seems likely that she will once again win an Oscar nomination"; WP "sensitive, vivid and handsomely nuanced"; V "standout"); both BAFTA winner Jenny Agutter (V "excellent") and BAFTA nominee Joan Plowright as the mother (V "marvelous"; S&S "strong") in *Equus*; Claire Bloom in *Islands in the Stream* (V "terrific"); Donna Pescow, who finished third in New York, in *Saturday Night Fever*; Geraldine Chaplin in *Welcome to L.A.* (NYT "impressive", "the only figure that does have life … the role, as written, is more winsome than moving, but Miss Chaplin gives it a genuine wildness, and a rhythm that sounds like static and feels like electricity … she is far better than anything else in the movie"; LAT "Miss Chaplin, who perhaps dominates the film, has never had a finer role, at least in American films"); both Globe nominee Ann-Margret (NYT "at the top of her magnificent form"; LAT "the centrepiece of 'Joseph Andrews' … she has become a very gifted actress/comedienne who here does a complicated and subtle accent so persuasively it could be her very own") and Beryl Reid (LAT "played to a rouged and quivering perfection") in *Joseph Andrews*; and Lisa Pelikan as the young Julia in *Julia* (LAT "played extremely well").

1977

BEST SUPPORTING ACTOR

ACADEMY AWARDS
Mikhail Baryshnikov as 'Yuri' in *The Turning Point*
Peter Firth as 'Alan Strang' in *Equus*
Alec Guinness as 'Ben "Obi-Wan" Kenobi' in *Star Wars*
• Jason Robards as 'Dashiell Hammett' in *Julia*
Maximilian Schell as 'Johann' in *Julia*

GOLDEN GLOBE AWARDS
Mikhail Baryshnikov – *The Turning Point*
• Peter Firth – *Equus*
Alec Guinness – *Star Wars*
Jason Robards – *Julia*
Maximilian Schell – *Julia*

BRITISH ACADEMY AWARDS
Colin Blakely – *Equus*
Robert Duvall – *Network*
• Edward Fox – *A Bridge Too Far*
Zero Mostel – *The Front*

NEW YORK – Maximilian Schell – *Julia*
LOS ANGELES – Jason Robards – *Julia*
BOARD OF REVIEW – Tom Skerritt – *The Turning Point*
NATIONAL SOCIETY – Edward Fox – *A Bridge Too Far*

The National Society of Film Critics named Edward Fox as Best Supporting Actor for his portrayal of Gen. Brian Horrocks in the war film *A Bridge Too Far* (NYT "quietly but brilliantly funny"; CT "steals the show"; WP "astonishing … does a brilliant turn … as far as I'm concerned, Fox should be given all the year's supporting actor awards by acclamation right now … the kind of rousing, delightful performance that seems to jump off the screen without jumping out of character"). Garnering 29 points, Fox finished ahead of Bill Macy in *The Late Show* with 23 points (NYT "fine"; LAT "Macy is also finally a creature of sympathy as the small-time loser") and both David Hemmings in *Islands in the Stream* (NYT "even better than his material") and Maximilian Schell as a courier in *Julia* (NYT "memorable … seems to have reduced himself in size to play a man of physical frailty and immense courage"; LAT "a small but handsomely done role"), each with 21 points.

1977

Surprisingly, two days later, Fox did not receive a single vote from the New York Film Critics Circle. The east coast group instead named Schell (his second win from the group) by a margin of 20 points to 17 over Macy with Hemmings a further three points behind in third place.

The National Board of Review honoured Tom Skerritt in *The Turning Point* (LAT "sympathetic in a difficult role"), while the Los Angeles Film Critics Association gave their inaugural supporting prize to Jason Robards for his portrayal of writer Dashiell Hammett in *Julia* (NYT "with Jason Robards as Hammett, these scenes are so good and occasionally so tough that one wishes the film were about Hellman and Hammett"; LAT "could well earn another Academy nomination for his brief but indelible portrait"; V "excellent"; S&S "impersonated with conviction").

Of these contenders, the Academy only recognised the two cast members of *Julia.* Also nominated were ballet dancer Mikhail Baryshnikov in *The Turning Point* (NYT "played with cheerful ease"; LAT "very engaging"; CT "played with a solid naturalness"; WP "Ross utilizes Baryshnikov's breathtaking abilities as a dancer and the attractive aspects of his personality, especially his foxy, amusing sexual assurance, while carefully obscuring potential weaknesses, like his accent and limited acting experience"); Peter Firth for reprising his stage success as the troubled youth in *Equus* (NYT "excellent"; LAT "he surely will be an Oscar contender … [a] tour de force"; WP "there is one bright spot in the film and that is Peter Firth as the stableboy … through his intense body movements, Firth draws all our attention to him … [a] haunting performance … convincing"; V "very impressive"; TT "extraordinary"; S&S "strong"); and Alec Guinness in the science-fiction blockbuster *Star Wars* (CT "save for Alec Guinness, the cast is unmemorable").

Others overlooked included: Richard Gere in *Looking for Mr Goodbar* (NYT "especially good"; CT "worth noting … stunning"; WP "well played"); John Gielgud in *Joseph Andrews* (NYT "hilarious"; LAT "a bright cameo"); BAFTA nominee Colin Blakely as the father in *Equus* (V "superb"; S&S "benefits from the camera and the chance to register emotions at odds with the flow of speech"); and Robert Fortier as the former stunt man in *3 Women* (NYT "noteworthy"; LAT "well-portrayed").

The Oscar favourite was Firth, the twenty-four-year old Golden Globe winner. On the night, however, the surprise winner was Robards. It was his second consecutive statuette in the category.

In London, it was NSFC prizewinner Fox who collected the BAFTA for his performance in *A Bridge Too Far.*

1978

BEST PICTURE

ACADEMY AWARDS

Coming Home
(Hellman, United Artists, 126 mins, 15 Feb 1978, $13.3m, 8 noms)
• ***The Deer Hunter***
(EMI, Cimino, Universal, 183 mins, 15 Dec 1978, $27.4m, 9 noms)
Heaven Can Wait
(Dogwood, Paramount, 101 mins, 27 Jun 1978, $49.4m, 9 noms)
Midnight Express
(Columbia, 120 mins, 7 Oct 1978, gr:$35.0m, 6 noms)
An Unmarried Woman
(Twentieth Century-Fox, 124 mins, 4 Mar 1978, 3 noms)

GOLDEN GLOBE AWARDS

(Drama)
Coming Home
Days of Heaven
The Deer Hunter
• ***Midnight Express***
An Unmarried Woman

(Comedy/Musical)
California Suite
Foul Play
Grease
• ***Heaven Can Wait***
Movie, Movie

BRITISH ACADEMY AWARDS

Close Encounters of the Third Kind
• ***Julia***
Midnight Express
Star Wars

NEW YORK – ***The Deer Hunter***
LOS ANGELES – ***Coming Home***
BOARD OF REVIEW – ***Days of Heaven***
NATIONAL SOCIETY – ***Préparez vos Mouchoirs (Get Out Your Handkerchiefs)***

Five days before the 1977 Academy Award nominations were announced, the early frontrunner for the various 1978 Best Picture accolades was released into North American cinemas: *Coming Home*, a drama about Vietnam War veterans. In The New York Times, Vincent Canby had only modest praise for the project saying it "starts beautifully" but "becomes soggy with good if unrealized intentions." Most reviews, however, were strong (LAT "intimate and moving … a passionate anti-war statement"; CT "what's best about 'Coming Home' are the moments when it loses its standard characters and becomes personal"; WP "sentimental"; V "excellent", "compelling and absorbing"; TT "emotionally charged"; MFB "benign"; S&S "intense"). Despite disappointing box office returns in the United States, *Coming Home* was entered in competition at the Cannes Film Festival.

Another American film in competition at Cannes was actor-writer-director Paul Mazursky's feminist drama *An Unmarried Woman* (WP "witty"; V "superb"). The film was released in the North America in March as was the drama *Straight Time* which star Dustin Hoffman publically disowned alleging First Artists had wrested away the creative control he had been promised. The film nonetheless earned strong reviews (NYT "an uncommonly interesting film"; LAT "riveting … a dramatic and unsentimental social document"; CT "a superior thriller … don't miss it if you like your movies tough and uncompromising").

With the phenomenon of 'summer blockbusters' becoming a dominant trend in the United States, two commercial and critical successes with mainstream appeal were released in June. The first was the musical *Grease*, which starred John Travolta and Australian singer Olivia Newton-John (NYT "a larger, funnier, wittier and more imaginative–than–Hollywood movie with a life that is all its own"; LAT "[a] sleazy and cynical piece of work … strident, cluttered, uninvolving and unattractive"; CT "flawed … it's exciting only when Travolta is on the screen"; WP "[a] mess … I've never seen an uglier large-scale musical"; V "an easy winner"). It became the year's top box office attraction. The second was *Heaven Can Wait*, a remake of the 1941 comedy *Here Comes Mr Jordan* (NYT "has a kind of earnest cheerfulness that is sometimes most winning"; LAT "[a] rousing remake … funny, lyrically romantic and optimistic [and] buoyantly cheerful … a fantasy that works beautifully"; CT "delightful … both surprisingly fresh and old-fashioned"; WP "appealing … it manages to preserve much of the charm and romantic fantasy that worked for its predecessor while freshening up some of the settings and details"; V "outstanding"; MFB "one of the most imperfectly remade remakes in many a moon"; SMH "although this romantic comedy is delightfully easy to watch, heaven help us if this picture should achieve what it has been nominated for – the Oscar as best picture of the year").

In early August, Woody Allen followed up the comedy *Annie Hall*, which had won the Best Picture and Best Director Oscars the previous year, with *Interiors*, a serious ensemble drama inspired by the work of American playwright Eugene O'Neill and Swedish film-maker Ingmar Bergman (NYT "an intelligent, beautifully composed and acted movie"; LAT "sombre, intense and stunning"; CT "more a sketch than a full realized story"; WP "the utterly sincere, inescapably preposterous result of Allen's irresistible impulse to create a movie in the Bergmanesque vein").

Upon its release in mid-September, Variety hailed Terrence Malick's *Days of Heaven* as "one of the great cinematic achievements of the last decade", saying the drama was "dramatically moving and technically breathtaking." While The New York Times again dissented, most critics heaped praised on the film (NYT "[an] intolerably artsy, artificial film"; LAT "an extraordinary and original visual experience and a movie which is thrilling in its uncompromised purity"; CT "a staggering experience … there is beauty and action in the film's every image"; WP "creates an enormous disparity between sensual and dramatic stimulation"; FQ "extraordinarily impressive"; S&S "masterful").

Late in the year, there was critical acclaim for three foreign-language releases by renowned directors: Claude Chabrol's drama *Violette* (NYT "a combination of stunning artistry and brute suspense", "an enthralling movie, virtually certain to become a classic"; LAT "astounding … a film of awesome beauty and mystery … remarkable, a genuine tour de force"); Ingmar Bergman's *Höstsonaten (Autumn Sonata)*, a drama about a professional mother and her neglected daughter, played by Ingrid Bergman and Liv Ullmann respectively (LAT "gruelling and exhausting but beautifully conceived and enacted"; CT "masterly"; V "fascinating"; TT "magisterial and exquisite"); and Bertrand Blier's *Préparez vos Mouchoirs (Get Out Your Handkerchiefs)* (NT "an exuberant and highly inventive comedy"; LAT "unquestionably an original, individual and eccentric work"; CT "unconventional"; WP "striking [and] wildly funny").

The biggest challenger to *Coming Home*, however, was another Vietnam War film which did not go into general release in North America until early 1979, nearly twelve months after its rival. Given a limited release in New York City and Los Angeles in December to qualify for the major critics' prizes and the Academy Awards was Michael Cimino's *The Deer Hunter*, starring Robert De Niro. The New York Times called it "a big, awkward, crazily ambitious, sometimes breath-taking motion picture." The response from other leading critics on both sides of the Atlantic was equally strong (LAT "an extremely ambitious and important film … a film of excellences"; CT "quite remarkable"; WP "melodramatic … has the outline of a great film and the appearance of a great film, but the banal, evasive writing undermines the director's potentially stirring edifice"; V "intense, powerful and fascinating"; HRp "a major achievement in American movies"; S&S "an impressive achievement"; MFB "brilliant, original [and] fascinating").

In mid-December, the Los Angeles Film Critics Association selected *Coming Home* as Best Picture. Three days later, the National Board of Review honoured *Days of Heaven* with *Coming Home* named runner-up. The day after that, the

1978

New York Film Critics Circle picked *The Deer Hunter* as Best Picture over *Days of Heaven* by 29 points to 24. The runners-up were *An Unmarried Woman* (20 points), *Coming Home* (15 points) and *Interiors* (9 points). At the end of the year, The New York Times included *The Deer Hunter* on its annual list of the year's ten best films along with *Days of Heaven*, *Straight Time* and *Violette*. In a major shock, however, *Coming Home* was not on the list at all.

Early in the new year, the last of the major critics' groups, the National Society of Film Critics, unexpectedly selected Blier's *Préparez vos Mouchoirs* by one point over both *The Deer Hunter* and *An Unmarried Woman* and then, a further three points adrift, *Days of Heaven*. According to Gene Siskel of the Chicago Tribune, the winner was "a reluctant compromise choice [as] factions within the group were unwilling to allow either the much better 'Days of Heaven' or 'The Deer Hunter' to take the top prize." As Blier's unconventional comedy was France's entry for the Best Foreign-Language Film Oscar and didn't open in a Los Angeles cinema until late in January 1979, it was ineligible for Best Picture consideration by Oscar voters until the following year.

At the Golden Globe Awards *Coming Home*, *Days of Heaven*, *The Deer Hunter* and *An Unmarried Woman* were all nominated for the Best Picture (Drama) award. In a surprise, however, they were bested by *Midnight Express*, a drama about a young American imprisoned in Turkey for drug offences (LAT "strong and shocking … [has a] terrific impact"; CT "a powerful film [but] melodramatic"; WP "outrageously sensationalistic … sets a new standard in shamelessness"; V "admirable"). Meanwhile *Heaven Can Wait* won the Globe (Comedy/Musical) ahead of a field that included *Grease*, and Bergman's *Höstsonaten (Autumn Sonata)* won the Globe for Best Foreign-Language Film.

Topping the list of Academy Award contenders, each with nine nominations, including mentions in the Best Picture category, were: *The Deer Hunter* and *Heaven Can Wait*. Completing the ballot for the top statuette were *Coming Home* with eight nods, *Midnight Express* with six and *An Unmarried Woman* (the only contender without a Best Director nomination) with three mentions.

On Oscar night, *Coming Home* stars Fonda and Voight won the Best Actor and Actress statuettes, but the Academy Awards for Best Picture and Best Director were won by *The Deer Hunter*. In the Best Foreign-Language Film category the Oscar was won by NSFC champ, *Préparez vos Mouchoirs*.

At the British Academy Awards, *Coming Home* was not even nominated for Best Film. Instead, *Close Encounters of the Third Kind*, *Midnight Express* and *Star Wars* were all cited, along with one of the previous year's unsuccessful Best Picture Oscar nominees: Fred Zinnemann's *Julia*. While Alan Parker won Best Director for *Midnight Express*, the Best Film award was won by *Julia*. The following year, *The Deer Hunter* was outpolled for the Best Film BAFTA by Woody Allen's black-and-white comedy *Manhattan*.

1978

BEST DIRECTOR

ACADEMY AWARDS
Woody Allen for *Interiors*
Hal Ashby for *Coming Home*
Warren Beatty and Buck Henry for *Heaven Can Wait*
• Michael Cimino for *The Deer Hunter*
Alan Parker for *Midnight Express*

GOLDEN GLOBE AWARDS
Woody Allen – *Interiors*
Hal Ashby – *Coming Home*
• Michael Cimino – *The Deer Hunter*
Terrence Malick – *Days of Heaven*
Paul Mazursky – *An Unmarried Woman*
Alan Parker – *Midnight Express*

DIRECTORS GUILD AWARD
Hal Ashby – *Coming Home*
Warren Beatty and Buck Henry
  – *Heaven Can Wait*
• Michael Cimino
  – *The Deer Hunter*
Paul Mazursky
  – *An Unmarried Woman*
Alan Parker – *Midnight Express*

BRITISH ACADEMY AWARDS
Robert Altman – *A Wedding*
• Alan Parker – *Midnight Express*
Steven Spielberg
  – *Close Encounters of the Third Kind*
Fred Zinnemann – *Julia*

NEW YORK – Terrence Malick – *Days of Heaven*
LOS ANGELES – Michael Cimino – *The Deer Hunter*
BOARD OF REVIEW – Ingmar Bergman – *Höstsonaten (Autumn Sonata)*
NATIONAL SOCIETY – Terrence Malick – *Days of Heaven*

For the first time since the Directors Guild of America began handing out its award in 1948/49, all of the nominees were first-time candidates: Hal Ashby for *Coming Home* (NYT "the pseudo-hip style of the movie is not appealing at all … [gives the film a] manner of smug self-importance barely tolerable after the first hour"; LAT "again and again Ashby and his associates seem to choose the right option … impeccably handled"; WP "Ashby seems to be trying to improvise 'Coming Home' into existence"; S&S "the makers have taken such an odd, indirect, almost metaphorical approach to their subject; MFB "Ashby has managed with a degree of success to abstract his theme [but shows] an excess of directorial sincerity"); Warren Beatty and Buck Henry for the remake *Heaven Can Wait* (LAT "you have the feeling that Beatty won most of the coin tosses, and that cinematographer [William] Fraker was a lot of help"; WP "[the film] lacks the finishing stylistic polish that a sophisticated and experienced director exercising clear authority might have contributed. There are slack passages and missed opportunities for intensified suspense and romance"; MFB "relentlessly plodding direction, which underlines all the foolishness a Forties director would have skipped through"); Los Angeles Film Critics Association prizewinner Michael Cimino for *The Deer Hunter* (NYT "impressive"; CT "a big achievement"); Paul Mazursky for *An Unmarried Woman* (LAT "as film-making, 'An Unmarried Woman' is impeccable … [Mazursky is] a marvelous social observer, with a novelist's eye and ear for significant details of place and speech and character"; WP "succeeds admirably and enjoyably up to a point – roughly the beginning of the last reel … [nonetheless] Mazursky's intimate style makes empathy so tangible"; S&S "likely to confirm Mazursky's initial promise as one of America's readily exportable directors of intelligence … his most smoothly achieved film"); and Alan Parker for *Midnight Express* (WP "outrageously sensationalistic").

Notable absentees were: New York Film Critics Circle and National Society of Film Critics award winner Terrence Malick for *Days of Heaven* (LAT "reaffirms on a much more ambitious scale all the promise and the particular gifts of his first feature … an awesome piece of film-making"; CT "as directed by Terrence Malick, [the film] is one magnificent shot after another …the real star [of the movie] is director Malick"; WP "neither the business nor the public is up to the curiously simplistic alienating challenge of his art"); Ingmar Bergman for *Höstsonaten (Autumn Sonata)* (CT "masterly"); Woody Allen for *Interiors* (NYT "has used careful, stylized solemnity to find his way into areas where comedy just won't go"; LAT "it is a perilous high-wire act [and] he has brought it off … an absolutely masterful use of space, shape and color to convey atmospheres and states of feeling … as a piece of the film-maker's art, it is thrilling"; WP "bloodless, superficial, derivative"); and Claude Chabrol for *Violette* (LAT "displaying a superb control of tone"; CT "masterful").

The Academy made one change from the DGA list: Allen, the previous year's Oscar winner, was included ahead of Mazursky. With the top three New York prize contenders – winner Malick, and runners-up Mazursky and Bergman – all excluded from consideration, the overwhelming favourite for the Oscar was DGA and Globe winner Cimino, who had finished fourth in New York.

On Oscar night, *The Deer Hunter* was named Best Picture and Cimino won the Best Director statuette. A month later, Malick was honoured as Best Director at the Cannes Film Festival for *Days of Heaven*.

1978

BEST ACTRESS

ACADEMY AWARDS
Ingrid Bergman as 'Charlotte Andergast' in *Höstsonaten (Autumn Sonata)*
Ellen Burstyn as 'Doris' in *Same Time, Next Year*
Jill Clayburgh as 'Erica Benton' in *An Unmarried Woman*
• Jane Fonda as 'Sally Hyde' in *Coming Home*
Geraldine Page as 'Eve' in *Interiors*

GOLDEN GLOBE AWARDS
(Drama)
Ingrid Bergman
– *Höstsonaten (Autumn Sonata)*
Jill Clayburgh – *An Unmarried Woman*
• Jane Fonda – *Coming Home*
Glenda Jackson – *Stevie*
Geraldine Page – *Interiors*

(Comedy/Musical)
Jacqueline Bisset
– *Who's Killing the Great Chefs of Europe?*
• Ellen Burstyn – *Same Time, Next Year*
Goldie Hawn – *Foul Play*
Olivia Newton-John – *Grease*
• Maggie Smith – *California Suite*

BRITISH ACADEMY AWARDS
Anne Bancroft – *The Turning Point*
Jill Clayburgh – *An Unmarried Woman*
• Jane Fonda – *Julia*
Marsha Mason – *The Goodbye Girl*

NEW YORK – Ingrid Bergman – *Höstsonaten (Autumn Sonata)*
LOS ANGELES – Jane Fonda – *California Suite* and ***Comes a Horseman*** and ***Coming Home***
BOARD OF REVIEW – Ingrid Bergman – *Höstsonaten (Autumn Sonata)*
NATIONAL SOCIETY – Ingrid Bergman – *Höstsonaten (Autumn Sonata)*

At the Cannes Film Festival, the Best Actress award was shared for the third year in a row. One of the co-winners was American Jill Clayburgh for her portrayal of a Manhattan housewife who discovers her independent identity after her husband leaves her for a younger woman in *An Unmarried Woman* (NYT "nothing less than extraordinary in what is the performance of the year to date", "superb"; LAT "proving that she is a superlatively versatile actress, able to move between comedy and drama or, as she does here, to combine both … [her performance] is beautiful to watch and it remains in memory"; CT "finally gets a feature film role worthy of her talent … challenging to watch"; WP "several brilliant moments of acting [although] in the later stages of the movie [her character] gets less talkative and Clayburgh's performance begins to resolve itself into a series of warming smiles and contented sighs"; V "outstanding"; MFB "a perfectly judged performance"; S&S "something exceptional, a performance that is at its best at precisely those points when the tiniest of false notes could collapse an entire sequence"). In his review of the film in The Washington Post, Gary Arnold declared, Clayburgh's performance "may establish her as the early-frontrunner for next year's Academy Award."

Sharing the Best Actress citation at the festival was French actress Isabelle Huppert for her performance as a teenager who poisons her parents in Claude Chabrol's *Violette* (NYT "superb", "persuasive"; LAT "stunning … believable, sympathetic even"; CT "masterful"). Huppert was eligible for Oscar consideration that year for her work in both *Violette* and the 1977 release *La Dentellière (The Lacemaker)* for which she won the Most Promising Newcomer to Leading Film Roles BAFTA at the 1978 ceremony in London (NYT "all too believable"; LAT "stunning"; WP "credit for the film's underlying tension must go to actress Isabelle Huppert [who] brilliantly masks the turbulent, repressed emotions [her character] must be feeling … she unfolds [her character] as slowly and imperceptibly as a blossom").

Also in contention at Cannes was Jane Fonda in the role of a marine's wife who becomes involved with a paraplegic Vietnam War veteran when she volunteers as a nurse, in *Coming Home* (NYT "immensely appealing"; LAT "acts with a self-effacing restraint that conceals the craft but suffuses the portrait with earnestness and warmth"; WP "the weakest performance of her career"; V "superb", "memorable and moving"; TT "quiet, charming acting"; S&S "has uncannily reincarnated herself"; MFB "an upright performance, slightly restrained"). Fonda's co-star, Jon Voight, won the Cannes Best Actor award.

At the end of the year, Fonda was named Best Actress by the Los Angeles Film Critics Association. In addition to her work in *Coming Home*, she was also cited for her performance in the drama *Comes a Horseman* (LAT "another marvelous portrayal … soul-deep conviction"; CT "she is tough without being a bore about it, tender without being condescending … it's her best performance since 'Klute'") and her contrasting turn in *California Suite*, a film version of Neil Simon's hit Broadway comedy (NYT "superlative"; LAT "for the third time this year she shows what an immensely versatile and talented actress she has grown to be … her portrait is as fine as anything she has yet done, which is saying a lot"; CT "as compelling as she has ever been"; WP "determined to bring emotional conviction to roles that simply can't accommodate it, [Fonda and Smith] seem to overpower the material"; V "demonstrates yet another aspect of her amazing range").

1978

The year's three other critics' awards were won by sixty-three year old Ingrid Bergman as a concert pianist exploring the troubled relationship with her daughter in Ingmar Bergman's *Höstsonaten (Autumn Sonata)* (NYT "superb", "exhilarating", "one's attention throughout the film is riveted by Miss Bergman, who has never before had a role to match this one"; LAT "absolutely enthralling to watch [in] what may well stand as her most impressive performance of all, a masterpiece"; CT "compelling"; WP "invests [her role] with undeniable emotional conviction and impact … spell-binding"; TT a "tour de force", "has never been so excellent"; S&S "extraordinary" and "admirable"; MFB "[a] beautifully modulated virtuoso performance"). It was Ingrid Bergman's final film appearance and came over forty years after she had made her debut in *Intermezzo*, also as a concert pianist. It was Bergman's third award from the New York Film Critics Circle and her second from the National Board of Review. She was also the runner-up to Fonda in the voting in Los Angeles. The accolades made her a strong contender for the Academy Award.

While some observers tipped Bergman, most backed an Oscar win by either Clayburgh or Fonda. They had finished as runners-up in the voting in New York; Bergman had garnered 24 points on the first ballot while Clayburgh received 4, and Fonda got 3 and 2 for *Coming Home* and *Comes a Horseman*, respectively.

At the Golden Globe Awards, Fonda was presented with the Best Actress (Drama) prize for the second year in a row, and for the third time in eight years. She outpolled both Bergman and Clayburgh, as well as Glenda Jackson as the late English poet Stevie Smith in *Stevie*, a performance for which she was named Best Actress at the Montreal Film Festival and that would eventually win her the 1981 New York Film Critics Circle award as Best Actress (NYT "extraordinary … splendid ... profoundly moving … the best performance by an actress to be seen in any film released so far this year … not since 'Sunday, Bloody Sunday' has she had a film role that so fully and efficiently utilizes the range of her intelligence and power as a dramatic actress … a special talent at the top of its form"; LAT "matchless … a tour de force performance … has never been so inward-looking, so vulnerable, so eloquent, and she has never been better … [a] very strong contender for [an] Academy Award nomination"; CT "an extraordinary performance"; MFB "a fine performance") and Geraldine Page as a mentally disturbed wife in Woody Allen's drama *Interiors* (NYT "marvelous", "her performance not only carries the movie but takes one's breath away"; LAT "simply unforgettable … she demonstrates the acting art to all who might have thought they knew it, and confirms that she is arguably the finest actress of her generation"; MFB "played with such highly charged hysteria that one repeatedly fears she may be on the point of self-parody").

There were two winners in the Comedy/Musical category: Ellen Burstyn reprising her Tony Award winning performance as a woman having a long-term affair in *Same Time, Next Year* (NYT "she brings so much sweetness to Doris's various incarnations that the character very nearly comes to life"; LAT "she makes Doris not a comedienne's cartoon but a real woman"; V "first-class") and Maggie Smith as an Oscar nominee in *California Suite*, a performance for which she won the Academy Award for Best Supporting Actress. Among the other nominees were: Goldie Hawn in *Foul Play* (LAT "carries it off majestically"; CT "thoroughly captivating"; V "superb"); and Olivia Newton-John in the hit musical *Grease* (NYT "simultaneously very funny and utterly charming"; CT "she hasn't been given much help, either by the direction or the script"; V "registers very impressively").

Overlooked for the Globes, and also subsequently for the Oscar, were: Ellen Burstyn as an imprisoned child murderer in *A Dream of Passion*, for which she placed third in the voting in Los Angeles (LAT "wrenchingly, harrowingly effective [in] the most demanding role an actress has faced all year … Burstyn's Brenda is the performance of a lifetime"; CT "she does everything required of her here perfectly, but because her characterization is so on target we are curiously unmoved by what she does"; WP "boldly inventive and shockingly convincing … gives a performance that makes your nerve ends shiver"; SMH "riveting [and] overwhelmingly powerful … [her] portrayal of madness is terrifying and believable"); Liv Ullmann as the daughter in *Höstsonaten* (NYT "positively searing"; LAT "absolutely enthralling to watch"; WP "invests [her role] with undeniable emotional conviction and impact … spell-binding"; TT a "tour de force"; S&S "extraordinary"; MFB "[a] beautifully modulated virtuoso performance"); and Simone Signoret in *La Vie Devant Soi (Madame Rosa)* (NYT "tremendous … her best role in years"; LAT "there is a grandeur and dignity about Signoret's portrayal and a kind of self-sacrificing surrender to the demands of the part that is in the highest and rarest tradition of her craft … astonishing and moving … altogether brilliant"; CT "fine").

Previous winners Bergman, Burstyn and Fonda were short-listed for the Academy Award, along with first-timer Clayburgh, and perennial 'bridesmaid' Page. The Globe result seemed to position Fonda as favourite for the Oscar, but on the eve of the ceremony, an article in the Los Angeles Times saw the paper's six movie reporters split evenly in predictions of victory for Bergman and Clayburgh. In the end, however, it was Fonda who collected the statuette, her second. Fonda's win saw Page equal the record tally of six unsuccessful Best Actress nominations set by Deborah Kerr.

Fonda's performance in *Coming Home* was eligible for the British Academy Awards, but she instead won the BAFTA for *Julia*, for which she had been an Oscar nominee the previous year. One of the other Best Actress Oscar nominees, Geraldine Page, won the Best Supporting Actress BAFTA for *Interiors*.

1978

BEST ACTOR

ACADEMY AWARDS
Warren Beatty as 'Joe Pendleton' in *Heaven Can Wait*
Gary Busey as 'Buddy Holly' in *The Buddy Holly Story*
Robert De Niro as 'Michael Vronsky' in *The Deer Hunter*
Laurence Olivier as 'Ezra Lieberman' in *The Boys from Brazil*
• Jon Voight as 'Luke Martin' in *Coming Home*

GOLDEN GLOBE AWARDS
(Drama)
Brad Davis – *Midnight Express*
Robert De Niro – *The Deer Hunter*
Anthony Hopkins – *Magic*
Gregory Peck – *The Boys from Brazil*
• Jon Voight – *Coming Home*

(Comedy/Musical)
Alan Alda – *Same Time, Next Year*
• Warren Beatty – *Heaven Can Wait*
Gary Busey – *The Buddy Holly Story*
Chevy Chase – *Foul Play*
George C. Scott – *Movie, Movie*
John Travolta – *Grease*

BRITISH ACADEMY AWARDS
Brad Davis – *Midnight Express*
• Richard Dreyfuss – *The Goodbye Girl*
Anthony Hopkins – *Magic*
Peter Ustinov – *Death on the Nile*

NEW YORK – Jon Voight – *Coming Home*
LOS ANGELES – Jon Voight – *Coming Home*
BOARD OF REVIEW – Laurence Olivier – *The Boys from Brazil* and **Jon Voight – *Coming Home***
NATIONAL SOCIETY – Gary Busey – *The Buddy Holly Story*

Jack Nicholson, Al Pacino and Sylvester Stallone all turned down the lead role of a disillusioned paraplegic Vietnam War veteran attracted to a volunteer nurse in *Coming Home*, a project that Jane Fonda had developed since commissioning the script in 1973. When Fonda told United Artists that she was giving the part to Jon Voight, who had already signed on to play the supporting role of the nurse's marine husband, the studio offered her a further one million dollars to secure a big-name star. She declined the money and stood by the casting of Voight. The other role went to Bruce Dern. When the film opened in February,

1978

Voight earned his best reviews since his Oscar-nominated turn in *Midnight Cowboy* nearly a decade earlier (NYT "immensely appealing"; LAT "Voight gives a mature and intelligent portrayal that is acting at its affecting and indelible best"; CT "excels"; WP "the film's greatest asset … the movie is rescued from potential disaster by Voight's glowing, robust masculinity"; V "his finest acting to date"; TT "quiet, charming acting"). Soon after, he was awarded with the Best Actor award at the Cannes Film Festival and became the favourite for the Academy Award when he won prizes from both the east and west coast critics' groups.

In New York, Voight won his second plaudit in a decade with 40 points on the second ballot, ahead of Gary Busey (who garnered 32 points) as the eponymous rock'n'roll singer in the biopic *The Buddy Holly Story* (NYT "it's Gary Busey's galvanizing solo performance that gives meaning to an otherwise shapeless and bland film"; LAT "the heart and soul and power of 'The Buddy Holly Story' is the uncanny, marrow-deep, robust, exhilarating, likable, superlative, overwhelmingly convincing portrayal by Gary Busey … one of those rare and stunning performances in which the person of the actor himself is totally lost to sight in his creation of someone else"; CT "compelling … [a] galvanizing performance"; WP "Busey's performance as Holly gives the movie an analogous conviction and distinction … [he] invests the title role with a personal charm so original and an emotional dedication so exhilarating that he seems to lift the material off its somewhat pedestrian feet"; V "a strong performance"; FQ "[a] sensitive and spontaneous portrayal"). Busey, who also finished as the runner-up to Voight in the voting by the Los Angeles Film Critics Association, subsequently won the National Society of Film Critics accolade for his portrayal (that group having previously named Voight as Best Actor in 1969). The support of the critics' groups early in the awards season was considered critical for Busey's chances of Oscar glory given the film's disappointing box office results. Only a few months earlier, influential critic Gene Siskel had written in the Chicago Tribune, "A prediction: Gary Busey will not receive an Academy Award nomination for 'The Buddy Holly Story'. That will happen not because Busey isn't deserving of the honor; on the contrary, his compelling performance is one of the finest of the '70s. Busey will be ignored because 'The Buddy Holly Story' is a small film that is doing poor business nationwide. Hollywood reveres only big films at Oscar time: small films that make big money are only exceptions."

Voight was also named by the National Board of Review, sharing the honour with Laurence Olivier as an ageing Nazi hunter in *The Boys from Brazil*, a performance that had divided critics (NYT "marvelous", "a constant delight … acting of a rare sort"; LAT "Olivier is interesting to watch as he builds a colorful characterization [but] in this context it is hard to see him except as actor Olivier, plying his trade"; WP "wonderful"; V "slips completely into the role"; MFB "dismaying").

At the Golden Globes, Voight's status as the Oscar frontrunner was confirmed when he won the Best Actor (Drama) award ahead of: twenty-nine-year old Brad Davis as the American imprisoned in a Turkish prison for drug offences in *Midnight Express* (LAT "reveals rather than tells … [at times] unconvincing [while] elsewhere is quite effective"; CT "[he] is simply not up to the lead role … appears unsure of himself and, like the film itself, overacts"; WP "a veritable encyclopaedia of mannerisms"; V "a strong performance"); Robert De Niro, who had finished third in the voting in both New York and Los Angeles, as a steelworker who fights in the Vietnam War in *The Deer Hunter* (NYT "vivid … some of his best work to date"; LAT "excellent [in] a markedly different characterization from [his last few films]"); Anthony Hopkins as a deranged ventriloquist in Richard Attenborough's British thriller *Magic* (NYT "Hopkins is too good an actor to be completely lost in this nonsense, but the best he can do is convince us of his intentions"; LAT "Hopkins' performance, or dual performance, as Corky the man and Fats the lethal dummy, is one of the year's best"; CT "Hopkins is most responsible for the magnetism of 'Magic'. It is a movie that stands or falls on the performance of one actor … [Hopkins] deserves an Academy Award nomination"; WP "struggling to sustain a characterization that veers from panicky to berserk over feature-length"); and Olivier's co-star in *The Boys from Brazil*, Gregory Peck as Nazi war criminal Dr Josef Mengele (LAT "the portrayal is intense and skilful, but it is simply overwhelmed by Peck's pre-existing image"; WP "reveals an unexpected flair for stiff-necked, intimidating villainy in the juicy role … often a righteous bore, Peck seems to have been powerfully stimulated by the opportunity to impersonate a seething, self-righteous moral monster").

Unsurprisingly absent from the list of candidates was Dustin Hoffman as a parolee in *Straight Time*, a film project he had put together but disowned upon its release claiming the production company had denied him a final cut as originally agreed (NYT "beautifully acted"; LAT "has less dimension than some of his earlier characterizations [but] it is more credible for being so little demonstrative"; CT "interesting"; WP "the fundamental problem seems to be Hoffman's suitability in the starring role … Hoffman cannot turn that crucial acting trick. He gives it a respectable try but in some unavoidable way he just doesn't look threatening and ruthless"; MFB "astute").

The New York prize runner-up Busey was nominated for the Globe (Comedy/Musical), but was outpolled by Warren Beatty as a professional football player who is taken to Heaven before he is due and is subsequently returned to life in another man's body in *Heaven Can Wait* (LAT "exudes a likable boyish charm that sustains the picture"; CT "as good a performance by

Beatty as any he has given"; V "excellent"; MFB "seems to be treading heavily"). The role had previously been played in the 1941 release *Here Comes Mr Jordan* by Robert Montgomery, who received a Best Actor Oscar nomination for his performance. Among the other nominees for the Globe were: Alan Alda as a man having an unusual, once-a-year, long-term affair in *Same Time, Next Year* (NYT "isn't terribly playful, and he reads every line as if it were part of a joke, which only accentuates the flatness of the script"; LAT "until Alda settles more comfortably into the character in its later surfacings, there is a considerable sense of performance, of lines being said rather than felt"; V "[a] first-class performance"); George C. Scott in the lauded parody *Movie, Movie* (NYT "superb … Scott is such a powerful actor that it's always a surprise he can be so wickedly funny"; LAT "his serene command of the ridiculous is very enjoyable to watch"; WP "ventures slightly out of [his] range"); and John Travolta as the cool highschool student in the musical *Grease*, the year's biggest box office hit (NYT "better than he was in 'Saturday Night Fever' … I'm still not sure if he's a great actor, but he's a fine performer"; CT "[the film's] exciting when John Travolta is on the screen"; V "excellent").

When the Academy announced its field of Best Actor candidates on 20 February 1979, previous winner Olivier became the first man to receive a tenth nomination in the acting categories and equalled Spencer Tracy's record nine mentions for the Best Actor prize. The Academy's Board of Governors subsequently announced that he would be presented with an honorary Oscar for career achievements, guaranteeing him another statuette regardless of the outcome in the Best Actor category. Also nominated were previous Best Supporting Actor winner De Niro (for the third time), Beatty and Voight (each for the second time), and Busey (for the first time). Voight was the overwhelming favourite. On the eve of the Oscar ceremony, four of the movie reporters in the Los Angeles Times tipped Voight to claim the Academy Award. The other two reporters backed De Niro. On Oscar night, Diana Ross announced that the Best Actor Academy Award had been won by Voight.

In London, the previous year's Oscar winner, Richard Dreyfuss in *The Goodbye Girl*, won the BAFTA ahead of Davis in *Midnight Express,* Hopkins in *Magic* and Peter Ustinov in *Death on the Nile* as Agatha Christie's Belgian detective Hercule Poirot, the role for which Albert Finney earned an Oscar nomination in *Murder on the Orient Express* four years earlier (NYT "a star doing the obligatory star-turn, which is exactly what's required"; LAT "it is distinctly an achievement ... he creates an amusing characterization and evokes some genuine laughter despite all those wads of inevitable, unavoidable exposition"; CT "beautifully played"; Obs "delicately judged … a confidently realised character"; S&S "monotonously mannered"). Although eligible, Voight was not listed among the nominees.

1978

BEST SUPPORTING ACTRESS

ACADEMY AWARDS
Dyan Cannon as 'Julia Farnsworth' in *Heaven Can Wait*
Penelope Milford as 'Viola Munson' in *Coming Home*
• Maggie Smith as 'Diana Barrie' in *California Suite*
Maureen Stapleton as 'Pearl' in *Interiors*
Meryl Streep as 'Linda' in *The Deer Hunter*

GOLDEN GLOBE AWARDS
Carol Burnett – *A Wedding*
• Dyan Cannon – *Heaven Can Wait*
Maureen Stapleton – *Interiors*
Meryl Streep – *The Deer Hunter*
Mona Washbourne – *Stevie*

BRITISH ACADEMY AWARDS
Angela Lansbury – *Death on the Nile*
• Geraldine Page – *Interiors*
Maggie Smith – *Death on the Nile*
Mona Washbourne – *Stevie*

NEW YORK – Maureen Stapleton – *Interiors*
LOS ANGELES – Maureen Stapleton – *Interiors* and **Mona Washbourne – *Stevie***
BOARD OF REVIEW – Angela Lansbury – *Death on the Nile*
NATIONAL SOCIETY – Meryl Streep – *The Deer Hunter*

The New York Film Critics Circle named Maureen Stapleton in Woody Allen's *Interiors* as Best Supporting Actress (NYT "beautifully projects the tone and feelings of a sweet, robust, coarse woman"; LAT "a matchless display of the acting arts"; CT "superb … Stapleton excels [and] makes her character someone to cherish"; WP "played with delightful, soul-restoring gusto"; V "wonderful"; S&S "excellent"; MFB "played with steamrollering ebullience"). The runners-up were Maggie Smith as an actress unsuccessfully nominated for an Oscar in *California Suite* (NYT "pricelessly funny", "now has a part that makes use of her unique gift for comedy", "[Smith and Caine] create characters of unexpected depth and compassion"; LAT "splendid … a comedienne whose self-mocking frailty is capable of melting hearts of steel"; WP "determined to bring emotional conviction to roles that simply can't accommodate it, [Fonda and Smith] seem to overpower the material"; SMH "elegantly played") and Meryl Streep in *The Deer Hunter* (NYT "a smashing film performance"; LAT "a welcome discovery, a warm and intelligent actress"). All three received other prizes during the season: Stapleton shared the Los Angeles Film Critics Association honour; Smith shared the Best Actress (Comedy/Musical) Golden Globe; and Streep won the National Society of Film Critics prize. All were nominated for the Oscar.

Also mentioned by the Academy were Globe winner Dyan Cannon as the wife in *Heaven Can Wait* (NYT "beautifully played"; CT "marvelous … scores again"; WP "played with brilliance … [she is] especially funny"; V "excellent") and Penelope Milford as the sister of a Vietnam veteran in *Coming Home* (LAT "very good … sympathetic [in] a brief but dimensional role"; CT "gives us a fresh portrayal of a fully competent young woman who runs into an emotional buzzsaw"; V "excellent").

Surprisingly overlooked were both National Board of Review winner and BAFTA nominee Angela Lansbury in *Death on the Nile* (LAT "very nearly commandeers the boat … a model of pure and amusing camp"; WP "skillful"; S&S "scene-stealing") and Los Angeles co-honoree Mona Washbourne in *Stevie*, a performance for which she would win the NBR award in 1981 (NYT "marvellously well played"; LAT "a performance of the deepest observation … [a] very strong contender for [an] Academy Award nomination"; CT "delightfully played"; V "charming and sympathetic"; S&S "[a] real triumph"; MFB "'Stevie' may be unreservedly commended on one count: the performance of Mona Washbourne … emerges as a character in her own right").

Also by-passed were: Stockard Channing in *Grease* (NYT "would (if it were possible) stop the show twice"; LAT "Channing has the most punishing female role, asked to be tough, promiscuous and vulnerably sympathetic in turn. It's a thankless chore done with high competence"; V "impressive"); Barbara Harris in *Movie, Movie* (NYT "marvelous"; WP "proves an invaluable addition"); both Lisa Lucas, who placed third in the voting in New York (CT "nicely played"; WP "smartly embodied") and Kelly Bishop (WP "the immediate pace-setter for best supporting actress") in *An Unmarried Woman*; Mary Beth Hurt in *Interiors* (NYT "very sweet and intense [and] appealing"; CT "the standout"; S&S "a striking debut"); and Stéphane Audran in *Violette* (LAT "[her] finest portrayal").

On the eve of the Academy Awards ceremony, the Los Angeles Times declare Globe winner Cannon to be the strong favourite for the statuette, but on the night Smith became the only person to win an Oscar for portraying an Oscar loser when she collected her second statuette. She was nominated for the BAFTA for *Death on the Nile* (S&S "scene-stealing") but was outpolled by unsuccessful Best Actress Oscar nominee: Geraldine Page in *Interiors*.

1978

BEST SUPPORTING ACTOR

ACADEMY AWARDS
Bruce Dern as 'Captain Bob Hyde' in *Coming Home*
Richard Farnsworth as 'Dodger' in *Comes a Horseman*
John Hurt as 'Max' in *Midnight Express*
• **Christopher Walken as 'Nikanor Chevotarevich'** ***in The Deer Hunter***
Jack Warden as 'Max Corkle' in *Heaven Can Wait*

GOLDEN GLOBE AWARDS
Bruce Dern – *Coming Home*
• **John Hurt –** ***Midnight Express***
Dudley Moore – *Foul Play*
Robert Morley – *Who's Killing the Great Chefs of Europe?*
Christopher Walken – *The Deer Hunter*

BRITISH ACADEMY AWARDS
Gene Hackman – *Superman*
• **John Hurt –** ***Midnight Express***
Jason Robards – *Julia*
François Truffaut – *Close Encounters of the Third Kind*

NEW YORK – Christopher Walken – ***The Deer Hunter***
LOS ANGELES – Robert Morley – ***Who's Killing the Great Chefs of Europe?***
BOARD OF REVIEW – Richard Farnsworth – ***Comes a Horseman***
NATIONAL SOCIETY – Richard Farnsworth – ***Comes a Horseman*** and **Robert Morley –** ***Who's Killing the Great Chefs of Europe?***

The glaring absentee from the list of Oscar nominees was Robert Morley as a gourmet magazine publisher in the comedy *Who's Killing the Great Chefs of Europe?* (LAT "walks away with [the movie] in the best part he's had in years – and is a sure bet to be remembered come Oscar nominations time … easily commands every scene he's in"; CT "excellent … entertaining as a credible villain"; WP "richly amusing … he's the perfect actor to endow Max's pomposity, sarcasm and self-pity with irresistible comic authority … Morley's performance could emerge as a favourite for the next Academy Award in the supporting actor category"; V "provides the film's finest moments"). Morley won the plaudit from the Los Angeles Film Critics Association, shared the National Society of Film Critics prize and received a Golden Globe nomination.

Others overlooked were: both Charles Grodin (NYT "beautifully played"; WP "played with brilliance"; V "excellent") and James Mason (CT "elegant … quite right") in *Heaven Can Wait*; E. G. Marshall in *Interiors* (NYT "fine"; LAT "an excellent performance"; CT "just right"; MFB "a nicely restrained, complementary performance"); Sam Shepard as the farmer in *Days of Heaven* (LAT "outstanding"); Michael Caine in *California Suite* (NYT "[Smith and Caine] create characters of unexpected depth and compassion"; LAT "Caine is here again an actor of nuance and sensitivity and he has not been better"); Barry Bostwick, who finished third in the voting in New York for *Movie, Movie* (NYT "marvelous … a standout"; WP "gives him his first chance [on screen] to display the charm and zest that have delighted Broadway audiences"); and both M. Emmet Walsh as the parole officer (NYT "marvelously well-played"; LAT "one of the most memorably hateable villains since Morgan Woodward's prison guard in 'Cool Hand Luke'"; WP "strong") and Harry Dean Stanton as an ex-con (NYT "beautifully acted"; WP "strong"; V "excellent") in *Straight Time*.

Ahead of these candidates the Academy nominated: Christopher Walken, winner of the New York Film Critics Circle prize and runner-up for the Los Angeles Film Critics Association accolade, as a young man destroyed by his experiences in the Vietnam War in *The Deer Hunter* (NYT "vivid … some of his best work to date"; V "a marvel"); New York runner-up and both National Board of Review and NSFC winner Richard Farnsworth as a ranch foreman in *Comes a Horseman* (NYT "touching", "very affecting"; LAT "[the film] is rustled cleaned away by Richard Farnsworth … he has delivered a portrayal of such naturalness, humor and sympathy that he is a prime contender for Best Supporting Actor next year"; V "altogether sympathetic"); Bruce Dern as the marine husband of a volunteer nurse in *Coming Home* (LAT "delivers [the role] with his usual high professionalism"; V "convincing"; TT "a vulgar piece of overacting"); Globe winner John Hurt as a Turkish prison inmate in *Midnight Express* (LAT "unforgettable … in the way superb actors can, Hurt seemed to have built the character of Max from the inside out, investing him with a past and persona only hinted at in the script"; V "very good"); and Jack Warden as the manager in *Heaven Can Wait*, the role for which James Gleason was nominated for playing in *Here Comes Mr Jordan* in 1941 (NYT "succeeds with ease"; LAT "a fine, calm performance which finds and holds a tone of light sincerity that never grabs for jokes or winks, metaphorically, at the audience"; CT "key to the film's success … plays the role with great enthusiasm"; V "excellent").

On Oscar night, Walken claimed the statuette for his part in the year's Best Picture Oscar winner. Although unsuccessful in Hollywood, Globe winner Hurt later won the British Academy Award in London. Walken was unsuccessfully nominated for the BAFTA the following year.

1979

BEST PICTURE

ACADEMY AWARDS

All That Jazz
(Columbia, Twentieth Century-Fox, 123 mins, 19 Dec 1979, $20.3m, 9 noms)

Apocalypse Now
(Zoetrope, United Artists, 153 mins, 15 Aug 1979, $37.9m / gr:$78.8m, 8 noms)

Breaking Away
(Twentieth Century-Fox, 100 mins, 17 Jul 1979, 5 noms)

• ***Kramer vs Kramer***
(Jaffe, Columbia, 105 mins, 19 Dec 1979, $62.9m / gr:$106.3m, 9 noms)

Norma Rae
(Twentieth Century-Fox, 110 mins, 1 Mar 1979, 4 noms)

GOLDEN GLOBE AWARDS

(Drama)
Apocalypse Now
The China Syndrome
• ***Kramer vs Kramer***
Manhattan
Norma Rae

(Comedy/Musical)
Being There
• ***Breaking Away***
Hair
The Rose
10

BRITISH ACADEMY AWARDS

Apocalypse Now
The China Syndrome
The Deer Hunter
• ***Manhattan***

NEW YORK – *Kramer vs Kramer*
LOS ANGELES – *Kramer vs Kramer*
BOARD OF REVIEW – *Manhattan*
NATIONAL SOCIETY – *Breaking Away*

For the first time, the major critics' circles on the east and west coasts of the United States selected the same film as Best Picture: *Kramer vs Kramer*, a drama about a Manhattan business man whose wife leaves him and then files for a divorce and for custody of their young son (NYT "fine, witty, moving"; LAT "as nearly perfect a film as can be … a motion picture with an emotional wallop second to none this year"; CT "one of the year's finest films"; WP "a triumph of partisan pathos ... astutely succeeds"; V "a perceptive, touching and intelligent film").

1979

The runner-up to *Kramer vs Kramer* in Los Angeles was Francis Ford Coppola's Vietnam War epic *Apocalypse Now*, an infamously troubled project which earlier in the year had shared the Palme d'Or at the Cannes Film Festival (NYT "a stunning work ... technically complex and masterful … may be the quintessential Hollywood film of the '70s"; LAT "a landmark in film history, a masterpiece … it towers over anything that has been attempted by an American film maker in a very long time"; CT "individually, these episodes are compelling and spectacular [but] together they play like some kind of laundry list of Viet Nam issues … in the last 25 minutes [it] dissolves into gibberish"; WP "stunning for nearly two hours [but then] gets bogged down in the most gaudily festooned moral mishmash you ever saw"; V "brilliant and bizarre").

The other honoree in Cannes had been Volker Schlöndorff's *Die Blechtrommel (The Tin Drum)*. The German drama won the Oscar for Best Foreign-Language Film and was subsequently eligible for the various critics' prizes and other Academy Awards the following year after receiving a North American release in April 1980.

In New York, *Kramer vs Kramer* triumphed by just a single point over *Breaking Away*, a low-budget comedy-drama and surprise box office hit about a teenage cyclist (NYT "a gentle, hilarious, thoroughly winning comedy", "wonderful … fresh and funny"; LAT "charming, ingratiating, funny, exciting and pleasing"; CT "thoroughly entertaining and a guaranteed good time … one of the year's best films"; WP "the year's most appealing American movie … modest, humorous, authentically stirring … so endearing that it could upset the blockbusters and star vehicles at the next Academy Awards … a happy, unpretentious artistic breakthrough"; V "thoroughly delightful"; MFB "fatally lacks a clear purpose and identity"). Finishing third was Woody Allen's *Manhattan* (NYT "extraordinarily fine and funny", "Allen's funniest, most serious, best film so far"; LAT "even better than his Oscar-sweeping 'Annie Hall' … his masterwork … profoundly affecting"; CT "remarkable … may turn out to be the year's best comedy and drama"; WP "sparkling … exhilarating … consistently amusing and discreetly affecting"; V "irresistible"; MFB "interesting [and] cracklingly funny"). *Manhattan* had led on each of the first two ballots.

Other films to receive votes during the balloting by the New York Film Critics Circle were Bob Fosse's semi-autobiographical *All That Jazz* (NYT "an uproarious display of brilliance, nerve, dance, maudlin confessions, inside jokes and, especially, ego"; LAT "[a] superbly spendthrift explosion of energy, imagination, autobiography, choreography, fantasy and all-stops-out celebration of the possibilities of film … engrossing and occasionally overwhelming entertainment"; CT "one of the year's most original films"; V "often compelling"; TT "brilliant razzle dazzle") and Blake Edwards' comedy *10* (NYT "frequently hilarious"; LAT "a comedy as hilarious as it is bitterly dark underneath"; CT "very funny"; WP "sporadically funny, marginally interesting"; V "a shrewdly observed and beautifully executed comedy of manners and morals").

The same group of films contested the National Society of Film Critics and National Board of Review Best Picture accolades, but with different results. *Breaking Away* claimed the NSFC award with 26 points, over *Kramer vs Kramer* with 20, *Manhattan* with 17 and *10* with 13 points. Allen's *Manhattan*, meanwhile, emerged as winner of the NBR prize.

Kramer vs Kramer followed up its strong showing in the critics' votes with a leading tally of seven nominations for the Golden Globe Awards, and confirmed its status as the Oscar frontrunner with a win in the Best Picture (Drama) category. It triumphed over a field of nominees that comprised most of the expected Academy Award contenders, including both *Apocalypse Now* and *Manhattan*, as well as *The China Syndrome*, the hit drama about a crisis in a nuclear power plant (NYT "smashingly effective, very stylish suspense melodrama"; LAT "stunning … truly suspenseful and disturbing"; CT "a very entertaining movie"; V "moderately compelling"; MFB "highly effective") and *Norma Rae*, Martin Ritt's film about a woman who campaigns for union representation of Southern textile factory workers (NYT "stirring"; LAT "a wonderful and judicious work", "an intimate drama"; CT "repeatedly crosses into the realm of melodrama … is unrealistic in many crucial instances"; V "a superb film"; MFB "heart-warming is probably the word for 'Norma Rae', a film which leaves no cliché unturned").

In the Best Picture (Comedy/Musical) category the NSFC champ *Breaking Away* triumphed over a field that included Edwards' *10*, as well as both *Being There*, which starred Peter Sellers as a half-wit gardener mistaken for a genius (NYT "a stately, beautifully acted satire"; LAT "a gentle, exquisitely funny film … thoroughly engaging and witty"; V "unusually fine"); and *The Rose*, a musical drama in which Bette Midler portrayed a self-destructive singer (NYT "the movie maintains its momentum even after its gone off the track"; LAT "there are films in which nothing else matters but the strong and thrilling central performance, and 'The Rose' is one of them"; CT "a routine show biz saga … all-too-predictable"; WP "peculiarly unstirring [with] abundant cliches").

When the Oscar nominees were announced, *Kramer vs Kramer* topped the list of contenders with nine nominations, including Best Picture and Best Director for Robert Benton. In something of a surprise, its tally was matched by Fosse's *All That Jazz*, a film that had been overlooked for a Best Picture nomination at the Globes. Included in the Best Picture category with these two frontrunners were: *Apocalypse Now* (with eight nods); *Breaking Away* (with five mentions); and, in another surprise, *Norma Rae* (with four nominations). In the

Los Angeles Times, Charles Champlin had considered both *Being There*, *The China Syndrome* and *Manhattan* as each more likely than *Norma Rae* to round out the list.

In the final lead-up to the Academy Award ceremony, the Directors Guild of America gave their annual accolade to Benton, which further consolidated the Oscar chances of his film. The DGA winner's film had won the Best Picture Oscar every year for the past decade. As expected, on Oscar night, the Best Picture statuette was won *by Kramer vs Kramer*, which also received four other awards, including Best Director and Best Actor.

The Best Foreign-Language Film Academy Award was won by Cannes honoree *Die Blechtrommel.* It was the first German film to ever claim the prestigious statuette. In the Best Picture category, meanwhile, the Academy overlooked another German-language release, Rainer Werner Fassbinder's farce *Die Ehe de Maria Braun (The Marriage of Maria Braun)* which The New York Times had included on its annual list of the year's top ten films (NYT "epically funny … may be Mr Fassbinder's most perfectly realized comedy to date … both an epic comedy and a romantic ballad"; LAT "superb … [a] remarkable, challenging and satisfying film"; CT "will someday be regarded as a seminal film in the creation of a new German cinema). Another notable omission was another international release: the 1975 Australian drama *Picnic at Hanging Rock* (NYT "the film has a hypnotic spell … it's a movie composed almost entirely of clues … Weir and his screenwriter deal in moods"; LAT "sensuous mystery [and] ravishing images"; WP "exquisite … absorbing albeit inconclusive"; S&S "a pure 'atmosphere' piece").

In London, the Best Film category at the British Academy Awards comprised the previous year's Best Picture Oscar winner *The Deer Hunter*, the Cannes Palme d'Or co-winner *Apocalypse Now*, *The China Syndrome* and *Manhattan.* Surprisingly, the BAFTA was won by the year's most glaring absentee from the Oscar list: *Manhattan.* At the 1980 Cannes Film Festival, meanwhile, *All That Jazz* was one of two films to share the Palme d'Or.

Finally, at the following year's BAFTAs, *Kramer vs Kramer* was among the nominees outpolled for the Best Film accolade by *The Elephant Man*, one of that year's unsuccessful Best Picture Oscar nominees.

1979

BEST DIRECTOR

ACADEMY AWARDS
• Robert Benton for *Kramer vs Kramer*
Francis Ford Coppola for *Apocalypse Now*
Bob Fosse for *All That Jazz*
Edouard Molinaro for *La Cage aux Folles (The Bird Cage)*
Peter Yates for *Breaking Away*

GOLDEN GLOBE AWARDS
Hal Ashby – *Being There*
Robert Benton – *Kramer vs Kramer*
James Bridges – *The China Syndrome*
• Francis Ford Coppola – *Apocalypse Now*
Peter Yates – *Breaking Away*

DIRECTORS GUILD AWARD
Woody Allen – *Manhattan*
• Robert Benton – *Kramer vs Kramer*
James Bridges – *The China Syndrome*
Francis Ford Coppola – *Apocalypse Now*
Peter Yates – *Breaking Away*

BRITISH ACADEMY AWARDS
Woody Allen – *Manhattan*
Michael Cimino – *The Deer Hunter*
• Francis Ford Coppola – *Apocalypse Now*
John Schlesinger – *Yanks*

NEW YORK – Woody Allen – *Manhattan*
LOS ANGELES – Robert Benton – *Kramer vs Kramer*
BOARD OF REVIEW – John Schlesinger – *Yanks*
NATIONAL SOCIETY – Woody Allen – *Manhattan* and **Robert Benton – *Kramer vs Kramer***

Apocalypse Now, Francis Ford Coppola's trouble-plagued Vietnam War epic, shared the Palme d'Or at the Cannes Film Festival (NYT "masterful"; LAT "a carefully and ingeniously orchestrated journey into madness … a dazzling piece of film making"). In the Best Director category, however, Coppola was by-passed in favour of Terrence Malick for *Days of Heaven*. The previous year Malick had been the Best Director choice of the New York Film Critics Circle but had been overlooked by the Academy. Despite this, Coppola was a strong early contender for the annual end-of-year Best Director accolades.

1979

The first major group to hand out its awards was the Los Angeles Film Critics Association, who cited Robert Benton for *Kramer vs Kramer* (NYT "packed with beautifully observed detail"; LAT "Benton's tact and delicacy reveal themselves in his handling [of the cast]"; CT "low-key, realistic touch"; V "smooth and effortless"; MFB "elegant"). Coppola was the runner-up.

Four days later, the east coast circle selected Woody Allen for his black-and-white comedy-drama *Manhattan* (LAT "has become one of the finest, most thoughtful and individual film-makers in America"; CT "Allen has become one of the few quality brand names in American films … there is a crystalline polish to his work"). It was Allen's second plaudit from the group in three years. The runner-up was Benton (by a vote of 28 points to 23). Finishing in third place was Bob Fosse for *All That Jazz* (NYT "seeks to operate on too many levels at the same time"; LAT "not all of it works well, an allowable shortcoming in so original a film … beautifully executed … masterful"; CT "Fosse is going to be accused of everything from arrogance to brilliance. But his achievement is neither"). Coppola did not feature among the serious contenders in New York.

In early January, Allen and Benton shared the Best Director trophy from the National Society of Film Critics (each garnering 22 points). The runners-up were Peter Yates (with 21 points) for *Breaking Away* (LAT "well crafted"; CT "proves to have a fine eye"; WP "lucid … neat but never overcalculated, unobjectionable but never innocuous … during most of the film, Yates does himself proud as a director of low-key comic naturalism and ensemble acting") and Blake Edwards (with 17 points) for the comedy *10* (NYT "Mr Edwards' comic gifts haven't been blunted by his recent series of 'Pink Panther' hits"; LAT "his direction is effortlessly graceful … may well rank as his best work"; CT "has a considerable reputation of a director of visual comedy [and also] has a serious side … well, both sides of Edwards' craft are on view in '10'"; WP "seems to take two dumb steps for every smart one … Edwards can't seem to resist the most miserable sight gags that occur to him").

The dissenter among the major critics groups was the National Board of Review. Although it named Allen's *Manhattan* as Best Picture, the group gave its Best Director prize to John Schlesinger for *Yanks* (NYT "beautifully realized"; LAT "subtle … the honesty of the handling stays true"; CT "has a fine eye [but] Schlesinger makes a fatal mistake"; WP "skillful"; MFB "has never done anything as touching, natural or well worked out in screen space before").

The lack of critics' prizes seemed to have stalled Coppola's campaign for a second Best Director Oscar, but his chances were dramatically revived in late January when he won his second Best Director Golden Globe in an upset over the highly-favoured Benton, whose film won the Best Picture (Drama) Globe.

A month later, Coppola and Fosse each received their third Best Director Oscar nominations. Also short-listed were Benton and Yates, each for the first time. In a shock, however, New York prizewinner Allen was overlooked in favour of Edouard Molinaro for *La Cage aux Folles (The Bird Cage)*, the year's most commercially successful European film (NYT "Molinaro and [his co-writers] go for gags at the expense of character – and humor"; LAT "amazing how [he has] managed to avoid obvious pitfalls]"; V "uneven direction").

Others omitted from the Academy's list were: James Bridges for *The China Syndrome* (LAT "skilfully executed … his most expert work by far"; WP "does not display miraculous resourcefulness [and] on the contrary, relies on the standard panicky cliches"); Martin Ritt for the Best Picture nominee *Norma Rae* (NYT "the film's principal appeal [is] in the way that Mr Ritt, his writers and his cast reveal the natural resources of the characters"; LAT "he is here again a craftsman both solid and sensitive"; WP "Ritt has certainly changed his tone … [his] leisurely, observant, cumulatively affecting style has been exchanged for an anxious, choppy, bombastic exposition"; V "firm but sensitive direction"; MFB "[Ritt shows his] feeling for character, and his unfailing eye for settings"); Hal Ashby for *Being There* (NYT "directs at an unruffled, elegant pace, the better to let Mr Sellers's double-edged mannerisms make their full impression on the audience"; LAT "ever so deftly … in a thoroughly contemporary and sophisticated low key"; WP "despite its shortcomings, director Hal Ashby has managed to transplant the undernourished narrative [of Jerzy Kosinski's novel] with remarkable success"; V "a significant achievement"); Ridley Scott for *Alien* (NYT "very stylish … executed with a good deal of no-nonsense verve"; LAT "surpassingly well-done … not a frame of 'Alien' is flat or casual or perfunctory"; CT "accomplished"; WP "stylish … builds and sustains a brilliant nightmarish tension … orchestrates [the suspense] with masterful visual and rhythmic command"; MFB "artful"); Peter Weir for *Picnic at Hanging Rock* (S&S "effortlessly welding space, time and setting into an indivisible whole"); and Rainer Werner Fassbinder's *Die Ehe de Maria Braun (The Marriage of Maria Braun)* (CT "director Fassbinder is the real star here. His skill is evident in matters as small as his camera movements to matters as large as Maria's deeply felt relationship with a heavy-set black American soldier").

Three weeks later, Benton emerged as the Oscar favourite when he was named Best Director by the Directors Guild of America. On Academy Awards night, *Kramer vs Kramer* was honoured with five statuettes, including Best Director for Benton.

At the British Academy Awards, the critics' winners Allen and Schlesinger were nominated alongside Coppola and the previous year's Oscar winner, Michael Cimino for *The Deer Hunter*. While *Manhattan* was named Best Film, the Best Director award went to Coppola. The following year, Benton was nominated for the BAFTA, but lost to Akira Kurosawa for *Kagemusha (The Shadow Warrior)*.

1979

BEST ACTRESS

ACADEMY AWARDS
Jill Clayburgh as 'Marilyn Homberg' in *Starting Over*
• Sally Field as 'Norma Rae' in *Norma Rae*
Jane Fonda as 'Kimberly Wells' in *The China Syndrome*
Marsha Mason as 'Jennie MacLaine' in *Chapter Two*
Bette Midler as 'Rose' in *The Rose*

GOLDEN GLOBE AWARDS
(Drama)
Jill Clayburgh – *La Luna (Luna)*
Lisa Eichhorn – *Yanks*
• Sally Field – *Norma Rae*
Jane Fonda – *The China Syndrome*
Marsha Mason – *Promises in the Dark*

(Comedy/Musical)
Julie Andrews – *10*
Jill Clayburgh – *Starting Over*
Shirley MacLaine – *Being There*
Marsha Mason – *Chapter Two*
• Bette Midler – *The Rose*

BRITISH ACADEMY AWARDS
• Jane Fonda – *The China Syndrome*
Diane Keaton – *Manhattan*
Maggie Smith – *California Suite*
Meryl Streep – *The Deer Hunter*

NEW YORK – Sally Field – *Norma Rae*
LOS ANGELES – Sally Field – *Norma Rae*
BOARD OF REVIEW – Sally Field – *Norma Rae*
NATIONAL SOCIETY – Sally Field – *Norma Rae*

There was never any doubt about who would win the Best Actress Academy Award. For years, Sally Field had struggled to shake her reputation as the star of two popular television series, 'Gidget' and 'The Flying Nun'. In 1976, she had won an Emmy for her performance as a schizophrenic woman with seventeen personalities in the television drama 'Sybil', and the following year found commercial and critical success in feature films with roles in the comedy *Smokey and the Bandit* and the drama *Heroes*, respectively. Her breakthrough, however, came in March 1979 when she played the eponymous young woman who campaigns for a trade union in the Southern textile factory where she works, in Martin Ritt's acclaimed drama *Norma Rae* (NYT "spectacular ... a performance that is firm and funny and full of risk [in] a role loaded with the kind of sentimental temptations that might sidetrack a lesser performer … [her performance] gives dimension to the film", "demonstrates once and for all that she is an actress of dramatic intelligence and force, someone who no longer need be referred to in terms of her television credits"; LAT "[a] beautifully conceived and sustained performance … extraordinary drive and vitality"; CT "[a] superior performance … thoroughly winning … that Field makes her character's enormous transformation believable is the main reason why 'Norma Rae' works"; WP "embodies the title character with considerable sincerity"; V "a tour-de-force ... [Field] now ranks among the finest contemporary actresses"). The New York Times declared that Field's portrayal "may well be the one that those of other actresses are measured against this year." Shortly after receiving acclaim from American critics, Field won the Best Actress accolade at the Cannes Film Festival. At the end of the year, she followed this win with a clean sweep of the major American-based Best Actress prizes. She claimed both the New York and Los Angeles critics' awards, the National Board of Review and National Society of Film Critics plaudits, the Golden Globe (Drama) and, finally, the Academy Award (at her first nomination).

At the Oscar ceremony at the Dorothy Chandler Pavilion, Field accepted the statuette from Richard Dreyfuss and said, "I'm going to be the one to cry tonight, I'll tell you that right now. They said this couldn't be done!" She reserved her greatest thanks to her director, Martin Ritt, commenting, "Marty Ritt is Norma Rae; he's fought all his life to put on films that have something to say". The victory firmly established Field as a leading star and five years later she collected a second Best Actress Academy Award for her performance as a widowed farmer during the Depression in *Places in the Heart*.

The only major Best Actress trophy that Field did not collect (in fact, she was not even a nominee) was the BAFTA, which was claimed by Jane Fonda for the second year in a row. Fonda was honoured for her performance as a television news reporter in *The China Syndrome*, a role originally written for a man, and which had initially been intended for Richard Dreyfuss (NYT "splendid … her performance is not that of an actress in a star's role, but that of an actress creating a character that happens to be major within the film. She keeps getting better and better"; LAT "commanding and convincing"; CT "absolutely convincing – and thoroughly entertaining … the galvanizing force of the film"; V "superior"; S&S "a precise but appealing ambivalent performance"; MFB "magnificent"). Fonda was among those actresses outpolled by Field at the Oscars (she had been nominated for a fifth time) and ironically, she was also one of several actresses, along with Faye Dunaway, who had turned down the lead role in *Norma Rae*.

Another of the actresses to decline the part of Norma Rae, Jill Clayburgh, was also an unsuccessful Oscar nominee that year. For her performance as a schoolteacher who becomes involved with a divorcee in *Starting Over*,

Clayburgh received her second consecutive mention from the Academy (NYT "delivers a particularly sharp characterization that's letter-perfect during the first part of the story and unconvincing in the second, through no fault of her own"; LAT "a beautiful performance"; WP "she makes Marilyn eccentrically adorable"). Prior to the announcement of the Oscar nominations Vincent Canby had predicted in The New York Times that the Academy would include Clayburgh on the ballot for Best Actress, but he had thought that she would be recognised for her turn in Bernardo Bertolucci's *La Luna (Luna)* (NYT "extraordinary", "depending on how the film fares with the Hollywood people as well as with the public, she could possibly win the [Academy] award"; LAT "Clayburgh's achievement is to make 'Luna' succeed better as a story than as the stylized and symbolic drama it also is"; V "hard-pressed to sustain the melodramatics"; MFB "at the beginning Clayburgh strikes one as lacking in the kind of inner resources demanded by the role; but her feisty New York manner usefully undercuts the plot's more outrageous excesses"). Clayburgh was nominated in the two Best Actress categories at the Golden Globes for her two contrasting performances.

Also garnering dual Globe nominations was Marsha Mason. She was included in the Drama category for her performance as the doctor in *Promises in the Dark* (LAT "soul-deep believability and accuracy … Mason is, as we watch her, a doctor rather than an actress playing at being a doctor, and it is an award-winning performance") and in the Comedy/Musical category for playing a character that had actually been based on herself in Neil Simon's *Chapter Two*, a semi-autobiographical dramatisation of the relationship between the actress and her Broadway playwright husband (NYT "a vibrant, appealing performance that minimizes the movie's troubles … sunny and intelligently appealing … there are no great depths to the performance, but there's a lot of fire"; LAT "whatever else the Oscar voters may conclude about 'Chapter Two', they seem certain to agree that Marsha Mason is once again very nominatable indeed. Her performance is simply remarkable in its range and its depth. From piquant charm to torrential rage, from amusement to anguish, she moves with intelligence, sensitivity and power"; V "tremendous"; TT "magnificent"). Mason had been the runner-up to Field in the voting in Los Angeles for her work in *Chapter Two* and it was for that performance that she was nominated by Academy voters.

Completing the list of Oscar nominees was Bette Midler, the runner-up to Field for the New York Film Critics Circle accolade. Midler, a popular singer and comedienne, was included in the category for her film debut as a wild and self-destructive rock singer in *The Rose*, for which she won the Globe (Comedy/Musical) (NYT "an unexpectedly alluring performance", "succeeds beautifully in giving her character depth and dimension", "her performance never seems strained or directed"; LAT "there are films in which nothing else matters but the strong and thrilling central performance, and 'The Rose' is one of them … what counts for everything is the power and the glory of Bette Midler's portrayal … [she] is a wonder and a stunner"; CT "Midler is very impressive in her feature film debut … she's always compelling, never boring, and she plays the part without ever once breaking character and playing her own stage persona"; V "should establish her as a first-rate dramatic actress").

The most notable omission from the Academy's list of candidates was the actress that had won Best Actress in Berlin and finished as the NSFC runner-up to Field: German actress Hanna Schygulla in *Die Ehe de Maria Braun (The Marriage of Maria Braun)* (NYT "[a] sweet, tough, brilliantly complex performance", "may be the single most riveting performance of the year"; LAT "Schygulla has the audacity to make Maria come vibrantly alive and to carry off with ease her every (and often melodramatic) act and gesture so that they reverberate with Fassbinder's serious implications"; CT "many critics have praised Hanna Schygulla's performance as Maria, but let's face it, this is a great role that many actresses could have played"). In The New York Times in October, Canby had declared, "with the opening this week of 'The Marriage of Maria Braun', there are now two women in competition for the Oscar that, next spring, will be given for the best performance by an actress in a leading role in 1979. Only two? Well, until the arrival of the Fassbender picture, in which Hanna Schygulla fives a mesmerizingly funny and touching performance as the sort of Mother Courage who wouldn't be caught dead pulling a cart, there was, in my estimation, only one: Sally Field, whose guts, humor and raised-consciousness illuminated Martin Ritt's 'Norma Rae'."

Others overlooked included: previous winner and BAFTA nominee Diane Keaton in *Manhattan* (NYT "superb", "marvelous"; LAT "excellent"; WP "brilliantly funny"; V "most convincing"; MFB "splendid"); Globe nominee Shirley MacLaine in the comedy *Being There* (NYT "beautifully acted"; LAT "MacLaine supplies the comedy – her attempt to vamp Sellers is a comic high point"; WP "delightful… witty and unerring"; V "subtle and winning"); and Globe nominee Lisa Eichhorn in *Yanks* (NYT "plays the English girl most persuasively, but she's so sweet that after a time one feels like ditching her"; LAT "a fine discovery … a good and subtle actress"; WP "radiant [and] extraordinary"; CT "a striking film debut … almost single-handedly makes the picture work. She is able, without resorting to histrionics, to communicate the duality of her feelings in a number of scenes … draws attention to her emotions, not to herself"; MFB "Eichhorn is so good you have to watch her closely, and so able to move from turmoil to calm in an instant that you are reminded of Margaret Sullavan").

Unsurprisingly, Sigourney Weaver's performance in the science fiction horror thriller *Alien* was also left off the Best Actress list by the Academy. (NYT “impressive”, “succeeds in creating an unusually interesting character”; LAT “Weaver, in her first feature, is notably individual and has a bright future”; CT “an auspicious debut”; WP “her movie debut may generate instant stardom … she brings an exciting combination of intelligence, bravery and sex appeal to the portrayal of warrant officer Ripley … Weaver never allows the character to degenerate into caricature”; V “carries it off well”). Although she had the lead role in the film, the previously unknown Weaver had been promoted by Twentieth Century-Fox for awards season recognition in the supporting category. When she reprised the role seven years later in the sequel *Aliens*, Weaver earned a Best Actress Oscar nomination.

1979

BEST ACTOR

ACADEMY AWARDS
• Dustin Hoffman as 'Ted Kramer' in *Kramer vs Kramer*
Jack Lemmon as 'Jack Godell' in *The China Syndrome*
Al Pacino as 'Arthur Kirkland' in *...And Justice For All*
Roy Scheider as 'Joe Gideon' in *All That Jazz*
Peter Sellers as 'Chance' in *Being There*

GOLDEN GLOBE AWARDS
(Drama)
• Dustin Hoffman
– *Kramer vs Kramer*
Jack Lemmon – *The China Syndrome*
Al Pacino – *...And Justice For All*
Jon Voight – *The Champ*
James Woods – *The Onion Field*

(Comedy/Musical)
George Hamilton
– *Love at First Bite*
Dudley Moore – *10*
Burt Reynolds – *Starting Over*
Roy Scheider – *All That Jazz*
• Peter Sellers – *Being There*

BRITISH ACADEMY AWARDS
Woody Allen – *Manhattan*
Robert De Niro – *The Deer Hunter*
• Jack Lemmon – *The China Syndrome*
Martin Sheen – *Apocalypse Now*

NEW YORK – Dustin Hoffman – *Kramer vs Kramer*
LOS ANGELES – Dustin Hoffman – *Kramer vs Kramer*
BOARD OF REVIEW – Peter Sellers – *Being There*
NATIONAL SOCIETY – Dustin Hoffman – *Kramer vs Kramer*

Nearly a decade after George C. Scott declined the Best Actor Oscar because he did not believe in making actors compete for prizes, the statuette was won by Dustin Hoffman, another actor who had long spoken out against awards for acting. Unlike Scott, however, Hoffman did not refuse the honour. Instead he appeared at the Oscar ceremony and graciously told that audience, "I'm up here with mixed feelings. I've criticised the Academy before, with reason. I refuse to believe that I beat Jack Lemmon, that I beat Al Pacino, that I beat Peter Sellers. We are part of an artistic family. There are six thousand actors in the Screen Actors Guild who don't work. You have to practise accents while you're driving a taxicab 'cause when you're a broke actor, you can't write and you can't paint. Most actors don't work and a few of us are so lucky to have a chance. And to that artistic family that strives for excellence, none of you have ever lost and I am proud to share this with you, and I thank you."

Hoffman received his first Oscar for his performance as a man suddenly deserted by his wife and left to care for his young son in *Kramer vs Kramer* (NYT "splendid [in] a delicately witty performance, funny and full of feeling"; LAT "the degree to which the principal performances [by Hoffman and Streep] seem never to be performances at all is not less than miraculous … [he] has given a number of disparate and extraordinary performances in his career but none more affecting than this one, none that seems more clearly to originate in his soul as much as in his art"; CT "one of his most memorable performances … he should win the Academy Award next April"; WP "[a] sensitive and wryly tender-hearted performance … Hoffman will be the front-runner for this year's best-actor Oscar … [a] vivid, urgent, sentimental performance"; V "credible and sympathetic", "his best [performance] in years"; TT "supercharged and glossy"). It was his fourth nomination and came after he had collected the New York Film Critics Circle and Los Angeles Film Critics Association prizes, the National Society of Film Critics plaudit and the Golden Globe for Best Actor (Drama).

The early frontrunner for the Oscar had been Jack Lemmon. He had won the Best Actor accolade at the Cannes Film Festival for his turn as a worker in a nuclear power plant determined to publicise the truth of a near-disaster in *The China Syndrome*, a role turned down by Jack Nicholson and Robert Redford (NYT "splendid"; LAT "a performance that equals his portrait of a man in extremis in 'Save the Tiger'"; WP "contributes a persuasively alarmed, resolute performance"; V "superior", "a remarkably well-rounded performance"; MFB "brilliant"). Although he missed out on a third Oscar from the Academy in Hollywood (it was his sixth nomination), Lemmon's performance did earn him a third award from the British Academy.

The darkhorse in the field of Oscar contenders was Peter Sellers, who was mentioned for the second (and final) time for his portrayal of a simple-minded gardener in *Being There* (NYT "played with brilliant understatement ... never strikes a false note"; LAT "Sellers hasn't been so terrific – or had such terrific material – in years … [a] most disciplined performance"; WP "[in] a tightrope act of enigmatic stupidity, Sellers tries to sustain a single-key performance, but he seems in and out of the appropriate monotone"; V "smashing"; TT "Sellers gives one of the most restrained, and so best, performances of his career"). Sellers won the Globe (Comedy/ Musical) and the National Board of Review award, and had been a distant runner-up to Hoffman for both the New York and NSFC prizes. Sellers had earned decidedly mixed reviews for his performances in his other release that year, *The Prisoner of Zenda* (NYT "when Mr Sellers appears the film really does come to life … [he] is dividing his energies between a serious character and a funny one … the serious performance is, in many ways, the more remarkable one … he performs a perfect balancing act, orchestrated so well that the funny character makes the serious one even more effective, and vice versa"; CT "lacklustre … the ultimate blame must go to Sellers, who breathes absolutely no life into the creaky old script"; WP "plays three roles with no vitality"; V "in good form").

The runner-up to Hoffman in Los Angeles was also among the Oscar nominees: Roy Scheider as a self-destructive, workaholic Broadway director and choreographer in *All That Jazz*, a character based on the film's director, Bob Fosse (NYT "key to the success of the production is the performance of Roy Scheider … with an actor of less weight and intensity, 'All That Jazz' might have evaporated as we watched it"; LAT "a wonderment whose portrayal of this life-splurging, death-obsessed man poses the Academy voters another mind-boggling decision"; CT "Scheider is a selfless actor [whose] dedication only enhances our regard for [the character]"; V "superb"). Scheider won the role when Richard Dreyfuss backed out prior to the start of filming. It was Scheider's second mention by the Academy, but his first in the major category.

Even though he was in contention for an Oscar for the fifth time in just eight years, the long-shot for the statuette was Al Pacino as a young lawyer in *...And Justice For All* (NYT "when the movie opens, Mr Pacino is behaving as if he were at the end of his rope, which leaves him no place to go except crazy with moral indignation"; LAT "the part is made to order for the most dramatic actor of the current cinema and Pacino leaves no brief unturned … often very funny in his chronic exasperation, but he also has some quiet and affecting moments"; CT "a failure … he repeats himself throughout the movie. He explodes once every reel and frankly, he gets a little boring"; V "a dynamite performance").

The most glaring omission from both the lists of Globe and Oscar nominees was Martin Sheen as the soldier sent to assassinate an insane officer during the Vietnam War in Francis Ford Coppola's *Apocalypse Now* (NYT "superlatively right … [his] weary eyes suggest much that is never adequately expressed by the script"; LAT "you can imagine [the role] having been written differently, not performed better"; V "extraordinary and extremely effective"). Despite being snubbed at the major Hollywood awards ceremonies, Sheen was nominated for the British Academy's Best Actor award in London.

Also overlooked for the Oscar were: BAFTA nominee Woody Allen in *Manhattan* (LAT "Allen is here more the actor than ever"); Globe nominee Dudley Moore in *10* (NYT "the movie belongs very much to Mr Moore, who manages to be funny without ever having to appear stupid"; LAT "[the film's] key strength"; CT "he succeeds both at performing physical comedy and at making George a sympathetic character"; V "deserves heavy credit"); Globe nominee Burt Reynolds in *Starting Over* (NYT "Mr Reynolds's performance begins very well, and very seriously [but later] it's time for Phil to show the strain, or to show the conflict, or to show something – and still Mr Reynolds lies low"; LAT "extraordinarily subdued"; WP "[an] endearing characterization … his acting is exquisitely balanced … navigates a tightrope that only the most experienced and astute film actors ever master"; V "underplays marvelously"); Globe nominee James Woods in *The Onion Field* (LAT "played with a grinning and malevolent charm … it is Woods who stays hauntingly in mind, not sympathetic but chillingly comprehensible"; V "superb", "chillingly effective"); Nick Nolte in *North Dallas Forty* (NYT "the uncontested star of the show … engaging and full of surprises"; LAT "by a long way his best and most charismatic performance so far"; CT "one can't deny that Nolte's leading performance is compelling … although the film has cracks in its believability, Nolte never falters in his character"; WP "Elliott is a demanding character for Nolte, and he delivers … [he] proves his versatility by embodying a sane, contemplative protagonist"); Michael Douglas as a cameraman in *The China Syndrome* (LAT "relative to the other roles, it is unshowy to the point of self-effacement, and the more useful for it"; CT "nicely underplayed"; V "superior"); Ben Gazzara in *Saint Jack* (NYT "maybe too good to be the kind of mythical icon that such a film demands. In style, he belongs to the films of today, not to the romances of yesteryear "; CT "contributing to the film's reality is Gazzara, who manages to turn in a nicely subdued performance for a leading role"; V "excels"; MFB "the failure here may be partly a mistake of casting – Ben Gazzara seems too efficient an operator for [the part]"); Dirk Bogarde in *Despair* (NYT "gives the performance of his career", "Bogarde's prissy gestures, mixed with expressions of alarm and lust that are always conscious, beautifully illuminate this seminal Nabokovian hero"; LAT "[a] commanding portrayal of a man disintegrating … most impressive"); and both Michel Serrault (NYT "energetic, broad, much too knowing and superficial … all too convincing as the hammy, temperamental transvestite … he minces more grossly than ever did Billy De Wolfe, and he lunges at pathos like someone playing right guard for the Rams"; LAT "at first, there's an uneasy feeling that the humor is going to be at the expense of Serrault's often shrieking transvestite – but Serrault can pull himself up proudly to become a self-aware figure of implacable dignity … wonderful"; CT "the film's best performance … genuinely touching") and Ugo Tognazzi (NYT "a fine actor, but here he looks as ridiculous as his role"; LAT "deftly underplays") in *La Cage aux Folles (The Bird Cage)* (CT "the film's only distinctive quality is the skill of its veteran actors in working with tired material").

1979

BEST SUPPORTING ACTRESS

ACADEMY AWARDS
Jane Alexander as 'Margaret Phelps' in *Kramer vs Kramer*
Barbara Barrie as 'Mrs Stohler' in *Breaking Away*
Candice Bergen as 'Jessica Potter' in *Starting Over*
Mariel Hemingway as 'Tracy' in *Manhattan*
• Meryl Streep as 'Joanna Kramer' in *Kramer vs Kramer*

GOLDEN GLOBE AWARDS
Jane Alexander – *Kramer vs Kramer*
Kathleen Beller – *Promises in the Dark*
Candice Bergen – *Starting Over*
Valerie Harper – *Chapter Two*
• Meryl Streep – *Kramer vs Kramer*

BRITISH ACADEMY AWARDS
Lisa Eichhorn – *The Europeans*
Mariel Hemingway – *Manhattan*
• Rachel Roberts – *Yanks*
Meryl Streep – *Manhattan*

NEW YORK – Meryl Streep – *Kramer vs Kramer*
LOS ANGELES – Meryl Streep – *Kramer vs Kramer* and ***Manhattan*** and ***The Seduction of Joe Tynan***
BOARD OF REVIEW – Meryl Streep – *Kramer vs Kramer* and ***Manhattan*** and ***The Seduction of Joe Tynan***
NATIONAL SOCIETY – Meryl Streep – *Kramer vs Kramer* and ***Manhattan*** and ***The Seduction of Joe Tynan***

"The first Academy Award presented tonight was no surprise," commented The New York Times, "Meryl Streep won as best supporting actress." Nominated for a second consecutive year, Streep won her first statuette for her portrayal of a woman who suddenly deserts her husband and young son in *Kramer vs Kramer* (NYT "one of the major performances of the year", "excellent"; LAT "the degree to which the principal performances [by Hoffman and Streep] seem never to be performances at all is not less than miraculous … gives us a portrayal that appears to be constructed of raw nerves and remembered pain"; CT "a wonder"; WP "[a] sensitive and wryly tender-hearted performance"; V "credible and sympathetic", "shines"; TT "supercharged and glossy").

Streep had also won praise from critics that year for her performances as the lesbian ex-wife in Woody Allen's *Manhattan* (NYT "beautifully played"; LAT "excellent … briefly but devastatingly seen"; MFB "splendid") and as the mistress of a US Senator in *The Seduction of Joe Tynan* (NYT "Streep's remarkable accomplishment is to keep both Tynan and the audience perpetually off balance, to turn a predictable affair into a source of constant surprise"; LAT "years from now, [the film] may be best remembered as the first film to give Meryl Streep full rein for her luminous talents … Streep plays her very, very delicately, with every ambiguity intact … it's a complex and fascinating performance"; CT "repeatedly a scene-stealer"; V "outstanding", "underplays beautifully"; MFB "slithering faultlessly through an impossible combination of femme fatale, Southern belle and New Woman"). "Rarely has an actress turned in such a remarkable string of performances in one year," observed Gene Siskel in the Chicago Tribune. It was for all three performances, that Streep won the Best Supporting Actress awards from the Los Angeles Film Critics Association, the National Board of Review and the National Society of Film Critics. For her turn in *Kramer vs Kramer* alone, she collected the New York Film Critics Circle plaudit and the Best Supporting Actress Golden Globe.

Also nominated for the Oscar were: Barbara Barrie as the mother in *Breaking Away* (NYT "superb … manages to be funny, wise, small-town and sexy all at the same time … doesn't play down to the character"; LAT "not least among the achievements of 'Breaking Away' is that [Barrie and Dooley] keep these roles [as the parents] from becoming wholly caricatures"; WP "delightful"); Candice Bergen as a talentless songwriter in *Starting Over* (NYT "one of the comic masterstrokes in 'Starting Over' is the casting of Candice Bergen as Jessica"; LAT "Bergen gives a fine, unselfconscious and multisided characterization [that is] edgy and funny"; WP "one of the [director's] minor triumphs is Candy Bergen's performance: for the first time she is exploited with satirical zest … you may not be quite sure how much of the performance is comic acting and how much sheer embodiment, but that doesn't make it less entertaining"; V "a career highlight"); New York runner-up Jane Alexander as the next-door neighbour in *Kramer vs Kramer* (NYT "superbly acted"; LAT "[a] careful and deep-running performance … her role is marginally more than a device but Alexander goes a long way toward making the woman an identifiable individual, not just a sympathetic type"; WP "excellent"; V "superior"); and Mariel Hemingway as the teenage drama student in *Manhattan* (NYT "superb", "marvelous"; LAT "excellent"; MFB "splendid [and] delightfully fresh"). The latter two were, of course, both co-stars of Streep.

Another of Streep's co-stars was a notable absentee from the list of nominees: the popular comedienne Barbara Harris had been the runner-up for the NSFC prize for her performance as the adulterous Senator's frustrated wife in *The Seduction of Joe Tynan* (NYT "Harris is particularly graceful in avoiding the stereotype of the politician's wife. Just as Miss Streep does, she shows the audience something new"; LAT "brings gallantry and warmth to the film's most difficult role. That she manages not to be shrill and catches our sympathy is no small feat"; WP "[a] superb and rounded characterization"; MFB "strong"). Variety commented that Harris "gives the performance of her career, one that certainly merits Academy Award consideration."

Also by-passed for consideration were: Rachel Roberts for both her BAFTA winning performance in *Yanks* (NYT "totally honest and at ease"; LAT "contributes one of her best characterizations in some time"; WP "'Yanks' may bring awards to Rachel Roberts") and her turn as the headmistress in *Picnic at Hanging Rock* (LAT "fine"); Valerie Harper in *Chapter Two* (LAT "very good"; V "highly effective"); Globe nominee Kathleen Beller for her arguably co-leading role as the dying teenager in *Promises in the Dark* (NYT "Beller has the worst of it, being required to smile bravely when a real first-rate tantrum, or some other form of identifiable despair, would be in order"; LAT "the girl is central to all else, and it is a superb piece of acting and a particularly thoughtful characterization … never seeming, despite a dramatic role, to be a performer at work"; WP "plays effectively"; V "first-rate", "heart-wrenching"); Barbara Baxley as the title character's mother in *Norma Rae* (NYT "very good"; LAT "splendid"); Ann Reinking as the mistress in *All That Jazz* (NYT "extremely good … a fine dancer and an excellent comedian"; LAT "real and affecting"); Mary Steenburgen in *Time After Time* (NYT "delightfully played", "emerges as a funny and affecting figure, one of the nicest surprises the movie has to offer"; LAT "she is, for want of a better word, wonderful"; CT "appealingly played"; WP "mannered"); Frances Sternhagen as the cheerful sister-in-law in *Starting Over* (NYT "gets the opportunity to demonstrate how truly funny she can be … the screenplay is full of wit and insight that Miss Sternhagen understands completely"; LAT "has some fine lines, approaching but avoiding caricature"); Priscilla Pointer in *The Onion Field* (NYT "[an] immensely resonant performance"; LAT "has immense dignity as Campbell's mother"); and Janet Leigh as the duty-bound daughter of an elderly couple in *Boardwalk* (NYT "creates a character who is vastly more complex, interesting and believable than the movie that surrounds her"; LAT "sensitive").

Over the following decades, Streep has become one of the leading actresses in American cinema. She has received more Academy Award nominations in the acting categories than any other actor or actress.

1979

BEST SUPPORTING ACTOR

ACADEMY AWARDS
• Melvyn Douglas as 'Benjamin Rand' in *Being There*
Robert Duvall as 'Lieutenant-Colonel Kilgore' in *Apocalypse Now*
Frederic Forrest as 'Houston Dyer' in *The Rose*
Justin Henry as 'Billy Kramer' in *Kramer vs Kramer*
Mickey Rooney as 'Henry Dailey' in *The Black Stallion*

GOLDEN GLOBE AWARDS
• Melvyn Douglas – *Being There*
• Robert Duvall – *Apocalypse Now*
Frederic Forrest – *The Rose*
Justin Henry – *Kramer vs Kramer*
Laurence Olivier – *A Little Romance*

BRITISH ACADEMY AWARDS
• Robert Duvall – *Apocalypse Now*
Denholm Elliott – *Saint Jack*
John Hurt – *Alien*
Christopher Walken – *The Deer Hunter*

NEW YORK – Melvyn Douglas – *Being There*
LOS ANGELES – Melvyn Douglas – *Being There* and *The Seduction of Joe Tynan*
BOARD OF REVIEW – Paul Dooley – *Breaking Away*
NATIONAL SOCIETY – Frederic Forrest – *The Rose*

In October, The New York Times film critic Vincent Canby commented that previous Academy Award winner Jack Lemmon "would seem to be odds on favourite for a nomination in the Best Supporting Actor category" for his performance as a nuclear power plant worker in the drama *The China Syndrome*. When the Oscar nominations were announced, however, Lemmon was included among the contenders for the Best Actor statuette.

The nominees for the supporting prize were: previous winner Melvyn Douglas (his third nomination) as the dying billionaire in the comedy *Being There* (NYT "superb"; LAT "supplies the pathos"; WP "delightful … witty and unerring"; V "almost steals the film with his spectacular performance"); Robert Duvall (his second nod) as a disturbed army commander in *Apocalypse Now* (NYT "superlatively right", "walks off with the film"); Frederic Forrest as an army deserter involved with a rock singer in *The Rose* (NYT "would be the surprise hit of the movie if Miss Midler didn't herself have dibs on that position"; LAT "a good, quiet portrayal"; MFB "perfect"); Justin Henry as the young boy caught between his divorcing parents in the drama *Kramer vs Kramer* (NYT "excellent"; NYDN "astonishingly natural"; LAT "[he] is splendidly and blessedly a small boy, never a winsome kid actor"); and Mickey Rooney (his fourth mention) as a veteran horse-trainer in the children's drama *The Black Stallion* (NYT "lends humor and humanity to the proceedings", "very funny [and] completely authentic"; WP "[the film] would merit at least half a dozen Oscars … most satisfying of all, Mickey Rooney for supporting actor … [his] endearing, elder statesmanly performance as a canny horse trainer surely deserves Hollywood's ultimate recognition"; V "excellent").

At eight years of age, Henry was at that time the youngest person ever nominated for an Academy Award in the competitive categories. After the little boy cried at losing the Golden Globe, Hollywood veteran and previous Best Supporting Actor Oscar winner Douglas (one of the co-winners of the Globe) told Helen Dudar at The New York Times, "[it] had to be heart-breaking. That's what's so silly about it. How absurd that this 8-year-old and this 80-year-old – practically – should be in competition. Utterly absurd." Douglas explained to Dudar, "I have mixed feelings about the whole business. I dislike intensely all the politicking that goes along with it." In addition to sharing the Globe, in the lead up to the Oscars, Douglas won both the New York Film Critics Circle and Los Angeles Film Critics Association prizes and finished as the runner-up for the National Society of Film Critics prize. He was cited by the west coast critics for his work in *The Seduction of Joe Tynan* (NYT "suitably alarming"; LAT "perfectly played"; MFB "strong") as well as in *Being There*. Illness prevented him from attending the ceremony in Hollywood where he once again prevailed, collecting his second golden statuette.

While some in Hollywood had favoured a sentimental Oscar win for veteran Hollywood star Rooney, in the weeks prior to Academy Awards night, the favourite for the statuette among leading pundits and industry observers had actually been Duvall, the actor with whom Douglas had shared the Globe. The other strong contender had been NSFC winner and New York runner-up Forrest.

The most notable absentee from the list of Oscar contenders was National Board of Review winner Paul Dooley as the bewildered father in *Breaking Away* (NYT "excellent", "superb"; LAT "not least among the achievements of 'Breaking Away' is that [Barrie and Dooley] keep these roles [as the parents] from becoming wholly caricatures … [he] is just right in a crucial role that could all too easily have been overplayed in any one of several wrong directions"; WP "delightful").

Also overlooked were: Wilford Brimley in *The China Syndrome* (LAT "the subsidiary casting is of considerable importance here, and one key player is Wilford Brimley"; CT "one supporting performance in the film is worth special mention. Wilford Brimley is excellent … a beautiful portrait"); John Forsythe as the villainous judge in *...And Justice For All* (LAT "dominates the film … Forsythe proves himself an actor of wider range than he is usually asked to show … the judge is a figure of courtroom melodrama but Fosythe brings him hatefuly and suavely alive"; WP "disarmingly effective"); Michael Murphy in *Manhattan* (NYT "beautifully played"; LAT "excellent in another difficult but rather thankless role"); Denholm Elliott as a gentle English businessman living in Singapore in *Saint Jack* (NYT "nicely played"; V "moving"); Ian Holm as an android in the science fiction horror film *Alien* (NYT "excellent"; LAT "very effective"; S&S "intriguing"); Pat Hingle as the title character's father in *Norma Rae* (NYT "very good"; LAT "splendid"); Harry Dean Stanton in *The Rose* (NYT "superbly played"); Franklyn Seales in *The Onion Field* (LAT "excellently portrayed … a greatly affecting performance"); James Mason as Dr Watson in *Murder by Decree* (NYT "superlative ... one of the best performances he has ever given"; LAT "the one real joy in the film … inspired"; CT "steals almost every scene … delightful"); and Mike Kellin as an ageing prisoner in *On the Yard* (NYT "the movie's standout performance is that of Mike Kellin … a performance to win awards"; LAT "Kellin has one of the best scenes of his career as he faces an impassive parole board, desperately trying for a self-confidence that rapidly unravels as he outlines his whole sorry life"; WP "registers vividly").

Although it appeared in cinemas in most part of the United States and opened in the United Kingdom the following year, the espionage thriller *The Human Factor* was given a limited release in Los Angeles in late December 1979. Despite this Oscar-qualifying run, the Academy ignored Robert Morley (WP "a miscalculation"; TGM "especially delightful"), Richard Attenborough (WP "admirable") and Derek Jacobi (WP "particularly impressive"; TGM "played rather spectacularly") for their performances (NYT all three "superb … have never been better"; BG "the acting is sublime").

Index

Index

Index

Index

Index

Index

Index

Index

Index

Index

Index

Index

Index

Index

Index

Index

Index

Index

Index

Index

Index

Index

Index

Index

Index

www.ingramcontent.com/pod-product-compliance
Lightning Source LLC
LaVergne TN
LVHW020523100826
845148LV00010B/1323

9780980490954